The managerial choice:
To be efficient and
to be human

The managerial choice

To be efficient and to be human

FREDERICK HERZBERG
Distinguished Professor of Management
The University of Utah

 DOW JONES-IRWIN *Homewood, Illinois* 60430

ISBN 0-87094-123-2
Library of Congress Catalog Card No. 76-8140
Printed in the United States of America

Preface

This is my fourth book on the psychology of people at work. The three preceding books were: *Work and the Nature of Man* (New York: Crowell Publications, 1966), *The Motivation to Work,* with Bernard Mausner and Barbara Snyderman (New York: John Wiley & Sons, 1959), and *Job Attitudes: Research and Opinion,* with Bernard Mausner, Richard Peterson, and Dora Capwell (Pittsburgh: Psychological Service of Pittsburgh, 1957).

There are two basic differences between this book and those preceding it. First, the underlying purpose of the first three was to present basic research and theory about man and his relationship to his work. In this book, the basic emphasis is on the practical applications of the theory. Second, this book is essentially an anthology of my most popular articles, the popularity being measured by the number of reprints and reprintings that have been requested and that have been published. An extensive listing of approximately 150 relevant personal references, from which I have chosen approximately 34 to include in this book, is given in the Bibliography. I have attempted to collate these separate writings in such a way that the ideas and materials expressed logically follow each other to provide a cohesive narrative that approximates the usual book form.

Despite the numerous publications, the many addresses and guest lectures I have given and consultations I have enjoyed, and appearances and mentions in various media, I find that I have still left people asking questions that I thought I had answered in these many excursions in communication. The problem with this assumption has been that my writings, films, and lectures, interviews, and other personal appearances, have been so scattered within and among so many different media that, although I know what I have been saying most of the time, few of my audiences have this varied knowledge of my work or easy access to the variety of sources in which the material is contained. In addition, textbook writers and other synopsizers have so distorted or so oversimplified what I have said that I felt it necessary to provide those who are interested with the originals of my works. This book, particularly if it is read along with my *Work and the Nature of Man* and *The Motivation to Work*, should provide a virtually up-to-date record of my theories, views, and practices.

The book is intended for the general public and the general manager as well as for personnel specialists. Chapter 5 deals with research criticisms of my theories; this is the one chapter I specifically included for personnel specialists in academia and industry.

The book is divided into six chapters, each of which includes published materials in their original or an adapted form. In some instances, new material that has not been previously published is included. All but two of the articles have been written or coauthored by myself. The two exceptions appear in Chapter 5, on answers to criticisms of Motivation-Hygiene Theory. These were written by my graduate students and a young colleague at Case Western Reserve University. Although I advised in the preparation of these articles, I preferred that these be written by others for a more objective analysis of the technical arguments which have raged around my work for the past ten years.

In the first chapter I write about society and work. While at Case Western Reserve University I established a doctoral and postdoctoral program of Industrial Mental Health, sponsored by the National Institutes of Health. It was my purpose to train industrial mental health specialists. I wished to help raise industrial and organizational psychology to a socially responsible level rather than an area of technocratic specialization for personnel departments of industry. From my World War II military experiences, particularly at Dachau Concentration Camp, I concluded that a society does not go insane because of the insane. Every society has at least an estimated 15 percent that are mentally deranged for one reason or another. But they account for only a minute amount of the pathologies that can grip any society. I believed at Dachau as an American soldier in 1945 and believe now 30 years later, more than ever, that a society goes insane when the sane go insane and, in truth, more problems are created by the sane who are *inept* or *unethical* than by the acknowledged insane and criminal. My emphasis in teaching my students in the Industrial Mental Health program was how they could contribute to our organizations by keeping the sane people sane.

This is quite a reversal from my behavioral science colleagues, who have always overemphasized the consequences of the mentally ill and overextended their energies in dealing with their treatment. This is not meant to disparage the treatment of the ill. It is only to suggest that society would gain more from greater attention to the healthy and in trying to maintain their health. I also instilled in my students the fact that managers are human beings, not giants, and there is a myth that we in the United States have had superb management. My professional career has spanned the years since World War II, and in my experience most companies were simply manager-proof. The demand was high and the jelly beans abundant. The paradoxical situation I found was that, despite so much management development and so many schools of management mushrooming, management in fact has been truly neglected during this growth period. Management became a nonconcept with a hell of a lot of teaching, but the real emphasis has been on the subspecialities and spoilers of organizations—the technocrats. Today, with the magic of growth pretty much dispelled and no longer an automatic underpinning for inept management, we truly need managers. People and social questions are *the* problems facing managers. The technology and know-how is there to accomplish the hardware production, but the management is falling way behind. In fact, management is worse today relative to its potentialities and its needs than at any time before.

In the second chapter I review very briefly the basic Motivation-Hygiene Theory principles, then proceed in subsequent articles to expand the elementary principles to the principles of specific application to management problems in organizations.

In the third chapter I take up Orthodox Job Enrichment which has been the pronounced application of my theories. I provide the principles underlying job enrichment and the variations on the themes that have taken place, and add striking examples of this approach to bringing efficiency and humanity to work.

The fourth chapter takes us into the realm of mental health. A new definition of mental health is suggested, and a new approach to dealing with the psychological problems people have is given. These new definitions and therapeutic approaches provide for a different perspective of sanity which is essential in trying to organize and manage sane people.

Chapter 5 deals with the technical problems of my theories and the technical criticisms and arguments about them, as well as the answers to these criticisms and arguments.

And finally in Chapter 6, I answer some of the most frequent questions that are asked of me, particularly in regard to basic theory concepts and job enrichment procedures and problems. The Bibliography, as I have indicated above, includes almost all of my relevant publications on people at work. Omitted are those publications into which I have strayed that are not pertinent to the subject matter of this book.

Within the book there is some redundancy, although much effort has been made to reduce it to a minimum. What redundancy has remained is that which I believe profits from repetition. It is the "Play It Again, Fred" refrain that I have had requested so often for my scenarios.

Salt Lake City, Utah   FREDERICK HERZBERG
August 1976

Acknowledgments

This is my first attempt at writing a book whose origin is the compilation of many separate writings that I have participated in over many years. Surprising to me has been the greater difficulty of putting together a book of readings than composing a straightforward book. It is easier to write direct ideas than to integrate published ideas and studies, therefore the assistance required in this sort of book is much greater than would generally be anticipated. Accordingly, the following acknowledgments are made with greater appreciation.

First, I wish to give my heartfelt gratitude to Marita Bolte who has handled everything of a "secretarial" nature in the highest sense of the word of a professional secretary. She has kept the book on track, typed the manuscripts with their many revisions, amassed the permissions, and checked, and checked, and checked. This forgotten breed of secretary, if resurrected in industry, I would predict would have an amazing impact on the efficiency of organizations. I thank you, Miss Bolte.

To my young colleague, Yoash Wiener, I am much indebted for his persistent analysis and rebuttals of criticisms. A theoretician gets bored with the continuous "shots" that are taken at his work and sometimes at him personally. Professor Wiener has had perhaps more patience than I have had and has met the adversaries in academia head on with his persistent and painstaking dissection of critical studies. He has defended my ideas in areas where I no longer wish to tread but which serve the purpose of making the academics act as academics.

My next acknowledgment is to my two current postdoctoral fellows, John N. Taylor and Alex Zautra, who have read and reread all of my works and were invaluable in helping to integrate these various works and provide for smooth transitions, which I believe has resulted in the manuscript becoming more than an anthology of Herzberg.

To Perry Pascarella, executive editor of *Industry Week* magazine, my thanks for insisting that I publish my ideas as they occur rather than waiting for the years that pass before they can all be assembled under one cover. This stimulus provided for immediate feedback on the value of the ideas and also forced me to continually generate new ones.

To Major General Edmund A. Rafalko of the Air Force Logistics Command, my respect and admiration for his helping me carry through one of the most ambitious job enrichment projects as yet reported within the most difficult of organizations, that of an Air Logistics Center at Hill Air Force Base. His managerial skill in getting such a program through in such delicate areas has given me renewed faith in what truly good managers can accomplish where depersonalized technology reigns supreme.

To the workers, staff, and executives of a large engine company for co-operating in the introduction of many of my ideas during the crucial time of the installation of a new plant, I am grateful for their permission to publish a consulting project and admire their desire for temporary anonymity in order that they may truly install a modern management system and forego the gratification of the public relations until the system is firmly established.

Also, I express my gratitude to the many other organizations that have tested my ideas in their companies.

I have had a number of teaching assistants as part of my professorial duties, particularly Jay L. Solomon, who was very helpful in collating material, suggesting ideas for improving individual articles, and overseeing the final compilation.

Last, I wish to express my appreciation to the many publishers of my works for their permissions to reprint:

Chapter 1

Be efficient and be human   Consolidation, with permission, of three articles published in *Industry Week:* "Be Efficient and Be Human" (June 8, 1970); "People Are Polarizing" (July 27, 1970); "Are Have Nots Entitled to Automatic Equality?" (March 15, 1971).

Management of hostility   Consolidation, with permission, of two articles published in *Industry Week:* "Management of Hostility" (August 24, 1970); "Black and White of Hostility" (September 21, 1970).

The end of obligation   Consolidation, with permission, of three articles published in *Industry Week:* "Swapping Managerial Garbage" (October 2, 1972); "The Equality of Ignorance" (October 9, 1972); "The End of Obligation" (October 16, 1972).

Reasons for pursuing success   Adapted, with permission, from "Why Bother To Work," *Industry Week,* July 16, 1973.

Economic crisis and work motivation   Edited, with permission, from *Industry Week,* February 25, 1974.

Managing people in an era of hopelessness   Edited, with permission, from *Industry Week,* November 11, 1974.

What people want from their jobs Reprinted, with permission, from *Industry Week,* October 19, 1970.

Chapter 2

The first psychologist Adapted, with permission, from *Industry Week* article entitled "Work and the Two Faces of Man," November 9, 1970.

One more time: How do you motivate employees? Part I Reprinted, with permission, in abbreviated form, from *Harvard Business Review,* January–February 1968. Copyright © 1967 by the President and Fellows of Harvard College. All rights reserved.

Motivational types: Individual differences in motivation Adapted from "Motivational Types," produced by Advanced Systems, Inc., Elk Grove Village, Ill., 1973.

Motivation-hygiene profiles: Pinpointing what ails the organization Reprinted, with permission, from *Organizational Dynamics,* Fall 1974. American Management Association.

The proper management of hygiene: Am I treated well? Adapted, with permission, from *Industry Week* articles entitled "Avoiding Pain in Organizations," December 7, 1970 and "More on Avoiding Pain in Organizations," January 18, 1971. Adapted from "Management of Hygiene," produced by Advanced Systems, Inc., Elk Grove Village, Ill., 1973.

The proper management of motivators: Am I used well? Adapted from *Industry Week* article entitled "Management of Motivators," February 15, 1971. Adapted from "Management of Motivators," produced by Advanced Systems, Inc., Elk Grove Village, Ill., 1973.

Chapter 3

Why job enrichment? Adapted from "What Is Job Enrichment?" produced by Advanced Systems, Inc., Elk Grove Village, Ill., 1974.

The wise old Turk Reprinted, with permission, from *Harvard Business Review,* September–October 1974. Copyright © 1974 by the President and Fellows of Harvard College. All rights reserved.

One more time: How do you motivate employees? Part II Reprinted, with permission, in abbreviated form, from *Harvard Business Review,* January–February 1968. Copyright © 1967 by the President and Fellows of Harvard College. All rights reserved.

Job enrichment pays off William J. Paul, Keith B. Robertson, and Frederick Herzberg. Reprinted with permission, from *Harvard Business Review,* March–April 1969. Copyright © 1969 by the President and Fellows of Harvard College. All rights reserved.

Efficiency in the military: The Hill Air Force Base project Frederick Herzberg and Major General Edmund A Rafalko. Reprinted with permission, from *Personnel,* November–December 1975, American Management Association, New York, N.Y.

An American approach to job enrichment Original paper not previously published.

The managerial choice   Parts of this article were reprinted with permission from *Industry Week* entitled "Job Enrichment's 'Father' Admits: Disparity Between Promise and Reality," November 25, 1975

Chapter 4

A motivation-hygiene concept of mental health   Frederick Herzberg and Roy M. Hamlin. Reprinted, with permission, from *Mental Hygiene, 45,* 1961.

The motivation-hygiene concept and psychotherapy   Frederick Herzberg and Roy M. Hamlin. Reprinted, with permission, from *Mental Hygiene, 47,* 1963.

Motivation and mental health: Some empirical evidence   Original paper prepared for this book.

Chapter 5

An analysis of studies critical of the Motivation-Hygiene Theory   David A. Whitsett and Erik K. Winslow. Reprinted, with permission, from *Personnel Psychology, 20,* 1967.

Has the research challenge to Motivation-Hygiene Theory been conclusive? An analysis of critical studies   Benedict Grigaliunas and Yoash Wiener. Reprinted, with permission, *Human Relations, 27,* No. 9, 1974.

Chapter 6

Managers or animal trainers? An interview with Frederick Herzberg by William F. Dowling. Reprinted by permission of the publisher from *Management Review,* July 1971. Copyright © 1971 by the American Management Association, Inc.

Questions and answers pertaining to Motivation-Hygiene Theory   Original paper prepared for this book. Retrospective commentary on Maslow's "A Theory of Human Motivation" reprinted by permission from Howard Thompson, *The Great Writings in Marketing* (Plymouth, Michigan: Commerce Press, Ltd., 1976).

Questions and answers regarding job enrichment   Original paper prepared for this book. Answers to Questions 3, 4, and 8 are taken from "Job Enrichment: A Pragmatic View," produced by Advanced Systems, Inc., Elk Grove Village, Ill., 1974.

Contents

chapter *1*

Social and psychological changes in society affecting the motivation to work

INTRODUCTION

Change is a cliché word, a hackneyed theme, and as with all clichés, the significance of what it says is gradually diminished and then lost. We certainly have been oversubjected to the topic of change throughout history, and as the past and present get closer together, this topic is discussed more frequently. With all the importance of change and with its continual history, the surprising thing is that we have never learned to cope with it adequately. This chapter is about change—specifically, the changes that have come about in the psychological fabric of our organizations.

The first article, "Be Efficient and Be Human," discusses some of these changes and how they affect the management of people. Today we are witnessing in organizational life a collapse of time in which advancements in technology, the heightened interdependence of national and multinational economies, and rapid shifts in geopolitics have dramatically reduced the margin of error, as well as the lead time available to correct management errors. This collapse of time requires an increased efficiency and competence from our organizations, but competence is also quickly overtaken by scientific and technological advances. Amidst these changes there is also a new set of beliefs and values: the national character is different from what it was, and workers and managers alike require human, not mechanistic, management. This change in the psychology of the

1

worker is not just another migraine headache for industry, but rather the kind of change that leads to the need for more competence in organizations and their willingness and ability to master the challenges inherent in these accelerating times. Yet, organizations have too often retreated from these changes, claiming that it is time to solidify their positions. This strategy amounts to protecting incompetence near or at the top of the hierarchy and crippling the effectiveness of the organization. This is the major thrust of this article; we must be efficient *and* human to meet the demands of change and the demands for competence among employees in the world of work today.

Polarization between people has grown and is more noticeable today, and with this change has come increased hostility toward organizations from employees and in society as a whole. While this hostility is a natural response to the many frustrations facing employees today, the manager frequently does not allow his subordinates to express it directly. In "Management of Hostility," the reasons for increased hostility and its consequences are discussed. The problem is not identifying how many "rotten apples" are sabotaging production and quality standards, but how management is to deal effectively with hostility from employees in order to prevent its escalation to sabotage of organizational and societal purposes.

Behavioral science has become lost in the maze while these changes have been taking place. Consequently, attempts to change organizations to make them more effective have been, for the most part, dismal failures. In "The End of Obligation," three prominent behavioral science failures are discussed: scientific management, the human relations movement, and industrial or democratic socialism. These approaches to the management of people have failed because they have misdiagnosed the psychology of the worker today. What they have missed is man's principal need for competence in his work. The simplification of tasks promoted by Tayloristic concepts, the interpersonal sensitivity found in human relations, and the concept of equality for the sake of socialistic ideals did not help meet this need. The employee no longer carries a sense of obligation to the company for the sake of tradition, ideologic beliefs such as the Protestant ethic, or an immigrant value system.

In "Reasons for Success," these changes in the psychology of the worker are expanded to answer the question haunting most management philosophies: Why do people work? The old justifications for success, based on power motives, desires for a better consumer existence, religious beliefs, Darwinian survival ethics, and meritocracy, linger on, but they are slowly losing their credibility among workers today. A new reason is needed, one not based on slogans and mythologies but which has its roots in the psychological realities facing employees today.

Some managements would like to retreat to the good old days, when job insecurity could be used as a means of ensuring worker productivity. Fear, however, has never been a motivator, and advanced social welfare policies restrict its use as even a temporary incentive. "Economic Crisis and Work Motivation" discusses how an economic crisis could provide increased productivity through a psychological return to work as a means of finding fulfillment in life. The escape routes of multiple life-styles, avocations, and recreation have been severely limited by energy restrictions and economic hardships. Without these escapes, the worker may begin to demand his right to be motivated on the job, a satisfying alternative to the wasteful way he attempts to manage the quality of his life outside the job.

In "Managing People in an Era of Hopelessness," the most difficult challenges brought about by rapid and accelerating changes in our society are presented. These changes have led to a number of paradoxes. We had hoped that technology could solve them, but the more technology we create, the more complex and paradoxical the problems become. Wisdom, not "scientism," is needed in order to resolve the dilemmas facing our society. The revolutionary changes in the psychological lives of the people have compounded the dilemmas, leading many to believe that we now live in an era of hopelessness. Searching for leadership, we find our leaders have not only feet of clay but heads of clay as well. The ten recommendations made at the end of this article may offer some alternatives to despair so that, with wisdom, we can face the challenges of the very difficult times in which we live.

This chapter ends with a brief article considering "What People Want from Their Jobs." This article, which concludes with the recognition that a different view of man's motivations is necessary, leads to the second chapter, on Motivation-Hygiene Theory.

Be efficient and be human

For industry to operate successfully, it is essential that efficient procedures be used to the maximum. This necessity has presented management with what appears to be mutually exclusive positions: It believes it cannot be both efficient and human. Because it is imperative that efficiency be maximized, the management process tends to overlook certain fundamental human needs—and, as is starkly evident today, to overlook environment and social welfare.

For many years, American management has believed that anarchy will result if work is humanized to the extent that good mental health is made operative. But the problems of humanizing job content must be solved in order that social needs as well as industrial needs are met. Management, in short, must be efficient, but at the same time it must be human.

WHY EFFICIENCY?

Let us consider the first point. Does industry really have to be efficient? Many of the young today have the romantic delusion that perhaps we need less efficiency in our lives. They long for a return to the uncomplicated days of our pioneering forefathers, and once again they bake bread at home. They say: Let us pause in this frantic quest for more and more efficiency and enjoy what we are doing and add style to our work life.

It is a tempting notion, but it is impossible to return to those glorious days that probably never existed. You cannot borrow from efficiency, simply because inefficiency leads not only to less production, to less salary or less profits, or to a decrease in the standard of living. Inefficiency leads to catastrophe.

We have built a technological society so demanding that inefficient operations ensure disaster, for example, in the launching of a spacecraft or in the designing of a supersonic plane. We no longer destroy only a crop by inefficient farming methods; we can ruin agriculture.

4

Man must not be incompetent today. In the past you were probably better off if you were wrong about important decisions, because you had so much company. But today society cannot afford to praise or even tolerate people who are wrong, for our very survival is at stake.

And the same is true in the smaller dimension of an individual company. Efforts must be made to be more productive, not only to raise industrial production goals but to avoid complete collapse. If it is agreed that it is a vital necessity for American management to be efficient, does it follow that the same management can also be human?

WHY HUMANITY?

Let us look at our present society and examine the reasons why it is imperative that management be human. First, we must face the knowledge that technology has grown to gigantic proportions in a very short period of time, grown so rapidly that man is not able to comprehend this growth with his sensory, intellectual, and emotional capacities. It is asking too much for the inhabitants of our universe to comprehend the entire solar system. Yet our technology makes this knowledge available and demands that it be incorporated into our daily experience. We no longer can absorb world events into our consciousness, despite the fact that we are participants in them via on-the-spot television coverage. But hiding from or denying what is too complex today will bring little psychological relief. It invites disaster.

Second, this enlargement of technology leads to the enlargement of organizations—the big unions, the giant corporate entities, the massive government agencies. This grossness of organizations further dwarfs the individual and leaves him with the necessity to exist within bigger systems while at the same time understanding them less.

Third, the acceleration of technology is forcing us to alter drastically our view of time. Consider college courses in history. "Western Civilization" taught the student to recognize the medieval period and to distinguish it from the Renaissance and to put boundaries to the era identified as the Age of Enlightenment. In this way it was easy to digest and analyze 300 years. Today, the rapid current of events has forced occurrences which previously developed slowly over a span of 300 years to be collapsed into a period of 25 years. My point is that our world—the world in which most of us reached maturity 25 years ago—is as different from today as the Middle Ages was from the Renaissance. But more important, the awesome fact is that 25-year-old cultural landmarks are unrecognizable to present-day observers.

These vast differences exist within my own life span, so that I must consider the relatively long voyage I must make from those years in which I gained recognition of the world to the world in which I live and manage today. Those of us in our forties and fifties are living in the same geographical spot on the globe, but figuratively our cognitive maps of the world locate us in the surroundings of 300 years ago. We react to events as if 25 years ago were just a quarter of a century in the past. The truth is that it is 300 years ago, relatively speaking, no matter what the calendar says. So we must relearn the world, relearn our way around this constantly developing planet, in order that our competency can maintain itself, in spite of the accelerated pace of the time machine.

Another failure is our inability to realize that the value system we acquired in our youth is vulnerable to attack. In the past, when there was disagreement about the importance of certain values, we proudly stood our ground. Our values were unimpeachable, even if others had to face the uncertain dimensions of their truths.

The collapse of time has shaken not only our concepts of the world but our concepts of what to believe. They are being battered by other cultures and subcultures in our society that are demanding recognition and in many instances are proving their worth. A lifetime of convictions is secure for only a half of a lifetime.

Today there is a decreasing amount of time available in which man can correct errors. Man has less and less lead time in which to change the course of events, both because of his own physical limitations and because of the tempo of the world in which he lives.

THREE LEVELS OF MAN

Let me illustrate this point with the three levels of man's existence: the biological, the psychological, and the existential. At the biological level the loss of lead time is exemplified by the nuclear stalemate. When someone pushes that "go" button, the last war of our civilization will start. There will be no time to gear American industry to a war footing and to send out an expeditionary force, as was done in the past. The only course of action in regard to a nuclear war is to prevent it; it cannot be corrected. Population and other geological problems are similarly left without much lead time for correction. Biologically, we are passing the point of no return for continued life on this planet.

This lead time has run out in another area of American life. It is apparent in the psychological implications of the civil rights battle cry "We want freedom now." When blacks say, "We want freedom now," society has gone beyond the point where it can safely turn back. We have lost the time in which to maneuver, and, since blacks cannot have all their political, social, economic and psychological freedom now, we must contend with an irreversible pathology.

The time loss required to correct errors is apparent also in the existential area of our lives. Witness the frantic activities of the religious mystery systems in their haste to refurbish theology and the institutions that market it. The ecumenical movement and the Vatican Council were attempts to act before their lead time runs out.

MANAGEMENT BY PREVENTION

How does the vitiation of lead time affect management? Since there is little time left for any institution to correct its errors, this points to a new concept: management by prevention, not by correction.

In the past, managers could earn "Brownie points" by choosing certain criteria in which they were sure to operate effectively. These criteria could be met at the expense of cutting into future operative time, that segment which belonged to their successors. Those who followed had to correct the pathologies that had been created in the past. This procedure is no longer possible, because the ills that managers create today are going to catch up with them tomorrow.

The question then arises: What factors can be found to evaluate a man who manages by prevention? The manager has a real problem. He has no extant criteria by which he can say, "Look what I did. I came in and corrected that situation." So business has no indexes for knowing how to judge a successful manager.

Much of the planning of organizations is concerned with what will happen ten years from now. With the complexity of organizations, with problems surfacing so rapidly and changes coming so fast, our managers are fighting fires all day. And when they are fighting fires, they cannot make a decision that will have preventive qualities for the next ten years. So, in our era of specialization, managing by prevention requires much more adaptability on the part of the manager.

Escalation of our problems to the catastrophic level, the rapid collapse of time, and the loss of lead time will force management to reexamine assumptions about human nature and the management of people.

CHANGES IN SELF-PERCEPTION

In addition to the changes that have taken place in the world, two very profound changes are emerging in man's self-perceptions. Man is the only organism which is a phenomenon to itself. He is an object as well as a subject. He asks questions about himself.

Since living in total reality can be the greatest insanity, he has to hide himself from some of the knowledge he finds. He distorts the world. Man does this in one of two ways. He pulls the wires, or he crosses the wires.

We can pull the wires. The heart is a pumping mechanism, the lung is an oxidating system, the kidney is a filtrating organ, the brain is built for making decisions. Formerly, when we did not like the decisions we made with our brains, we could pull the wires and invent a new organ called faith or intuition or autism. You cannot do that today, because there is no lead time to correct errors by plugging the wires back in the proper position. Few people will fly with a pilot who believes he can navigate an airplane by prayer instead of radar.

We can cross the wires. We can say, "I don't like the information coming in, so I'll switch the connections and see what I would like to see, rather than what is really there." At one time we credited people who did this with superior and unusual perception; we call this mental illness now.

NO HIDING FROM REALITY

Today you can no longer pull the wires with impunity, and you can no longer cross the wires at will. Therefore, you can no longer hide man from reality. Now you must treat each person as a whole, not with the wires pulled or crossed. This requires a new way of treating people.

The radical and accelerated changes in the world have brought two antagonistic existential questions into open competition. The existential question of man in a slow-moving society is the meaning of death, the past, the remembered traditions. The existential question of man in a changing society is the meaning of life and the future. While it is the young who are most often asking, "How am I spending my life at work?" more older workers are becoming aware that tradition is a very tenuous pillar on which to attach life's significance. Two basic psychological developments—the need for reality testing and the emergence of a present-future life orientation—are polarizing the world in many basic dimensions that will have profound effects on the management of man.

DIMENSIONS OF POLARIZATION

People are becoming more unalike; we are polarizing at an extreme speed in most critical dimensions of man's life. Today there are more people starving to death than ever before, and there are more people who own three automobiles. Furthermore, the difference between the haves and the have-nots can no longer be hidden. Added to this is the fact that the basic economic thrust of modern society is to make people feel deprived. Never have so many people felt so deprived in so many areas. The level of feelings of deprivation is escalating with incredible speed. Management will need to cope with ever-increasing feelings of dissatisfaction.

There is also an increase in polarization between the competent and the incompetent. The competent are gaining more competencies, while the incompetents are becoming less able. There are 750 million illiterates in the Free World—and at the same time postdoctoral education is becoming a necessity in many areas! Thirty years ago an unskilled laborer could pump gasoline in a service station, but today that has become a public relations job, suitable for the man who wears the star and appears in the TV commercial. The range of ability that is to be managed today is becoming beyond management.

SANE-INSANE POLARIZATION

There is another polarization which has taken place, and that is between the sane and the insane. A major difference between the sane and the insane person is that the sane person is adaptable, and the insane person is not. The sane person has a repertory of behavior that he can bring to bear as the occasion demands. The insane person is stereotyped, constricted in his behavior. He can only repeat the same patterns of performance.

How does this polarization between the normal and the abnormal man affect present management problems? With the tremendous technological changes that have taken place, the competency life of man has been drastically reduced; the "half-life" of an engineer is about eight years. This means that within one lifetime, the engineer can operate from a repertory of behavior that ranges from competency to incompetency.

Let us say a man has a competence for A, B, and C, which he acquired earlier in life. Now he must know D and E to be competent; A, B, and C are no longer effective. What can he do? He proclaims his skills in A, B, and C in more strident tones, and he reacts with the same type of psychodynamics as does a child who throws a temper tantrum or a mental patient in an asylum. But the difference between the child, the psychotic, and the worker is not apparent. The man looks normal; he does not have the visible characteristics of abnormality. He makes a good appearance; he dresses well; he is articulate. He has a self-image of competency. The masquerade is successful—until operational demands are made. Then the mask can no longer hide the truth.

PRAGMATISM AND IDEOLOGY

The American managerial system has been the most successful the world has ever known, for at least one basic reason. We have been pragmatic. When we have a problem we use know-how to solve it, then add to the know-how and let the fallout become our ideology—the American Way.

"Honesty is the best policy," we say, but, "business is business" and a businessman would be a fool if he didn't cover his hand. Progress, we believe, is our future, but we also fervently suggest that the good old ways are the best. All men are created equal in our society, but too many also say "a nigger is a nigger." You can go right down the line and you will find ours is the most schizophrenic nation in the world. Why?

Because what we believe is what works. Our ideology is a fallout of our know-how.

The communist countries developed consistent ideologies and hoped that the fallout from those ideologies would be know-how. How to farm? Read what Lenin said about communist beliefs, or, today, read "The Thoughts of Mao Tse-tung." Ideologs are consistent in their beliefs, but they are terrible managers.

OUR NEW IDEOLOGICAL OUTLOOK

Incredibly, Americans are becoming ideological. One of the reasons we are doing this is that in our affluent society, with its high feeling of deprivation and its tremendous polarization of talent, we are creating more and more A, B, and C people, with limited knowledge. A man who does not have knowledge can become a man of principles. And so, unfortunately, we are getting more and more people who turn to principles as a substitute for knowledge, and principles are hard to fight.

Most of our social problems today are not problems of ideology but rather problems that require working knowledge. In the past, industry has faced this situation in the area of labor relations. The future suggests the possibility of more and more interference from ideology in many other areas of corporate life.

Perhaps the most significant change that has taken place is in the definition of a human being. In the past, dominant institutions defined people by the way they needed them to be, and this need always was based on the specific ideology of the defining institution. The Army has its idealized version of the proper man, the church its version, the state its version. And since the Industrial Revolution, industry has allowed its ideology to outline the basic nature of a human being to meet its own needs.

Technology today, however, is going to force us to look at the way man is, rather than the way we need him to be, if we are going to survive by managing the talents of human beings.

ARE THE HAVE-NOTS ENTITLED TO
AUTOMATIC EQUALITY?

A most significant psychological attitude prevalent throughout the world today is having a serious negative effect on work motivation. This attitude is the growing acceptance by the have-nots that the haves are obligated to give them consumer equality.

As the world continues to polarize between these two groups, the press of this feeling of obligation becomes stronger. In those countries that the political scientists call the Third World—newly independent, under developed, and, with few exceptions, under dictatorial government.—

policy of undisguised blackmail has characterized their foreign policies. At first this policy was justified as payment for past exploitation during the days of colonialism. Today, however, such justification is not felt to be necessary. Instead, economic equality is simply considered to be a natural right, rather than a reward for human effort.

Israel, for example, has lost the political support of much of the Third World because it is considered to be a have nation, as judged by its relatively high consumer standard of living. The hostility of the Arabs to the Jewish nation is the hostility of the less fortunate toward those who are presently better off.

HOSTILITY: NORMAL AND IRRATIONAL

The greater the discrepancy in well-being that can be attributed to the differences in human achievement, the more dangerous the hostility. Hostility that is a product of the exploitation of one people by another can be considered normal. However, hostility that is based on the need to sustain one's pride becomes irrational, and while it can serve to provide for some temporary psychological comfort, in the long term it may lead to further psychological disability.

Evidence of exploitation no longer is necessary or even assumed. If you are successful, then you owe me—a simple belief that becomes dominant in the minds of the affected people. It is not a philosophy of something for nothing; rather it is a philosophy of an automatic right to equality.

This belief has been fostered by the have nations and segments of society, partly from a genuine feeling of guilt for past and continued wrongs. It is also partly due to the social and political realities of a world divided into strong, competing national and special interests, buttressed by outdated ideologies. Modern marketing and advertising methods which suggest that everyone is entitled to the good things in life and which excite appetite without ambition and faith without works are also partly responsible.

RATIONALIZING UNSUCCESS

Thus it comes about that developed nations are in debt to underdeveloped nations because they are developed. Successful companies are in debt to inefficient companies because they are successful. Professors are in debt to their students because they have the knowledge, and skilled workers owe skilled jobs to the unskilled because they are skilled. The accepted view becomes that of little admiration for achievements and great condemnation for the economic and social inequality that results.

The achievement of building a nation is denied to the Israelis because it led to inequality with their less achieving Arab neighbors. The cry of exploitation is the rationalization for denying Israel its accomplishments, for the belief is that achievement does not have a force of its own in propelling human behavior; it is a motive derived only from less lofty human goals.

In the philosophy of an automatic right to equality, a star football guard or a great surgeon is really satisfying latent sadistic needs, and an architect is only sublimating suppressed sexual urges. College professors did not become scholars through study and the joy of learning; rather they are only the academic establishment denying power to students. The master craftsman's long years as an apprentice and journeyman are dismissed, and he is cursed for denying opportunities to blacks. Companies did not develop and effectively market desired products; rather they were successful in deceiving the public.

Certainly in each of these representative instances many wrongs have been committed on the way to success. But to view all success as based on wrongs and to assume, in addition, that success produces unacceptable inequality results in denial of the value of achievement itself.

ACHIEVEMENT IS MINE

The communist philosophy attempted to bridge the belief in consumer equality with respect to human achievement by proclaiming a motto of each giving according to his ability and each receiving according to his needs. This motto attempted to separate achievement from rewards by substituting personal need as the criterion for individual treatment. People were to be given food because they were hungry, not because they had earned it.

One reason for the failure of the communists to build a humane society has been their replacement of group goals as the value for achievement rather than the individual goals of personal psychological growth and personal satisfaction in one's accomplishment. It made public a private experience that cannot be vitiated by group sharing if it is to sustain man's need for psychological income. If a human being cannot own his own growth, then there is little left to distinguish one individual from another, and personal identity is compromised.

THE NEED TO PRESERVE INDIVIDUAL ACHIEVEMENT

As we seek improved social justice, we must preserve individual achievement as one of man's most rewarding motives. Pride in personal achievement can easily be sacrificed by the need to assuage the hurt pride of nonachievers. If Israel were destroyed tomorrow, the positive material gains to the Arabs would be very slight indeed. Perhaps 100,000 Arabs would gain some economic benefits, but in Egypt, for example, approximately three fourths of the population would still be suffering from schistosomiasis (a crippling parasitic disease) and an equal number would still be illiterate. Similar social problems would remain with all the Near East Arab peoples.

However, the immense burden of negative feelings that the Arabs presently feel for themselves would be considerably lightened. The removal of negative feelings becomes the justification for equality, worthy of itself, but a subtle substitute for the enhancement of one's self through positive achievement.

The attempt to produce industrial democracy that is being preached by so many social scientists today must recognize that democracy does not mean the enhancement of human values by eliminating negative feelings about one's self, but rather the enlargement of the opportunity for human accomplishment for all employees. Otherwise, democracy will be identified with mediocrity.

A "mediocracy" that is dressed up with the most beloved humanistic slogans is devastating to the creative force in society. The slogans tend to become so removed from reality that people are forced to believe them with greater fervor in order to sustain their psychological equilibrium. The disease of the Arabs in the Middle East has been just this confusion between their rhetoric and the extant reality, and the resulting character disorder further ensures the lack of development of an achievement motive among them.

SELF-RESPECT VERSUS SELF-HATE

As the underprivileged fight for their social justices and as the more affluent in society assist them in this struggle, which is not only morally justified but highly pragmatic, we must be careful to see that they are helped to achieve self-respect. This achievement is *not* the opposite of the removal of self-hate.

Of more importance is the prevention of this psychological turnabout among the relatively privileged groups in our society. New Left members, products of an affluent middle class, are as psychotic in their sloganeering as the worst of the Arab demagogues. They perceive inequality to be a direct result of success and therefore believe achievement and success are to be devalued. Tear down the establishment and it will be replaced by something. By what they cannot say, because they have no achievement experience or content in their programs. Removal of self-hate and social inequality are believed to be the equivalent of positive accomplishment.

Traditional middle America blue-collar and white-collar slogans are equally guilty in their antiintellectualism and resistance to the genuine achievement aspirations of minorities. Black pride through black achievement requires opportunities for its realization. The boring tasks and restrictions in employee initiative that are a part of bureaucratic organizational structures can serve to create doubt in any person regarding ability and a consequent loss of respect for human achievement motivation.

SURVIVAL WITH SOCIAL JUSTICE

Our survival as a free society in a physically and psychologically healthy country will depend on the maintenance of our historic achievement motivation, not at the expense of social justice and not without social justice. But social justice at the expense of respect for individual achievement is less than human justice. This is perhaps the greatest challenge that will face the managers of our organizations.

Management of hostility

Every newspaper front page published today depicts some potential catastrophe related to a story of hostility. As challenges to our social, political, and economic systems increase, so will latent hostility. Managers today and increasingly in the future will have to understand the psychological laws of hostility and the appropriate management of hostility.

In this article I will summarize briefly the most important laws of psychological hostility and their implications for managers. The second part deals with a specific example of hostility—that of blacks for white people and their institutions.

The simplest (although very incomplete) statement of the basic law of psychological hostility is called frustration-aggression. Simply put, if someone hurts you, you will get mad at him. (If you don't get mad when someone hurts you, you are what the psychologists technically call a "nut.") Hostility is not an ephemeral or abstract psychological term; rather, it is the substance of a biochemical change in the human body manifested by the secretion of neurohormones at nerve fiber connections. As in any biological imbalance, the surplus biochemicals must be transformed or neutralized. For example, too much acid in the stomach must be removed by some alkaline action (such as Rolaids). Similarly, at the behavioral level you must energize and transform the hostility that results from frustration. You have to walk it off, shout, throw something, but you must in some way express hostility.

KEEPING THE MIND HEALTHY

What is the mentally healthy thing to do when your boss frustrates you? *Tell him to go to hell.* Seriously, if you tell your boss to go to hell when he frustrates you, you will be mentally healthy—and fired. And what does firing do to you? It just increases your frustration. You see how hard it is to be mentally healthy?

What can you do? If you express your hostility to the frustrating

15

object, your boss in this instance, it only results in increased frustrations. The psychological law, however, states that you must express hostility. One solution is to go home and yell at your wife, a technique psychologists call displacement. This basic mechanism operates, very obviously, in prejudice. The bigoted person is frustrated, but should he express his hostility to the frustrating object he would be clobbered, so he therefore finds a convenient scapegoat on which he can release the hostility with relative impunity. But (returning to our example) if you go home and yell at your wife, you will be mentally healthy—but she will not be. Then what happens if she has all the money? She leaves you, taking all the money with her, and furthers your frustration.

If you cannot express your hostility directly at the person who is frustrating you and you cannot displace your hostility to another person, and all other avenues for expression of your hostility are blocked, where can the hostility go? Only one direction is possible: The hostility must be directed back into yourself. Psychologists call this internalization. When hostility is directed toward oneself, it leads to depression, self-hate, self-degradation and, ultimately, psychological suicide. If we look around us in industry today, we can see employees who no longer have any interest in what they do, who merely respond as automatons on their jobs, and who have indeed been forced to commit psychological suicide. In this final solution for the individual lies a great hidden cost for the organization.

FRUSTRATION IS THE NAME OF THE GAME

Implicit in the psychological work contract between a manager and his subordinate is the clause, "If you work for me, I'm going to have to frustrate you sometimes." Any time you manage people you have to frustrate them—it's the name of the game, and no amount of agonizing is going to negate this reality. However, the danger to the organization lies in extending this tacit contract to include the statement, "When I do frustrate you, don't you dare express your hostility to me—I am the boss. Go home and kick your dog, go join a kook organization, or go eat your heart out—that is, turn the hostility back on yourself."

With greater personal freedom we decrease the likelihood, particularly among new college graduates, that they will go home and kick their dogs or eat their hearts out. It is now more likely (and will be increasingly so in the future) that they will tell the manager who frustrates them to go to hell. Many college-trained people are in a very real sense telling industry to go to hell as a reflection of their anticipation that their creative needs will be frustrated.

Even today where job opportunities are less abundant this attitude will prevail. The form of the hostility, however, will change from the more aggressive manifestations of the past (the 1960s) to the more invidious type—passive hostility. Passive hostility is a procedure of showing aggression with plausible denial. Plausible denial is seeming to be helpful when in reality the person is being harmful to the organization. The issue facing management is to avoid forcing the employee to displace or internalize hostility and to accept and handle the direct expression of hostility.

MANAGERS OF COMPETENCE AND OF SLOGANS

What type of manager will be able to accept this direct expression of hostility without blowing his cool? It will be the manager of competence. Contrariwise, it will be the manager of slogans who will not be able to tolerate the hostility of his subordinates. If you attack a manager of competence, he will accept it as a challenge, but if you challenge a manager of slogans, he will consider it to be a personal attack. The manager of competence is not destroyed by hostility, but the manager of slogans finds hostility dismantling his smoke screen and cannot withstand the challenges to his ability.

What does a manager of slogans do when he is confronted by the hostility of subordinates? One thing he can do is to come back with counterhostility—the familiar backlash. And what does he accomplish by this counterhostility? The good people, particularly the young, will leave the organization, and those that do remain will tend to become housebroken. Either way, the organization loses.

What does a manager of slogans do when he cannot use backlash for self-protection? He gets his subordinates to displace their hostility to someone else in or outside the company. He gets the heat off him by getting them to blame the labor unions, top management, other divisions, social and political problems. Displacement succeeds in protecting the manager of slogans from the threat of being discovered, but it has terrible consequences. Let us see more clearly what happens with displaced hostility.

HOSTILITY MULTIPLIED

The poor white tenant farmer in the Deep South was frustrated by the white power structure, but he found it too dangerous to express his hostility to the frustrating object, so he displaced it to the Negro. When Negroes were lynched, it was because a moderate amount of frustration had led to an extreme amount of hostility. The Germans in the thirties were frustrated, and they displaced their hostility to the Jews. When the Germans burned six million Jews it was an incredible increase of hostility over provocation.

The second law of hostility states that displaced hostility increases the amount of hostility exponentially. If your boss frustrates you and you have to go home and take it out on your wife, you will multiply the hostility toward your boss by an incredible factor and you will yell at your wife longer. The scapegoat is always punished viciously in order to hide the fact that he or she is an innocent victim. The same process is also in effect when hostility is internalized. Managers who succeed in getting their people to displace their hostility, because they do not have competence enough to accept a challenge to their authority, increase the amount of hostility that will need to be managed in an organization.

Many companies and managers are bewildered by the extreme negative consequences that seem to be generated by inconsequential provocations. A personal slight leads to a work stoppage; an unanswered phone call leads to paranoic reactions; a minor, foolish company policy leads to work dissatisfaction on the part of the employees. Companies run morale surveys and waste a lot of money to pinpoint the inconsequential instigators of bad morale; it's a wild goose chase.

If a man has had a fight with his boss but must go home and take it out on his wife, then silly but serious consequences can occur. If he discovers that what he is having for dinner is what he had for lunch, this provocation can cause an extreme marital fight. An independent observer of this scene would easily conclude that the provocation of the duplicate menu was not sufficient to have such terrible consequences. The independent observer would also easily conclude that the hostility being expressed by the husband to the wife was displaced hostility.

In a company, any time personnel consequences are out of line with the seeming provocation, you know that you are dealing with displaced hostility. It is a futile exercise to try to correct the manifest reason.

OBSCURED SOURCES OF POOR MORALE

Managers of slogans not only increase the amount of hostility in a company that must be managed, they also obscure the sources of poor personnel morale. In a larger picture, KITA management (the carrot and stick approach)[1] is management via frustration, but since the employee wants and needs the "jelly beans" the organization is tempting him with, he cannot express his hostility to the organization. Those people who play the organization's game of jumping for the rewards, while maintaining outward organization loyalty, must be displacing their hostility, but they do this subtly. Their seemingly good behavior and good performance are more than offset in hidden ways that hurt the company.

The danger and costs of displaced hostility to the organization are threefold. First, displaced hostility is evidence that the organization is

---

[1] The KITA concept will be explained in the article "One More Time: How Do You Motivate Employees?" *Harvard Business Review*, January–February 1968, reprinted (in two parts) in Chapters 2 and 3.

being managed by title rather than by talent. Second, these managers create mentally unhealthy employees by not allowing the open expression of hostility. Finally, the alternative mechanisms of displacement and repression of hostility increase the amount of hostility and can at some point do severe damage to the organization.

The direct expression of hostility is much saner, safer, more open, and infinitely less damaging to an organization than displaced hostility. The mentally sick and the emotionally frightened may be willing to displace their hostility, but encouraging these groups to turn to scapegoats in a modern society or organization invites catastrophe. The greatest barrier to a free, democratic, and sane organization is managers who cannot stand any hostility directed at them. This inability is directly correlated with their low self-confidence. The competent manager has a higher tolerance to frustration.

THE BLACK AND WHITE OF HOSTILITY

Beyond the mismanagement of endemic hostility within the organization, the presence of certain forces in our society makes the appropriate management of hostility critical to industry today. Perhaps the most obvious area where greater understanding of the dynamics of hostility is needed is in the revolt of blacks to continued frustration.

For 200 years in America we have frustrated the hell out of a number of minority groups, particularly the blacks. If American technical know-how and managerial skill ever deserved an E for excellence, it is for the expertise with which we have degraded such a high percentage of our population.

The frustration of blacks led quite naturally to their hostility toward whites. But if the black expressed this hostility to the frustrating object —the white man—he was lynched. In fact, not only did we frustrate the blacks in our population, we went one step farther. Every legitimate avenue of hostile expression which the blacks attempted to use to release their frustrations was effectively blocked. An impermeable barrier to the black man's expression of hostility was erected.

Where did the hostility go? It went in the only direction possible— back into the blacks themselves. The black denigrated himself. When hostility is directed toward one's self it leads to depression and self-hate and, in social situations, to group apathy and group disintegration. The crime rate among blacks directed toward blacks reflects the intrapunitive nature of black hostility.

This is the final treason. You frustrate a population, then you succeed in having the members turn the resultant hostility back on themselves, and in this way you encourage them to commit psychological suicide. This is what the civil rights leadership saw—the blacks were destroying themselves. Now they are fed up with blaming themselves; they are no longer willing to wait for the Kingdom of Heaven to receive their just rewards.

No population rises up when it is frustrated. If this were what happened, we would have revolutions every day. Rather, a population rises up when continued frustrations lead to self-destruction. It revolts to survive psychologically.

First, the blacks' attempt at survival was through the juridical procedures of this society—Supreme Court decisions, the ballot box, and other legal maneuvers. The second attempt was through economic pressure, particularly as illustrated by the boycott of the buses in Montgomery, Alabama, led by Martin Luther King, Jr. Third, there is the technique of passive resistance or nonviolence, again illustrated by Dr. King's methods.

In psychology this is called passive hostility, a most powerful form. For example, if a man has a wife who constantly fouls him up and gets him into all kinds of difficulties and, when he calls her on it, responds with a plaintive, babyish disclaimer of "What can you expect from poor little me?" this is an example of passive hostility. In reality, the facts are she is shafting him. What can he do? She has him in the unenviable position of being a bastard if he does anything. Today, kids frustrate the hell out of cops, and when the cops react, they are the bastards.

The final technique used by blacks is outright militancy, as practiced by the Black Panthers.

FREEDOM AND HOSTILITY

All these pressures from black people forced the enaction of legislation ensuring more political, social and economic freedom to the black population of our country. What is the result of this increased freedom? To the bewilderment of many of our citizens, it has been an increase in the manifest hostility of black people to white people and their institutions.

Why, when freedom is increased, is the result this increased hostility? The answer is simply that increased freedom permits the direct expression of hostility.

All totalitarian regimes require their subjects to displace their hostility, to find scapegoats for the frustrations that exist. If there is an economic downturn in Russia, the government says, "Don't you dare blame us: let's have a hate-America campaign or an anti-Semitic campaign. Hate them, not us!" The essence of freedom is the right to be mad at the person who hurts you, rather than being forced to hate someone else or yourself to release the tension of built-up hostility.

As we increase freedom in our society, and as we democratize our political, social, economic, religious, and military institutions, we should be prepared for an increased direct expression of hostility. Black hostility is being directed to the frustrating object—white society—more and more, and increasingly this hostility has escalated to violence. While in 1976 the violence has subsided in the United States, this is perhaps only temporary. Rhodesia is a more contemporary illustration of the rise of violence. It must be understood that when past hostility does not lead to change, this magnifies present hostility.

As a symbol of past repressions, the black ghetto has borne the impact of much of black violence. The magnitude of this violence is also a function of the fact that the hostility is displaced from the original frustrating object—white society—to the more visible and convenient black ghetto. Unless white America ceases to merely appease its conscience with racial tokenism and begins to share real economic and political power with the black man, the frustrations of blacks will continue to increase. We will see more frequent and greater violence in our society directed to the real source.

AND THEN THERE'S THE GRADUATE

For management, however, the problem of black hostility is less a societal phenomenon than one which has its roots in know-how. Today, management must not only be able to deal with and understand black hostility; it must also differentiate this hostility from the hostility it is facing from other new employees, particularly college graduates.

A recent perplexing phenomenon in industry has been the emergence of a new breed of bright, competent, and openly aggressive college graduates. Unwilling to kowtow to established company policies, to respect superiors who have outgrown their competencies, and to accept routine work, the new employees are openly reacting to these sources of frustration. To meet this challenge from these "kids," competent management today must respond by changing outmoded rules, replacing outmoded managers, and redesigning outmoded jobs. If they do not, the organization will slowly die.

Unfortunately, most black hostility is not similarly based on frustrated competence. By treating blacks in this country "as a peasant population" for the last 200 years, we have ensured that the black will be incompetent in today's technological world. To be sure there are other incompetent groups today, and more and more people are becoming more incompetent as our technological and informational "explosion" continues. For example, we can view the "hard hat" phenomenon and associated sloganeering as the displaced hostility of the lower middle-class white to being replaced by automated machinery on his construction job. Other than the blacks (and the Indians), however, no other group has historically been forced into being incompetent.

INCOMPETENCE IS NOT BEAUTIFUL

As a result of this incompetence, most efforts at black inclusion into society have failed. To develop community action groups and build a political power base for black participation in the white power structure, effective organizational mechanisms must exist. While there certainly are many powerful and effective black leaders, the scarcity of competent black rank-and-filers hinders such strategies. You cannot have an organization without an infrastructure on which to build that organization.

As the manager who has become obsolete unwittingly uses slogans to mask his incompetence, so does the black. Black sloganeering, however, has twofold indications. Certainly, "Black Power" and "Black is beautiful" are necessary concepts for increased black awareness of black identity. However, these slogans must not be used as a substitute for competence. Slogans will not make a black a better worker, because they cannot teach him how to do a better job. Management should accept black slogans as a means for blacks to minimize the pain of living in what now is essentially a white, hostile environment. They should not, however, accept black slogans as a justification for doing poorly on a job.

With the passage of civil rights legislation, the black has achieved legal equality within the system. The danger is in allowing this equality to substitute for achievement on a task. Giving equality of opportunity has ensured an inequality of achievement for blacks. This will remain so until efforts are directed at making the black competent to achieve on his job. Recent educational requirements for high school graduation and college entrance in California and New York are an admission by our educators of the necessity for these recommended efforts.

This is not a form of the "white man's burden." The working-age black population in this country, both male and female, forms a labor pool which must be fully tapped before both the economy and the country can be totally healthy.

Despite the family hour on television designed to restrict hostility to mature audiences, very little is being done to educate the population, particularly managers, on the need to understand and manage hostility. Detente is still overshadowed by an escalation of hostility throughout the world.

The end of obligation

THREE FAILURES OF BEHAVIORAL SCIENCE

Everywhere in the world today management people are looking at two problems: How do you manage people? Why do people work? These questions used to spark intellectual repartee among the academically minded behavioral scientists, but industry no longer can afford to test out all the answers, however convoluted or well packaged they may be. To survive economically, organizations need the right answers now. While behavioral science has attempted to provide these answers, the more industry needs them, the farther away behavioral science gets from providing the right ones.

If we review the applications of behavioral science over the past 50 years or so we find three major failures in their efforts. These failures, coming from their own lack of understanding about the motivations of people, have confused industry more, when it needs confusion least.

THE FAILURE OF SCIENTIFIC MANAGEMENT

One is the failure of behavioral science founded on scientific management principles—often referred to as Taylorism. The revolt against the assembly line is not actually new. Remember Charlie Chaplin's indictment in the 1930s film *Modern Times?* What has happened today is that this revolt has found its time; it has become psychologically, socially, and, perhaps, for a practical world, economically relevant.

The work stoppage at the General Motors Corporation Vega assembly plant at Lordstown, Ohio, was not a warning of things to come; it was rather an illustration that the change had already arrived. Both the union and management conceded that they were surprised by the depth of the resistance. A young spot welder commented in a news report: "What they are doing, they are trying to take away our dignity. Maybe they could do that in the thirties, but this generation and myself won't let it happen here."

The activist youngsters have made all the change they are going to make—which has been considerable, but far short of Abbie Hoffman's revolution. The next revolution will come from the working "straights." The same news article reports that management has attempted to conciliate by instituting sensitivity training sessions in which groups of workers can air their gripes—tender loving concern for boredom.

The assembly line's days are numbered. Its efficiency is no longer persuasively defended; it is the lack of alternatives that sustains its use. And companies will soon run out of countries where they will be able to find cheap and willing hands.

Many of the personnel techniques that have accompanied Taylorism are also in trouble: testing for square pegs, rigid job descriptions, job evaluations, time and motion procedures, incentive systems, performance appraisals, personality assessments, and interest, attitude, and morale surveys.

The abuses of these procedures have long been silently recognized as personally degrading. Often their validity has relied mostly on the games that personnel psychologists play. Now they are becoming economically ineffective.

THE SOCIALIST TRAGEDY

Behavioral science founded on ideology has also failed. In Europe and elsewhere the socialist ideologists believed and hoped that as a result of the establishment of a socialist system people would be willing to work, to cooperate, to run efficient societies. It was believed that the difficulty in managing people lay in the capitalist system itself. Once a society had produced socialism or believed in socialist ideology, the natural cooperativeness of man would get people to work efficiently and harmoniously together.

The ideology of socialism has been one of the tragic failures in answering the question: How do you manage people effectively in organizations? Nationalized industries in Western democracies are certainly no models for work motivation. And certainly the productivity of Russia cannot be considered a claim for the success of Communism in motivating workers.

The failure of all the utopian notions is inherent in the belief that man can be defined and approached in terms of an ideal society. The group becomes the unit to be served, rather than the individual. If the primacy of the group coincided with the primacy of the individuals' needs, ideologists would not need their slogans, indoctrination, and physical persuasions to convince the individual of his best interest.

Ideology has been revealed to be what I call a KITA—a kick in the pants. And KITA leads to movement, not to motivation.

HUMAN RELATIONS FALLS SHORT

Behavioral science failed, too, when it was linked with the human relations movement. In the United States we used our ideology more as a cultural noise, not to be taken too seriously in practical application. We have been essentially a pragmatic nation. For example, human relations was not genuinely considered to be a value system but rather a technology to be mastered.

Handling people was regarded as a skill that can be taught and learned. From Dale Carnegie to sensitivity training and now, transactional analysis, we taught managers how to deal with people from a practical body of know-how. This, too, has failed. I have invented my own form of group encounter therapy for managers. We all sit around with our clothes on.

What we now are beginning to recognize is that people's attitudes are more a consequence of their behavior than precursors to behavior. Attitudes are the rationalizations, confirmation, and justifications of the behavior that our abilities and opportunities essentially permit.

In this sense, then, the attitudes of workers are appropriate to what they can do. A worker on an assembly line who has a responsible attitude toward his work must be either mentally retarded or mentally sick. You are asking him to be a responsible idiot.

Human relations technology was an attempt to create an inappropriate attitude among workers toward the behavior they had to manifest. Little wonder then that failure has resulted.

Scientific management defined man as an extension of machines and organizations. Socialist ideologies defined man with qualities that would perfect group behavior. And the behavioral scientists defined man in terms that matched their diagnostic, therapeutic, and manipulative techniques—joining with the ideologist for a humanist rationalization for their procedures and joining the Taylorists for acceptance by management.

The human relations, group dynamics, and organizational development movement has been used by industry as a psychological humanitarian veneer to Taylorism, just as the amelioration of physical conditions was the focus of the industrial humanitarian movement following the labor reforms of the first third of this century.

SWAPPING MANAGERIAL GARBAGE

The failure of socialist hopes in Europe has led to the massive importation of U.S. human relations technology, whereas the failure of the same techniques in the United States is leading to the importation of ideologic-sponsored suggestions for our industry.

Participative industrial democracy is the most persuasive of these new imports. However, I find that the tempting notion of democratizing our organizations is still based on the wishful-thinking psychology that underlies the socialist ideology.

Let us examine a socialist system that has lived up to its loftiest idealistic values and avoided human obscenities on the way to its goals but now is in trouble. I am referring to the Israeli kibbutz. With about 3 percent of the population, the Israeli kibbutzim have reclaimed the desert and swampland, wrought agricultural miracles (and, recently, similar miracles in factory production), provided the political and military leadership of the country, secured a high standard of living for its members, and, most important, avoided a drug counterculture among its hard-working youth.

THE EQUALITY OF IGNORANCE

What is happening to this most promising experiment? During the Turkish period and then in the British mandate times, the Israeli kibbutzim were started by socialist ideologists who came from many nations. They were inspired by two dreams: the establishment of a national home for Jews and the perfection of a socialist egalitarian society.

These pioneers represented many occupations and stations in life: doctors, lawyers, shoemakers, laborers. They shared all the work, the living conditions, and the fruits of their labor equally. In fact the goal of part of the Zionist movement was to create a Jewish proletariat in opposition to the professional, merchant, petty artisan, and shopkeeper roles that social, religious, and political persecution had forced them into.

So the doctor would spend his time working in the fields and orchards and with the dairy cattle and take his turn with such less attractive chores as kitchen and latrine duty. Similarly, the unskilled laborer would rotate from farming to household duties. In fact they were all equal— *equally ignorant*. The doctor and the shoemaker and the laborer were equally ignorant about how to develop an orange grove or how to run a dairy farm.

SPECIALIZATION BREEDS INEQUALITY

As they learned and as the family communal farm prospered and grew into a factory in the field, the equality of ignorance disappeared. There now is a Ph.D. in animal husbandry in charge of the dairy cattle. Whereas before the kibbutz manager was chosen for his accepting personality and empathic nature, he now spends a year or two at the Ruppin Institute studying for the equivalent of a Master of Business Administration before assuming his position.

Whereas before all members shared equally in the work, the Ph.D. in animal husbandry and the kibbutz leader who is a graduate of the Ruppin Institute can condescendingly agree to serve their day in the kitchen. But the laborer or the shoemaker cannot run the dairy farm, plan the marketing of the fruits and vegetables, arrange for bank loans, negotiate trade agreements, or do all the other managerial and technical tasks that a modern factory farm requires.

There now is a specialization and a hierarchy of labor. It is a techno-logic system, and a technologic system depends on a specialization of knowledge and a consequent inequality in decision making. There can be equality only in emotions or in work environment, but technology does not understand emotions. Even in the job environment inequalities must occur. Certain positions now have requisite appurtenances of office: private telephones and automobiles, travel abroad, and even appropriate business dress. The inequality spreads.

It might be mentioned that the modern women's liberation movement started in the kibbutz, because the women were completely equal to men. As in all pioneer societies, they were needed as equals. Now the young women are leaving the kibbutzim as the specialization of labor relegates them more and more to working in the kitchen and the children's houses. It is interesting to note that as the women are reverting to the more traditional roles, more kibbutz members are opting for having their children live with them rather than in the traditional communal chil-dren's houses.

To deal with the discontents arising from these changes, the kibbutz leaders are inviting human relations experts from the United States to teach their members how to get along with one another through sensi-tivity training sessions. Here is a system that originated in the idea of people getting along with one another, based on ideology, which is now depending on U.S. human relations technology to do the job.

DIFFERENCES MUST BE RECOGNIZED

Democracy is a most inefficient system for running a technologic or-ganization. Democracy in management decisions works best when there is an equality of ignorance. The communes of the young people or certain religious groups can succeed as a return to primitiveness for an individual style of life. But there is no going back to a supposed romantic past for an industrial society. The technologic base is so complex that the result is more likely to be catastrophe than romance.

Does this mean that we must have only authoritarian-managed or-ganizations? By no means—a difference in or inequality of knowledge does not mean there must be inferiority in terms of equitable treatment of employees or the opportunities to enjoy meaningful and prestigious work. However, participation alone does not remove differences in ability and practice.

Americans have differed from Europeans in that we have placed a higher priority on pragmatism than on our ideology. We have, however, not been lacking in revolutionary zeal. Our ideas have been revolutionary while our implementation has been pragmatic, whereas in the socialist nations there have been pragmatic ideas but revolutionary implementa-tion. The elimination of gross unfairness, exploitation, unearned privilege, and corruption are pragmatic ideas of ways to improve society. But their implementation becomes idealistic and inefficient when they result in the nationalization of companies run by incompetent party functionaries, forced cooperation, suspension of individual freedoms and ideas, and the use of slogans as substitutes for know-how and as excuses for mistakes. Let us not confuse slogans for know-how as we face the need for change in the management of our organizations.

A NEGATIVE RETURN IN PRODUCTIVITY

These newer approaches to the management of people—the human relations technology and social and industrial democracies—have arisen out of real concerns of management, but the approaches fall short. They use old concepts from antiquated geographies to map the psychology of the worker. Monetary manipulating magic, the controls vise, and the Phase 1, Phase 2, and extended Phase 2 of 1972 did little to reduce unemployment or stabilize prices and permit a return to a free economy.

The real name of the game is worker productivity, and we will have to come to grips with the elementary economic fact that employees are, in a great part, providing a negative return for the investment made in them. This is the problem facing management today, and no amount of human relations or socialistic equity seeking can resolve it.

What has happened to the willingness of workers to be productive? Where has our work ethic gone?

I believe, as stated previously, that the overall cause for the apparent loss of the work ethic is a change that has come about in the focal existential question of life that is being posed by our society. It is not articulated well by most workers, but it is felt by a majority of them.

In a nondeveloped society the central existential question has dealt with the meaning of the past, the meaning of *traditions,* and the meaning of death. In contrast, for a modern affluent society the central question revolves around the meaning of the present, the meaning of the future, and the meaning of life.

The question being asked today is "What kind of life am I leading?" rather than "What kind of traditions can I uphold?" It reflects a search for an awareness of oneself, with an acceptance of the right to own one's own existence. Whereas such a question was the doubtful luxury of a few in the past (though latent in all men at all times), it has become the cornerstone of thought for the majority today.

THE END OF OBLIGATION

When a significant life becomes more important, the upholding of traditions at the expense of the quality of living is no longer an obligation.

We see this end of obligation very clearly in attitudes toward the Vietnam War. When our military and our national "patriotic" traditions were first in our psychological hearts, we could expect our young men to give their lives for these traditions. But when life itself is the main concern, young men feel no obligation to destroy it for what they consider secondary and somewhat irrelevant values under the present circumstances. This is not the thinking of a radical. Former President Nixon had created an all-volunteer army by 1973, suggesting, with the end of the draft, an end of the obligation for citizens to serve their country in a military capacity.

This end to obligation is also seen in the various rights movements. The black no longer feels obligated to be the "nigger" for some of the white man's traditions. Women no longer feel obligated to live their traditional lives through their husbands and their children. Many clergy no longer feel obligated to give up living what they consider to be a more valid religious life for the traditions of their respective churches.

Similarly, workers no longer feel obligated to diminish their lives to uphold the free enterprise system, just as workers in Russia no longer feel obligated to a nonconsumer existence to uphold the slogans and traditions of Communism.

IMMIGRANTS AND THEIR CHILDREN

The obligation to traditions is a product of an immigrant labor mentality, be it the labor migrating from the farms to the city, political and religious refugees fleeing their native countries, or migrants seeking opportunities in another country. Migrants affected much of our past and now are present in Europe, with southern nationalities entering the northern industrial economies.

The immigrant laborer was seeking security and a future for his children. This, along with the hope of consumerism, meant a successful work life. He would bear his life on a Mickey Mouse job and gather his psychological income from his social, ethnic, religious, political, and family traditions.

His children, however, find these traditions wanting when compared with their desire for personal fulfillment and significance in what they do. For them, security and consumerism are more rights than rewards. As members of the new generation face the dull routine of their jobs today, they lack the substitute psychological income of their parents' traditions, so they see their whole life as Mickey Mouse.

They are consequently under no personal obligation for productivity, work quality, or work discipline. Each of these would require more effort at the cost of further debasing their self-esteem. They want more money irrespective of performance, as much out of anger as out of equity. And no reciting of traditional Protestant ethic slogans of work as therapy, as character building, or as noble effort is going to influence them much. (Remember, too, the Protestant ethic is in reality a negative KITA, or kick in the pants, as its traditional justification for hard work was to avoid sin, not to attain the satisfaction of personal achievement.)

This attitude is characteristic not only of youth—it has caught the older worker as well. Many employees in their fifties, with early retirement policies facing them, are finding that their traditions have become rather weak pillars upon which to rest the remainder of their lives.

MAKING WORK LIFE MEANINGFUL

Forget about obligation as a management lever.

If the central existential question is the meaning of life, then industry, must make the work life more meaningful if it is to achieve its sought-after productivity. Industry will need to be concerned with this psychological aspect of industrial relations. No society can exist without dependable obligations. Pious, sincere attempts to build these obligations through human relations, love, and ethics, while always necessary, are grossly inadequate today.

Structural changes in our world of work are required to build obligations to society through the obligations of the individual to his own meaningful activity and development. Our work must be redesigned to enable the employee to derive intrinsic satisfaction from its performance. It must include large amounts of education and training and be considered as much leisure as it is work.

This combination of work, education, and leisure is the future. Our managerial and behavioral science efforts need to be directed toward preparations for the organizational structures, management know-how, and labor legislation necessary to deal with the new significance and a new style of work.

Reasons for pursuing success

We are just coming through one of the most ambitious periods in American life. For over a quarter of a century, since the end of World War II, Americans have attempted five Herculean national tasks:

1. The reconstruction of Europe and the defense of the world.
2. The generation of maximum economic growth.
3. The attempt to nation build in Southeast Asia.
4. The attempt to people build among minorities in this country.
5. A beginning of earth building in our new awareness of the ecological problems that have emerged.

Those who lived through this quarter of a century were caught up in the challenge of these immense tasks, and many found in them justification for their strivings. Now, however, we have faced the end of the Vietnam War, followed by Watergate, with a sense of national dullness and fatigue, disillusionment, and an inability to work out our feelings. It seems the present generation of young people will face mostly a philosophy of negativism as they seek guidelines for their own strivings. In particular, they must search out new reasons to achieve success.

THE FIVE JUSTIFICATIONS

Historically, there have been five justifications for the success of some people and the failure of the rest. Let us examine these five justifications to see where they stand today.

First is the justification of power—power from whatever source it may arise. This justification is one of the earliest, most pervasive rationales for the success-failure differences among people, and certainly it is the most continuous one. Today, as we have seen illustrated so painfully in Vietnam, power has reached its limit of effectiveness. Its escalation in all parameters of life has concomitantly stretched its use so that it yields counterproductive results, or goes to the point of overkill. The limits of power seen at the national level also are reflected in the limitations of power at the organizational and individual levels.

What we have learned as a nation, through profound tragedy, the young people will have to learn as individuals. Success will be just as likely to limit their power to influence others, to influence events, and most of all, to influence their own lives as it once was believed to enhance these influences.

The second obvious reason for pursuing success is the desire for a better life. The consumer society has indeed become a worldwide phenomenon, extending, at least in terms of aspiration, to the remotest regions of the earth. A primitive native who inhabited hut No. 4 in clearing No. 6 in the thickest jungle of Africa once felt deprived if his neighbor had two elephant's teeth and he only had one. Now, with modern communication facilities, he has the whole consuming world to compare his lot with, and his deprivation level has soared to astronomical levels. The wants of a ghetto child encompass the wants of the most affluent segments of our society. Psychological perimeters stretch vastly beyond geographical boundaries.

Yet in the 1960s, the affluent child became disillusioned with the values and the costs of the so-called better life. His achieving parents also began to experience the seamier side of their better life—hippy children, soaring divorce rates, alcoholism, and sheer boredom. The quality of life became an issue, in opposition to the post–World War II devotion to the quantities of life. The historic philosophical dedication to the good life has surfaced again to temper the validity of increased consumption as a reason for striving for success. The children of postwar achieving parents began to wonder: Is success worth it? They began to explore alternatives to careerism and to reject their parents as models for their future lives.

The third reason for pursuing success historically has been religious in character. The most famous of these was the Protestant ethic, which suggested that a clue to one's predestination was the measure of earthly success for some, particularly in economic areas, and God's design of damnation for the rest. Business was religion, and religion became business. Or as the proverb had it, "Seest thou a man diligent in his business —he will stand before kings."

Religious purposes too are failing as a reason for pursuing success. Whatever your private beliefs are, from a psychological, public-health point of view of society, they are no longer such a potent force in justifying individual behavior in the pursuit of success. I can suggest two obvious reasons for the dissipation of religion as a motive force and a rationale for individual endeavor.

The first reason can be found in the explosion of knowledge, and in particular its accompanying technology. In addition to the intellectual conflict this growth of knowledge and technology has created between religious and "scientific" beliefs, more importantly it has made it impossible for the individual to permeate his daily life with religious convictions. Religion, by necessity, has had to become a part-time activity, where once it entered all aspects of life. This is not a matter of intellectual or moral conviction. It has become a necessity to disestablish religion in the practical affairs of coping with modern technology.

The other reason for the weakening of religious values as a justification for success or failure has been the idiosyncratic nature of religious morality, and often there is immorality in the translation of religion from the sermon to the realities of social responsibility. Again, this is not at the intellectual or faith level but at the level of practicality. As a result, religion has become too preoccupied with defining its position and has lagged behind nonreligious moral leaders and thought. This historic lag of religion in moral leadership makes the reactive retreat to fundamentalism seem more defensive than sincere.

The fourth reason for pursuing success that no longer sustains an achieving society is the 19th-century concept of social Darwinism. It was believed that success or failure is dictated by inexorable laws in the social and economic spheres of life, paralleling the inexorable laws of biology. The economic and social jungle was equated to the biological jungle, where biological fitness determines success or failure. Modern awareness of economics, sociology, and psychology has pretty much debunked this self-serving determinism. Children in the ghetto are there because of social and economic deprivation; they are not inevitably the products of some universal, intractable law of social science. Rather, they are more probably the products of the social diseases produced and made communicable by man.

The fifth reason for pursuing success that is becoming increasingly difficult to maintain as a rationale has been the 1950s and early 1960s concept of meritocracy. This idea maintained that those with better plans, better motivation, and better capability, and those who successfully jumped the academic and social hurdles, had proved themselves worthy of their positions. I suspect that part of the student revolution of the 1960s here and abroad, particularly the 1968 revolution in France, stemmed more from an objection to the antiseptic nature of meritocracy than from disillusionment with the morality of society in general. The rhetoric dealt with the latter, but I believe that the disruptive force of these student revolutions was more related to their disillusionment with the psychology of meritocracy.

The strange failure of meritocracy lay in cheating the achiever of his sense of achievement. Achievement was not a measure of individual personal worth and growth; it became the sterile beating of others. No satisfaction ensued. It was only, "I am better than they." Richness of learning and personal growth were vitiated. The merit scholar found himself an uncreative product of an academic and business assembly line. He became an instrumental man with little goal- or value-choosing freedom.

CONTINUING INFLUENCE

All of these reasons—power, consumerism, religion, social Darwinism and meritocracy—no longer seem to the introspective (and not too introspective) person to be psychological justification for the pursuit of personal success. They will obviously linger on, but primarily as half-hearted slogans. They will continue to exert a force in our society because of a lack of alternatives and especially because of the excesses of the objections that have been made to them.

As a result of our Vietnam experience, power has been denounced as totally evil and wrong. This has led to demands for complete demilitarization and isolation as a national policy. The reaction to this naivete will serve to sustain power as a motive force in our society. In our organizational life, the demand for complete participative democracy will encourage the applications of power and autocratic hierarchy to defend organizations against anarchy and mediocrity as the norm. With such a norm, modern technology in organizations cannot survive; technology recognizes that the only equality is the equality of ignorance.

An economic recession, continuing inflation, and rising taxes have all combined to stall the movement away from consumption to other values in life. The older generation has become obsessed with holding onto what they have, and in just a few years, as a result of the realization that the gravy train of assured good jobs is not automatically coming, the younger generation has climbed back onto the bandwagon of careerism and consumerism. I have witnessed the quickest third act in the scenario of student protest; in the space of one year, the concern with quality and purpose of education has succumbed to the greed for grades. This reversal in goals has been a demonstration of how quickly reality testing catches up with one in life.

The reaction against the force of religion has led to the extremes of social disorganization, the end of obligation, and the most grotesque protest—the drug culture. To protect ourselves from these overreactions, religion can proclaim the negative value of being a shield against this sort of human debasement.

The manifest failure of much economic, sociological, and psychological theory, particularly as it was translated into social engineering, will to some extent sustain the social Darwinist's beliefs in the inherent inequality of man. The search will be intensified for locating success-failure differences in the genes.

Finally, meritocratic beliefs will be sustained by the effort to bring about an equality of results, as opposed to equality of opportunity.

A FRESH REASON

People of all ages will need a fresh reason for pursuing success. As I have indicated, the five traditional justifications have been found wanting and are surviving only as warmed-over motives, in response to the extreme reactions they have produced. As our society settles down and can take time to sort out its feelings, the personal achievement motive may emerge as a justification. By this I mean a pure achievement motive, not an advertising slogan.

Economic crisis and work motivation

There has been a persistent view among the more tradition-oriented and depression-scarred managers that the "return" of worker motivation must await a "good" economic recession or depression. With the economic crisis creating more unemployment and a consequent increase in the feelings of job insecurity, it was believed by some that we could anticipate proper worker motivation and productivity. I concur that this could happen, but fear will not be the reason. Fear has never been a motivator, but rather a temporary incentive for worker compliance.

The reason I believe that work motivation can be improved is that the economic crisis is restricting the worker's opportunity to escape from unrewarding jobs into the frantic pursuit of recreational activities that was so characteristic of the last decade. The tolerance of the worker for his unrewarding job, in order to be able to take his boat to a lake or his camper to a park or his family to a resort, will not be as great as it was before.

Consequently, people will need to find more enjoyment at their workplaces, rather than just suffering their jobs in order to find compensation in the previously available recreational escapes. And, of course, if people start to truly enjoy their work, they will become more efficient. However, this will depend upon whether industry will make the necessary effort to redesign work so it is something the worker can enjoy.

If this comes about, then the energy crisis may be a serendipitous benefit to the nation. For too long we have relegated the world of work to a secondary, disagreeable aspect of life, to be endured in order to enjoy afterwork hours. With the alternative of compensatory recreational and avocational opportunities reduced, we will need to give more priority to work as of major psychological significance to people. This should provide the benefits to organization of greater productivity and all-around efficiency.

Job enrichment efforts will have an additional incentive, for the pressure from employees for meaningful work undoubtedly will be greater. This pressure will more than offset the traditional fear of employees during recessions, which results in poor performance stemming from job insecurity.

In an expanding economy where waste, both of materials and human effort, can be afforded, there is a reluctance to experiment with making the work itself a satisfying activity. Instead, there is a tendency to consider work as just an instrumental act—a means to extrawork satisfactions. The pressure for meaningful work will become—in addition to an economic necessity—more of a psychological demand.

CRISIS BRINGS BACK ETHICS

In a time of shortages and economic crisis such as in World War II, waste, inefficiency, and slovenly work become ethically abhorrent, not only to managers but to the workers themselves. A different psychology arises during an expanding economy, as opposed to an economy beset by shortages. In an expanding, growth economy the major conflict centers on who is going to get more. In a shortage and crisis economy, the major question is who is going to get hurt more.

It is this last question which will reintroduce the need for ethics in the relationships between workers and their organizations. Ethics, which is essentially a concept of fairness, is a feature more of a society in stress than of a society of abundance. To be sure, the society beset by shortage limitations will produce the opportunistic chiseler and the "smart operator," but these types are no longer looked upon as representing the norm. Rather, they are regarded as deviates.

So, hopefully, poor performance by employees will not have the sanction of general acceptance that a wasteful society generally provides. Rather, the poor performance will be regarded as unethical behavior.

Perhaps, too, we will begin to distinguish between ethics and morals. The former is a question of fairness, whereas morals is mostly a question of taste. The social upheaval of the 1960s can be viewed as an attempt to make this distinction. We have confused the two and, as has been historically the case, justified the relaxation of ethics by arguing and propounding the rightness of one group's tastes (morals) over another group's tastes (morals).

The Watergate affair is a prime example of those who preach their own morals to the country, but preach them less as an uplifting value to be emulated and more as a pretext or justification for the relaxation of ethical (fair) behavior. There are, of course, legitimate moral concerns which a society must consider, but too often, as has happened in the United States recently, moral preachment has been a disguise for the absence of ethics.

If the social protests of the 1960s have succeeded in opening the society to an acceptance or even a tolerance of the varied tastes found in our people, perhaps the ethics of the society can be put in their proper perspective as a guide to human behavior. Shortages and sacrifices are more demanding of the ethics of a society than of its morals.

UPLIFT OR SLOWDOWN?

Conscientious work restructuring may be accelerated in our organizations, and our business, religious, and particularly political leaders may begin to stress ethics as the paramount virtue of our institutions, rather than their idiosyncratic moralities. If so, I can predict a most rewarding return to our economy of motivated behavior on the part of our work force.

If, however, the economic crisis is turned into a job security club to be wielded over the employees, and this is combined with a Billy Graham style of pontification on the moral (taste) characteristics of workers, then I can predict a supercrisis in our economy and a social system like England's.

If we do meet the challenge of work problems, organically by job enrichment and psychologically by a reaffirmation of ethics, we may reap a still more valuable human bonus. When meaningless jobs, consumerism, and moral indignation characterized the essential components of our society, the result was a loss in many important dimensions of our lives about which we have felt helpless in recent years.

When such a central aspect as our work life is depleted of psychological income, it creates an overloading effect on our other activities. Leisure, for example, certainly became overloaded. Rather than being a fulfilling experience in its own right, it became a compensation for the psychological deadness of work. Accordingly, most people rarely enjoyed their leisure; more accurately, they consumed it.

Interpersonal relationships were another critical area that became overloaded, in great part due to the psychological impoverishment of work. The husband who was bored on his job sought to make up for its lack of meaning by seeking psychological rewards from his wife that were beyond her capacity to fulfill, and he concluded that she was failing him. Similarly, the wife, bored with the routine of housework, became increasingly demanding of her husband in their social and psychological relationships, and he could not provide for her overloaded compensatory demand. Consequently, there was a sense of mutual failure. It is obvious that they were asking too much of each other. Tender loving care is not an antidote to boring activities.

This overloading of human relations eventually led to the debasement of this most human experience and need. Natural human relationships were changed into therapeutic encounters, and the richness and enjoyment of relations with other people were diverted to psychotherapeutic rituals.

The dinner party lost its intellectual stimulation and its interpersonal charm and became a group therapy session. The art of conversation was lost, and substituted for it was the development of communication skills, an offshoot of the human relations technology we developed when we dehumanized our institutions.

Perhaps with more interesting occupational lives, more ethical behavior, fewer hangups on the variety of human tastes, and less transportation available to separate ourselves from one another, we may recapture the pleasure of human company. The return to the enjoyment of human company stripped of the human relations skill component should reduce the interpersonal conflicts that plague our organizations. I suspect that the artificiality of the human relations technology that guides so much of our behavior in organizations produces subtle conflicts more than it succeeds in preventing or resolving manifest conflicts.

Should the economic crisis lead to more tolerance for individual tastes, more fairness among people in our organizations, and richer work assignments, worker motivation will be greatly improved.

Managing people in an era
of hopelessness

In the preceding articles of this chapter I have commented on many of the changes which have occurred in our society, and I have suggested that the most basic of these changes have taken place in the central existential questions of life. Historically, the revolutions shaping the minds of men and women have come about when two competing existential questions of life are interchanged. Our psychological lives are now turned toward such revolutionary purposes. I have suggested that we stop asking the older question: What is the meaning of the past, the meaning of traditions, the meaning of death? Instead, we can pose a second question: What is the meaning of the present, of the future, of living?

There is a desire for a more human existence today—a human existence that is defined as material *and* psychological well-being. Spiritual well-being (a tradition-oriented societal goal) is now considered to be a derivative of material and psychological well-being. Spiritual sustenance has remained for too long a semantic "noise," without sufficient hardness to support the material and psychological needs of modern man.

This change and others accompanying it have led to a series of paradoxes in our society, for one of the basic dynamics of change does create paradoxes. These paradoxes pose dilemmas for us which are at once inescapable and uncompromising in their double-edged challenges to our understanding. In turn, these dilemmas have led to a feeling of hopelessness in dealing with problems and to the dismissal of attempts to cope with them. Nevertheless, to cope with the problems of managing people today, we must look at people's dilemmas.

The dilemmas today are still the historic ones. They appear in every morality play—from Biblical allegories, Greek tragedies, medieval ghost stories, American cowboy pictures, to even the mod antihero art forms. But man's dilemmas today are compounded by an incredible acceleration in change. The wisdom of society has been able to cope sufficiently with the dilemmas of the human condition thus far, but change is coming so fast that conventional wisdom (or even sophisticated wisdom) is no longer effective. This projects a dismal future for the management of people.

Society throughout history has been built, nearly collapsed, and then rebuilt; it resembles a sine function. But now the periods of history have been so compressed that the past and the present are getting closer together, and we find it difficult if not impossible to predict the future. The particular question is: Will there be an upswing in the crucial dimensions of society, or will the sine function break at its trough, so we have to start again from ruins? With the knowledge that changes now are often irreversible, we must act with the same dedication of purpose as the community epidemiologist who is successful only through prevention of epidemics; he has failed once they occur. Epidemiology is the only major area of society where we have managed by prevention rather than by correction.

The present existential struggle for a human existence has led to a psychological revolution that must be coped with in the management of organizations today. Psychological science cannot help; it has failed miserably in making our organizations effective. Instead, I am hoping that a return to wisdom, something that has gotten lost in the psychological disciplines, may save us, our health and our sanity, by helping us cope with change. Without wisdom in the management of people today, we find blind alleys for the perplexed and pessimism for the dismayed.

PEOPLE OBSOLESCENCE

One of the most profound changes that is occurring is people obsolescence. The aspirations arising from a growth technology have led to increased material wealth but an acceleration of "unacceptable" jobs. For a more educated population, or at least a more *aware* working population, this compromise is unacceptable. The unskilled worker may not be educated, but he is no longer dumb. He now strongly objects to boredom, and he is very politically conscious about it.

At a recent international conference on the Sociology of Work in Toronto, Canada, a social scientist from East Germany offered a solution. He suggested that a productive worker is one who has the *proper social ideals;* responsible work means good *patriotic spirit.* Under such a regime, the individual who does not work hard gets a reeducation in political manners. Well, the workers in a free society do not buy this ideology any longer. They want the benefits now, both monetary and motivational, from their organizations.

Concomitant with the deskilling of work has been the upgrading of skilled professional work to the point of extreme specialization. The result is a polarized work force in which there exists a severe discontinuity of advancement opportunities. At the Toronto conference a Swedish scientist noted the increase in those who have stopped looking for employment. These people no longer have the skills to do the increasingly specialized work. They have also given up on jobs that offer them none of the motivators.

These trends, with the accompanying social welfare demands of modern society, have created a new class of workers, the *militant motivational unemployables*. These people will not do Mickey Mouse work, even if that is all they can do. Countries are running out of immigrant labor to perform boring jobs, and companies are running out of countries to run to for higher productivity at lower human costs.

Those who are skilled are becoming victims of specializations; more narrow training leads to professionally titled "idiot savants." The desire of this group of educated elite is to become renaissance men and women, but this is impossible, for their education, especially at the graduate level, has been vocational. They carry a Doctor of Philosophy degree, an M.D., or an M.B.A., and their know-how puts them in positions of managing, but they know nothing of the world. They run efficient enclaves in organizations but err badly outside of their highly sophisticated domains. Within the organizations, their narrow training leads to quick obsolescence of their talent, and they, too, become "ideological" in defense of their incompetence. More damaging still, the halo of their professional titles remains and continues to mislead the population. It is for these reasons that peer review in the medical profession has such strong supporters and such dogmatic antagonists.

The more educated population that we have produced since World War II has become more educated in the sense of *what they do not know*. This awareness has increased their feeling of being manipulated, and, then, more sophisticated manipulations have been attempted. The understandable reaction from the public is that they have been turning off—part of the reason for the end of obligation we find so prevalent today. Paradoxically, the demands for humanness have required more personal participation of all employees in organizational affairs and the democratization of our organizations. Yet the trend toward specialization contradicts this desire, and the competence of the people attempting to make management decisions in a committee composed of people differing in know-how is challenged. The result has been that employees have felt increasingly manipulated as our attempts to democratize our institutions have become, more and more, a human relations charade.

Specialization has increased the necessity for cooperation, which, of course, has increased the necessity for more organization. The result has been again paradoxical: The increased cooperation necessary to get a job done has had an antigravitational effect in human relations. What has occurred is simply a psychological overcrowding in our lives. People are seeking relief from other people.

We have here another paradox, because the single most pressing health problem we face is that we have to deal with more people in the world today. We are classifying more people as human beings with wants and rights, and the definition of a human being continually escalates to a more expensive organism. The consumer society indeed has become a worldwide phenomenon. It is said that we are approaching zero population growth in the United States. Nonsense! If we double the consumerism of our population, it is like doubling the population. What we have seen in our society, and it is true in other countries as well, is that more *wants* have become *rights,* and conversely, previous rights have become wants. Good medical care is now a right, and clean drinking water and fresh air have become wants.

CHANGES IN ORGANIZATIONS

The organizations have become bigger, and, as they have, the commercial and business aspects of these burgeoning organizations have increased exponentially. If we are to treat our employees more humanly, it would appear that these employees will need, on their part, a greater understanding of business principles.

Listening to doctors establishing an HMO (Health Maintenance Organization) or other group practice, you wonder how soon it will be before the traditional humanities education given in our preprofessional educational institutions will be the Master of Business Administration program. Tax shelter sophistication courses will replace courses in art appreciation in the undergraduate curriculum. This switch has already occurred in our professional organizations. They originally were begun in order to maintain professional and ethical standards, and they have turned into *trade associations.* As we strive not to live our lives by bread alone, we are forced more and more to become "economic man." That is the paradox.

Another change is in organizational objectives. In almost every organization in our society there has been a profound alteration of its professed objectives or in the objectives which it is being forced to consider.

We have seen the churches being completely disrupted because of changes in their objectives. What are their goals? Salvation, human decency, power competition? These all have been historic objectives of the church, but today this multiplicity of objectives is not only known by the hierarchal few but by most members of the church's organization and its constituency. We have seen business organizations veer from straight economic considerations to social action, not in the traditional sense of paternalism and welfare capitalism but as a primary goal to be served. The Army has become extremely confused as to what its primary objectives are. The modern volunteer Army is serving more political and social goals than defense goals; clearly this is an illustration of multiplicity of values within organizations that once were separated between organizations. These changes in objectives in organizations confuse employees and increase psychological disruptions among them as greatly as when technology and skill changes occur.

We are also witnessing in our professions horrendous changes in values. Nowhere else is this seen more than in the medical and legal professions. The change has been so rapid that it has resulted in obvious conflicts between traditionalists and liberalists. You will have to manage organizations with just such wide splits in values among your employees. And remember, values are not precursors to behavior. They are the results of behavior. You develop a behavior pattern, and then you develop an attitude and a value system that justify your behavior. All values do is enable you to read the environment to see whether your behavior is acceptable.

WHERE ARE THE HEROES?

Finally, who are the models and heroes that all society needs as guides to their lives? Are there corporate executives who provide this function for our young, middle-aged, and older employees? Certainly the political arena is no place to look! Even down to the nuclear family level we are hard pressed to find models or heroes. The boss is recognized as a mixed-up person. The switch that has come about is that models and heroes are not considered to have feet of clay, but rather they are considered to have *heads* of clay.

It seems that we have more answers in this world and, paradoxically, bigger and more unanswerable questions. But this is the nature of human enlightenment. The escalation of this paradox, however, is becoming a bit overwhelming.

We find that progress is man running around in bigger circles. Let me offer some recommendations, mindful that they are not easily implemented but are necessary alternatives to the paradoxical methods we now employ.

First, for organizations to be productive, the work must be intrinsically satisfying, not instrumental or "compensatory" for nonwork values. We need better enriched jobs and more training for these jobs.

Second, vocational training must be accompanied by human education. Paramedics, although they do not have all the know-how necessary to be a physician, can read Shakespeare.

Third, ethics must partially replace human relations courses in education and in industry. We need to know about how to live ethically more than we need to know how to understand and manipulate more effectively.

Fourth, the "now" generation must be enjoyed, not tasted by the leisure society. Motivation is now, not something you have to do on weekdays.

Fifth, we need to restore some traditions to give continuity of meaning and value to life. Traditions are misleading as guides for how to act, but they do tell us of our origins. It must be taken out of the hands of the marketeer. While nostalgia is a pleasant experience, today it has become a commercial enterprise or a political slogan. Although we cannot return, we can remember.

Sixth, sanity must be permitted and given its place in society. We have become too clinical in our observance of others, finding and expanding "blemishes" so that a person is known not for what he does well but for what he does not do, or does poorly or absurdly.

Seventh, and this is a part of our need to return sanity to our society, we need to have more respect for neurotics who feel guilty about their success, and to show more directly our disrespect for those with "character disorders" who are successful without guilt. The psychopath has far too long captured our imagination at our own expense, in all levels of leadership.

Eighth, we need renaissance men as leaders to be models for humans, not robotlike calculators. We need those who have a broader perspective of the world to guide us; the technologist is not equipped to solve these problems.

Ninth, we need to be decent, not to get something in return, not to make someone like us, but rather just to be decent. People want to be treated fairly; they do not want to be seduced into doing something they do not want to do in return for decent treatment.

Tenth, and finally, we need to restore education as a place to find doctrines that stress the permanence of change and the expectancy of nonchaos in one's life.

With these understandings we may yet, with wisdom, cope with change.

What people want from their jobs

Some years ago I had the opportunity to lecture on my theory of work motivation at the University of Leningrad in the Soviet Union. I was asked to offer any comments I had with respect to the first empirical job attitude investigation which had been conducted in the Soviet Union.

The Russians appear to have amended their convictions regarding the answers that can be derived from their ideology. In this instance, they seemed to have learned that the problems of people do not disappear once the communist ideology is accepted. Problems of people, the Soviets now realize, require "scientific" answers; hence their concern with such things as morale surveys. They are concerned with them because of absenteeism, labor turnover, productivity lapses, alcoholism—for all the reasons that we conduct such surveys. But particularly, they are seeking information to help them educate young workers to a socialist attitude to work.

Neither acceptance of the free enterprise system by the Americans nor belief in the communist system by the Russians seems to have absolved the industry of either nation from the need to be more rational about the problems of managing people. And it is more than coincidence that industrial relations research in the United States receives its greatest support during periods of highest economic success. For the Russians, too, such research began to appear only when the consumer society was getting underway.

WHAT HUMANS NEED

In accounting for this seeming relationship between economic success and the increased presence of social scientists in industry, a possible explanation lies in theory of motivation set forth by the late Abraham Maslow, an American psychologist. He proposed a theory of human motivation which suggests the following needs, which he listed in hierarchical order: physiological needs, safety needs, the need for belonging and love, the need for esteem, and, at the apex of human requirements, the need for self-actualization.

He further concluded that once a lower order need was satisfied it would no longer act as a motivator of behavior. Consequently, the individual would come under the stress of the next higher need in the hierarchy. Simply put, if I am not hungry, thirsty, cold, or in other ways in physical distress, the rewards in these areas will not serve to motivate my actions, but instead (and in the general case) I will be concerned with the need to protect and safeguard my social and psychological condition. Similarly, when I feel reasonably safe, I will seek rewards from interpersonal relationships. Then, in return, I will desire the ego satisfactions of reflected personal worth and, finally, intrinsic personal worth from my own sense of accomplishment, as contrasted with what others think.

Good evidence for the support of this notion of human wants comes from an examination of the historical development of the areas emphasized by industrial relations. With the rise of industry as the dominant institution of Western society, the primary view of the needs of man assumed by industry was that these needs are overwhelmingly economic. The concern of both management and labor was with how much money each could receive or hold on to as its share. Money meant survival and, out of the philosophy of social Darwinism, money became the symbol of the survival of the fittest in the economic jungle. That philosophy was considered to be a description of the fundamental nature of society.

AFTER MONEY, WHAT?

Next, industrial relations programs began to point to those needs that cater to the security fears of employees. Starting with the basic security goals that are served by safety programs, workmen's compensation, seniority guarantees, and union representation, management and unions inaugurated the era of fringe benefits. These fringe benefits have continued to widen and to cover more and more of the security demands of the work force. They now include such expanded security benefits as retirement plans, unemployment compensation and supplementary unemployment benefits, illness protection, early retirement, and the current concern with job retraining to meet the challenge of automation.

With the economic man firmly entrenched in the minds of management and manifestly also in the minds of the workers, and with the arrival of welfare capitalism or paternalism as an accepted industrial philosophy for meeting the security needs of employees, the next order of Maslow's needs cropped up to push management. It was the landmark studies at the Hawthorne (Chicago area) plant of Western Electric Company which first called attention to the social or belongingness needs of workers.

The Hawthorne studies demonstrated that the workers were capable of restricting output, to their own economic detriment, in order to be accepted by their fellow workers. In many ways it was shown that membership in a work group affected the plant's operation, contrary to expectations of the formal management system. These findings were instrumental in ushering in the age of human relations. So it was that Maslow's next higher need became a potent force in industrial relations programs.

As the human relations programs in industry became more sophisticated, managements began to concern themselves with more than the social needs of work groups. Industry started to serve the higher or ego needs partially included in the Maslow level of self-esteem. Instruction in personality dynamics—from the primitive courses offered to foremen to the deeper group therapy of sensitivity training for higher levels of management—have now become a common practice in American companies.

ENTER THE BEHAVIORAL SCIENTIST

Finally, today, self-actualizing, self-fulfilling achievement and growth needs have come to the fore. They represent the major theme of industrial relations exhortation, as in the writings of this author and Chris Argyris, Douglas McGregor, and David McClelland. In less than 100 years, the workers of this country have been credited with all five ranks of Maslow's system, which seem to have been recognized and provided for in a sequential order, although with some overlapping. The rise in the standard-of-living index does show a reasonable parallel with the hierarchy of needs of workers, and these needs demand satisfaction. As more needs, and particularly higher ordered ones, come into play, the behavioral scientist becomes more relevant.

MASLOW'S MISTAKES

The Maslow system, then, does seem appropriate, but it has holes in it. Lower-order needs never get satisfied, as witness the constant demand for physiological and security guarantees, the continuing socialization of our society, and the never-ending search for status symbols. This is evident even though we have recognized the importance of self-actualization as a potent force in the motivational makeup of people.

The Maslow system stresses the material needs of man as primary to his more "human" moral motives. The system has not worked in application because the biological and psychological needs of man are parallel systems, rather than either one assuming initial importance. A new theory of how the material and moral motives of man act together in work motivation is needed.

chapter 2

Motivation-Hygiene Theory

INTRODUCTION

Motivation-Hygiene Theory, one of the most controversial theories in industrial psychology, is an attempt to view the needs of man in a completely new light. This new view is a prerequisite to the formulation of more effective managerial procedures regarding human activity, which are so necessary today. The theory was first presented in *The Motivation to Work*, published in 1959,[1] and I further developed it in *Work and the Nature of Man*, published in 1966.[2] Those who wish to gain a more complete understanding of the development, research methods, and basics of the theory should consult these two books.

In this chapter only a very brief synopsis of the theory is presented. The first of the two articles in this synopsis ("The First Psychologist") introduces the two concepts of man which underlie the theory with the biblical archetypes of Adam and Abraham.

The second article illustrates the congruence of the two archetypes of man with the nature of job attitudes. The material for this second article was taken from the first half of the most reprinted article ever in the *Harvard Business Review*, "One More Time: How Do You Motivate Employees?"[3]

The next two articles in the chapter deal with individual and organizational differences in Motivation-Hygiene Theory terminology. Following

---

[1] Frederick Herzberg, Bernard Mausner, and Barbara Snyderman, *The Motivation to Work* (New York: John Wiley & Sons, 1959).

[2] Frederick Herzberg, *Work and the Nature of Man* (New York: Thomas Y. Crowell Co., 1966).

[3] Frederick Herzberg, "One More Time: How Do You Motivate Employees?" *Harvard Business Review,* January–February 1968, pp. 53–62.

the basic theory presentation and the articles on individual differences ("Motivational Types") and organizational differences ("Motivation-Hygiene Profiles") are two articles on the application of Motivation-Hygiene Theory principles to management in organizations. The first of these application articles, entitled "The Proper Management of Hygiene" deals with the question of how to treat people in organizations, while the last article, "The Proper Management of Motivators" addresses the question of how to use people in organizations.

The first psychologist

How did God define man's goals? The Old Testament presents us with two distinctly different versions of the strivings of man. The earlier concept is in the story of God's creation of the first human being, Adam, and the other version is found in the covenant he makes with Abraham and later with Moses.

Adam is presented as God's crowning achievement, to lord it over all his works. However, we are also told that Adam was feebleminded because he lacked the capacity for knowledge: "And the Lord God commanded the man, saying, "Of every tree of the garden thou mayest freely eat, but the tree of knowledge of good and evil, thou shalt not eat of it; for in the day thou eatest thereof thou shalt surely die" (Genesis 2:16).

Adam's punishment for standing psychologically upright and eating of the fruit of knowledge was being cast out of his "paradise" by God. This episode has had the enduring and powerful effect that man's life is viewed as an exercise in suffering. But, to those less pessimistically inclined, it symbolizes the moment when man accepted his own personality, destiny, and responsibility—"to fly with his own wings."

The former interpretation, however, has dominated throughout recorded history. With few exceptions, the consensus in most every culture has been that man's basic nature is that of an avoidance organism, somewhat less than the perfect human first constructed. He now shares kinship with all living matter in seeking to attune himself to his environment in order to survive. The environment is the source of danger and consequently the source of his unhappiness.

For lower animals, the environment to which they must adjust is predominantly physical, but for man the psychological environment becomes the major source of his dissatisfaction. The hygiene factors to be described in the next article are those aspects of the environment of work that man, in the image of Adam, seeks to avoid.

We find later on in the Bible God's additional acknowledgement that man is to be more than a contented innocent. He is also to be a striving, creating organism that would produce civilizations: "And when Abraham was ninety years old and nine, the Lord appeared to Abraham, and said unto him: I am God almighty; walk before Me, and be thou whole-hearted. And I will make My covenant between Me and thee and will multiply thee exceedingly . . . and thou shall be the father of a multitude of nations (Genesis 12:2)."

This statement to Abraham, later reaffirmed with Moses, was that man is capable, that he has been given the potential for an active mission to fulfill the Grand Design. The idea that man is created in the image of God can be construed as evidence that man is capable because he has been given divine abilities. Man, it would seem, is endowed with a nature that also impels him to utilize and to fulfill those capabilities that are distinctive of his position in the phylogenetic hierarchy.

Which view of man is correct? Man is obviously both Adam and Abraham, but, as each view has a different origin, satisfying the needs of one has little effect on the needs of the other. Adam is the nature of man which is concerned with unhappiness, and Abraham is the nature of man which seeks happiness. Both Adam and Abraham have to be served, and certainly one cannot be a substitute for the other. You cannot find happiness by avoiding pain, nor can you avoid pain by finding happiness.

One more time: How do you motivate employees? Part I

How many articles, books, speeches, and workshops have pleaded plaintively, "How do I get an employee to do what I want him to do?"

The psychology of motivation is tremendously complex, and what has been unraveled with any degree of assurance is small indeed. But the dismal ratio of knowledge to speculation has not dampened the enthusiasm for new forms of snake oil that are constantly coming on the market, many of them with academic testimonials. Doubtless this article will have no depressing impact on the market for snake oil, but since the ideas expressed in it have been tested in many corporations and other organizations, it will help—I hope—to redress the imbalance in the aforementioned ratio.

"MOTIVATING" WITH KITA

In lectures to industry on the problem, I have found that the audiences are anxious for quick and practical answers, so I will begin with a straightforward, practical formula for moving people.

What is the simplest, surest, and most direct way of getting someone to do something? Ask him! But if he responds that he does not want to do it, then that calls for a psychological consultation to determine the reason for his obstinacy. Tell him? His response shows that he does not understand you, and now an expert in communication methods has to be brought in to show you how to get through to him. Give him a monetary incentive? I do not need to remind the reader of the complexity and difficulty involved in setting up and administering an incentive system. Show him? This means a costly training program. We need a simple way.

Note: I should like to acknowledge the contributions that Robert Ford of the American Telephone and Telegraph Company has made to the ideas expressed in this paper, and in particular to the successful application of these ideas in improving work performance and the job satisfaction of employees.

Every audience contains the "direct action" manager who shouts, "Kick him!" And this type of manager is right. The surest and least circumlocuted way of getting someone to do something is to kick him in the pants—give him what might be called the KITA.

There are various forms of KITA, and here are some of them:

Negative physical KITA

This is a literal application of the term and was frequently used in the past. It has, however, three major drawbacks: (1) it is inelegant, (2) it contradicts the precious image of benevolence that most organizations cherish, and (3) since it is a physical attack, it directly stimulates the autonomic nervous system, and this often results in negative feedback—the employee may just kick you in return. These factors give rise to certain taboos against negative physical KITA.

The psychologist has come to the rescue of those who are no longer permitted to use negative physical KITA. He has uncovered infinite sources of psychological vulnerabilities and the appropriate methods to play tunes on them. "He took my rug away"; "I wonder what he meant by that"; "The boss is always going around me"—these symptomatic expressions of ego sores that have been rubbed raw are the result of application of:

Negative psychological KITA

This has several advantages over negative physical KITA. First, the cruelty is not visible; the bleeding is internal and comes much later. Second, since it affects the higher cortical centers of the brain with its inhibitory powers, it reduces the possibility of physical backlash. Third, since the number of psychological pains that a person can feel is almost infinite, the direction and site possibilities of the KITA are increased many times. Fourth, the person administering the kick can manage to be above it all and let the system accomplish the dirty work. Fifth, those who practice it receive some ego satisfaction (one-upmanship), whereas they would find drawing blood abhorrent. Finally, if the employee does complain, he can always be accused of being paranoid, since there is no tangible evidence of an actual attack.

Now, what does negative KITA accomplish? If I kick you in the rear (physically or psychologically), who is motivated? *I* am motivated; *you* move! Negative KITA does not lead to motivation, but to movement. So:

Positive KITA

Let us consider motivation. If I say to you, "Do this for me or the company, and in return I will give you a reward, an incentive, more status, a promotion, all the quid pro quos that exist in the industrial organization," am I motivating you? The overwhelming opinion I receive from management people is, "Yes, this is motivation."

I have a year-old Schnauzer. When it was a small puppy and I wanted it to move, I kicked it in the rear and it moved. Now that I have finished its obedience training, I hold up a dog biscuit when I want the Schnauzer to move. In this instance, who is motivated—I or the dog? The dog wants the biscuit, but it is I who want it to move. Again, I am the one who is motivated, and the dog is the one who moves. In this instance all I did was apply KITA frontally; I exerted a pull instead of a push. When industry wishes to use such positive KITAs, it has available an incredible number and variety of dog biscuits (jelly beans for humans) to wave in front of the employee to get him to jump.

Why is it that managerial audiences are quick to see that negative KITA is *not* motivation, while they are almost unanimous in their judgment that positive KITA *is* motivation? It is because negative KITA is rape, and positive KITA is seduction. But it is infinitely worse to be seduced than to be raped; the latter is an unfortunate occurrence, while the former signifies that you were a party to your own downfall. This is why positive KITA is so popular: it is a tradition; it is in the American way. The organization does not have to kick you; you kick yourself.

MYTHS ABOUT MOTIVATION

Why is KITA not motivation? If I kick my dog (from the front or the back), he will move. And when I want him to move again, what must I do? I must kick him again. Similarly, I can charge a man's battery, and then recharge it, and recharge it again. But it is only when he has his own generator that we can talk about motivation. He then needs no outside stimulation. He *wants* to do it.

With this in mind, we can review some positive KITA personnel practices that were developed as attempts to instill "motivation":

1. *Reducing time spent at work.* This represents a marvelous way of motivating people to work—getting them off the job! We have reduced (formally and informally) the time spent on the job over the last 50 or 60 years until we are finally on the way to the "6½-day weekend." An interesting variant of this approach is the development of off-hour recreation programs. The philosophy here seems to be that those who play together, work together. The fact is that motivated people seek more hours of work, not fewer.

2. *Spiraling wages.* Have these motivated people? Yes, to seek the next wage increase. Some medievalists still can be heard to say that a good depression will get employees moving. They feel that if rising wages don't or won't do the job, perhaps reducing them will.

3. *Fringe benefits.* Industry has outdone the most welfare-minded of welfare states in dispensing cradle-to-the-grave succor. One company I know of had an informal "fringe benefit of the month club" going for a while. The cost of fringe benefits in this country has reached approximately 25% of the wage dollar, and we still cry for motivation.

People spend less time working for more money and more security than ever before, and the trend cannot be reversed. These benefits are no longer rewards; they are rights. A 6-day week is inhuman, a 10-hour day is exploitation, extended medical coverage is a basic decency, and stock options are the salvation of American initiative. Unless the ante is continuously raised, the psychological reaction of employees is that the company is turning back the clock.

When industry began to realize that both the economic nerve and the lazy nerve of their employees had insatiable appetites, it started to listen to the behavioral scientists who, more out of a humanist tradition than from scientific study, criticized management for not knowing how to deal with people. The next KITA easily followed.

4. Human relations training. Over 30 years of teaching and, in many instances, of practicing psychological approaches to handling people have resulted in costly human relations programs and, in the end, the same question: How do you motivate workers? Here, too, escalations have taken place. Thirty years ago it was necessary to request, "Please don't spit on the floor." Today the same admonition requires three "please"s before the employee feels that his superior has demonstrated the psychologically proper attitudes toward him.

The failure of human relations training to produce motivation led to the conclusion that the supervisor or manager himself was not psychologically true to himself in his practice of interpersonal decency. So an advanced form of human relations KITA, sensitivity training, was unfolded.

5. Sensitivity training. Do you really, really understand yourself? Do you really, really, really trust the other man? Do you really, really really, really cooperate? The failure of sensitivity training is now being explained, by those who have become opportunistic exploiters of the technique, as a failure to really (five times) conduct proper sensitivity training courses.

With the realization that there are only temporary gains from comfort and economic and interpersonal KITA, personnel managers concluded that the fault lay not in what they were doing, but in the employee's failure to appreciate what they were doing. This opened up the field of communications, a whole new area of "scientifically" sanctioned KITA.

6. Communications. The professor of communications was invited to join the faculty of management training programs and help in making employees understand what management was doing for them. House organs, briefing sessions, supervisory instruction on the importance of communication, and all sorts of propaganda have proliferated until today there is even an International Council of Industrial Editors. But no motivation resulted, and the obvious thought occurred that perhaps management was not hearing what the employees were saying. That led to the next KITA.

7. *Two-way communication.* Management ordered morale surveys, suggestion plans, and group participation programs. Then both employees and management were communicating and listening to each other more than ever, but without much improvement in motivation.

The behavioral scientists began to take another look at their conceptions and their data, and they took human relations one step further. A glimmer of truth was beginning to show through in the writings of the so-called higher-order-need psychologists. People, so they said, want to actualize themselves. Unfortunately, the "actualizing" psychologists got mixed up with the human relations psychologists, and a new KITA emerged.

8. *Job participation.* Though it may not have been the theoretical intention, job participation often became a "give them the big picture" approach. For example, if a man is tightening 10,000 nuts a day on an assembly line with a torque wrench, tell him he is building a Chevrolet. Another approach had the goal of giving the employee a *feeling* that he is determining, in some measure, what he does on his job. The goal was to provide a *sense* of achievement rather than a substantive achievement in his task. Real achievement, of course, requires a task that makes it possible.

But still there was no motivation. This led to the inevitable conclusion that the employees must be sick, and therefore to the next KITA.

9. *Employee counseling.* The initial use of this form of KITA in a systematic fashion can be credited to the Hawthorne experiment of the Western Electric Company during the early 1930's. At that time, it was found that the employees harbored irrational feelings that were interfering with the rational operation of the factory. Counseling in this instance was a means of letting the employees unburden themselves by talking to someone about their problems. Although the counseling techniques were primitive, the program was large indeed.

The counseling approach suffered as a result of experiences during World War II, when the programs themselves were found to be interfering with the operation of the organizations; the counselors had forgotten their role of benevolent listeners and were attempting to do something about the problems that they heard about. Psychological counseling, however, has managed to survive the negative impact of World War II experiences and today is beginning to flourish with renewed sophistication. But, alas, many of these programs, like all the others, do not seem to have lessened the pressure of demands to find out how to motivate workers.

Since KITA results only in short-term movement, it is safe to predict that the cost of these programs will increase steadily and new varieties will be developed as old positive KITAs reach their satiation points.

HYGIENE VERSUS MOTIVATORS

Let me rephrase the perennial question this way. How do you install a generator in an employee? A brief review of my Motivation-Hygiene Theory of job attitudes is required before theoretical and practical suggestions can be offered. The theory was first drawn from an examination of events in the lives of engineers and accountants. At least 16 other investigations, using a wide variety of populations (including some in the communist countries), have since been completed, making the original research one of the most replicated studies in the field of job attitudes.

The findings of these studies, along with corroboration from many other investigations using different procedures, suggest that the factors involved in producing job satisfaction (and motivation) are separate and distinct from the factors that lead to job dissatisfaction. Since separate factors need to be considered, depending on whether job satisfaction or job dissatisfaction is being examined, it follows that these two feelings are not opposites of each other. The opposite of job satisfaction is not job dissatisfaction but, rather, *no* job satisfaction; and, similarly, the opposite of job dissatisfaction is not job satisfaction, but *no* job dissatisfaction.

Stating the concept presents a problem in semantics, for we normally think of satisfaction and dissatisfaction as opposites—i.e., what is not satisfying must be dissatisfying, and vice versa. But when it comes to understanding the behavior of people in their jobs, more than a play on words is involved.

Two different needs of man are involved here. One set of needs can be thought of as stemming from his animal nature—the built-in drive to avoid pain from the environment, plus all the learned drives which become conditioned to the basic biological needs. For example, hunger, a basic biological drive, makes it necessary to earn money, and then money becomes a specific drive. The other set of needs relates to that unique human characteristic, the ability to achieve and, through achievement, to experience psychological growth. The stimuli for the growth needs are tasks that induce growth; in the industrial setting, they are the *job content*. Contrariwise, the stimuli inducing pain-avoidance behavior are found in the *job environment*.

The growth or *motivator* factors that are intrinsic to the job are: achievement, recognition for achievement, the work itself, responsibility, and growth or advancement. The dissatisfaction-avoidance or *hygiene* (KITA) factors that are extrinsic to the job include: company policy and administration, supervision, interpersonal relationships, working conditions, salary, status, and security.

A composite of the factors that are involved in causing job satisfaction and job dissatisfaction, drawn from samples of 1,685 employees, is shown in Figure 1. The results indicate that motivators were the primary cause

Figure 1

Factors affecting job attitudes, as reported in 12 investigations

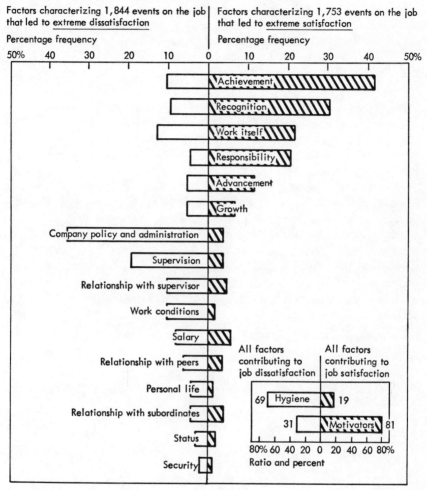

Factors characterizing 1,844 events on the job that led to extreme dissatisfaction

Factors characterizing 1,753 events on the job that led to extreme satisfaction

Percentage frequency

Percentage frequency

50% 40 30 20 10 0 10 20 30 40 50%

Achievement
Recognition
Work itself
Responsibility
Advancement
Growth
Company policy and administration
Supervision
Relationship with supervisor
Work conditions
Salary
Relationship with peers
Personal life
Relationship with subordinates
Status
Security

All factors contributing to job dissatisfaction

All factors contributing to job satisfaction

69 Hygiene 19
31 Motivators 81

80% 60 40 20 0 20 40 60 80%
Ratio and percent

of satisfaction, and hygiene factors the primary cause of unhappiness on the job. The employees, studied in 12 different investigations, included lower-level supervisors, professional women, agricultural administrators, men about to retire from management positions, hospital maintenance personnel, manufacturing supervisors, nurses, food handlers, military officers, engineers, scientists, housekeepers, teachers, technicians, female assemblers, accountants, Finnish foremen, and Hungarian engineers.

They were asked what job events had occurred in their work that had led to extreme satisfaction or extreme dissatisfaction on their part. Their responses are broken down in the exhibit into percentages of total "positive" job events and of total "negative" job events. (The figures total more than 100% on both the "hygiene" and "motivators" sides because often at least two factors can be attributed to a single event; advancement, for instance, often accompanies assumption of responsibility.)

To illustrate, a typical response involving achievement that had a negative effect for the employee was, "I was unhappy because I didn't do the job successfully." A typical response in the small number of positive job events in the company policy and administration grouping was, "I was happy because the company reorganized the section so that I didn't report any longer to the guy I didn't get along with."

As the lower right-hand part of the exhibit shows, of all the factors contributing to job satisfaction, 81% were motivators. And of all the factors contributing to the employees' dissatisfaction over their work, 69% involved hygiene elements.

Why do the hygiene factors make for job dissatisfaction? Because man is Adam, and as Adam he is an animal with an overriding goal to avoid pain from the environment. The hygiene factors describe the job environment. Why do the motivators make man job satisfied? Because man is Abraham, and as Abraham he is a *human* with an overriding goal to use his human talents for psychological growth, which is the source of human happiness. The motivators are the nutrients for psychological growth. It is what man can accomplish that makes him human, and what he can accomplish on the job will determine his human feelings.[1]

---

[1] This paragraph has been added to the original article by the author.

Motivational types: Individual differences in motivation

I have suggested that man is a duality, that the normal human being has two parallel and equal need systems. As Adam he is an animal, and as an animal he must adjust to the environment for survival and for comfort. I have called this the individual's hygiene requirements. On-the-job hygiene refers to the following environmental factors:

1. The company policy and administration which determine so much about where the individual works and under what conditions he works.
2. That very important environmental factor, who the man reports to, his supervisor.
3. All the various forms of interpersonal relationships he experiences at his place of work.
4. The working conditions, the salary, and all the other financial payments he receives.
5. The increasing number and variety of status feelings he experiences on his job.
6. Job security.

A deprivation in these factors can lead to job dissatisfaction, but their amelioration does not lead to job satisfaction. Pain can be relieved, but this is not in the ordinary or healthy sense a source of personal gratification. Normalcy requires that we avoid being hurt. It is all right to cry when you are hurt, but there is more to normalcy than just this.

As Abraham, man is a human being who must make an adjustment to himself. He continually strives for personal fulfillment and psychological growth.

On-the-job motivators encompass the nature of the tasks the individual performs and his opportunities to be challenged by the organization of these tasks.

Are there achievement possibilities in his job? Can he come home at night after having accomplished something on the job? Or does he just come home from a boring routine to rest and return again tomorrow, without the satisfaction of having done something with his training and education, and with his abilities unused or underused?

Is recognition given for those achievements that he does make? Or is recognition given, as it is so often in organizations, for simply being housebroken, not rocking the boat, never making a mistake which would be embarrassing to someone in the organization?

Is the work actually interesting, challenging, and worthwhile? Or does the organization just use these terms as cultural noises to buy or seduce the person into feeling important while doing a dumb job?

Does he have responsibilities as an adult, or are those responsibilities he really has better reserved for children?

Is he going anywhere? Is there professional advancement in where he is going in the organization? Is he going to do new things—tougher things?

Is he growing as a person on the job, or is the job just a place to spend the rest of his years before retirement?

These motivators characterize the needs that man has as a human being.

NORMAL PROFILES

If we are to understand the attitudes people have toward their jobs, we must know two things about them. First, does the person seek his satisfactions on two dimensions? Is he seeking psychological growth as well as freedom from physical and psychological discomfort? Second, how successful is he at meeting these two separate and equal need systems? Let us look at four prototypes of normal people at work.

The first type is the individual who exists in the best of all possible worlds (Figure 1). Here we have depicted an individual who is very

Figure 1

The best of all possible worlds

NORMAL PROFILE

Hygiene factors   Motivator factors

Needs fulfilled

high on hygiene fulfillment. He has a good salary, good fringe benefits, a wonderful boss to work under, nice subordinates and peers, a beautiful office. We can even extend this to his family life; he has a big house, a charming wife, lovely children, even a boat. He is *not unhappy*, he hurts very little, and he is a fortunate man indeed because he is also high on his motivators. His work is interesting, meaningful, challenging. He accomplishes something on his job, and he is growing psychologically. He is *very happy*.

In motivation-hygiene terms, we would describe this person's job attitudes as being *very happy* and *not being unhappy*. He meets the four requirements of living in the best of all possible worlds. He is seeking growth from either his job or his avocations, and he is finding growth

Figure 2

The starving artist

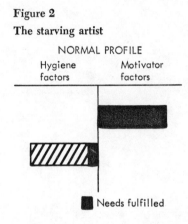

from either his job or his avocations. He is seeking the avoidance of pain from his environment, and he is also very successful in avoiding pain in his life.

Let us look at another situation where the individual is also a normal human being. This person is on the hygiene continuum, that is, seeking the avoidance of pain, and he also has motivator needs. He is on both need systems. This dual motivational pattern is what makes him normal. However, circumstances arise to make his hygiene very bad. He is unhappy, but he does have very good motivators. This is the starving artist illustration (Figure 2). If you ask a starving artist "How do you like your job?", he is likely to say, "I love my job but I hate starving." The point is, you do not give him a 50 percent morale score. If you do, you miss the whole point. He answered correctly: He said he was happy about what he was doing in life but was unhappy about the circumstances under which he must live. He was *happy* and he was *unhappy*.

There is also the "I'm all right, Jack" situation (Figure 3), in which the normal worker feels he is being treated all right. He is *not unhappy*.

However, he also feels he is doing meaningless, stupid, insipid, Mickey Mouse work. That is, he is *not happy*. Again, we do not give this man a 50 percent morale score. Unfortunately, this is the situation that characterizes too many workers in our industrial society today.

Finally, let us look at one of those tragic situations that a normal worker can find himself in: the down and out situation (Figure 4). A person can have very poor hygiene and at the same time very few motivators on his job. He can be starving and washing toilets. He can be very *unhappy* and in addition have very little *happiness*. He can be down and out but still fighting. Unfortunately, this situation has typified

Figure 3
"I'm all right, Jack."

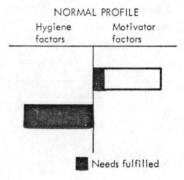

NORMAL PROFILE

Hygiene factors   Motivator factors

■ Needs fulfilled

many of our minority-group workers for too long a time, but remember, it also characterizes many other groups in our organizations and in society today.

ABNORMAL PROFILES (INVERSIONS)

What is an abnormal person in Motivation-Hygiene Theory? He is solely Adam. He is a person who exists solely on the hygiene dimension. His only goal in life is to avoid pain. It is important to remember that hygiene is as necessary as the motivators, but for different reasons. As I have said, it is all right to cry when you are hurt. It is perfectly normal to want money because it makes you less unhappy.

This point is one of the most misunderstood in all of Motivation-Hygiene Theory. A professor wrote an article entitled "Ominous Trends in Wage and Salary Administration," in which he said I did not believe in money and therefore companies should shy away from my theory.[1] Surprisingly enough, and for the obverse reason, many companies picked

---

[1] David W. Belcher, "Ominous Trends in Wage and Salary Administration," *Personnel* (American Management Association), September–October 1964.

this up and said, "Wonderful! wonderful! Herzberg doesn't believe in money so we can act accordingly," and I had to run around to all these companies and say, "This is not true, this is sheer misinterpretation." But they insisted, "No, Herzberg, you don't believe in money." So, in desperation to prove my point, I had to double my consulting fees.

It's perfectly normal to want more money because it makes you less unhappy, but it is abnormal to seek money for happiness. It is normal to want more status because you will feel less psychological pain. But to seek status in the hope of happiness is again abnormal.

Love is one of the most important hygiene factors in life. We have tried to build a civilization based on it, and all we seem to be doing is increasing the obscenities in life. Let me illustrate love to you. Picture in

Figure 4

The down and out situation

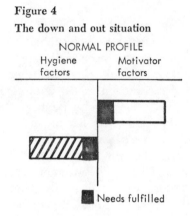

your mind a husband home from a deadening job, sitting down, trying to relax and read the newspaper. His wife, from across the room, quietly asks, "Do you really, really, really love me?" I could also say, Do you really understand me? Do you really, really, understand me? (I'll give you two really's in life and quit.) *There is an indeterminancy to all interpersonal relationships.* What is she trying to do? She is trying to find positive meaning in life by exaggerating her need for avoiding the feeling of not being loved. This is an inversion in Motivation-Hygiene Theory. The hygiene seeker substitutes increased hygiene for a motivator deficiency (Figure 5), and since this is a non sequitur, the hygiene seeker is doomed to a lifetime of frustration, suffering, and knowing only pain or its temporary absence. The simple hygiene seeker experiences no satisfiers. This is what is abnormal.

I would like to describe some of the typical characteristics of simple hygiene seekers so that you can learn to recognize them and their dilemma. They are essentially motivated by the nature of their environment and transfer all motivator need fulfillment to this end. They, therefore,

Figure 5

Simple hygiene seeker

ABNORMAL PROFILE (INVERSION)

Hygiene   Motivator
factors   factors

Nonexistent

manifest a chronic, heightened dissatisfaction with their job surround-ings. They will show an overreaction of exuberance and boasting when their hygiene is good and an overreaction of depression and complaining when their hygiene is bad. They derive very little satisfaction from their accomplishments. That satisfaction which does come from accomplish-ment comes from beating someone else (status). They have very little interest in the worthwhileness or quality of their work. Therefore, they are very cynical about the positive aspects of work and life in general.

Since it is the hygiene that concerns simple hygiene seekers and not what they do or how they do it, they do not profit professionally from experience. They do not grow psychologically. They are prone to cultural noises. They are either ultraliberal or ultraconservative. They tend to parrot management's philosophies, and if they are in middle management, they act more like top management than top management does. The dilemma of the simple hygiene seeker is that he is usually quite tech-nically competent at his current level but will never grow. We often mistake his sterile competence for the real thing, and then we commit an organizational atrocity—we promote him.

Figure 6

Monastic hygiene seeker

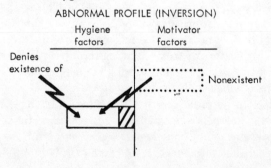

ABNORMAL PROFILE (INVERSION)

Hygiene   Motivator
factors   factors

Denies
existence of

Nonexistent

There is another type of hygiene seeker—the monastic type (Figure 6). He understands the dilemma of the simple hygiene seeker in that no amount of avoidance in life will give him happiness. So what does he do? He says, "I will deny my hygiene needs. I will do without and be proud of it, I will flagellate myself, I will starve, and then I will find accomplishment in defeating these mundane aspects of life." He finds achievement in denial.

This attitude is sick for two reasons: first, it denies Adam. Adam is real. And second, how do you grow psychologically by starving yourself? Again, it is a non sequitur. In industry, the monastic is manifested in those who revel in tough, poor, dirty, dangerous working conditions. They are the ones who say, "This job has a lot of pressure. This job really tests one's mettle." The issue then becomes how much one can endure rather than what one can do.

Finally, there is the Protestant ethic hygiene seeker (Figure 7). If you

Figure 7

Protestant ethic hygiene seeker

ABNORMAL PROFILE (INVERSION)

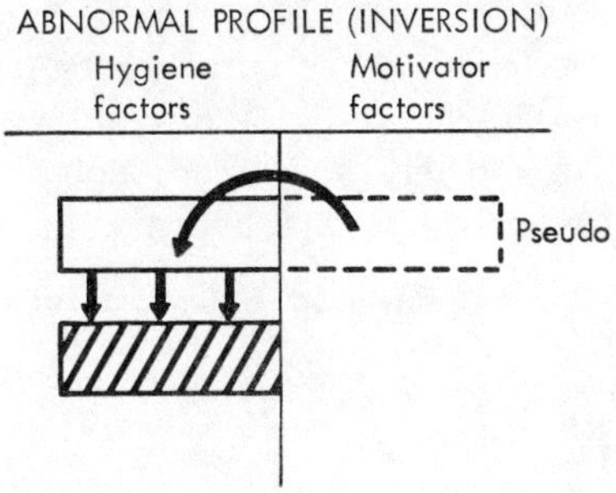

remember in the Protestant ethic you work hard not for the joy of achievement but to avoid sin. Today, people no longer use work to avoid sin, but the same work psychology is used to avoid personal problems. Work is therapy for the workaholic who wishes to avoid the problems of personal inadequacies.

This behavior is abnormal also. This hygiene seeker is doing the right thing for the wrong reasons and finds no solution to his problem in doing so. He hopes that by pursuing work with a vengeance, he'll find the motivators, but what he gets is fool's gold, pseudomotivators, imaginary achievement with no sustenance. "Look how hard I work, how dedicated I am, how much work I turn out. People must think I'm good." This form of hygiene seeking or inversion substitutes the appearance of motivators to meet a hygiene deficit. He looks good because of his hard work and diligence and many small achievements. But since his efforts are in the service of hygiene avoidance he does not metabolize these achievements into growth. His appearance justifies promotion; however, the promotion that ensues is the Peter Principle.[2]

These are the abnormal types in Motivation-Hygiene Theory: the simple hygiene seeker who exaggerates hygiene for the motivators, the monastic who denies his hygiene for the pseudomotivation, and the Protestant ethic hygiene seeker who fantasizes the motivators in order to avoid his hygiene problems.

If a man appears to do well on the job because of hygiene, what difference does it make? It makes a big difference. First, he is dying on the job. You have lost a valuable resource, a person who has much more to offer. Second, he will let you down in a pinch. He is only motivated for short periods of time, and only when external or interpsychic hygiene rewards are to be had. Third, in an emergency he will not come through, especially if he is in a key position and must take risks that require confidence. Fourth, and most damaging, he will instill in his subordinates his own motivational characteristics and values. If managers are to develop future managers, this kind of mold must be broken.

I hope this will give you some better understanding of the behavior and the resultant attitudes that people display in organizations and in life in general. Too often we think of the normal person as abnormal and the hygiene seeker as the ideal, normal type of employee and manager.

An organization, like a society, goes wrong not when the few abnormal people go wrong but when the normal become abnormal.

---

[2] See Laurance J. Peter and Raymond Hull, *The Peter Principle* (New York: William Morrow & Co., 1969).

Motivation-hygiene profiles: Pinpointing what ails the organization

Organizations are like people, and their motivator-hygiene needs can be depicted in similar-type profiles. Now that the Motivation-Hygiene Theory methodology has been replicated so often, it is possible to recognize employee morale problems from the profiles elicited by such an organizational study.[1]

There are three reasons that discrepancies from the classic profile occur, not the least of which is experimental error. Because all techniques contain the potential for error, slippages are often found in the results, with a hygiene item reported as satisfying or the lack of a motivator reported as dissatisfying. Second, individual differences in motivation can also account for discrepancies. Essentially, these differences suggest that the people interviewed were not "normal," and studies of clinical populations reported in the motivation-hygiene papers on mental health deal with these individual motivational problems. Another kind of deviation from the norm may appear, not because of any experimental error or because of any "personality" problems, but because of the climate of the organization itself and how it manages people. The motivation-hygiene interview procedure can reveal characteristics of the company that generate attitudes among its employees that are less than normal.

DEVELOPING THE PROFILE

The motivation-hygiene profile of an organization is constructed from the responses to a sequence-of-events survey of employees' feelings.

Note: The author wishes to acknowledge, with appreciation, the assistance of Alex Zautra, research associate at the University of Utah, in the preparation of this article.

[1] This paragraph is a substitution made by the author to the original article.

A representative group of employees from an organization or department report a time when they felt either exceptionally good or exceptionally bad about an event that occurred on their job. Asking the question in this manner assures the investigator that he is pinpointing events that describe a change in feeling state, and that the change is a critical one. Responses of this type are more likely to reveal a significant motivational pattern of the respondent than other types of questioning, because the focus is put on the specific event leading to the change in the employee's attitude. Thus first-hand information on activities that involved the respondent is obtained, rather than the rationalizations that are often given in response to attitude scales.

During the interview, the investigator concentrates on the event and asks the respondent to describe, in detail, what took place. The events are classified into factors that are essentially shorthand notations of what was going on during these periods of exceptional feelings. By grouping the data from all interviews within a single organization, it is possible to determine how often each factor is reported as satisfying or dissatisfying.

In profile analysis, these factors are ranked by frequency, *not* importance. All hygiene factors are potentially of equal importance, because you cannot meaningfully differentiate one type of pain as greater than any other. Nor can you equate the pain caused by the same factor in two different individuals.

To illustrate: The most common dissatisfier is company policy and administration; the least frequent, security. Remember that frequency is the key. An employee must deal every day with people on the job, mainly his supervisor and co-workers, and it is a rare day when all these experiences in interpersonal relations are positive. Also, he will be constrained almost every day in some way by company policy and administration. These are high-frequency dissatisfiers. Status and security, which by their nature evolve slowly, occur less often in day-to-day activities; therefore, they account for few responses in the interviews.

Similarly, with the motivators, achievement and recognition for achievement in an employee's life are much more likely to occur than are more interesting work assignments or job advancement. This distinction between frequency and importance is one of the most misinterpreted aspects of Motivation-Hygiene Theory. All hygiene factors are equally important, depending on the circumstances; however, the most important motivators occur with the least frequency. Personal growth is the end goal of the motivators, while achievement is the starting point for any personal growth. (For further explanation of this hierarchy of motivators and the equality of the hygiene factors see my book *Work and the Nature of Man.*)

A "normal," or classic, profile derived from numerous studies of employees, ranging from the highest to the lowest level jobs and representing various cultures, is illustrated in Figure 1. We can compare the findings

Figure 1

Classic profile of motivators and hygiene factors in an organization

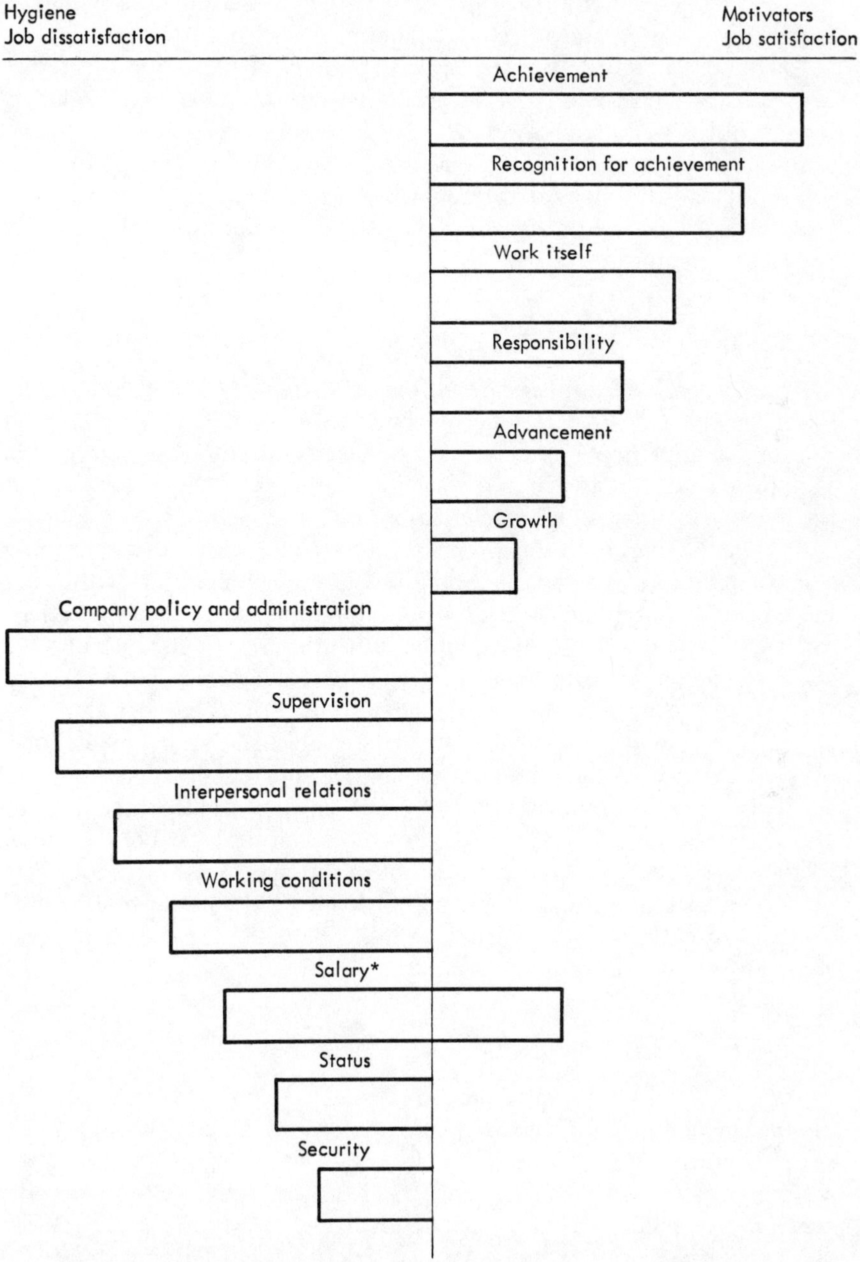

Hygiene
Job dissatisfaction

Motivators
Job satisfaction

Achievement

Recognition for achievement

Work itself

Responsibility

Advancement

Growth

Company policy and administration

Supervision

Interpersonal relations

Working conditions

Salary*

Status

Security

° Because of its ubiquitous nature, salary commonly shows up as a motivator as well as hygiene. Although primarily a hygiene factor, it also often takes on some of the properties of a motivator, with dynamics similar to those of recognition for achievement.

from specific companies or any unit of an organization with this profile and analyze significant deviations. With this procedure it becomes possible to generalize about the climate of the organization as a whole in terms of motivation and hygiene dynamics.

There are six organizational profiles that are particularly representative of the major kinds of difficulties encountered in organizations. Four of these problems originate with the mismanagement of hygiene, and two arise out of inattention to motivational needs. The six descriptions that follow lay bare the dynamics responsible for the resultant aberrant profiles. Such profiles can be used as diagnostic classifications of problems within the organization.

A DEVELOPING HYGIENE PROBLEM

The first problem, which can be found in almost all companies, is the mismanagement of one specific hygiene factor. In the profile shown in Figure 2 a single hygiene factor is significantly displaced in comparison with the classic profile. We use salary as an example, although any one of the hygiene factors would serve equally well.

In organizations with this profile, a single source of pain is disturbing a large number of employees. Some inequity in comparison with other organizations is implied by a factor that is "out of step" with the others. We would expect salary, for example, to be a source of dissatisfaction in social service organizations, where professional salaries are below the national average or less than those offered by private corporations for similarly qualified people. The hygiene problem is a legitimate one, albeit not critical to the present functioning of the organization.

Typical morale survey ratings of salary or any of the other hygiene factors can be regarded as a general comment on the status of the factor in the organization. In contrast, a motivation-hygiene study showing a significant increase in discontent with a hygiene factor can be accepted as *real*. Corrective action can then be taken before that factor becomes a major disruptive source of discontent.

A SPECIFIC HYGIENE CRISIS

As a result of consistently poor treatment of employees in terms of a specific hygiene complaint, the company may be faced with a hygiene crisis. In this case, as is shown in Figure 3, one hygiene factor, supervision, is elevated at the expense of all other factors. Otherwise, the motivational pattern remains similar to that of the classic profile. What has happened here is that a particular grievance has become so painful to the employees that the other concerns fade in comparison, just as a vicious headache can mask all other bodily pains. This problem can be severe enough to cause a walkout or work slowdown.

Figure 2

Profile of a developing hygiene problem in an organization

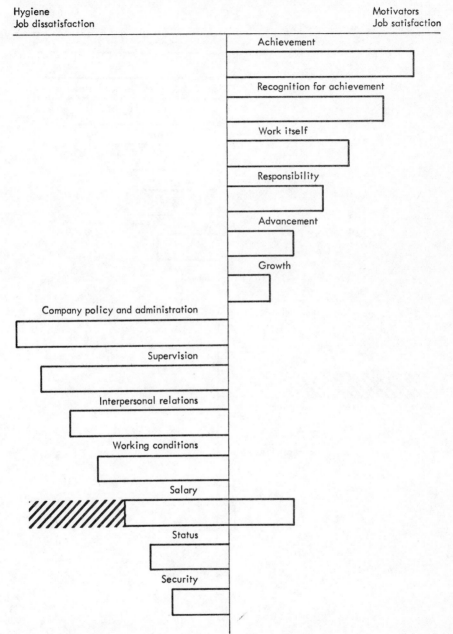

Figure 3

Profile of a hygiene crisis in an organization

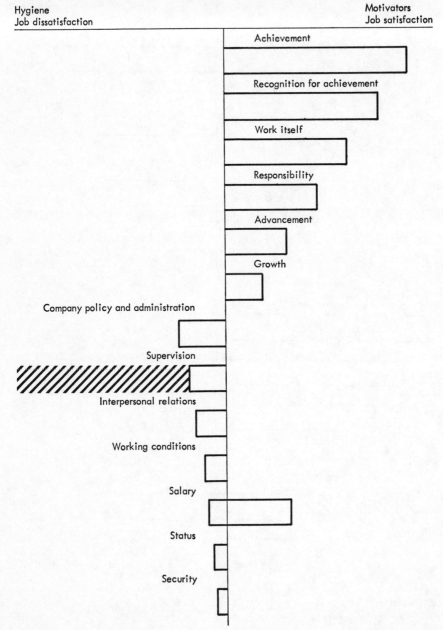

Although the crisis is often cured quickly—perhaps by the resignation or dismissal of the supervisor responsible for it—there are some long-term psychological side effects. The employees remain sensitive to the particular hygiene concern, and often the company finds it necessary to placate employees in ways that are both unnecessary and expensive once the situation has reached crisis proportions. The danger lies in just this overcompensation. The company should only rectify the complaint and avoid the temptation to provide something compensatory in addition. If it does go further, it is treating a legitimate complaint as a "tantrum," and this will in turn create a "tantrum" strategy among its employees.

The tantrum strategy may be illustrated by a situation in which we find employees seeking hygiene through manipulating the conscience of management. For example, a new supervisor is sent in to replace the man who caused the hygiene problem, and his employees immediately begin to complain. The new "grievances" go not to the new supervisor but to his superior. Unless management refuses to "baby" the employees and expresses confidence in the man it chose to improve supervision, the hygiene seeking will be exacerbated. The likely outcome is the appointment of committee after committee to study the problems, thus taking up valuable production time.

A SATISFYING HYGIENE EVENT—THE BOOMERANG EFFECT

Management's problems are not over after solving a hygiene crisis or correcting a chronic and painful condition. The immediate outcome of such a change is shown in Figure 4, which demonstrates what the motivation-hygiene profile would look like after a sudden improvement in company policy and administration. A significant inversion is observed as a result of the employees' misinterpretation of their feelings of relief from pain as a source of satisfaction. It is as if the company had stopped hitting its employees over the head with a hammer and subsequently was praised for the pain relief.

How long the boomerang inversion of the hygiene factor involved will remain as a source of job satisfaction will depend on two conditions. First, it is a question of how long the hygiene pain went on—the shorter the duration of the bad situation, the shorter the time will be when the relief from pain will be interpreted as satisfying. Second, and of greater concern, is the role management plays in prolonging this response by maintaining an essentially unhealthy condition in the organization.

If the company encourages this inversion by expecting increased performance and satisfaction with the job as a result of the alleviation of pain, serious and long-term motivational problems will develop. Let us consider a change in job security, for example. Suppose a company has experienced a severe economic slowdown and is threatened by the possi-

Figure 4

Profile of an organization after correction of a serious hygiene problem

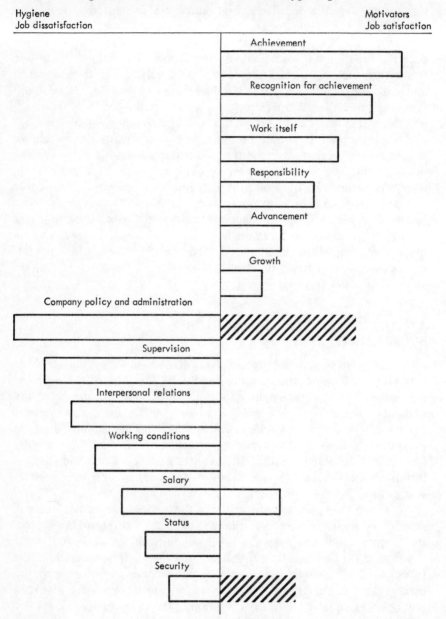

bility of across-the-board staff reductions. Fortunately, a new product or market develops, and the employees are no longer afraid of losing their jobs. The profile would then resemble the one shown in Figure 4, with job security and company policy and administration reported as motivational. In a few months, however, this inversion should subside, and the profile should return to normal.

On the other hand, if the company continues to remind the employees that, since their jobs are no longer vulnerable, everyone should naturally want to work harder, the inversion would stabilize. The employees would then be working to pay off management for making their jobs secure, and not for the intrinsic value of the work itself. The resulting adjustment pattern is one of increased expectancies of hygiene improvements, and conformity to rules and procedures (doing things the right way rather than the best way). Finally, in many cases, hostility is directed at the company for its failure to recognize the real motivational needs of its employees. This syndrome is the one most frequently observed in the management of people.

HYGIENE SHOCK

Hygiene shock occurs whenever there is a serious threat to the integrity of the organization. The resultant profile is one that represents psychological chaos in the organization. As shown in Figure 5, the motivators are depressed. Motivator inversions may occur, as well as significant displacements of the hygiene factors. In fact, the profile may not even resemble the normal organization of satisfiers and dissatisfiers. What has happened is a damaging series of events in which the nervous system of the organization has been jolted by a shock wave, leaving employees psychologically dazed and disoriented as regards both hygiene and motivator factors. Like the impact of a death in the family on an individual, the organization is experiencing a loss of catastrophic proportions.

A perceived gross injustice in any hygiene area can set off hygiene shock. There are too many possibilities to list all the recurring hygiene shock situations in an organization, but they almost always arise from extremely inept handling of a labor grievance or from what is interpreted as a vindictive or callous new company policy or practice. A familiar example is the autocratic attempt by a company to enforce an unpopular policy by "stonewalling" it as if there had been infringements of "divine" management rights. Another is a company that forces early retirement on longer-term employees or uses a totem-pole merit-rating program coupled with an up-or-out tenure policy.

Hygiene shock demands of management the most open and honest communications with its employees and the best of cool leadership qualities. Management's overriding job is to not lose control of the situation and to initiate decisive actions dealing only with the essential hygiene

Figure 5

Profile of hygiene shock in an organization

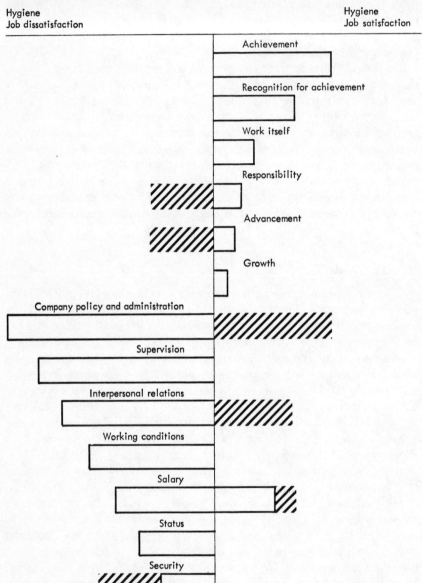

amelioration needed by the employees. In short, simply stop the bleeding. The mistakes management frequently makes are either to delay action while it searches for all the facts via morale surveys, task force studies, reviews of company policies and procedures, or to do nothing and hope to ride out the storm. Very often the failure to act is prompted by the fear of making a mistake. Any action—and the quicker the action the better—will involve casualties, but the failure to act at all may threaten the survival of the organization.

THE ASSEMBLY-LINE SYNDROME

Companies with many jobs of limited motivational potential are common to the world of work. This condition is represented on the motivation-hygiene profile as a significant increase in two motivational factors, achievement and recognition for achievement, while the other motivators are depressed, as is shown in Figure 6. The hygiene factors follow the classic sequence, with one or two possible inversions. The problem here is that the job is impoverished, and the only motivators that are available are those of short duration and high frequency, such as achievement and recognition for achievement.

The assembly line is the place where we most often find this motivational problem. Frequently, the only available motivator is the degree to which working faster fosters feelings of achievement, along with the recognition for achievement built into exceeding the standard piece rate set for the job and earning incentive pay. Evidence suggests that these motivators move only a minority of assembly-line workers. Soldiering on the job is more common behavior than rate busting. Inevitably, a dependence on these less nutritious motivators increases the need for "atta boys" from the supervisor, with subsequent inversion of hygiene items such as interpersonal relationships with the supervisor. The work is psychologically empty of growth, and, in order to compensate, the employee attempts to fulfill his motivational needs with hygiene factors.

Morale surveys, and even critical-incident surveys, would suggest that these blue-collar workers have less motivation than their white-collar counterparts. In fact, these employees want and need a motivating job more. The results are in direct contradiction to the facts. It is only the severe constraints placed on opportunities for growth among assembly-line workers that make it appear that they are less interested in motivators. Motivation becomes a myth to these employees, and self-actualization a concept conceived in an intellectual's fairyland. There is both a popular and a "scientific" literature in which it is asserted that lower-echelon employees desire more hygiene and fewer motivators than higher-level employees. We suggest, and our research confirms, that the reality of the situation is quite the opposite. The problem is that some

Figure 6

The assembly-line profile

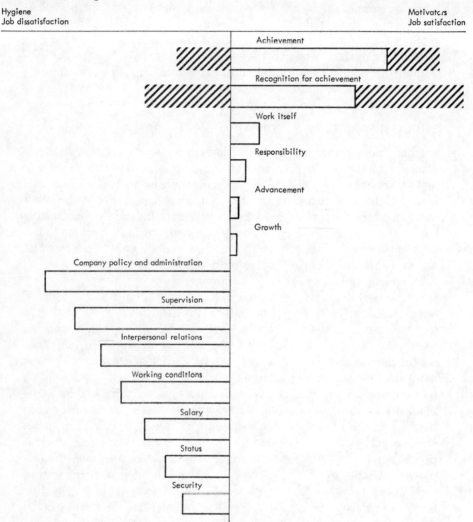

| Hygiene
Job dissatisfaction | | Motivators
Job satisfaction |

Achievement

Recognition for achievement

Work itself

Responsibility

Advancement

Growth

Company policy and administration

Supervision

Interpersonal relations

Working conditions

Salary

Status

Security

behavioral scientists cannot recognize the self-fulfilling prophecies in their own data.

ABILITY WITHOUT OPPORTUNITY

Another common failing of organizations is the underutilization of the available talents of their employees. In the previous motivational problem (the assembly-line syndrome), the workers did not have sufficient opportunity and/or training to express all their motivator needs. In this case,

Figure 7

Profile of an organization with ability but without opportunity

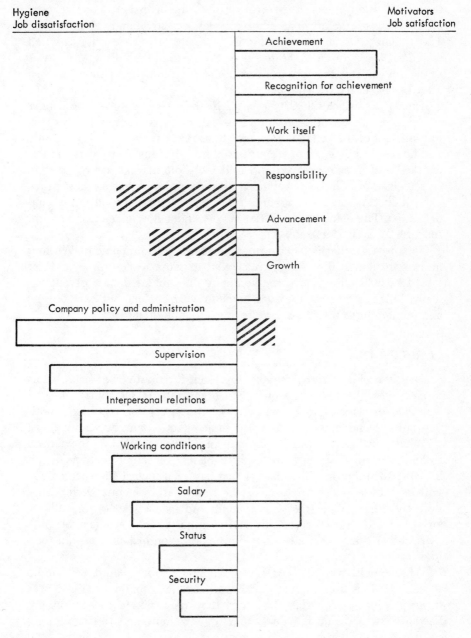

the employees have learned the necessary skills, but they have not been given the responsibilities commensurate with their abilities. The profile of the organization shown in Figure 7 displays the inversion of one or more of the motivator factors in an otherwise classic motivation-hygiene profile. The organization has recruited highly motivated people, yet it has failed to redesign jobs to meet the needs of these employees. Frequently, this profile will mirror the responses of a college graduate six months or so after he has joined the company.

The job classification that was adequate 15 years ago is no longer suited to the skills of the new employee. The inversion describes the dis-illusionment of the young employee who is ready to work diligently, only to find he has few, if any, responsibilities for his own work. He is checked and double-checked and told more often what not to do than what he can do. The company may tell the employee that he must prove himself first before moving on to a job with real responsibility and discretion. The employee's reaction is to wonder how he can prove himself in a Mickey Mouse job.

This organization is a prime candidate for job enrichment. Without improvements in jobs that increase the employees' control over their jobs, they will either leave the company outright or depart psychologically. In the latter case, they will come to work on time but be apathetic and indifferent to their jobs. And who can blame them?

CONCLUSION

The six profiles discussed above represent the most common problems in employee attitudes encountered in organizations. Of course, no two "normal," or classic, profiles will ever be the same, since no single motivator or hygiene factor will have the same effect on any two individuals.

What must be stressed is that the problems revealed by deviations from the "normal" profile are real problems, reflecting as they do an in-depth theory of human behavior that has been replicated repeatedly— with employees at every level of the organization hierarchy, in many different organizations, large and small; and in many cultures, authoritarian as well as democratic. This analysis reports actual events in people's lives, rather than their "attitudinal" rationalization of behavior and feelings.

What should we do about these problems? How should we handle these deviations from the normal? Each problem is singular and requires its own solution. Together, however, they demonstrate the continuing need to assess dissatisfaction within organizations and the continuing need to use ingenuity both in increasing the overall supply of hygiene factors and in distributing them equitably among employees. As I have written previously, there are no permanent solutions for sanitary engineers.

The motivator problems discussed in the last two profiles represent a different kind of challenge. Managements that are not prepared to provide whatever motivators are possible in the job are not prepared to meet the challenge of managing adults. Over time, the goals of an organization run by such managers become directed to the worker who is hygiene oriented rather than to the worker who is motivator oriented. The cost to the organization in diminished creativity and spirit is inestimable.

The proper management of hygiene: Am I treated well?

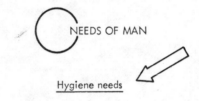

NEEDS OF MAN

Hygiene needs

Job dissatisfaction ◄——————Animal avoidance needs ———————— No job dissatisfaction

Motivator needs

No job satisfaction ——————Human activity needs ————————► Job satisfaction

Because human beings seek to satisfy two basic need systems, the management of people involves two problems—the proper management of hygiene needs and the proper management of the motivators. Hygiene deals with the question of how well you treat your employees, and the motivator question is concerned with how well you use your employees. We will limit this discussion to the proper treatment of employees (meeting their hygiene needs) and the proper management of this treatment.

LEVELS OF PERFORMANCE

An employee can provide his employer with three general levels of performance (see Figure 1). The most common level is average performance. This is much below the individual's capabilities, but it is still found acceptable by management. This level represents a kind of psychological contract which the employee makes with his employer to give so much work for an agreed-upon caliber of treatment. Industrial psychologists, unions, and working people commonly refer to this level as a fair day's work.

Another level is poor performance. This level, which is much below the fair day's work, will occur when the hygiene factors are considered to be inadequate. Improvement of hygiene in these circumstances does not lead to good performance, but rather to a temporary removal of a decrement in performance from the fair-day's-work level. Very often companies that install hygiene programs think they have improved the

Figure 1

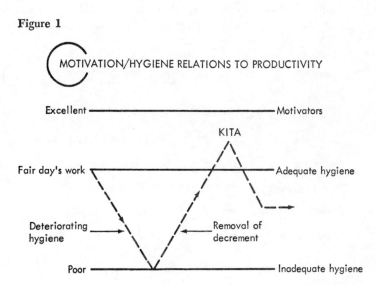

performance of their employees, when in reality all that has been accomplished is a removal of a decrement in performance.

The final level is good, or motivated, performance. This can result in as much as twice that given by a fair day's work. This level can be achieved by employees only through opportunities to experience the motivators and not by an increase in hygiene.

NO HYGIENE ANSWER

In a real sense there is no good hygiene, on the job or in all of life, as I will explain later in the section "The Dynamics of Hygiene." However, there is bad hygiene. Despite the fact that there are no conclusive answers to hygiene needs, the more serious problems that arise in an organization stem from the way hygiene programs are initiated and administered, and it is in this area that much improvement can be made.

The proper administration of hygiene first requires an understanding of the basic types of dissatisfiers found in companies. The employee will not always tell you where he hurts, especially when there are organizational penalties for expressing certain types of dissatisfactions. Often, too, he reports a problem that management may see as merely an acceptable complaint, but if the primary source is not discovered, the aggravations will continue and escalate.

MAJOR TYPES OF HYGIENE CONCERNS

There are six major types of hygiene concerns, as outlined in Figure 2. The simplest form of hygiene deprivation arises from consumatory needs. Inequitable salary administration is the usual cause. Salary, like

Figure 2

TYPES OF HYGIENE CONCERNS

Consumatory Hygiene	Salary
Facilitating hygiene	Supervision and company policy
Escape hygiene	Fringe benefits, paid vacation
Revenge hygiene	Status, interpersonal relations
Remembered hygiene	Job security
Ghost hygiene	All factors

all hygiene, is a relative concern which is psychologically determined by past earning power, wage rates for the same work in other companies, and expected rates of increase in pay.

Facilitating hygiene concerns are those that surround the performance of the job, notably supervision and company policies. Here the employee is not getting the supervisory support that he needs. It is the red tape, the procedure manuals, or the stopwatch of the time study expert which interfere with getting the job done. These complaints are frequently heard in companies, but they may also be substitutes for less acceptable dissatisfactions. Management must also be careful not to expect motivation simply through better supervision, fewer irritating company policies, or what is often referred to as Theory Y type management. The results of such improvements in hygiene are not going to last long, and the supervisor who boasts to his employees about all he has done for them often gets the reply, "But what have you done for me lately?"

A form of hygiene that was first used to alleviate pain in high-pressure jobs such as air traffic controller is concerned with the need to *escape*. Forms of this type of hygiene now are extended to all company jobs, through provision for paid vacations and fringe benefits to provide relief from the environmental pressures surrounding the work. It is a curious statement about such jobs when the companies accent escape needs in the hope of obtaining increased motivation from their employees. In this situation, a new policy is handed down stating that the worker has to stay on his job only until he meets his quota for the day. The company, in effect, is telling the worker that he works in order not to work. On top of that, the productivity of the worker is being artificially and, in most cases, arbitrarily, restricted. How such a paradoxical strategy as this can increase employee motivation escapes me.

The next form of hygiene concern is with *revenge*. This type can be particularly damaging to the company. Passive resistance, acts of sabotage, and even costly lawsuits result from employees needs to seek revenge for the wrongs done to them by the company. Usually the source of the problem is status or interpersonal relations. Criminal damage suits based on discriminatory promotion practices exemplify the form these attempts to satisfy this hygiene need take, and parallels can be found in the more violent underground activities in some authoritarian regimes. The revenge takes on milder forms as well; for example, the just-tenured college professor who stops preparing for his classes and starts crediting his publications as from outside his department.

Remembered hygiene concerns also arise from a past deficit, and a personal history of job insecurity in the company usually brings about this type of hygiene problem. Here the employee remembers his past fears and behaves *as if* he were facing the same threats to his job. Often he trades in his creativity and decision-making authority for a safe job. The company losses in initiative and talent are considerable from this proverbial "paper pusher."

Finally, there are the *ghost* hygiene concerns, the typical results of a companywide morale survey. The company attempts to chase down aggravations which are embedded within the history of the organization. The ghosts can take on any form, ranging from company policy and administration to status and security needs. These classifications are of little consequence in the minds of the employees until the company, on a fishing expedition, renews them with survey questions like, "How satisfied are you with . . . ?" These ghosts are best left lying in their graves with the pain that has stopped hurting long ago.

THE DYNAMICS OF HYGIENE

Although the content of each hygiene factor is different, the dynamics of all hygiene needs are the same, and these dynamics are summarized in Figure 3.

The underlying dynamic of hygiene is the *avoidance of pain from the environment* (APE), or in organizational terms, job dissatisfaction. Second, there are *infinite sources of pain*. In other words, man has a limitless variety of dissatisfactions from which to choose. With ten billion nerve cells in his central nervous system, he has a potential for misery unheralded in the history of biological life forms.

Another characteristic of hygiene is concerned with the element of time. All hygiene needs of man are very short term. I breathe, but I must breathe again very quickly. Similarly, if I receive a salary increase, I will not be unhappy after the increase, but most assuredly I will become very unhappy with my salary once again in a surprisingly short time. Therefore, any improvements in hygiene only result in a short-term removal of,

Figure 3

___

THE DYNAMICS OF HYGIENE

- The psychological basis of hygiene needs is the avoidance of pain from the environment—APE

- There are infinite sources of pain in the environment

- Hygiene improvements have short-term effects

- Hygiene needs are cyclical in nature

- Hygiene needs have an escalating zero point

- There is no final answer to hygiene needs

___

or prevention of, dissatisfaction. For example, the average length of time that employees are not dissatisfied with their salary after a salary increase is about six months, if even that much.

Hygiene is also based on the *cyclical* nature of man's basic needs. Since all primary drives of man are cyclical, they come back to the zero point. I breathe, but I must breathe again as much as I breathed in the past; I cannot store breaths. No matter how many salary increases I have received in the past, when I want a salary increase, I want a salary increase. Management must learn to live with the employee demand: "What have you done for me lately?"

The third characteristic dynamic of hygiene is that all hygiene has an *escalating zero point*. As I note in my popular film *Motivation through Job Enrichment,* a colonel who wants to become a general in the Army feels as deprived in status as a private who is bucking to become a corporal.[1] An employee who gets a $1,000 increase in salary one year and

___

[1] *Motivation through Job Enrichment,* BNA Communications, Inc., Rockville, Maryland, 1967.

only receives a $500 increase the next year has psychologically taken a $500 cut. The new zero point is $1,000.

In summary, hygiene is short term and cyclical in nature and has an escalating zero point. Given the premise that all hygiene is only temporarily served and goes back to zero, as the zero point escalates the obvious question of "How do you treat people well?" becomes a dilemma. What is good hygiene in an organization? Specifically, there is *no overall answer*. There is no answer to pain in life. Read the Book of Job or Ecclesiastes in the Old Testament if you are biblically oriented.

I know of no salary plan that will guarantee against eventual employee dissatisfaction with pay. I can conceive of no working conditions that will keep people from complaining about their working environment. Man has never succeeded in developing human relations techniques that have come anywhere near solving the personal problems of interpersonal relations. When I am asked to examine a morale problem in a company and my investigations show that people there are unhappy, I diagnose it as a hygiene problem. The company has failed to make its employees feel that they are being treated fairly. I advise the organization to set about cleaning up the hygiene problem; turn it over to the personnel department, which is the organization's sanitarian.

IMPROPER HYGIENE ADMINISTRATION

In order to consider the proper implementation of hygiene programs in a company, it is first necessary to examine the various kinds of hygiene practices that I do not recommend. These practices are listed in Figure 4. There is, first, KITA (kick in the pants) hygiene, the use of good treatment (instead of the motivators) to induce people to achieve higher performance levels. In KITA hygiene, good treatment is not practiced in order to keep people from hurting. That is, people are treated decently not because they are entitled to decent treatment but in order to get them to do something extra. For example, if the boss who comes back from a human relations training program says, "Look, I have learned something about handling people and their feelings, and I am going to try to be more decent to you because I don't want you to hurt," this is a perfectly good and normal hygiene practice. But if he says, "Now look, you ought to work harder because I treat you so well," this is a kick in the pants.

Typical hygiene KITAs are incentive systems, bonus schemes, and sales campaign promotions. The problem with these programs is that they are designed to use hygiene to stimulate the employee to do something more, rather than to prevent him from feeling dissatisfied. Hygiene cannot motivate, and when used to achieve this goal it can actually produce negative effects over the long run.

Two deleterious consequences in particular can occur from the improper use of KITA hygiene. The first is the denigration of the work ethic and the substitution and promotion of contrasting materialistic value systems as the only justification for work achievement. Second, another look at Figure 1 shows that KITA hygiene leads to a lowering of the level of a fair-day's-work performance. Ordinary treatment then will give a smaller return to the employee, and over the long run it will cancel out the initial gains achieved by the temporary spurt in performance as a reaction to a "big bag of jellybeans." Therefore, hygiene can be correctly recommended only to keep people from being treated unfairly, and not as a stimulus to activate performance above the fair-day's-work level.

Figure 4

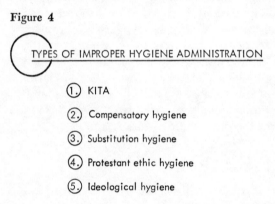

TYPES OF IMPROPER HYGIENE ADMINISTRATION

1. KITA
2. Compensatory hygiene
3. Substitution hygiene
4. Protestant ethic hygiene
5. Ideological hygiene

A second kind of ineffective hygiene practice is *compensatory* hygiene, the improving of hygiene to make up for a past deprivation in it. When the organization deprives the individual employee by giving him less than deserved treatment, with the promise that the company will make it up to him in the future, this is delayed compensatory hygiene.

A common example is offering the employee an initial low starting salary that will be compensated for in the future by a promise of a large bonus. This approach leads to the same kind of psychology that is seen among people who are deprived very early in life and then spend the rest of their lives trying to make up for the remembered deficiency. Even though they may presently have more than they will ever need, they still anxiously seek more money in the hopeless attempt to satisfy a past deprivation, a remembered pain.

Similarly, a low-status or low-caste position in childhood leads to an insatiable appetite for status as an adult. The psychological damage is evident in the desire to seek revenge on those who perpetrated the early pain. This can occur even when the person's present situation is now quite the opposite; there may be no deprivation any longer. What has happened is that the individual continues to pursue money in order to remove a remembered pain. Companies that deprive people of normal hygiene create a remembered pain which cannot be removed later on, no matter how much compensatory hygiene is given.

Companies that practice this kind of compensatory hygiene build up a revenge psychology among their employees that manifests itself in deep-seated distrust of the company, general low morale, lingering doubts of the company's honesty, failure in emergency situations, and excessive, irretractable demands during negotiations.

When management has a long-term policy of hygiene deprivation, the individual employee may also insist on compensatory hygiene as a means for retaliation. After an extended period of hygiene deprivation, the employee wants more than a simple redress of a past injustice and an alleviation of his present pain. The overuse and abuse of compensatory hygiene becomes a means to inflict pain on the organization and management. Again, this is revenge psychology.

Another common form of hygiene malpractice is *substitution* hygiene, that is, substituting one hygiene factor for another. Offering job security or increased status as a substitute for good pay is a common industrial and military example.

In organizations this type of treatment leads to exaggerated bureaucratic responses from employees and rigid, intolerant, and protective behavior. They become martinets, using their status and hanging on to their prerogatives because the status that is given to them is not for status purposes, but rather to compensate for the lack of adequate pay. If a person is hungry, offering him increased amounts of water in compensation for not giving him food obviously not only does not remove the source of his dissatisfaction, which is hunger, it heightens the attractiveness of water as well. No dissatisfaction is removed, and a second possible source of dissatisfaction is created. The level of tolerance for mismanagement of hygiene has now been decreased in the individual, as regards a brand new hygiene factor. Management can get by for a short period of time with this delusional practice, but it will be haunted by the substitutions later on. Because management may not recognize why the individual seems to have such a heightened need for a new hygiene factor he has just received, it tends to discount these needs as exaggerated. But it is perfectly explainable in terms of the normal dynamics of hygiene.

Then there is the appeal to the old *Protestant ethic*—"Work is good for you. Hygiene seeking is a frivolous activity. Devotion to duty is man's greatest goal." While much movement will be achieved by this approach, the basic dynamic underlying this kind of behavior is the fear of retribution or fear of not behaving according to some idealistic value system. The individual achieves a great deal, but the achievement does not lead to any personal growth. There is no nutriment in such endeavor. Often people who seem to be most dedicated to work, putting in 18 to 20 hours a day, never metabolize their achievement into growth, but because of their hard work they are promoted to responsible positions that they cannot handle. This is one explanation for the Peter Principle. Another negative result is that Protestant-ethic types have no appreciation for their subordinates' hygiene needs, and they create employee dissatisfaction as a consequence.

The last kind of improper hygiene practice, *ideological* hygiene, is the source of numerous "value" conflicts between company objectives and those of the employees. Here, the organization ascribes higher meaning to the tasks and offers the individual some tired slogan from which he is expected to derive satisfaction. We see this in the Peace Corps's appeals, the dollar-a-year man in government, and more frequently in the church and in the Army.

The problem is that such a practice will get people to work hard and achieve a great deal, but often contrary to the goals of the organization. Peace Corps kids may be devoted and motivated in their labors, but their goals may not be those of our State Department. In the military, senior officers who are inadequately paid for their level of responsibility often devote much of their energy and lives to doing a good job, but for goals which serve the military and not necessarily the nation. Organizations can hire idealistic people and they will work hard, but for goals that may be contrary to the profit and loss statement. When all there is for sustenance is ideology, each person will select the flavor that suits him best.

RULES FOR PROPER ADMINISTRATION OF HYGIENE

If these hygiene practices are, in the long run, ineffective ways to manage employee dissatisfaction, what then is good hygiene administration? Well, rather simply, it is recognition that man's animal nature makes him hurt and that it is all right to cry when something hurts. The five rules for properly administering to the pain are outlined in Figure 5.

First of all, *identify the type of hygiene problem* you have in the company. An error in diagnosis leads to waste of resources and heightens conflicts between management and labor through failure to understand the problem. It is also the quickest way I know for a manager to lose his effectiveness with his employees.

Second, *give hygiene for hygiene purposes*. Many managers make the mistake of trying to capitalize on their new "gifts" to the worker, expecting the fringe benefits of increased worker productivity and job satisfaction to result. Once again, solutions to hygiene problems alleviate pain or help the employee to avoid pain—reducing job dissatisfaction but not affecting the motivators. All too often companies decide to substitute one form of hygiene for another. If the employee has a bad job you cannot bribe him into productivity with higher pay or better physical surroundings. The job of management in hygiene areas is to be decent, not as a manipulative strategy but simply in order to be decent.

Third, *give hygiene for what hurts.* Because there are infinite sources of pain, substituting one form of hygiene for another or using compensatory hygiene only create new sources of dissatisfaction and do not solve the original problems. Good hygiene management requires responsible attention to the avoidance needs of employees, not elitist perspectives on what employees "ought" to need.

Fourth, *keep hygiene administration simple.* The more complex a hygiene program becomes, the more potential for dissatisfaction. Wage and salary administration is a good example. A straight salary system provides no overall answer because there is none. Yet it is better than an incentive system, which provides dissatisfactions not only with salary

Figure 5

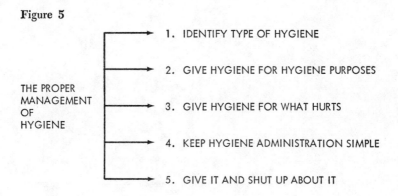

THE PROPER
MANAGEMENT
OF
HYGIENE

1. IDENTIFY TYPE OF HYGIENE

2. GIVE HYGIENE FOR HYGIENE PURPOSES

3. GIVE HYGIENE FOR WHAT HURTS

4. KEEP HYGIENE ADMINISTRATION SIMPLE

5. GIVE IT AND SHUT UP ABOUT IT

but also with the way the program is organized and administered. Simplified hygiene practices lead to simple solutions in the future; complex practices lead to increasingly complex problems in identifying and solving future hygiene problems.

Fifth (and finally), *give it and shut up about it.* Companies outdo themselves in advertising their decency to their employees. It reminds me of some of the relationships between the younger generation and their parents. The father proclaims that he has given his son all of the advantages, yet still the son did not turn out the way he wanted. His son replies, "Dad, I thought you were decent to me because you loved me. Now I see that you were only kicking me in the pants." There is no stronger claim of mistreatment than that made against a company that has boasted about its decency.

Throughout his history, man has been searching for answers to unanswerable questions. But the great tragedies and societal obscenities have not been the result of the failure to produce such answers; rather, they stem from the belief that such answers are available. These guidelines will be of very little help in suggesting final solutions to hygiene problems. They do provide answers which will reduce the sources and amounts of pain in organizations, and allow for fewer intolerable "solutions" to the Adam needs of man.

The proper management of motivators: Am I used well?

NEEDS OF MAN

Hygiene needs

Job dissatisfaction ◄──────── Animal avoidance needs ──────── No job dissatisfaction

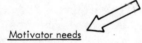

Motivator needs

No job satisfaction ──────── Human activity needs ──────► Job satisfaction

In organizations where the employees are dissatisfied and performing at less than a fair-day's-work level, the problem is usually a hygiene problem which should be cleaned up simply and quietly. If, however, the treatment of employees is reasonably good but they express few positive attitudes toward their work and are unwilling to extend any extra effort for the company, then the organization has a motivation problem. In this instance, two further questions must be explored.

The first question is: Is the employee's lack of satisfaction and lack of concern for work performance beyond the "get by" level caused by technical incompetence? It is not possible to motivate anyone to perform well who does not have the ability to do so. You cannot motivate someone to fly an airplane if he does not have the requisite skills. It should be recognized that most people are more willing to suggest that they are **not** being motivated than to admit that they cannot do something. Employees will use motivation as a smoke screen behind which to hide their lack of know-how. It is easier and more generous to one's ego to suggest that the company is not providing sufficient reasons to work hard than to admit to a personal deficiency in ability.

Very often when I am asked to look at a "motivation" problem in a company I have to report back to management that there is no problem of motivation—the employees just simply do not have the knowledge necessary to perform the job. Training, therefore, can be one of the most powerful motivators a company has in its repertoire. Proper selection and classification can also work wonders on the motivation of new employees. Continuous education and training will go a long way to sustain the motivation to work.

However, if the company has good talent but no motivation, then the second question must be asked: Is the available talent being sufficiently used? If the capabilities of employees are not being challenged, then the jobs that they do are sick. Just as the environment must be cleaned up when a company has a hygiene problem, so must the job be cleaned up when the company has a motivator problem among capable employees. Rehabilitating jobs is called job enrichment, not to be confused with the older concept of job enlargement, which was aimed at giving the employees more work to do rather than better work to do.

BARRIERS TO THE PROPER USE OF PEOPLE

To understand the concept underlying successful job enrichment, we must first examine the barriers which have served to circumvent the proper use of people in the past and see why they exist. These barriers consist of two widely held belief systems on which management has been operating for many years. These two popular management beliefs just happen to be wrong.

Scientific Management

The first stems from the old concept of Taylorism. This concept seems to have been built on a condescending "democratic" belief, the equality of man, gone wild. Instead of allowing each individual the opportunity to succeed according to his abilities, it provided a system in which individuals were saved from failure despite their disabilities. In practice, it went something like this:

It was correctly diagnosed that all the people did not have all the required skills, and, in fact, some of the people could not learn all the required skills. However, most of the people could learn *one* of the skills. This led to jobs being fractionated to their most simple skill level and the workers being given just one skill to perform (see Figure 1). It was felt that the shorter the cycle of the skill, the more efficiently it could be performed and the less the training that would be required. This amputation of human talent not only prohibits people from acting as adults and human beings on their jobs, it has also been very costly to management—despite the fact that management seems to think it has thereby achieved efficiency.

One of the reasons Taylorism was so heartily accepted by management was that it seemed, on the surface, to be the proverbial stone which can kill two birds. In this case, work simplification methods promised not

Figure 1

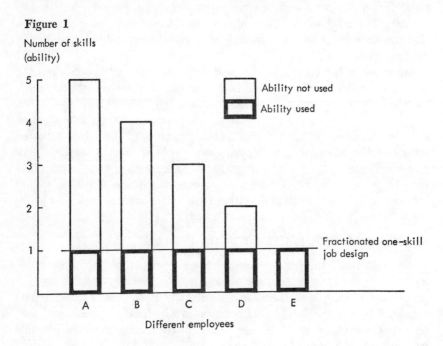

only to take full advantage of the practice effect, the advantage gained when people perform simple tasks over and over again in succession, but also to save a bundle on training costs. An addendum to this, of course, is that with the training costs per employee reduced, the employee was eminently replaceable; hence the interchangeable people working on the interchangeable parts of the interchangeable assembly lines became a reality. Turnover costs in such a system are minimal.

Industry also reaped an additional benefit from the extreme rationalization of work. It could get along with checkers instead of managers. From this "cheap" management cadre came the myth of the "man in the middle" dilemma which industrial psychologists have spent so much futile energy bemoaning. The people were not managers, nor could they be. They could only be, and were, checkers. It is true that the most agonizing job is really having nothing of your own to do. That was and is the real dilemma of the man in the middle.

So we ended up with excruciatingly monotonous jobs repeating their mindless insult to the worker who had to perform this type of work. What was saved in training costs has been lost through higher than expected turnover, rampant absenteeism, theft of company property by alienated employees, increased grievance procedures, and outright sabotage. While management seemed comfortable with the delusion that it had achieved efficiency, it was, in fact, sold down the river. It has lost more in the long run than it ever even dreamed of gaining in the short run. Scientific management is extremely efficient in producing waste, both in human and physical resources. We no longer can afford or permit waste. Workers no longer accept being wasted, and commodity shortages make waste too expensive.

Attitudes and behavior

The second barrier is much more important because it makes for a fundamental change in our concept of what happens in affecting people's behavior. The traditional belief states that the behavior of people is greatly determined by the attitudes they hold—that attitude leads to behavior. Attitudes of employees, it is believed, are the key to their work performance, and therefore employee relations efforts must be directed toward determining what these attitudes are and developing programs to modify them. Proper changes in an employee's attitudes should then lead to the desired behavior.

So we have introduced more and more attitude-change programs in companies, in the hope that if these people would just get the proper attitude, they would behave in the way we needed them to. Think of all the signs, slogans, speeches, and gimmicks you have been subjected to with such an emphasis: "Quality Starts Here"; "Do It Right The First Time"; "Pride Makes the Difference," and so forth. Unfortunately, this approach does not work. We have never changed attitudes to get motivated behavior. Incredible sums of money have been spent by organizations on morale surveys and attitude-change programs, ranging from elaborate communications systems to group psychotherapy. This has been a scandalous waste. The whole premise is wrong. Attitudes do not lead to behavior. It is the other way around: *Behavior leads to attitudes.* Attitudes are a psychological confirmation, justification, and rationalization for the behavior that an individual manifests. Once an attitude has been developed to conform to one's behavior, it then serves the function of enabling one to read other situations with an eye focused on whether one's behavior will be acceptable.

For example, if a child is brought up in a community that forces segregationist behavior, that child will develop attitudes appropriate to such behavior. These attitudes in turn will later enable this individual to appraise colleges for policies that will conform to his or her behavior pattern with respect to blacks. While at the discriminatory college, he will develop new behaviors toward social, political, economic, and interpersonal situations and form correlating attitudes. The constellations of all these attitudes become his value system, which serves essentially to justify his pattern of behaviors in all relevant life situations.

In other words, we develop attitudes which are in conjunction with the behavior we manifest. Therefore, *all attitudes are the proper attitudes*. If a man has an attitude of irresponsibility on the job, it is the right attitude if the job is a Mickey Mouse job. Management wants people to have attitudes which are actually incongruent with the behavior the people are expected to show. If they have to manifest idiotic behavior, they should have an infantile attitude and be irresponsible.

WHAT DETERMINES MOTIVATED BEHAVIOR?

If attitudes do not lead to motivated behavior, then what does determine it? Essentially three things: what an individual can do, what he is permitted to do, and what is reinforced when he does do something. For example, behavior with respect to playing the piano will depend on whether or not the individual *can* play the piano and whether or not he has a piano to play. If a person has a positive attitude toward playing the piano but does not know how to play it, it is a meaningless attitude, a throw-away attitude. This is a *training problem*. If the individual can play the piano, then it is necessary to have a piano to play. An individual cannot be motivated to play a piano if there is no piano available. Similarly, a person cannot be motivated to do a good job if there is not a good job available to be done. This is an *opportunity problem*.

Moreover, if the person can play the piano very well but has been provided with only a 44-key piano instead of 88 keys, his attitude will be the same as those now prevalent among other high-talent people who are not used well. It will range from boredom to open hostility. I have witnessed organizations where this policy acted as a reverse selection device. All the high-potential people left to find more progressive organizations, and only those who were unable or uninterested in doing more stayed behind. The organization was actually allowing one of its greatest assets to trickle through its fingers.

The attitudes that people have toward their work are the appropriate attitudes, regardless of whether or not they are beneficial to the company. A bacterial infection of the body should produce a fever. The fever is a normal reaction to such an infection, not an abnormal symptom, despite the fact that it produces great discomfort in the sick person. Similarly, the indifferent and irresponsible attitudes of so many employees toward their jobs are functional for the kinds of work they are asked to do.

What management expects from employees is psychologically impossible —attitudes that are contrary to the behavior that employees are forced to show. *Motivation at work is an attitude that justifies the behavior that arises when people are given a combination of ability to do a good job and the opportunity to have a good job. The attitude of motivation impels people to seek appropriate arenas where their ability can be enhanced by the opportunity to put it to use, in the expectation that there will be further development of that ability.*

The third determiner of motivated behavior is concerned with which behavior is reinforced and how. The child plays the piano well for his mother. What does mommy do? If she says, "Son, you played that piece very well . . . mommy's very happy," who and what is being reinforced here? Mommy's happiness, and the child will learn to play well in order to make mommy happy (an inversion). If the child plays a piece very well and mommy says, "You played that very well, dear . . . you must feel very happy," she has reinforced his internal generator, his own feelings of satisfaction through the recognition of his own growth.

As a specific example, let us compare the results which occur when people's motivated behaviors are reinforced with hygiene and with motivators. With the motivator reinforcement, the person who does a good job is rewarded by his supervisor as follows: "You did a great job and because you show a lot of talent, we are going to give you the opportunity to use more of your talents." That is rewarding motivated behavior with the possibility for more motivators. Should the individual be paid more? The answer is yes, not as a bonus or incentive, but because in this situation if he is not paid more, he will feel that he is not being treated as fairly as other people who achieve. We summarize this approach by saying, "You did a great job. You show a great deal of talent, and because of that, we are going to give you an opportunity to use more of your talent. By the way, so you will not be unhappy in your new situation, you are going to receive more money." Here we respect the person as a human being and have compassion as well for him as an animal.

In KITA hygiene, compensatory hygiene, or inverted hygiene, the same situation comes out: "You did a great job. Here is your bonus." This is like throwing peanuts to monkeys at the zoo. Here the person is seen just as an animal to be moved. You throw him a KITA to move him. Both approaches will come out the same monetarily, but the psychology is quite different, and so are the long-term results. In one we see the individual as a human and an animal, and in the other we see him just as an animal.

It is this incorrect application or reinforcement that contaminates so many of the appraisal systems in our companies. Most company appraisal systems reinforce the hygienes rather than the motivators. A constant question every organization should ask itself is: Are the people in the organization being reinforced for "going along," being "yes" men, or for how well they actually do their jobs?

MOTIVATION ON THE JOB

How do you motivate people on a job? First, by selecting talent and then developing that talent. Second, by maximizing the use of the talent. It is this second proposition that recommends the practice of job enrichment, which consists of installing motivators in jobs that lack sufficient ingredients for psychological growth. These motivators are: achievement opportunity, recognition for achievement, interesting work, responsi-

Figure 2

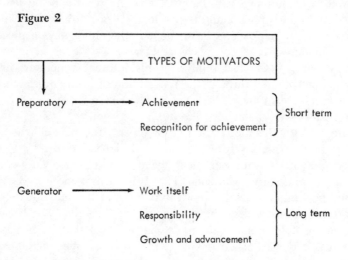

bility, and growth opportunity. Third, by reinforcement of motivated behavior through providing opportunities for psychological growth.

As outlined in Figure 2, there are two types of motivators, preparatory and generator. The first, preparatory, includes the motivator factors of achievement and recognition for achievement. These two factors I consider preparatory because they provide the stimulation (reinforcement) for more complex tasks that lead to psychological growth. The behavior during such growth I call motivation and characterize as providing the internal generator. The motivator factors can also be depicted with a time dimension, as I have done in Chapter 4, Figure 1 of the article entitled "The Motivation-Hygiene Concept and Psychotherapy." From this figure it can be seen that the preparatory motivators are relatively short term in effect, while the generator motivators are comparatively long term in effect. This difference in duration has significant implications for determining which motivators to emphasize.

Workers today expect good treatment as a matter of right, not as a

Figure 3

THE DYNAMICS OF HYGIENE	THE DYNAMICS OF MOTIVATION
• The psychological basis of hygiene needs is the avoidance of pain from the environment—APE	• The psychological basis of motivation is the need for personal growth
• There are infinite sources of pain in the environment	• There are limited sources of motivator satisfaction
• Hygiene improvements have short-term effects	• Motivator improvements have long-term effects
• Hygiene needs are cyclical in nature	• Motivators are additive in nature
• Hygiene needs have an escalating zero point	• Motivator needs have a nonescalating zero point
• There is no final answer to hygiene needs	• There are answers to motivator needs

reward for good behavior. But the cost of a fair day's work is becoming quite unfair to the company and to the consuming public. Real opportunity for personal achievement (not the cultural slogans that are often used as a substitute) is the hidden resource for future management. We will achieve better and healthier work results from making the work itself a rewarding experience. When we look at the dynamics of the motivator factors in contrast to the dynamics of the hygiene factors (Figure 3), we must wonder why management clings to hygiene as its life jacket.

Man is an animal which suffers not only from physical distress but from an infinite number of psychological hurts. He requires decent treatment to prevent him from doing harm to himself and the organization. Man is equally a human being when he finds positive satisfaction in the exercise of his human talents. When permitted to do so, he will provide the organization with the kind of extra performance that is essential to long-term success.

chapter 3

Job enrichment

INTRODUCTION

Chapter 2 presented the technical framework of Motivation-Hygiene Theory. My purpose was to put the plight of both modern workers and organizations in perspective and to begin to unscramble the seemingly incomprehensible attitudes and behavior of people at work. Here I will discuss the most public application of Motivation-Hygiene Theory in the organizational world—job enrichment.

While most managers want motivation, they often get only movement from their employees because they fail to recognize that the dynamics of motivation are different from those of movement. The first article, "Why Job Enrichment?" defines some of the current pressures that stem from the worker alienation and the consequent poor work quality that are a result of excesses of management in movement and ergonomics: the breaking of the jobs down to the lowest common denominator of skill. The motivation formula I present here calls for the reversal of this traditional industrial engineering practice by suggesting that we *enrich* the jobs rather than denude them.

Perhaps because of the difficulty in understanding how to provide psychologically meaningful work, major work philosophies have continued to view work as a burden rather than as a potential source of satisfaction. In addition, when management has tried to improve the quality of work life it is confused by the various approaches to work improvement that have been advocated. In the article "The Wise Old Turk" I have attempted to unscramble the major approaches to humanization of work that are current today and to give, in addition to a description of these various approaches, their unique advantages and disadvantages. This article concludes with a preference for the Orthodox Job Enrichment approach to work design.

The next article is the second part of the most reprinted publication in *Harvard Business Review* history. "One More Time: How Do You Motivate Employees?" describes the first criteria that I have published for true job enrichment and differentiates the earlier concept of job enlargement from my newer concept of job enrichment. This article also includes the first detailed, published example of job enrichment, which was conducted among the stockholder correspondents employed by the American Telephone and Telegraph Company.

The next article discusses a series of five classic experiments concluded at Imperial Chemical Industries in Great Britain, as described in the *Harvard Business Review* article "Job Enrichment Pays Off." These early experiments, conducted over different types and levels of jobs, succeeded in empirically verifying the concepts that had been introduced in the American Telephone and Telegraph Company. They also showed the capability of Orthodox Job Enrichment to improve work performance.

Since the publication of "Job Enrichment Pays Off," numerous job enrichment projects have been undertaken by many companies in the United States and elsewhere. These projects frequently were initiated quickly and quietly, and job enrichment evolved as the accepted way to manage people effectively throughout a company. Often research evidence was collected to test the concepts, but this work was usually done internally and without publicity. Occasionally a company release would allude to the job enrichment programs by such remarks as: "At our company people have satisfying jobs."

As the job enrichment process began to take on the characteristics of a political movement, like all such movements it attracted many splinter groups and, unfortunately, some opportunists. In contrast to the low profiles of many actual job enrichment projects, other programs operating under the guise of job enrichment have received more public notice.

The next article in this chapter, "Efficiency in the Military," presents one of the most ambitious Orthodox Job Enrichment programs that I have personally initiated. This program was introduced as an experiment within the Air Force Logistics Command. It emphasizes the rapidity and the payoff as well as the ubiquity of job enrichment processes that can be achieved, without going through the tortuous process of organizational development as a prelude to job redesign.

In order to contrast the social and individual approaches to organizational change in humanization of work, the article "An American Approach to Job Enrichment" compares the situation at the Volvo plant in Sweden, where the celebrated Socio-Technical Systems approach was applied, with a reasonably similar situation in a major engine company in the United States.[1] In the latter instance I tried to incorporate Ortho-

---

[1] Some Socio-Technical Systems theorists may object to classifying the Volvo experiments as sociotechnical.

dox Job Enrichment procedures where the technology seemed to require a sociotechnical approach similar to Volvo's.

The two projects (the Ogden Air Logistics Center and the "Engine Company") reported on are quite dissimilar in the methods and techniques they used to implement job enrichment. Each company had to respond to the unique demands of its organization in deciding how to implement Motivation-Hygiene Theory. Consequently, their ways of doing things differed considerably. At the Engine Company, the entire operation of a new plant was organized, based on the motivation-hygiene concepts, but the job enrichment method had to be constructed around the technology of group assembly of engines. At the Ogden Air Logistics Center, the strict demands for fail-safe defense systems required careful testing of pilot projects throughout the base before Orthodox Job Enrichment could be fully accepted. The results in both organizations were dramatic, and they demonstrate the advancements in job enrichment which have taken place quietly over the years since the concept began to pay off.

This chapter ends with a brief article entitled "The Managerial Choice." It addresses the question of the alternatives society faces— changing work to bring about a new "work ethic," or continuing to hope that the old tried and tested procedures still have validity. This article also lists the major barriers to implementing Orthodox Job Enrichment programs in organizations.

Why job enrichment?

The purpose of job enrichment is to assist in *motivating* employees to good work performance, not just to *move* them. Moving employees by external threats or rewards is no longer giving us a good performance, or even a fair day's work. If companies are to survive, they will have to change from management by movement to management by motivation.

You have experienced the many uses of movement in your organizations because people often confuse movement for motivation. However, the main distinction between movement and motivation is their time duration. A moved worker does not get far before he has to be moved again, while a motivated worker moves much further under his own initiative. Motivation is a more durable attribute. It focuses upon the basic nature of man and thus produces greater efficiency in the long run.

MOVEMENT AND MOTIVATION

Let me explain this with formulas which illustrate these two concepts more clearly. First, movement. Movement can be expressed as a function of extrinsic fear and extrinsic reward:

$$\text{Movement} = f \text{ (extrinsic fear and extrinsic reward)}$$

What is important to remember about this formula is that for man the two variables, fear and reward, are very short lived. They may at times have great amplitude, but they are of short duration. Even when they are added, their summation only produces a short-term effect—*movement.*

Now contrast the following formula for motivation with the previous one for movement:

$$\text{Motivation} = f \left(\frac{\text{Ability}}{\text{Potential}}; \ \frac{\text{Opportunity}}{\text{Ability}}; \ \text{What is reinforced} \right)$$

The formula for motivation is a function of ability over potential, opportunity over ability, and what is reinforced.

The first ratio of ability over potential determines what the individual is capable of doing. The more a person is capable of doing, the more you can motivate him to do. The less he can do, the less he will want to do, and the more it will cost the company to stimulate the extra effort that will be necessary for him to perform work that is not a reflection of his present capability. This ratio naturally leads to the procedures of personnel selection and classification of employees, which are concerned with getting the people into the right jobs where their abilities can be manifested. The ability/potential ratio is most relevant to training programs, especially today when fast technological changes produce a quick obsolescence of talent. Today's work environment requires a more flexible work force, one which is constantly learning.

The second ratio, opportunity over ability, determines how much of an individual's talent or capability is permitted to come forth on the job. You cannot motivate anyone to do a good job unless he has a good job to do. This ratio is reflected in the personnel and industrial engineering practices of job design, job enrichment, and work advancement. This ratio is the focus of job enrichment.

The last variable affecting the motivation of people at work is the nature of the feedback or reinforcement that is given to them for their performance. Typically, the responses that many companies have emphasized have been extrinsic rewards and punishments, based upon good or bad performance, rather than the personal satisfactions or nonsatisfactions to be derived from work behavior. Appraisal systems in most organizations emphasize the extrinsic consequences of work performance rather than the intrinsic ones. Too often the employee reports back to his wife what the company did *to* or *for* him, not what he personally accomplished!

While each ratio in the formula has its independent procedures and consequences, they must all be integrated to provide an effective motivation program within a company. There is no sense in training if you cannot offer opportunity, no sense in offering opportunity if you cannot offer training, and no sense in training and offering opportunity if you are going to reinforce solely with extrinsic rewards and punishments, or what I call "hygiene." We are emphasizing the opportunity/ability ratio and job enrichment, but it must be clearly understood that this ratio cannot be substantially improved without effective programs in selection, classification, training, and performance appraisal.

ALIENATED WORKERS AND COMPANY COSTS

Let us review *why* motivation through job enrichment has become so important today. I do this to emphasize that we are not dealing with an academic subject but rather with the name of the game for organizations today—*efficiency*. Unfortunately, efficiency is seen by an increasingly alienated work force as the source of their frustration. They see the monotony of their job, the routinization of their tasks, and the total absence of any meaningful input into the system as the price they are paying for the organization to be efficient. Yet the organization is paying an even greater price.

Managers in all kinds of functions say they cannot turn out their products or services cheaply enough to generate a profit without inflationary price increases. A Gallup Poll found 56 percent of a sample of first-line employees reporting they could produce more each day if they tried.[1] This is not limited to first-line employees; 70 percent of managers surveyed also felt they could produce more if they tried.[2] What we are faced with is: Why don't they try? Why aren't they motivated?

A decrease in quality is another symptom of worker alienation. The cost of quality control is staggering. An electrical assembly plant I recently visited has two line inspectors checking each unit processed and a quality assurance division to inspect each unit again. We have checkers checking the checkers! Even when zero defects programs are implemented, they show only a temporary improvement. We generally wind up with the same poor quality and with even more checkers!

Climbing absenteeism rates provide further indicators of the disillusionment-with-work phenomenon. Statistics from the federal government indicate that on a national scale absenteeism climbed over 0.7 percent in five years.[3] This rise means over 700,000 more workers absent from their jobs each year. One estimate for a plant with only 1,000 workers put the price tag on a one percentage point rise in absenteeism at $150,000.[4]

Growing disillusionment with the modern job is not relegated to the unskilled worker. In a recent survey of a cross-section of white-collar workers, only 43 percent (including professionals) would voluntarily choose the same work if given another chance.[5] A U.S. Department of Labor survey of 641 companies found that blue-collar workers failed to show up 57 percent more often than did white-collar workers, and even more alarming, the rate of increase in absenteeism among white-collar workers shot up almost 16 percent in just five years.[6]

Today's white-collar workers experience the same boredom on their jobs because their work has become fractionated. The consequences of the white-collar "blahs" are significant Turnover rates have climbed to 30 percent annually in some industries, and office workers are producing

---

[1] Reported in the *Salt Lake City Tribune*, April 1, 1973.

[2] *Work in America*, Report of a Special Task Force to The Secretary of Health, Education, and Welfare (Cambridge, Mass.: M.I.T. Press, 1973), p. 41.

[3] *U.S. News and World Report*, November 27, 1972.

[4] Ibid.

[5] *Work in America*, p. 16.

[6] *U.S. News and World Report*, November 27, 1972.

at only 55 percent of their potential. Other factors, such as company loyalty, have decreased 34 percent, while white-collar union membership increased 46 percent in ten years.[7]

Blue-collar blues and white-collar blahs can result in antisocial behavior, as demonstrated by hostility toward the family and inability to integrate into community activities. Alcoholism and drug abuse are just two of the job-related pathologies observable in our society. Other symptoms are political hostility, violence, aggression, mental illness, and many physical illnesses. Too many employees drink their lunch in order to face their jobs in the afternoons. In addition, the use of heroin and other hard drugs is widespread; 15 percent of the workers in an automobile plant employing 3,400 union members were reported to be addicted to heroin.[8] In a current study on work problems it was shown that the worker, in order to release his hostility towards his job and the system, will resort to sabotage and theft.[9] Deliberate waste and disruption and intentional poor service are also symptoms of worker frustration. Thieving has become one of the main ways to release hostility. In some jobs it has become a "fringe benefit," and this is not limited to the assembly-line worker. The executive who abuses expense accounts is also releasing some of his hostility toward his organization because of job-related frustrations. In addition to the direct cost of these pathologies, there is the lost energy of the worker in trying to beat the system rather than producing the goods or services.

All these symptoms of worker alienation are costing industry billions of dollars each year. These costs combined with the now pressing economic competition from abroad make the need for efficiency a vital concern. The problem has been that while industry has long recognized it cannot afford to waste its material resources, it has given only lip service to its greatest resource, and that is its people. To fully utilize this resource, you must create jobs which will motivate people to do a better job because they have a better job to do.

COPING WITH JOB BOREDOM

The problem of job boredom and the resultant job dissatisfaction, with all its ramifications (strikes, sabotage, poor quality, high turnover, high absenteeism, etc.), is a fashionable subject for behavioral scientists. Accordingly, all the popular news magazines (*Life, Newsweek,* and *U.S. News and World Report*) had feature stories on boredom,[10] and the Department of Health, Education and Welfare issued a report on job dis-

---

[7] *Work in America,* pp. 39–40.

[8] Ibid., p. 86.

[9] Ibid.

[10] *Life,* September 1, 1972; *Newsweek,* March 26, 1973; *U.S. News and World Report,* December 25, 1972.

satisfaction and its resulting consequences.[11] However, concern for worker boredom has always been there, and the consequences have always been there. What we are discovering today is not new. I reported in 1957 that the leading contributor to lost man-years in industry was mental illness.[12] A fad of concern for the mental health of workers has developed. But let me assure you, we are not dealing with a problem created by either the news media or overzealous social scientists.

The slaves who built the pyramids undoubtedly suffered from boredom, but who did they have to complain to? The workers in the factories of 19th-century England also suffered from boredom, but the need to survive by retaining a job was of more immediate concern. Henry Ford gave $5 a day to relieve his workers of their pain. Such techniques of compensatory pain relief were used to overcome the workers' dissatisfactions.

Today these techniques will no longer work. Management has realized that movement is too costly—it must truly motivate its workers. It is beneficial for you to examine how you have traditionally dealt with the problems of absenteeism, turnover, poor productivity, poor quality, and worker alienation. How does your company attempt to solve these problems? What have been the traditional attempts to solve worker motivation problems?

One traditional attempt has been Taylorism, or maximizing efficiency by reducing jobs to their lowest common denominator of skill. It has worked in the past, so why isn't it working today? Among the many sociopsychological changes that have taken place are increasing education and decreasing skill requirements for jobs. We are overeducating for current job designs. From 1940 to the present our population has gone from less than 40 percent high school graduates to nearly 80 percent high school graduates,[13] and as a result of such efforts as work simplification, the skill remaining in many jobs requires little of the formal education employees now have. If we superimposed the rise in education levels on the deskilling of jobs, we would get a graph showing an increase in wasted talent. We have educated people more and more to do less and less.

Another traditional attempt to solve employee motivational problems has been to buy people off with various hygiene techniques, such as benefits, shorter work weeks, more holidays, longer vacations, bonuses and incentives, communications packages, and human relations training for supervisors and managers. As a result of these attempts to bribe people to work harder by treating them better, it is costing us more and more to get employees to do less and less.

---

[11] *Work in America.*

[12] Frederick Herzberg, Bernard Mausner, Richard Peterson, and Dora Capwell, *Job Attitudes: Research and Opinion* (Pittsburgh: Psychological Services of Pittsburgh, 1957), p. 229.

[13] *Newsweek,* March 26, 1973.

The dispersion and sharing of power among various groups in our society has reduced the effectiveness of threats as a potent force to move people. For example, try firing a man with high seniority in a unionized plant! Industrial engineers have long realized that the focus of the problem really lies in the work itself. They attempted job redesign in the hope of dealing with the focus of the infection, that is, boring jobs. They began a job enlargement movement which resulted in what I have called the "horizontal loading" of jobs, and this resulted in compounding the felony by seeming to introduce more variety and interest. They really succeeded only in increasing the dimensions of boredom.

All of the efforts by industrial engineers can be summed up by saying that they fractionated the job vertically and tried to enlarge it horizontally. The job enlargement movement by the industrial engineer and the behavioral scientist represents a miscomprehension of the problem. The theoretical basis was that employees are functions rather than people. The traditional approach to job design has led to jobs created by geniuses to be accomplished by idiots. This approach has only added insult to injury.

The wise old Turk

When Zorba the Greek was asked if he had a wife, he replied, "A wife, children, a house, the whole catastrophe." And some organizations, having tried many of today's behavioral science interventions, feel that they, too, have had "the whole catastrophe." But not quite; it is beginning to look as if a new catastrophe that organizations are facing is job enrichment.

The term "job enrichment" is firmly lodged in the vocabulary of managers, behavioral scientists, and journalists. Managers are beginning to accept the basic theory behind job enrichment, but only at a cocktail-party level of understanding of human behavior. Behavioral scientists, ever ready to jump on a bandwagon, often have an equally shallow understanding, but a better vocabulary. And journalists have a new movement to misinterpret.

The result has been that job enrichment now represents many approaches intended to increase human satisfaction and performance at work, and the differences between all the approaches are no longer clear. The confusion, misuse, and subsequent bandwagon effect of job enrichment have led some companies, managers, and workers to conclude that they are merely caught up in a new word game. But job enrichment is a reality, and it is necessary because it will improve jobs and organizations.

Today we have several strategies aimed at improving the design of work in our organizations. I discern four distinct current approaches: Orthodox Job Enrichment, Socio-Technical Systems, participative management, and industrial democracy. Each has a different theoretical or philosophical base and, therefore, leads to different actions with different goals. Thus each technique is more relevant to some situations than to others. But although these approaches have their own unique emphases, in practice they actually overlap. And all are subject to distortion and misuse.

In an effort to clear up the current "enrichment" confusion, we could

Note: I wish to acknowledge with appreciation the assistance of Dan Prock, Research Fellow, University of Utah, and Major John N. Taylor, U.S. Army, and Research Fellow, University of Utah.

consult the "wise old Turk," Zorba's reputed source of all practical wisdom. First, however, let us take a look at each of these approaches in turn, to see what the advantages and disadvantages of each might be and to see how organizational development might relate to the whole subject of job enrichment. In looking at these approaches, it is important to keep in mind that academics, consultants, and managers most often operate from an eclectic point of view.

ORTHODOX JOB ENRICHMENT

The original intent of job enrichment—the installation of motivator factors into an individual job—I now prefer to call "Orthodox Job Enrichment." The motivator factors are a direct derivation of the connections I have observed between the quality of motivation and hygiene and the quality of job performance.[1] The basis of the idea is that motivators are the factors that meet man's need for psychological growth, especially achievement, recognition, responsibility, advancement, and opportunity. These factors are concerned with the job content—the work itself. The hygiene factors are concerned with the job environment—conditions and treatment surrounding the work, specifically company policy and administration, supervision, relationships with others, salary, personal life, status, and security. Their underlying dynamic is the avoidance of pain within the work environment. Motivators are concerned with using people well and, when combined with a good hygiene program, with treating people well.[2] The result will be motivated performance.

Orthodox Job Enrichment's motivation concept is based on observed relationships between ability and both potential and opportunity and on results of performance reinforcement. The first relationship (ability to potential) determines what an individual can do. The more ability employees have to do a job, the more they can be motivated to do it well. It is obvious that to get good performance from an individual, he or she must have or be able to acquire the necessary capability.

This relationship naturally leads to the procedures of personnel selection and classification; that is, getting people into the jobs where their abilities can be manifested, and into training programs that will develop the abilities they may lack to do their jobs well. Today, when rapid technological change is forcing people into early obsolescence, training to maintain work motivation is especially important. A person who has lost

---

[1] Frederick Herzberg, Bernard Mausner, and Barbara Snyderman, *The Motivation to Work* (New York, John Wiley & Sons, 1959); see also my book, *Work and the Nature of Man* (New York, Thomas Y. Crowell Co., 1966).

[2] See my articles, "Avoiding Pain in Organizations," *Industry Week*, December 7, 1970, p. 47; and "More on Avoiding Pain in Organizations," *Industry Week*, January 18, 1971, p. 152. These articles are the basis of "The Proper Management of Hygiene" in Chapter 2.

competence is much more resistant to motivating behavior than is a person just beginning to learn a job.

The second relationship (ability to opportunity) determines how much of the individual's talent is permitted to show itself. Managers cannot motivate a person to do a good job unless there is a good job to do. Here lies the fractionated job "crunch." Most people have more ability, or potential ability, than their fractionated jobs allow them to use or develop.

The last variable affecting the motivation of people at work is the nature of the reinforcement that results from job performance. First, do appraisal systems reinforce growth behavior that often involves a risk for the individual? They should. And second, do appraisal systems reinforce growth and achievement behavior with opportunities for further growth and achievement? Unfortunately, appraisal systems in most organizations emphasize the extrinsic consequences of work performance—pay, bonuses, and so on. A more effective reinforcer for achievement is the opportunity for further achievement through new opportunities for challenge.

These factors must be integrated into a systematic motivation program. Obviously, there is no sense in providing training without opportunity, no sense in offering opportunity without training, and no sense in offering both training and opportunity if the reinforcement is solely by hygiene procedures.

The implementation of Orthodox Job Enrichment is realized through direct changes in the work itself, permitting the motivator factors to emerge. The exact ingredients of an enriched job module that provide these factors vary with individual characteristics, professions, situations, and so on. Nevertheless, I would like to suggest a number of ingredients that, from the experience of the past few years, seem to lead to better jobs and better motivation.

INGREDIENTS OF A GOOD JOB

In looking at these different ingredients we should remember that they are not necessary to Orthodox Job Enrichment alone, but that they are primary to that approach and not to the others that will be discussed later. The eight ingredients are: direct feedback, a client relationship, a learning function, the opportunity for each person to schedule his own work, unique expertise, control over resources, direct communication, and personal accountability.

1. *Direct Feedback.* One basic principle of the psychology of learning and performance is that knowing the results of one's behavior is essential to efficient learning and performance. This is usually referred to as "feedback." Without going into the total psychology of feedback systems, I would like to suggest that two of the most important ingredients of a good job are (1) that the results of a person's performance be given directly to him rather than through any supervisor, performance review, or bureaucratic administrative innuendo, and (2) that this feedback be nonevaluative and timely. When the boss tells them how they are doing on a job, most people tend to interpret the message as a characterization of themselves, not of their performances. Thus nonevaluative behavior on the part of the boss can increase the learning impact of feedback by reducing the personal threat to the employee. Also, the more timely the feedback on performance, the more potent and accurate is the content of the message.

A very simple example of the proper use of feedback in job enrichment comes from the military—the training of marksmen on rifle ranges. Targets consist of electronically controlled silhouettes scattered at varying distances which fall instantly when struck by a bullet. If the target is missed, there is no ridiculing by target spotters—the target just stands there until it gets hit. Feedback here is direct, instantaneous, and nonevaluative. Success with this method has been dramatic in terms of savings in both money and time needed to train effective marksmen.

2. Client Relationship. A second ingredient of enriched jobs is that the individual has a customer or client to serve, whether external to the organization or inside it. Too often the customer is either a bureaucratic regulation or a supervisor. This leads to the individual's evaluating his job in terms of how well "housebroken" he is. Is the boss pleased? Are procedures maintained? Is he consistent with the company policy and image?

Let me illustrate the concept of having a customer. An electronics firm, unhappy with the performance of its workers on an important subassembly, changed the system only slightly to increase performance. Instead of merely filling a preestablished quota for the day, the workers were assigned to a particular group of unit assemblers who needed the product to complete their own work. A customer relationship was thus established.

The fallout of this arrangement has been a greater appreciation of the problems of relating parts to total assembly and a greater cooperation between the two sections. This increased cooperation has in turn led to an increase in the intrinsic interest in the subassembly operation.

3. New Learning. An essential ingredient of a good job is the opportunity for individuals to feel that they are growing psychologically. All jobs ought to always provide an opportunity for the worker to learn something purposeful and meaningful. Keep in mind that learning can also be viewed as either horizontal or vertical, like job loading.[3] A worker

---

[3] For the distinction between horizontal and vertical loading of jobs see my article, "One More Time: How Do You Motivate Employees?" *Harvard Business Review*, January–February 1968, p. 58. Part I of this article is reprinted in Chapter 2, and Part II appears as the next article.

can learn a horizontal series of new facts, but that in itself does not produce coherence or psychological growth.

A situation that quite vividly highlights purposeful learning and the impact of psychological growth took place in a chemical company. In the research department there were three major categories of employees: laboratory assistants, laboratory technicians, and scientists. The laboratory technician was the focus of the motivational problem. Though he was very well trained and experientially qualified for greater responsibilities, his job consisted solely of setting up the equipment for the scientists' experiments and then serving as a helper to the assistants. The growth potential in this setting was at a very low level until some job enrichment changes were made.

The technicians were given responsibility for the research reports. This responsibility created the opportunity for them to analyze and evaluate data and to learn to write scientific reports. Then they shared in the research planning, which provided a vent for creativeness, and were involved in the hiring, firing, and training of lab assistants, which gave new management dimensions to their work. And finally, they were given an opportunity to do some experiments on their own. This was the perfect chance for the technicians to try out and reinforce their new learning.

4. Scheduling. Another ingredient frequently present in successful job modules is the opportunity to schedule one's own work. The tendency in organizations to preprogram a person's job schedule is rarely dictated by any efficiency motive besides that of simplifying the supervisor's checking process. The person who does the job is the one most aware of the time he has available to spend on various aspects of his work. Allowing the employee to schedule his day in the sequence that he feels most appropriate will make him responsible for the work—not responsible to the schedule. This does not mean that the employee sets the deadline; he sets his own pace to meet it.

Recently, a most illustrative example of employee attitudinal changes was related to me. Workers overhauling aircraft had previously been told when they could take coffee, rest, and lunch breaks. Management felt that if it controlled rest periods, it would have a better chance of controlling work and meeting the scheduled deadlines. This system was changed: workers were held accountable only for meeting the item deadlines. A month or so after the change had been implemented, overtime had dropped slightly and failures to meet deadlines had dropped significantly. One of the "old Turks" on this team was asked how it felt to take all the time he wanted to rest and have a cup of coffee. His reply was revealing: "Hell, I wouldn't know. I've been too busy to worry about taking all those breaks like we used to. I get going on a job and I like to finish it. Whenever I beat the standard and finish early, I take a rest."

5. Unique Expertise. In this day of homogenization and assembly-line mentality, when everyone is judged on sameness, there exists a countervailing need for some personal uniqueness at work—for providing aspects of jobs that the worker can consider as "doing his own thing."

This idea can be seen at work in an electrical plant where the team concept is being applied to small generator assembly. Each individual on the team assembles, inspects, and marks his own generator. Individuals who finish their work ahead of schedule are allowed to use these blocks of company time to their own advantage. One might expect these workers to goof off during this period, but more gratifying results have come forth. Some examples of the use of this time are: learning from plant quality control what detailed technical checks might cause their work to be rejected; spending time with new employees and showing them how to do the job; working out better ways to assemble the generators; and visiting the engineering group to get a better understanding of its procedures.

6. *Control over Resources.* One of the more serious complaints that managers make of employees is that they are indifferent to costs. Responsible cost control, however, can only come when someone truly has responsibility for costs. Often, by providing employees with minibudgets to run their operations, managers will succeed in having them take responsibility for costs.

Conceptually, the way this is done is to push cost and profit centers down as low as is organizationally feasible. There are very few instances when cost centers in their simplified form cannot be used at the individual or team level. An example of such an action occurred when design engineers at a plant were given authority to spend the money allocated to a particular project. All administrative limits, such as those requiring approval for expenditures of more than a set amount, were removed. The costs rapidly became more realistic.

7. *Direct Communications Authority.* The greatest single loss of administrative time to get anything done in an organization is caused by rules that require ten people to communicate when only two people need to. For example, if an employee needs to talk to another employee in another division, department, or section, he has to go through his supervisor, who communicates with the supervisor of the person the employee needs to deal with, and then the reverse will occur. Along with the time necessary to make all these connections, a lot of good content is lost in this complex communications network.

Direct communications authority is also the facilitating vehicle for all the other enriched-job characteristics previously mentioned. Giving an employee a customer or client without direct access to that customer is providing a fictitious customer. Direct communications also enhance the growth potential of a job by providing the worker with new avenues of information. For many jobs, giving an employee the responsibilities of work scheduling and cost control without giving him the opportunity to communicate directly with the system is asking him to plan without knowing the facts—a proven formula for failure. If the creative value in doing one's own thing is to be gained for the organization, direct communications are vital.

8. *Personal Accountability.*   The last ingredient of a good job, personal accountability, can be usefully viewed both as an ingredient of job enrichment and as an effect of it. Because of the human relations era's stress on personal fairness, we have become so afraid to hold someone accountable for his job that we have denuded jobs of anything that anyone would want to be accountable *for*. We provide no organizational mechanism for personal accountability other than slogans and cutting remarks. The point is, it is pointless to hold someone accountable for performing an "idiot" job.

Administrative procedures that guard against hypothetical errors and imaginary irresponsibility breed the very carelessness and inefficiency that they were intended to prevent. Too many controls divide responsibility until it gets lost and no one is responsible. Fingers point in endless circles. A real method of instilling the potential of accountability is to remove the crutch of inspection and instead directly identify the performance of the work with the individual. The level of accountability is thus related to individual competence; and in every job there is room for individual competence for at least a portion of the work module.

The better the job, the more personal accountability it has. Thus an excellent indicator for managers to use when evaluating job enrichment efforts is the level of personal accountability achieved. It manifests itself in numerous ways: increasing pride in workmanship, skill, and service; a more positive and constructive acceptance of errors, mistakes, and training shortfalls; an increased level of creative effort; more individuals speaking out and challenging less effective practices and rules; a less uniform and monolithic work force; and an increased sensitivity of employees to any movement of the organization away from excellence.

These are some of the ingredients that go into an enriched job module. What these ingredients have in common is that they attempt to build into a job motivators that allow the individual to stand up in the hierarchy and be recognized for both what he does and how he does it.

The implementation of Orthodox Job Enrichment is a systematic but gradual approach to organizational structural change. It offers motivators to individuals but does not force changes upon them. Gradually, with hard work, an Orthodox Job Enrichment program can convert the fractionated job bureaucracy to an interlocking system of meaningful job designs. The result of such a program will be increased motivation and performance at the individual level, and a more effective organization.

The remainder of this article investigates other, different (but overlapping) approaches to job enrichment. Figure 1 compares the advantages and disadvantages of four different job-design methodologies, and

Figure 1

Job design methodologies—advantages and disadvantages

	Major advantages	*Major disadvantages*
Orthodox Job Enrichment	Lasting individual growth and competence Quickly implemented Minimizes new hygiene problems	Older employees adapted to impoverished jobs cannot change Increased employee defensiveness for incompetence Assumed lack of motivators can become alibis
Social approaches		
Socio-Technical Systems	Not limited by technology More variety (horizontal loading of jobs) More willingness to follow through on decisions	Tyranny of group over individual Slowly implemented Less likelihood of job enrichment
Participative management	Improves hygiene factors Better supervisor/subordinate communication More willingness to follow through on decisions	Can become human relations manipulation Slowly implemented Less likelihood of job enrichment
Industrial democracy	Theoretical reduction in organizational conflict Greater congruence of job rights with social and civil rights More willingness to follow through on decisions	Produces an equality of ignorance* Slowly implemented Less likelihood of job enrichment

* See Frederick Herzberg, "The Equality of Ignorance," *Industry Week*, October 9, 1972, p. 50. This is one of the sources of the article "The End of Obligation" in Chapter 1.

Figure 2 highlights the major differences between Orthodox Job Enrichment and the other more social approaches to job design.

SOCIAL JOB-DESIGN APPROACHES

The ingredients of a good job covered in connection with Orthodox Job Enrichment do, as mentioned, show up in other work environments as the result of other approaches. The three approaches I discuss next have some of these characteristics, but their basic philosophies are different. In general, these approaches try to deal primarily with the job in the context of the whole organization rather than, as with Orthodox Job Enrichment, in relation to the individual at work.

Examples, drawn from various sources, will be used to illustrate the main essence of each approach. It should be noted that the examples given in some of the referenced articles may be at variance with reality.

Figure 2

Major contrasts between job enrichment approaches

Orthodox Job Enrichment	Social approaches to job design
Basis is individual psychology (Motivation-Hygiene Theory)	Basis is group psychology, human relations, or social philosophy
Predominate human need is individual growth	Predominate human need is social acceptance, personal involvement, or political rights
Human relations is a hygiene factor	Human relations is a motivation factor
Primary goal is individual growth	Primary goal is group effectiveness
Method is individual job change	Method is group development, interpersonal competence development, or introduction of managerial/political consultation structures
Job design change precedes social system change	Job design change follows social system change
The job content is determinate: the social system is indeterminate	The job content is indeterminate: the social system is determinate
Training emphasizes individual competence	Training emphasizes group effectiveness
Talent decides who trains and who judges	Ideology decides who trains and who judges
Present organizational structures become hierarchies for talent and personal responsibility rather than hierarchies for control	Present organizational structures become democratic decision-making and performance groups

Conclusions as to success or failure of an enrichment program, or even as to what was really done, generally require a closer look than is reported in most published descriptions.

Socio-Technical Systems

Following World War II, London's Tavistock Institute of Human Relations developed an organizational social psychology that later spawned another successful job-design method. Sociotechnical theorists see the heavy applications of scientific management and advanced technology to lower organizational levels as having resulted in work processes—cycles of interdependent component tasks—that do not allow parallel sets of worker interrelationships to develop. Consequently, they see the answer to worker dissatisfaction as the redevelopment of interdependent relationships within the work group.

This sociotechnical approach works to rebuild interworker social relationships by establishing a semiautonomous work group. Within the group, job rotation or "enlargement" provides a greater variety of tasks and gives individuals a big picture of the whole process.

The actual worker task relationship is viewed as, and often is, determined by the technology involved. Sociotechnical theorist Fred Emery shares this point of view: "Thus, although an individual may find his immediate task distasteful, and this is probably the most typical case at operative levels in modern industry, he may gain some compensatory satisfaction from those other aspects of his role that concern his relations to fellow workers, supervisors, and the enterprise."[4]

The sociotechnical approach, therefore, attempts to compensate for the deficient worker/task relationship by suggesting that an individual can attain a sense of personal worth and achievement from the achievements of the group and the social relationships within that group.

Some aspects of the sociotechnical approach, however, do provide portions of a good job module as I defined it in connection with Orthodox Job Enrichment. Within the autonomous group, decisions can be made as to production levels, job rotation, and hiring into the group, and there is generally more internal control over the assigned work. So what we see is that while the worker/task relationship in its primary definition cannot be modified, many important secondary decisions are controlled by the group. This management of internal affairs does amount to an "enriched group module."

One of the best publicized illustrations of the sociotechnical form of enrichment can be found at the Volvo Company in Sweden. Its most aggressive attempt at a Socio-Technical System is at the assembly plant in Kalmar. Based on the idea that "bored people build bad cars," the objective is to build the atmosphere of a small "family" workshop within the large-scale organization of a car factory. The plant makes extensive use of the sociotechnical group in architecturally distinct assembly areas. Volvo press information describes how the work teams function:

The production team or group work system has been devised to give increased delegation of decision making and to provide improved cohesion of working teams in basic groups.

A production team is thus a group of employees within a particular supervisory subdivision having a common work assignment. The group elects its own chargehand, who acts as the spokesman and maintains contact with the supervisory function.

The team is given a particular assignment for a limited period (for example, a week) and is paid for the overall performance. The actual jobs are divided up by mutual agreement within the team. The team is responsible for planning its own production output, distribution of work, and quality control. This

---

[4] See Fred Emery, "Characteristics of Socio Technical Systems," in *Design of Jobs,* ed. Louis E. Davis and James C. Taylor (Middlesex, England: Penguin Books, 1972), p. 188.

means that the team forms a closely knit unit and is able to solve many problems internally.[5]

Here the overriding objective is the design of a social system to facilitate both task accomplishment and employee social satisfaction at work.

A major problem with the sociotechnical approach is the possibility of group tyranny. The group approach concentrates power into what can easily become a political structure, and the results may not always be beneficial for the organization or for the individual. This sociotechnical approach is less than ideal, but many work situations are also less than ideal. Where the technology of the work process, such as that in assembly lines, precludes a general return to individually oriented jobs, group enrichment may be all that is possible. In this method individuals must adjust to the group processes to function effectively. And while this adjustment may subvert valuable individual talents, the technological assets make it practically necessary.

Participative management

One outgrowth of the human relations movement, participative management, is the third contemporary approach used to improve work. Supporters of participative management assume that the overriding need of the worker is to be involved in decisions affecting his work. This primary need for personal involvement can be attained through worker participation and will provide the commitment necessary to motivate him.

Thus giving the worker more meaningful job content is seen as secondary to his legitimate needs for being consulted and involved in decisions that affect him. Naturally, some decisions in which he participates will concern his job content, and only in these cases can concrete job design changes happen through participation. Most often, however, the manager is in effect saying to the subordinate, "Since you don't have a responsible, meaningful job, I'll let you visit my job, but you will have to return to yours."

Donnelly Mirrors Company declares that its well-publicized change to participative management is so successful that it now markets a workshop on how this was done. The company claims to have raised its profits 20 percent annually in recent years and lowered prices 25 percent since 1952, as a result of its change to participative management policies.[6]

Participative policies usually begin with a form of the well-known Scanlon Plan,[7] a perfect example of participation in hygiene matters. The

---

[5] Volvo press information—via personal communication.

[6] *Time,* November 9, 1970, p. 74.

[7] See Fred G. Lesieur and Elbridge S. Puckett, "The Scanlon Plan Has Proved Itself," *Harvard Business Review,* September–October 1969, p. 109.

employees establish compensation packages and make commitments to pay for them by reducing waste, eliminating redundant jobs, or improving work methods or equipment.

Employees do, however, also participate in more substantive job decisions. For example, workers are involved in setting their own work standards (note that they do not *set* the standards, but are involved in the setting of standards). Also, in some cases machine operators may travel with purchasing agents to inspect new equipment. The purpose of this is to get operator commitment to the proper use of the machinery at a later time. The participation here effectively involves the operator in management decisions, but it does not change his job. When the machine arrives, the job will continue to be that of an operator. His opportunity for future influence and decision making remains at the convenience of management.[8]

So the difference between participation and enrichment is a difference in kind. Consultation does not give a subordinate the chance for personal achievement that he can recognize as his own, and denies him the chance of self-development to the point where he might become an executive himself.

Industrial democracy

Another approach to changing the structure of jobs is contained in a Europe-based philosophy known as industrial democracy. The industrial democracy advocates contend that, with most of life's institutions operating in a democratic manner, the institution of work should also be democratic. In order to maintain democracy at work, it is necessary to initiate programs where workers are represented in all the decision-making bodies within an organization.

A major assumption of this philosophy is that when workers are given a representative voice in making decisions about the operation of their organizations, they will become more committed to its democratically developed goals. At the individual job level no redesign or enrichment is included in the philosophy. But managements do admit that some type of change is needed, and in effect say to workers, "If you will visit me outside the hierarchy, we can discuss it." The fallout of these visits can be job redesign, typically in the form of sociotechnical groups.

The Grangesberg Company, in Sweden, has for years been moving forward in implementing the philosophy of industrial democracy. Personnel Director Karl-Johan Edstrom has said that the goal is to get rid of the "Papa knows best" autocratic management system. Edstrom says, "We

---

[8] William J. Paul, Jr., Keith B. Robertson, and Frederick Herzberg, "Job Enrichment Pays Off," *Harvard Business Review,* March–April 1969, p. 61. This article is reprinted below in this chapter.

want to give every individual influence in every job, and the old organization (structure) just won't do."[9]

In the attempt to realize this goal, Grangesberg has structured complex networks of boards, groups, and councils, all topped by the Granges Council, which is composed of 41 members, 13 representing management and 28, the employees. This system was used, for example, at one plant to determine how most of a $200,000 improvement program would be spent. Other operational policies include equal group pay programs, participation in day-to-day decisions, and a "no firing" policy. The company estimates that 10 percent of the more than 25,000 employees are directly engaged in some phase of the democratic machinery.[10]

It is often difficult to differentiate between the industrial democracy and sociotechnical approaches in operation. The difference was pointed out for me in conversation with Einar Thorsrud, an advocate of industrial democracy. I expressed to him some concerns about where a totally democratic approach might stop. Thorsrud replied that "one doesn't know where it will stop; we think that's good." In the sociotechnical approach, limited work-group control is a means to better production and satisfaction. In industrial democracy, work-group control is an ultimate end in itself.

This approach commands respect for the notion that work ought to be improved for the congruence of civil, social, and work rights. But in practice, the management/worker consultation system has proved to be a complex and time-consuming method of attempting organizational improvement. This approach shows some merit for widening democratic institutions, but in view of the necessity for rapid change, its slow political evolvement of job redesign relegates this method to secondary consideration.

Indeed, the main objective here seems to be to redefine the hierarchy itself rather than the jobs within the hierarchy. Therefore, it and the other social approaches are more akin to organizational development (OD) than to job enrichment itself. But as OD certainly has an effect on jobs within an organization, it might itself be considered an eclectic fifth approach.

ORGANIZATIONAL DEVELOPMENT—
A FIFTH APPROACH?

Frankly, I am not totally sure what organizational development is, and many of its practitioners do not seem to know either. Probably least sure of all are some OD client organizations.

---

[9] David Jenkins, *Job Power, Blue and White Collar Democracy* (New York: Doubleday, 1973), p. 266.

[10] Ibid., p. 268.

Organizational development views the lack of effectiveness in today's organizations as a result of ineffective human processes—that is, communication, decision making, conflict management, collaboration for problem solving, and others. Consultants in OD observe individual and group process behavior in organizations and help managers and subordinates diagnose ineffective ways of behaving. The "change agent" then attempts to educate individuals and groups in the use of effective behavioral skills such as risk taking in interpersonal encounters, communicating openly, making use of feedback, "owning up" to particular behaviors, using a participative leadership style, and confronting conflicts. This is done through various sorts of training programs and group meeting strategies. Typically, the change agent models effective behavior and helps establish behavioral skills as group norms in the organization. Theoretically these strategies will result in a reorientation of basic values and a more humanistic view of man. These changes, in turn, will facilitate organizational processes and performance.

One of the more successful organizational development efforts is in a large glass company. Its organizational development is a mixed bag of Orthodox Job Enrichment and such organizational and interpersonal interventions as organizational diagnosis, group development meetings, project teams, business management teams, role clarification meetings, and intergroup meetings. All these procedures are designed to facilitate communication between and within groups by diagnosing the effects of behavior on performance. If these programs sound ambiguous—they are.

But even if one accepts the operational OD assumption that most organizational problems are problems of interpersonal behavior, such behavior is very complex and hard to analyze. Behavioral problems often involve ethical issues, differentials in ability, structural situations that create the interpersonal problems, and even lack of the behavioral skills necessary for interaction.

OD approaches to the ethical issue emphasize the humanistic values. The assumption is that there is a certain ethical relationship, a sense of fairness, that must exist between people in order for them to perform well. But it is very easy for people to learn to use behavioral skills in order to preserve nonhumanistic ethics or values. Without humanistic ethics as the basis of behavioral skills, the result will be mushrooming levels of manipulation.

Also, differentials of ability partially determine the content of interpersonal relationships. People protect themselves from their own incompetencies. For example, if another person is an expert on a certain subject and I am not, our interaction is limited by my knowledge or lack of it. This is not an issue of the behavioral skill of risk taking, but of the simple fact that regardless of the other's basic acceptance of me, I lack ability for certain forms of interaction. Here my nonability acts as a constraint on the interpersonal relationship.

Next, interpersonal problems arise, as I have suggested, from the work structure. Attempts to change people's job behavior apart from the job content have, in the past, proved largely unsuccessful. If a checker in a production process is given the skills needed to interact with production workers, nothing has actually changed. Behavioral skill may make the situation a little more bearable, but someone is still checking someone else. The behavior is the same, and attitudes appropriate to it will continue.

Poor behavioral skills account for only a small percentage of the interpersonal problems in organizations. An example illustrating misconception of the cause of interpersonal problems can be taken from the movie *Cool Hand Luke*. After an escape attempt prisoner Luke is beaten, rather reluctantly, by a prison warden. "What we have here," says the warden, "is a failure to communicate."

For organizations to overemphasize interpersonal processes and risk taking at the expense of job redesign, effective selection, placement, and technical training efforts is unwise and will not result in the improvements desperately needed today.

"THE WHOLE CATASTROPHE"

There is massive confusion existing today among the different job-enrichment approaches. My research and experience have led me to believe that Orthodox Job Enrichment is the most promising of the organizational improvement strategies. But many other theorists and managers emphasize one or more of the other approaches.

If this analysis is reasonably true, what can we expect? With luck, we will proceed without the expectations of panaceas and will learn to improve our management systems. For managers who are faced with the confusion of "What do I do?"; "Whom do I rely on to bring about needed organizational change?" I would like to recommend a new intervention. Use the behavioral scientist to find out what it is he is saying (or selling) —then get rid of him. The behavioral scientist knows about the organization's human resource problem in an intellectual sense. But he knows nothing of the history of jobs in his client organization. Here is where we might consult Zorba's source of practical wisdom, the "wise old Turk." There are many companies with forgotten "wise old Turks" who know— concretely, visually, and experientially—the history of numerous jobs. Many have had their jobs lifted out from under them by behavioral science, and have come through the ranks, experiencing the various levels of organizations. They know what mindless work is, and that it has often been the result of changes made in the name of efficiency.

These "old Turks" are a valuable source of information for job enrichment, and they are already on the payroll. A behavioral scientist or a manager wishing to enrich a job should start by finding them and asking: What past changes in the job, made in the name of efficiency, should be eliminated? Many times, when discussing job enrichment in industry, I have been told by a "wise old Turk," "Hell, that's the way we used to do it."

One more time: How do you motivate employees? Part II

ETERNAL TRIANGLE

There are three general philosophies of personnel management. The first is based on organizational theory, the second on industrial engineering, and the third on behavioral science.

The organizational theorist believes that human needs are either so irrational or so varied and adjustable to specific situations that the major function of personnel management is to be as pragmatic as the occasion demands. If jobs are organized in a proper manner, he reasons, the result will be the most efficient job structure, and the most favorable job attitudes will follow as a matter of course.

The industrial engineer holds that man is mechanistically oriented and economically motivated and his needs are best met by attuning the individual to the most efficient work process. The goal of personnel management therefore should be to concoct the most appropriate incentive system and to design the specific working conditions in a way that facilitates the most efficient use of the human machine. By structuring jobs in a manner that leads to the most efficient operation, the engineer believes that he can obtain the optimal organization of work and the proper work attitudes.

The behavioral scientist focuses on group sentiments, attitudes of individual employees, and the organization's social and psychological climate. According to his persuasion, he emphasizes one or more of the various hygiene and motivator needs. His approach to personnel management generally emphasizes some form of human relations education, in the hope of instilling healthy employee attitudes and an organizational climate which he considers to be felicitous to human values. He believes that proper attitudes will lead to efficient job and organizational structure.

There is always a lively debate as to the overall effectiveness of the approaches of the organizational theorist and the industrial engineer. Manifestly they have achieved much. But the nagging question for the behavioral scientist has been: What is the cost in human problems that eventually cause more expense to the organization—for instance, turn-over, absenteeism, errors, violation of safety rules, strikes, restriction of output, higher wages, and greater fringe benefits? On the other hand, the behavioral scientist is hard put to document much manifest improvement in personnel management, using his approach.

The three philosophies can be depicted as a triangle, as is done in Figure 1, with each persuasion claiming the apex angle. The Motivation-Hygiene Theory claims the same angle as industrial engineering, but for opposite goals. Rather than rationalizing the work to increase efficiency, the theory suggests that work be *enriched* to bring about effective utiliza-tion of personnel. Such a systematic attempt to motivate employees by manipulating the motivator factors is just beginning.

Figure 1

Triangle of philosophies of personnel management

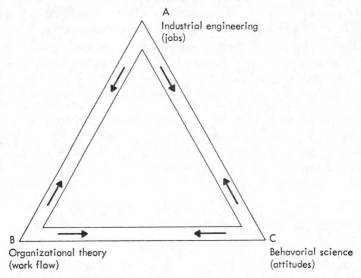

A
Industrial engineering
(jobs)

B
Organizational theory
(work flow)

C
Behavorial science
(attitudes)

The term "job enrichment" describes this embryonic movement. An older term, "job enlargement," should be avoided because it is associated with past failures stemming from a misunderstanding of the problem. Job enrichment provides the opportunity for the employee's psychological growth, while job enlargement merely makes a job structurally bigger. Since scientific job enrichment is very new,[1] this article only suggests the principles and practical steps that have recently emerged from several successful experiments in industry.

---

[1] Note that this article was published in 1968.

JOB LOADING

In attempting to enrich an employee's job, management often succeeds in reducing the man's personal contribution, rather than giving him an opportunity for growth in his accustomed job. Such an endeavor, which I shall call horizontal job loading (as opposed to vertical loading, or providing motivator factors), has been the problem of earlier job enlargement programs. This activity merely enlarges the meaninglessness of the job. Some examples of this approach, and their effects are:

Challenging the employee by increasing the amount of production expected of him. If he tightens 10,000 bolts a day, see if he can tighten 20,000 bolts a day. The arithmetic involved shows that multiplying zero by zero still equals zero.

Adding another meaningless task to the existing one, usually some routine clerical activity. The arithmetic here is adding zero to zero.

Rotating the assignments of a number of jobs that need to be enriched. This means washing dishes for a while, then washing silverware. The arithmetic is substituting one zero for another zero.

Removing the most difficult parts of the assignment in order to free the worker to accomplish more of the less challenging assignments. This traditional industrial engineering approach amounts to subtraction in the hope of accomplishing addition.

These are common forms of horizontal loading that frequently come up in preliminary brainstorming sessions on job enrichment. The principles of vertical loading have not all been worked out as yet, and they remain rather general, but I have furnished seven useful starting points for consideration in Figure 2.

A SUCCESSFUL APPLICATION

An example from a highly successful job enrichment experiment can illustrate the distinction between horizontal and vertical loading of a job. The subjects of this study were the stockholder correspondents employed by a very large corporation. Seemingly, the task required of these carefully selected and highly trained correspondents was quite complex and challenging. But almost all indexes of performance and job attitudes were low, and exit interviewing confirmed that the challenge of the job existed merely as words.

A job enrichment project was initiated in the form of an experiment, with one group, designated as an achieving unit, having its job enriched by the principles described in Figure 2. A control group continued to do its job in the traditional way. (There were also two "uncommitted" groups of correspondents formed to measure the so-called Hawthorne effect—that is, to gauge whether productivity and attitudes toward the job

Figure 2

Principles of vertical job loading

Principle	Motivators involved
A. Removing some controls while retaining accountability	Responsibility and personal achievement
B. Increasing the accountability of individuals for own work	Responsibility and recognition
C. Giving a person a complete natural unit of work (module, division, area, and so on)	Responsibility, achievement, and recognition
D. Granting additional authority to an employee in his activity; job freedom	Responsibility, achievement, and recognition
E. Making periodic reports directly available to the worker himself rather than to the supervisor	Internal recognition
F. Introducing new and more difficult tasks not previously handled	Growth and learning
G. Assigning individuals specific or specialized tasks, enabling them to become experts	Responsibility, growth, and advancement

changed artificially merely because employees sensed that the company was paying more attention to them in doing something different or novel. The results for these groups were substantially the same as for the control group, and for the sake of simplicity I do not deal with them in this summary.) No changes in hygiene were introduced for either group, other than those that would have been made anyway, such as normal pay increases.

The changes for the achieving unit were introduced in the first two months, averaging one per week of the seven motivators listed in Figure 2. At the end of six months the members of the achieving unit were found to be outperforming their counterparts in the control group, and in addition they indicated a marked increase in their liking for their jobs. Other results showed that the achieving group had lower absenteeism and, subsequently, a much higher rate of promotion.

Figure 3 illustrates the changes in performance, measured in February and March, before the study period began, and at the end of each month of the study period. The shareholder service index represents quality of letters, including accuracy of information, and speed of response to stockholders' letters of inquiry. The index of a current month was averaged into the average of the two prior months, which means that improvement was harder to obtain if the indexes of the previous months were low. The "achievers" were performing less well before the six-month period started, and their performance service index continued to decline after the intro-

Figure 3

Shareholder service index in company experiment (three-month cumulative average)

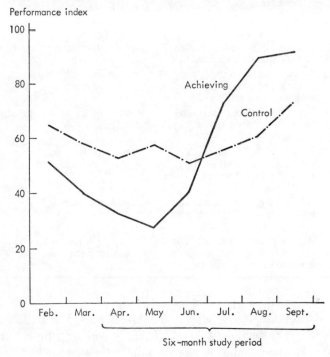

Performance index

Six-month study period

duction of the motivators, evidently because of uncertainty over their newly granted responsibilities. In the third month, however, performance improved, and soon the members of this group had reached a high level of accomplishment.

Figure 4 shows the two groups' attitudes toward their job, measured at the end of March, just before the first motivator was introduced, and again at the end of September. The correspondents were asked 16 questions, all involving motivation. A typical one was, "As you see it, how many opportunities do you feel that you have in your job for making worthwhile contributions?" The answers were scaled from 1 to 5, with 80 as the maximum possible score. The achievers became much more positive about their job, while the attitude of the control unit remained about the same (the drop is not statistically significant).

How was the job of these correspondents restructured? Figure 5 lists the suggestions made that were deemed to be horizontal loading, and the actual vertical loading changes that were incorporated in the job of the achieving unit. The capital letters under "Principle" after "Vertical loading" refer to the corresponding letters in Figure 2. The reader will note that the rejected forms of horizontal loading correspond closely to the list of common manifestations of the phenomenon on page 130.

Figure 4

Changes in attitudes toward tasks in company experiment (changes in mean scores over six-month period)

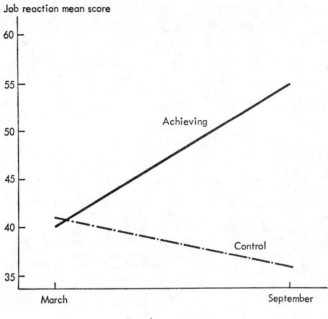

Job reaction mean score

Time between surveys

STEPS TO JOB ENRICHMENT

Now that the motivator idea has been described in practice, here are the steps that managers should take in instituting the principle in their relations with their employees:

1. Select those jobs in which (a) the investment in industrial engineering does not make changes too costly, (b) attitudes are poor, (c) hygiene is becoming very costly, and (d) motivation will make a difference in performance.

2. Approach these jobs with the conviction that they can be changed. Years of tradition have led managers to believe that the content of the jobs is sacrosanct and the only scope of action that they have is in ways of stimulating people.

3. Brainstorm a list of changes that may enrich the jobs, without concern for their practicality.

4. Screen the list to eliminate suggestions that involve hygiene, rather than actual motivation.

5. Screen the list for generalities, such as "give them more responsibility," that are rarely followed in practice. This might seem obvious, but the motivator words have never left industry; the substance has just been rationalized and organized out. Words like "responsibility," "growth,"

Figure 5

Enlargement v. enrichment of correspondents' tasks in company experiment

Horizontal loading suggestions (rejected)	Vertical loading suggestions (adopted)	Principle
Firm quotas could be set for letters to be answered each day, using a rate which would be hard to reach.	Subject matter experts were appointed within each unit for other members of the unit to consult with before seeking supervisory help. (The supervisor had been answering all specialized and difficult questions.)	G
The women could type the letters themselves, as well as compose them, or take on any other clerical functions.	Correspondents signed their own names on letters. (The supervisor had been signing all letters.)	B
All difficult or complex inquiries could be channeled to a few women so that the remainder could achieve high rates of output. These jobs could be exchanged from time to time.	The work of the more experienced correspondents was proofread less frequently by supervisors and was done at the correspondents' desks, dropping verification from 100 to 10 percent. (Previously, all correspondents' letters had been checked by the supervisor.)	A
The women could be rotated through units handling different customers and then sent back to their own units.	Production was discussed, but only in terms such as "a full day's work is expected." As time went on, this was no longer mentioned. (Before, the group had been constantly reminded of the number of letters that needed to be answered.)	D
	Outgoing mail went directly to the mailroom without going over supervisors' desks. (The letters had always been routed through the supervisors.)	A
	Correspondents were encouraged to answer letters in a more personalized way. (Reliance on the form-letter approach had been standard practice.)	C
	Each correspondent was held personally responsible for the quality and accuracy of letters. (This responsibility had been the province of the supervisor and the verifier.)	B, E

"achievement," and "challenge," for example, have been elevated to the lyrics of the patriotic anthem for all organizations. It is the old problem typified by the pledge of allegiance to the flag being more important than contributions to the country—of following the form, rather than the substance.

6. Screen the list to eliminate any *horizontal* loading suggestions.

7. Avoid direct participation by the employees whose jobs are to be enriched. Ideas they have expressed previously certainly constitute a valuable source for recommended changes, but their direct involvement contaminates the process with human relations *hygiene* and, more spe-

cifically, gives them only a *sense* of making a contribution. The job is to be changed, and it is the content that will produce the motivation, not attitudes about being involved or the challenge inherent in setting up a job. That process will be over shortly, and it is what the employees will be doing from then on that will determine their motivation. A sense of participation will result only in short-term movement.

8. In the initial attempts at job enrichment, set up a controlled experiment. At least two equivalent groups should be chosen, one an experimental unit in which the motivators are systematically introduced over a period of time, and the other one a control group in which no changes are made. For both groups, hygiene should be allowed to follow its natural course for the duration of the experiment. Pre- and post-installation tests of performance and job attitudes are necessary to evaluate the effectiveness of the job enrichment program. The attitude test must be limited to motivator items in order to divorce the employee's view of the job he is given from all the surrounding hygiene feelings that he might have.

9. Be prepared for a drop in performance in the experimental group the first few weeks. The changeover to a new job may lead to a temporary reduction in efficiency.

10. Expect your first-line supervisors to experience some anxiety and hostility over the changes you are making. The anxiety comes from their fear that the changes will result in poorer performance for their unit. Hostility will arise when the employees start assuming what the supervisors regard as their own responsibility for performance. The supervisor without checking duties to perform may then be left with little to do.

After a successful experiment, however, the supervisor usually discovers the supervisory and managerial functions he has neglected, or which were never his because all his time was given over to checking the work of his subordinates. For example, in the R&D division of one large chemical company I know of, the supervisors of the laboratory assistants were theoretically responsible for their training and evaluation. These functions, however, had come to be performed in a routine, unsubstantial fashion. After the job enrichment program, during which the supervisors were not merely passive observers of the assistants' performance, the supervisors actually were devoting their time to reviewing performance and administering thorough training.

What has been called an employee-centered style of supervision will come about not through education of supervisors, but by changing the jobs that they do.

CONCLUDING NOTE

Job enrichment will not be a one-time proposition, but a continuous management function. The initial changes, however, should last for a very long period of time. There are a number of reasons for this:

1. The changes should bring the job up to the level of challenge commensurate with the skill that was hired.
2. Those who have still more ability eventually will be able to demonstrate it better and win promotion to higher-level jobs.
3. The very nature of motivators, as opposed to hygiene factors, is that they have a much longer-term effect on employees' attitudes. Perhaps the job will have to be enriched again, but this will not occur as frequently as the need for hygiene.

Not all jobs can be enriched, nor do all jobs need to be enriched. If only a small percentage of the time and money that is now devoted to hygiene, however, were given to job enrichment efforts, the return in human satisfaction and economic gain would be one of the largest dividends that industry and society have ever reaped through their efforts at better personnel management.

The argument for job enrichment can be summed up quite simply: If you have someone on a job, use him. If you can't use him on the job, get rid of him, either via automation or by selecting someone with lesser ability. If you can't use him and you can't get rid of him, you will have a motivation problem.

Job enrichment pays off

William J. Paul, Jr.
Keith B. Robertson
and
Frederick Herzberg

In his pioneering article "One More Time: How Do You Motivate Employees?" Frederick Herzberg put forward some principles of scientific job enrichment and reported a successful application of them involving the stockholder correspondents employed by a large corporation.[1] According to him, job enrichment seeks to improve both task efficiency and human satisfaction by means of building into people's jobs, quite specifically, greater scope for personal achievement and its recognition, more challenging and responsible work, and more opportunity for individual advancement and growth. It is concerned only incidentally with matters such as pay and working conditions, organizational structure, communications, and training, important and necessary though these may be in their own right.

But like a lot of pioneering work, Herzberg's study raised more questions than it answered. Some seemed to us to merit further consideration, particularly those in regard to the (1) generality of the findings, (2) feasibility of making changes, and (3) consequences to be expected. Consider:

1. *Generality.* Can similarly positive results be obtained elsewhere with other people doing different jobs? How widespread is the scope or need for equivalent change in other jobs? Can meaningful results be obtained only in jobs with large numbers of people all doing the same work and where performance measures are easily available?

2. *Feasibility.* Are there not situations where the operational risk is so high that it would be foolhardy to attempt to pass responsibility and

---

[1] *Harvard Business Review*, January–February 1968, p. 53. The article is reprinted in two parts above.

scope for achievement down the line? Because people's ability and sense of responsibility vary so much, is it not necessary to make changes selectively? Do all employees welcome having their jobs enriched, or are there not some who prefer things to be left as they are? Can one enrich jobs without inevitably facing demands for higher pay or better conditions to match the new responsibilities? And, in any case, is not the best route to motivational change through participation?

3. *Consequences.*   In view of so many possible difficulties in the way, are the gains to be expected from job enrichment significant or only marginal? Do they relate primarily to job satisfaction or to performance? What are the consequences for supervision if jobs are loaded with new tasks taken from above—i.e., does one man's enrichment become another's impoverishment? Finally, what are the consequences for management if motivational change becomes a reality? Is the manager's role affected? If so, how? And what are the implications for management development?

There are undoubtedly more questions that could be raised and investigated. But these seem particularly important from a corporate point of view if job enrichment is to take place on a widespread basis, as part of management practice rather than as a research activity. Accordingly, the purpose of this article is to probe into the complexities of job enrichment in an attempt to shed light on these questions and to determine how the concept may be most effectively applied in furthering the attainment of corporate business objectives.

In order to do this, we shall report in Part I on five studies carried out in Imperial Chemical Industries Limited and other British companies. Two of the studies—covering laboratory technicians in an R&D department and sales representatives in three companies—will be examined in some detail. The other three—encompassing design engineers, production foremen on shift work, and engineering foremen on day work—will be summarized. In Part II, the main conclusions emerging from the studies will be presented in the form of answers to the questions raised at the beginning of this article.

Each study was initiated in response to a particular problem posed by management, and the conclusions drawn from any one can be only tentative. Among them, however, they cover not only widely different business areas and company functions, but also many types and levels of jobs. Collectively, they provide material which adds to our understanding of both theory and practice.

PART I: THE JOB ENRICHMENT STUDIES

As in all studies on job satisfaction and performance, the need to measure results introduced certain constraints which do not exist in normal managerial situations. Consequently, three main features were common to the studies we are reporting in this discussion:

First, the "hygiene" was held constant. This means that no deliberate changes were made, as part of the investigation, in matters such as pay, security, or working conditions. The studies were specifically trying to measure the extent of those gains which could be attributed solely to change in job content.

Second, recognition of the normal hygiene changes led to the need to have an "experimental group" for whom the specific changes in job content were made, and a "control group" whose job content remained the same.

Third, the studies had to be kept confidential to avoid the well-known tendency of people to behave in an artificial way when they know they are the subject of a controlled study. Naturally, there was no secret about the changes themselves, only about the fact that performance was being measured.

All studies set out to measure job satisfaction and performance for both the experimental and control groups over a trial period following the implementation of the changes. The trial period itself generally lasted a year and was never less than six months. The performance measures always were specific to the group concerned and were determined by local management of the subject company. To measure job satisfaction, we relied throughout on a job reaction survey which measures the degree of people's satisfaction with the motivators in their job as they themselves perceive them.

LABORATORY TECHNICIANS

Managers in an industrial research department were concerned about the morale of laboratory technicians, or "experimental officers" (EOs). This group's job was to implement experimental programs devised by scientists. The EOs set up the appropriate apparatus, recorded data, and supervised laboratory assistants, who carried out the simpler operations. The EOs were professionally qualified people, but lacked the honors or doctorate degrees possessed by the scientists.

The average age of the experimental officers was increasing. A quarter of them had reached their salary maximums, and fewer now had the chance to move out of the department. Their normal promotion route into plant management had become blocked as manufacturing processes grew more complex and more highly qualified people filled the available jobs. Management's view of the situation was confirmed by the initial job reaction survey. Not only were the EOs' scores low, but many wrote of their frustration. They felt their technical ability and experience was being wasted by the scientists' refusal to delegate anything but routine work.

Against this background, the research manager's specific objective was to develop the EOs into "better scientists." If job enrichment was to be useful, it would have to contribute to the attainment of that goal.

Changes and experimental design

Here is the specific program of action devised and implemented for the experimental officers:

Technical. EOs were encouraged to write the final report, or "minute," on any research project for which they had been responsible. Such minutes carried the author's name and were issued along with those of the scientists. It was up to each EO to decide for himself whether he wanted the minute checked by his supervisor before issue, but in any case he was fully responsible for answering any query arising from it.

EOs were involved in planning projects and experiments, and were given more chance to assist in work planning and target setting.

They were given time, on request, to follow up their own ideas, even if these went beyond the planned framework of research. Written reports had to be submitted on all such work.

Financial. EOs were authorized to requisition materials and equipment, to request analysis, and to order services such as maintenance, all on their own signature.

Managerial. Senior EOs were made responsible for devising and implementing a training program for their junior staff. In doing so, they could call on facilities and advice available within the company.

Senior EOs were involved in interviewing candidates for laboratory assistant jobs, and they also acted as first assessor in any staff assessment of their own laboratory assistants.

These changes drew on all the motivators. Each one gave important chances for achievement; together, they were designed to make the work more challenging. Recognition of achievement came in the authorship of reports. Authority to order supplies and services was a responsibility applying to all the EOs involved. The new managerial responsibilities reserved to senior EOs opened up room for advancement within the job, while the technical changes, particularly the opportunity for self-initiated work, gave scope for professional growth.

Some 40 EOs in all were involved in the study. Two sections of the department acted as experimental groups ($N = 15$) and two as control groups ($N = 29$). One experimental and one control group worked closely together on the same type of research, and it was anticipated that there would be some interaction between them. The other two groups were separate geographically and engaged on quite different research.

The changes were implemented for the experimental groups during October and November 1966, and the trial period ran for the next twelve months. After six months, the same changes were introduced into one of the control groups, thus converting it into an experimental group ($N = 14$). This was done to see whether a similar pattern of performance revealed itself, thereby safeguarding against any remote possibility of coincidence in the choice of the original groups.

Research work is notoriously difficult to measure, but as the aim was to encourage more scientific contribution from EOs, this was what had to be judged in as objective a way as possible. All EOs were asked to write monthly progress reports of work done. Those written by experimental and control group EOs were assessed by a panel of three managers, not members of the department, who were familiar with the research work concerned.

Reports were scored against eight specifically defined criteria thought to reflect the kind of growth being sought: *knowledge, comprehension, synthesis, evaluation, original thought, practical initiative, industry,* and *skill in report writing.* Whenever the assessor found particular evidence of one of these qualities in a report, he would award it one mark, the total score for a report being simply the sum of these marks.

In order to establish a base line for clarifying standards and testing the assessors' consistency of marking, reports were collected for three months prior to the introduction of any job enrichment changes. The very high consistency found between the marking of the three assessors encouraged confidence in the system. The assessors, naturally, were never told which were the experimental and control groups, though it became easy for them to guess as the trial period went on.

The other main measure was to use the same system to assess research minutes written by the EOs. These were compared against an equivalent sample of minutes written by scientists over the same period, which were submitted to the panel for assessment, again without identification.

Motivational results

The assessment of monthly reports written by the experimental officers is given in Figure 1, which compares the mean score achieved by all experimental group EOs each month with that achieved by all control group EOs. On occasions when a monthly report had obviously suffered because of the attention devoted to writing a research minute covering much the same ground, a marginal weighting factor was added to the score, depending on the quality of the minute concerned. Both experimental and control groups improved their monthly report scores at about the same rate during the first five months. There is no doubt that with practice all were getting better at report writing, and it may be that the mere fact of being asked to write monthly reports itself acted as a motivator for both groups.

Once the changes had been fully implemented in the experimental groups, however, performance began to diverge. Although the reports of the control groups continued to improve for a time, they were far outpaced by those of the experimental groups. With some fluctuations, this performance differential was maintained throughout the rest of the trial period. When, after six months, the motivators were fed into one of the

Figure 1

Assessment of EOs monthly reports

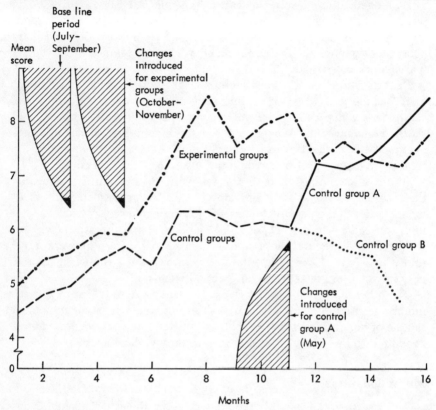

two control groups, its performance improved dramatically, following the pattern achieved by the original experimental groups. Meanwhile, the performance of the other control group, unaffected by what was happening elsewhere, began to slip back toward its original starting point.

During the 12 months of the trial period, a total of 34 research minutes were written by EOs, all from the experimental groups, compared with 2 from the department as a whole during the previous 12-month period. There were also a number of minutes jointly authored by scientists and EOs, which are excluded from this analysis. Of the 34 being considered, 9 were written by EOs in the control group which was converted into an experimental group, but all came from the time after the changes had been introduced.

It is one thing for laboratory technicians to write research minutes, but whether the minutes they write are any good or not is a different matter. Figure 2 shows the quality of the EOs' minutes compared with that of

Figure 2

Assessment of EOs research minutes

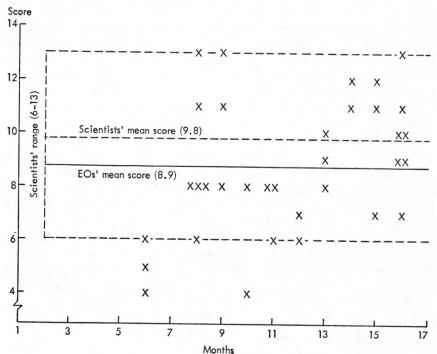

the scientists'. The EOs' mean score was 8.9; the scientists' 9.8. All EO scores except three fell within the range of scores obtained by the scientists; the three exceptions were written by one man. Three of the EOs' minutes, one in fact written by a laboratory assistant with guidance from an EO, were judged to be as good as the best of the scientists' minutes.

Encouraged by the success of a training scheme designed for laboratory assistants, the EOs initiated one for themselves. It aimed to give them the opportunity to come to terms with the ideas and terminology of chemical engineering. Managers judged it to have been of considerable value, and one EO summed it up by saying, "A couple of pages of chemical engineering calculations and formulas won't frighten us off now."

One original idea followed up, as the changes now permitted, by an EO from an experimental group resulted in an important discovery with possible applications in certain kinds of national emergency. The idea was investigated further by a government department, which described it as the most promising of some 200 ideas submitted on that topic.

Three staff assessments on EOs were carried out—at the beginning, middle, and end of the trial period. Each followed the normal company procedure. The only group which showed a consistent improvement was one of the experimental groups.

The job reaction survey was given both before and after the trial period. In the initial survey, experimental and control group EOs could not be specifically identified, and so an exact comparison of the before and after scores of each group cannot be made. The overall mean score attained by all EOs in the department was no higher at the end of the trial period than it had been at the beginning. Although managers believed there had been a positive change in job satisfaction, that is not a conclusion which can be supported with data.

An internal company report, written by the personnel officer who managed and coordinated the study throughout, concluded that there had been definite evidence of growth among the EOs, particularly in one group, and that much useful work had been accomplished during the exercise. One of the experimental groups had been able to keep abreast of its commitments even though it lost the services of two of its six scientists during the trial period and functioned without a manager for the last five months of the study. There can be little doubt that job enrichment in this case helped to further the research manager's objective of tackling a morale problem by getting at the root of the matter and developing experimental officers as scientists in their own right.

SALES REPRESENTATIVES

To investigate the potential of job enrichment in the sales field, work has been done in three British companies dealing with quite different products and markets, both wholesale and retail. In only one study, however, were experimental conditions strictly observed.

The company concerned had long enjoyed a healthy share of the domestic market in one particular product range, but its position was threatened by competition. A decline in market share had been stabilized before the study began, but 1967 sales still showed no improvement over those of 1966. So far as could be judged, the company's products were fully competitive in both price and quality. The critical factor in the situation appeared to be sales representatives' effort.

The representatives' salaries—they were not paid a commission—and conditions of employment were known to compare well with the average for the industry. Their mean score in the job reaction survey, like that of other groups of salesmen, was higher than most employees of equivalent seniority, which suggested that they enjoyed considerable job satisfaction.

The problem in this case, therefore, was that for the vital business objective of regaining the initiative in an important market, sustained extra effort was needed from a group of people already comparatively well treated and reasonably satisfied with their jobs. Here, job enrichment would stand or fall by the sales figures achieved.

Changes and experimental design

Here is the specific program of action devised and implemented for the sales representatives:

Technical. Sales representatives were no longer obliged to write reports on every customer call. They were asked simply to pass on information when they thought it appropriate or request action as they thought it was required.

Responsibility for determining calling frequencies was put wholly with the representatives themselves, who kept the only records for purposes such as staff reviews.

The technical service department agreed to provide service "on demand" from the representatives; nominated technicians regarded such calls as their first priority. Communication was by direct contact, paperwork being cleared after the event.

Financial. In cases of customer complaint about product performance, representatives were authorized to make immediate settlements of up to $250 if they were satisfied that consequential liability would not be prejudiced.

If faulty material had been delivered or if the customer was holding material for which he had no further use, the representative now had complete authority, with no upper limit in sales value, to decide how best to deal with the matter. He could buy back unwanted stock even if it was no longer on the company's selling range.

Representatives were given a discretionary range of about 10 percent on the prices of most products, especially those considered to be critical from the point of view of market potential. The lower limit given was often below any price previously quoted by the company. All quotations other than at list price had to be reported by the representative.

The theme of all the changes was to build the sales representative's job so that it became more complete in its own right. Instead of always having to refer back to headquarters, the representative now had the authority to make decisions on his own—he was someone the customer could really do business with. Every change implied a greater responsibility; together they gave the freedom and challenge necessary for self-development.

The company sold to many different industries, or "trades." In view of the initial effort needed to determine limit prices and to make the technical service arrangements, it was decided that the study should concentrate on three trades chosen to be typical of the business as a whole. These three trades gave a good geographical spread and covered many types of customers; each had an annual sales turnover of about $1 million.

The experimental group ($N = 15$) was selected to be representative of the sales force as a whole in age range, experience, and ability. An important part of each member's selling responsibility lay within the nominated trades. The rest of the sales force ($N = 23$) acted as the control group. The changes were introduced during December 1967, and the trial period ran from January 1 to September 30, 1968.

The background of static sales and the objective of recapturing the market initiative dictated that sales turnover would be the critical measure, checked by gross margin. The difficulties of comparing unequal sales values and allowing for monthly fluctuations and seasonal trends were overcome by making all comparisons on a cumulative basis in terms of the percentage gain or loss for each group against the equivalent period of the previous year.

Since they were selling in the same trades in the same parts of the country, the performance of all the representatives was presumably influenced by the same broad economic and commercial factors. In two of the trades, the experimental group had the bigger share of the business and tended to sell to the larger customers. In these cases it may be surmised that prevailing market conditions affected the experimental group's performance, favorably or unfavorably, more than the control group's. As it happened, in one of these trades commercial trends were favorable, while in the other they were distinctly unfavorable. In the third trade, the experimental and control groups were evenly matched. Taken together, then, the three trades give as fair a comparison as can be obtained between the performances of sales representatives under those two sets of conditions.

Motivational results

During the trial period the experimental group increased its sales by almost 19 percent over the same period of the previous year, a gain of over $300,000 in sales value. The control group's sales in the meantime declined by 5 percent. The equivalent change for both groups the previous year had been a decline of 3 percent. The difference in performance between the two groups is statistically significant at the 0.01 level of confidence.

Figure 3 shows the month-to-month performance of the two groups, plotted cumulatively. It can be seen that the control group in fact started the year extremely well, with January/February sales in the region of 30 percent above the equivalent 1967 figures. This improvement was not sustained, however, and by May cumulative sales had dropped below their 1967 level. By the last five months of the trial period, performance was running true to the previous year's form, showing a decline of about 3 percent.

The experimental group, on the other hand, started more modestly, not exceeding a 20 percent improvement during the first quarter. During the second quarter, outstanding results in May compensated for poorer

Figure 3

Sales turnover within trades chosen as typical of the business as a whole

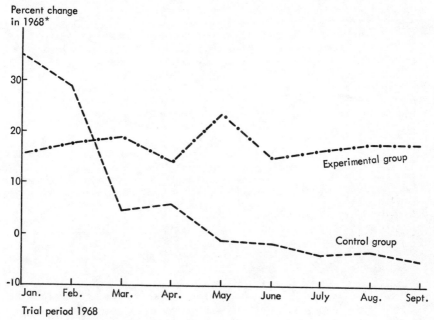

Percent change
in 1968*

Trial period 1968

* Against corresponding 1967 period, plotted cumulatively.

figures in April and June. The third quarter showed a steady, if slight, rise in the rate of improvement over 1967. This sustained increase of just under 20 percent was in marked contrast to the previously declining performance of the trades as a whole.

Comparisons with other trades suffer from the disadvantage that different economic and commercial factors affect the various parts of the business. Nevertheless, the experimental group's performance was consistently between 6 percent and 7 percent better than that for the rest of the business. Figure 4 shows the month-to-month picture. It can be seen not only that the experimental group maintained a higher rate of improvement than the rest of the business throughout the trial period, but that the gap widened, if anything, as time went on. At the 1967 rates of turnover, this performance differential in all trades would be worth $1.5 million in sales value in a full year.

In view of the greater negotiating authority granted to the experimental group representatives, it is important to check whether their substantial increase in turnover was achieved at the expense of profit. As all quotations other than at list price were reported by the representatives, it was possible to analyze the gross margin achieved by both groups. The analysis showed without doubt that the gross margin of the experimental

Figure 4

Sales turnover: experimental group and rest of business

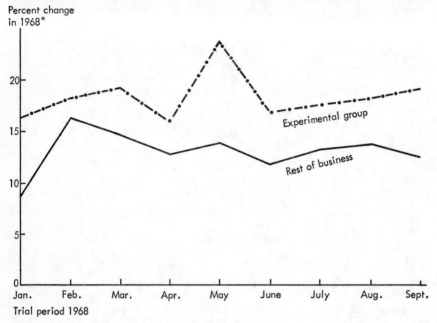

Percent change
in 1968*

Trial period 1968

* Against corresponding 1967 period, plotted cumulatively.

group's sales was proportionally as high, if not higher, than that of the control group's sales.

Managers had the impression that representatives actually used their price discretion less often than they had previously asked for special prices to be quoted by the sales office. Also, in the sales manager's view, once the representatives were given real negotiating authority, they discovered that price was not the obstacle to sales which they had always imagined it to be. Under the new arrangements, they were able to assess more completely what the true obstacles to sales were in each individual case.

Over the trial period the control group's mean score in the job reaction survey remained static. In contrast, the experimental group's score rose by 11 percent.

DESIGN ENGINEERS

The engineering director of one of the divisions of ICI wanted to see whether the job of design engineer might lend itself to motivational change. His design department faced an increasing work load as more design work for the division's plants was being done internally. The situation was exacerbated by difficulties in recruiting qualified design engineers. People at all levels in the department were being overloaded, and development work was suffering.

Changes and experimental design

Here is the specific program of action devised and implemented for the design engineers:

Technical. Experienced engineers were given a completely independent role in running their projects; the less experienced technical men were given as much independence as possible. Occasions on which reference to supervision remained obligatory were reduced to an absolute minimum. The aim was that each engineer should judge for himself when and to what extent he should seek advice.

Group managers sponsored occasional investigatory jobs, and engineers were encouraged to become departmental experts in particular fields. They were expected to follow up completed projects as they thought appropriate.

When authority to allocate work to outside consultants was given, the engineers were to have the responsibility for making the choice of consultants.

Financial. Within a sanctioned project with a budget already agreed on, all arbitrary limits on engineers' authority to spend money were removed. They themselves had to ensure that each "physical intent" was adequately defined and that an appropriate sum was allocated for it in the project budget. That done, no financial ceiling limited their authority to place orders.

Managerial. Engineers were involved in the selection and placing of designers (drawing office staff). They manned selection panels, and a recruit would only be allocated to a particular engineer if the latter agreed to accept him.

Experienced engineers were asked to make the initial salary recommendations for all their junior staff members.

Engineers were allowed to authorize overtime, cash advances, and traveling expenses for staff.

Motivational results

In summary fashion, these are the deductions that can be drawn from this study:

Senior managers saw a change in both the amount and the kind of consultation between experimental group design engineers and their immediate supervisors. The supervisors' routine involvement in projects was much reduced, and they were able to give more emphasis in their work to technical development. Some engineers still needed frequent guidance; others operated independently with confidence. The point is that not all were restricted for the benefit of some; those who could were allowed to find their own feet.

The encouragement of specialist expertise among design engineers was a long-term proposition, but progress was made during the trial period.

The removal of any financial ceiling on engineers' authority to place orders within an approved project with an agreed budget proved entirely effective. Whereas before the design engineers had to seek approval from as many as three higher levels of management for any expenditure over $5,000—a time-consuming process for all concerned—now they could, and did, place orders for as much as $500,000 worth of equipment on their own authority.

There is no evidence of any poor decision having been taken as a result of the new arrangements. In fact, at the end of the trial period, none of the senior managers concerned wanted to revert to the old system.

The changes involving the engineers in supervisory roles were thought by the senior managers to be at least as important as the other changes, possibly more so in the long term.

There was no doubt about the design engineers' greater involvement in the selection process, which they fully accepted and appreciated. Significantly, they began to show a greater feel for the constraints involved in selection.

The responsibility for overtime and travel claims was fully effective and taken in people's stride. There was no adverse effect from a budgetary control point of view.

The involvement of design engineers in making salary recommendations for their staff was considered by the senior managers to have been a major improvement. If anything, engineers tended to be "tighter" in their salary recommendations than more senior management. There was general agreement that the effectiveness of this change would increase over time.

Senior managers felt that none of the changes of its own accord had had an overriding effect, nor had all problems been solved. But there was no doubt that the cumulative effect of the changes had been significant and that the direction of solutions to some important problems had been indicated.

The changes may have been effective, but in this particular study the important question was whether they had a significant impact on job satisfaction. Some of the motivators introduced into the experimental groups had been in operation in the control group for some time; others—because of the specialist nature of the control group's work—were not as important to it as to the experimental groups. The control group had scored high in the initial job reaction survey, while the experimental groups had both achieved very low scores. If the experimental groups' scores did not improve, doubt would inevitably be cast on the relationship between job content and job satisfaction. As it turned out, comparison results of the before and after job reaction surveys revealed that the mean scores of the two experimental groups had increased by 21 and 16 percent, while those of the control group and all other design engineers in the department had remained static.

FACTORY SUPERVISORS

The final two studies, one in ICI and one in another British company, concerned factory supervisors: production foremen on shift work fabricating nonferrous metals, and engineering foremen on day work providing maintenance services. As the two studies seem to be complementary, they are considered jointly.

In both cases management was concerned about the degree to which the traditional role of the foreman had been eroded in recent years. The increasing complexity of organizational structures, plant and equipment, and industrial relations had left the foreman isolated. Decisions in the areas of planning, technical control, and discipline—originally in his province—were now passed up the line or turned over to a specialist staff. Many managers believed that as a consequence small problems too often escalated unnecessarily, managers were being overloaded, and day-to-day relationships between the foreman and his men had been weakened.

Changes and experimental design

Here is the specific program of action devised and implemented for the production and engineering foremen:

Technical. Foremen were involved more in planning. Production foremen were authorized to modify schedules for loading and sequencing; engineering foremen were consulted more about organizational developments, given more responsibility for preventive maintenance, and encouraged to comment on design.

All were assigned projects on specific problems, such as quality control, and could draw on the necessary resources for their implementation.

Other changes included giving foremen more "on the spot" responsibility, official deputizing for engineers, the writing of monthly reports, and more recognition of foremen's achievement of plans.

Financial. Engineering foremen were given complete control of certain "on cost" budgets. Production foremen were encouraged to make all decisions on nonstandard payments.

Managerial. Production foremen were given the authority to hire labor against agreed manning targets. They interviewed candidates for jobs and made the decision on their selection.

All the foremen were given complete disciplinary authority, except for dismissal. They decided what disciplinary action to take, consulted the personnel department if they thought it necessary, conducted the interviews, and kept the records.

All were given formal responsibility for the assessment, training, and development of their subordinates, and in some cases for the appointment of their own deputies. On the production side, a newly appointed training officer acted as a resource person for the foremen. Engineering foremen were involved more in the application of a job appraisement scheme and in joint consultation and negotiation with union officials.

The objective of integrating the foreman more fully into the managerial team dictated that responsibility should be the motivator chiefly concerned in these changes. Control of his own labor force, backed up by more technical and financial responsibility, was designed to give the foreman more opportunities for achievement and personal growth in the job. The main issue in these studies was whether foremen would prove themselves capable of carrying the increased responsibility. Thus, in monitoring the effectiveness of the changes, the aim was primarily to detect any instability or shortcomings in performance.

Motivational results

In summary fashion, these are the deductions that can be drawn from this study:

In six months the production foremen recruited nearly 100 men and were judged by the personnel officer to be "hiring a better caliber of man at an improved rate." Their immediate supervisors were categorical in their approval and noted that the foremen were taking special care to "design their own shifts." Recruitment interviews were said to have improved the foremen's ability to handle encounters with existing staff and shop stewards.

Training was handled equally successfully by the production foremen. For each job it was specified that there should be a certain number of men trained to take over in an emergency. During the trial period, the margin by which the target number was missed was reduced from 94 to 55; the number of operators unable to do another's job fell by 12 percent, and the number of assistants unable to do the job of the man they assisted fell by 37 percent. No comparable improvement was achieved in the control group.

It became clear from both studies that foremen were fully capable of carrying disciplinary responsibility. An analysis of all cases arising during the trial year showed that there had been a reduction in the number of "repeat offenses" among employees with poor disciplinary records and a substantial reduction in short-term work stoppages. The analysis concluded that foremen were not prone to take one kind of action rather than another, they had developed a purposeful approach to such problems, and there had been no adverse union reaction.

About 50 percent of the engineering foremen's monthly reports during the trial year referred to consultation and negotiation with union officials—this on a site not noted for its harmonious industrial relations. Topics included demarcation, special payments, and the easing of bans imposed on "call outs." The incidence of such reports was spread evenly throughout the experimental group; their frequency increased during the trial period as the foremen became more confident of their abilities. All such matters appear to have been handled capably.

From both studies came evidence, confirming what has long been demonstrated in training courses, that special investigatory projects give foremen much needed opportunity to contribute their experience and expertise to the solution of long-standing technical and organizational problems. In only three cases where financial evaluation was possible, the estimated annual savings totaled more than $125,000.

Regarding the engineering foremen's control of budgets, in some cases the aim was to meet the target exactly; in others it was to reduce costs as much as possible. Both aims were achieved by the foremen at least as well as they had been by the managers. There is no evidence that plant efficiency or work effectiveness suffered in any way as a result of cost savings achieved by the foremen.

In the case of the engineering foremen, the experimental group's staff assessments at the end of the trial year were markedly better than those of the control groups. Despite the attempt made in the initial selection of experimental and control groups to achieve as good a balance as possible in ability and experience, there can be little doubt that the experimental group did in any case contain some more able men. But no one anticipated that such a large difference would show itself at the end of the trial period. As evidence of development, 45 percent of the experimental group's assessments referred to significant improvements in performance during the year, and 36 percent made particular mention of how effectively the foreman had dealt with increased responsibility received during the year. These assessments were written by managers who were not party to the study.

In the production foremen's study, superintendents reported that the new conditions were "separating the wheat from the chaff"; some of those who had previously been thought to be among the best of the foremen had not lived up to their reputations in a situation which placed little value on compliance, while others had improved enormously.

The production foremen's job reaction survey scores showed no particular improvement over the trial period. In the case of the engineering foremen, the experimental group's mean score showed a 12 percent increase, while the control group's had only risen by 3 percent.

PART II: THE MAIN CONCLUSIONS

What has been described in the first part of this article is the consistent application of theory in an area where custom and practice are normally only challenged by individual hunch or intuition. As we have seen, each study posed a separate problem concerning a different group of employees; the only common element among them was the conceptual framework brought to bear on the problem, enabling a specific program of action to be devised and implemented. Much was learned in the process, by ourselves and managers alike.

Now in Part II, the main conclusions which emerged from the job enrichment studies are presented in the form of answers to the questions raised at the beginning of this article.

GENERALITY OF FINDINGS

Can similarly positive results be obtained elsewhere with other people doing different jobs?

Yes. The studies reflect a diversity of type and level of job in several company functions in more than one industry. From the evidence now available, it is clear that results are not dependent on any particular set of circumstances at the place of study. Our investigation has highlighted one important aspect of the process of management and has shown that disciplined attention to it brings results. The findings are relevant wherever people are being managed.

How widespread is the scope or need for equivalent change in other jobs?

The scope seems enormous. In brainstorming sessions held to generate ideas for change in the jobs covered by the studies, it was not uncommon for over a hundred suggestions to be entertained. The process of change in these particular jobs has started, not finished. In many places it has not even started. Though there probably are jobs which do not lend themselves to enrichment, we have never encountered a level or a function where some change has not seemed possible. It is difficult to say in advance what jobs are going to offer the most scope; the most unlikely sometimes turn out to have important possibilities. We have certainly not been able to conclude that any area of work can safely be left out of consideration.

The need is as deep as the scope is wide. The responsiveness of so many people to changes with a common theme suggests that an important and widespread human need has indeed been identified in the motivators. Moreover, it would seem to be a need which manifests itself in a variety of ways. If, from a company point of view, a gain once demonstrated to be possible is accepted as a need, then the performance improvements registered in these studies would seem to betray an organizational need which is far from fully recognized as yet.

Can meaningful results be obtained only in jobs with large numbers of people all doing the same work, and where performance measures are easily available?

No. Meaningful results can be obtained in situations very far from the experimental ideal. Indeed, the very awkwardness of many "real-life" situations leads to perceptions which could not come from a laboratory experiment.

Organizational changes are made, work loads fluctuate, people fall sick, managers are moved, emergencies have to be dealt with. The amount of attention which can be given to managing changes designed to enrich people's jobs is often slight. When a man's immediate supervisor does not even know that a study is taking place, there is no vested interest in its success. In circumstances such as these, whatever is done stands or falls by its own merits.

In few of the studies could members of the experimental groups be said to be doing exactly the same work. Changes sometimes had to be tailor-made to suit specific individual jobs. Yet from the diversity of application came an understanding of the commonality of the process. Although laboratory technicians were engaged in quite different kinds of research, they were all doing research work; although foremen were looking after radically different operations, they were all supervising.

The changes that seemed to have the most impact were precisely those which related to the common heart and substance of the role played by people whose jobs differed in many important details. More than this, it became clear that all of them—the laboratory technician following up an original idea, the design engineer buying equipment, the foreman taking disciplinary action, the sales representative negotiating in the customer's office—are essentially in the same situation, the crux of which is the private encounter between an individual and his task. Only a change which impacts on this central relationship, we believe, can be truly effective in a motivational sense.

Real-life conditions not only give an investigation authenticity; they highlight the problem of measurement. What is most meaningful to a manager, of course—a foreman's proprietary attitude toward his shift, for example—is not always quantifiable. An important discovery, however, was that the better the motivator, the more likely it was to provide its own measure. Employees' "sense of responsibility," judged in a vacuum, is a matter of speculation; but the exercise of a specific responsibility, once given, is usually capable of meaningful analysis. Laboratory technicians may or may not be thought to have innate potential; the number and quality of their research minutes can be measured. Several times managers commented that job enrichment had opened up measurement opportunities which not only allowed a more accurate assessment of individual performance, but often led to a better diagnosis of technical problems as well.

FEASIBILITY OF CHANGE

Are there not situations where the operational risk is so high that it would be foolhardy to attempt to pass responsibility and scope for achievement down the line?

Probably there are, but we have not encountered one. The risks attached to some of the changes in the sales representatives' study seemed frightening at the time. Few managers who have not tried it can accept with equanimity the thought of their subordinates placing orders for $500,000 worth of equipment on their own authority, even within a sanctioned project. The research manager in the laboratory technicians' study concluded that a change was only likely to be motivational for his subordinates if it made him lose sleep at nights.

Yet in no case did disaster result. In reviewing the results of the studies with the managers concerned, it was difficult in fact for us as outsiders not to have a sense of anticlimax. By the end of the trial period, the nerve-racking gambles of a few months before were hardly worth a mention. The new conditions seemed perfectly ordinary. Managers had completely revised their probability judgments in the light of experience.

Theory provides an explanation for the remarkable absence of disaster experienced in practice. Bad hygiene, such as oppressive supervision and ineffectual control systems, constrains and limits performance, and may even lead to sabotage. Administrative procedures that guard against hypothetical errors and imaginary irresponsibility breed the very carelessness and apathy which result in inefficiency. With too many controls, responsibility becomes so divided that it gets lost. Hygiene improvements at best lift the constraints.

The motivators, on the other hand, make it possible for the individual to advance the base line of his performance. The road is open for improvement, while present standards remain available as a reference point and guide. When a man is given the chance to achieve more, he may not take that chance, but he has no reason to achieve less. The message of both theory and practice is that people respond cautiously to new responsibility; they feel their way and seek advice. When responsibility is put squarely with the person doing a job, he is the one who wants and needs feedback in order to do his job. His use of the motivators, not our use of hygiene, is what really controls performance standards.

As managers, we start having positive control of the job only when we stop concentrating on trying to control people. Mistakes are less likely, not more likely, than before; those which do occur are more likely to be turned to account, learned from, and prevented in the future, for they are seen to matter. Monitoring continues, but its purpose has changed. Now it provides the jobholder with necessary information and enables management to see how much more can be added to a job rather than how much should be subtracted from it. That way, continual improvement, while not being guaranteed, at least becomes possible as the scope for the motivators is extended. It is the nearest thing to a performance insurance policy that management can have.

Such is the theory, and from the evidence of the studies, practice bears it out. If the studies show anything, they show that it pays to experiment. No one is being asked to accept anything on faith; what is required is the courage to put old assumptions and old fears to the test. For the manager, the process is like learning to swim: It may not be necessary to jump in at the deep end, but it surely is necessary to leave the shallow end. Only those who have done so are able to conquer the fear which perverts our whole diagnosis of the problem of managing people.

Because people's ability and sense of responsibility vary so much, is it not necessary to make changes selectively?

No. To make changes selectively is never to leave the shallow end of the pool. We are in no position to decide, before the event, who deserves to have his job enriched and who does not. In almost every study managers were surprised by the response of individuals, which varied certainly, but not always in the way that would have been forecast. As the job changed, so did the criteria of successful performance change. Some people who had been thought to be sound and responsible under the old conditions turned out merely to have been yes-men once those conditions were changed; their performance was the same as it had always been, but now compliance was no longer valued so highly. At the other extreme was one classic example of an awkward employee, about to be sacked, who turned out to be unusually inventive and responsible when he has given the opportunity to be so.

In one study, not reported, a promising set of changes brought relatively disappointing results—the changes had been implemented selectively. When pressed to explain the grounds on which people had been chosen, the manager quoted as an example someone who had already carried similar responsibility in a previous job. It is exactly this kind of vicious circle that job enrichment seeks to break.

When changes are made unselectively, the genuinely good performers get better. Some poor performers remain poor, but nothing is lost. Because the changes are opportunities and not demands, all that happens is that the less able ignore them and go on as before. Some people, however, develop as they never could under the old conditions, and do better than others originally rated much higher. This is the bonus from job enrichment. Not only is overall performance improved, but a clearer picture emerges of individual differences and potential.

So long as a foundation of new job opportunities available to all is firmly established, there is no harm in restricting certain changes to the more senior of the jobholders. Such changes can be seen in both the laboratory technicians' and the design engineers' studies. This is a very different matter from introducing changes selectively in the first place. It is a way of providing scope for personal advancement within the job and recognizing the achievements of those who build well on the foundation of opportunity already provided.

Do all employees welcome having their jobs enriched, or are there not some who prefer things to be left as they are?

Individual reaction to job enrichment is as difficult to forecast in terms of attitudes as it is in terms of performance. Those already genuinely interested in their work develop real enthusiasm. Not all people welcome having their jobs enriched, certainly, but so long as the changes are opportunities rather than demands, there is no reason to fear an adverse reaction. If someone prefers things the way they are, he merely keeps them the way they are, by continuing to refer matters to his supervisor, for example. Again, there is nothing lost.

On the other hand, some of the very people whom one might expect to duck their chance seize it with both hands, developing a keenness one would never have anticipated. In attitudes as well as in performance, the existence of individual differences is no bar to investigating the possibilities of job enrichment.

Can you enrich jobs without inevitably facing demands for higher pay or better conditions to match the new responsibilities?

Yes. In no instance did management face a demand of this kind as a result of changes made in the studies. It would seem that changes in working practice can be made without always having a price tag attached.

Here, as in the matter of operational risk, what is surprising in practice is easily explicable in terms of theory. The motivators and the hygiene factors may not be separate dimensions in a manager's analysis of a situation, but they are in people's experience. It is time that our diagnosis of problems took more account of people's experience. The studies demonstrate again that, when presented with an opportunity for achievement, people either achieve something or they do not; when allowed to develop, they either respond or stay as they are. Whatever the result, it is a self-contained experience, a private encounter between a person and his task.

It is something quite separate when the same person becomes annoyed by his poor working conditions, worries about his status or security, or sees his neighbors enjoying a higher standard of living. The cause-effect relationship between hygiene and motivation scarcely exists. Motivation is not the product of good hygiene, even if bad hygiene sometimes leads to sabotage. Higher pay may temporarily buy more work, but it does not buy commitment. Nor does commitment to a task, by itself, bring demand for better hygiene.

Managers often complain of their lack of room for maneuver. In doing so, they are generalizing from the rules of the hygiene game to the total management situation. There is little evidence that the work force in fact prostitutes its commitment to a task, although incentive bonus schemes, productivity bargaining, and the like assiduously encourage such prostitution. Before the process goes too far, it seems worth exploring more fully the room for maneuver freely available on the motivator dimension.

This is not to say, however, that the motivators should be used as an alibi for the neglect of hygiene. If people genuinely are achieving more, taking more responsibility, and developing greater competence, that is no reason to take advantage of them for a short-term profit. Any tendency to exploitation on management's part could destroy the whole process.

Is not the best route to motivational change through participation?

Yes and no. We have to define our terms. So far as the process of job enrichment itself is concerned, experimental constraints in the studies dictated that there could be no participation by jobholders themselves in deciding what changes were to be made in their jobs. The changes nevertheless seemed to be effective. On the other hand, when people were invited to participate—not in any of the reported studies—results were disappointing. In one case, for example, a group of personnel specialists suggested fewer than 30 fairly minor changes in their jobs, whereas their managers had compiled a list of over 100 much more substantial possibilities.

It seems that employees themselves are not in a good position to test out the validity of the boundaries of their jobs. So long as the aim is not to measure experimentally the effects of job enrichment alone, there is undoubtedly benefit in the sharing of ideas. Our experience merely suggests that it would be unwise to pin too many hopes to it—or the wrong hopes.

Participation is sometimes held, consciously or unconsciously, to be an alternative to job enrichment. Instead of passing responsibility down the line and possibly losing control, the manager can consult his subordinates before making a decision, involve them, make them feel part of the team. It all seems to be a matter of degree, after all. Participation, in this sense of consultation, is seen as a safe halfway house to job enrichment, productive and satisfying to all concerned.

A multitude of techniques are available to help the manager be more effective in consultation: he can be trained to be more sensitive to interpersonal conflict, more sophisticated in his handling of groups, more ready to listen, more oriented toward valuing others' contributions. Better decisions result, especially in problem-solving meetings that bring together colleagues or opponents in different roles or functions.

But in the specific context of the management of subordinates, it is worth asking who is motivated in this kind of participation. The answer would seem to be the person who needs a second opinion to make sure he comes to the right decision—the manager, in fact. The subordinate does not have the same professional or work-inspired need for the encounter, for he is not the one who has to live with responsibility for the decision. It is doubtful whether his "sense of involvement" even makes him feel good for long, for an appeal to personal vanity wears thin without more substance. However well-intentioned, this halfway-house kind of participative management smacks of conscience money; and receivers of charity are notoriously ungrateful. In the case of professional staff it is downright patronizing, for the subordinate is paid to offer his opinion anyway.

Theory clarifies the position. It is not a matter of degree at all. The difference between consultation and enrichment is a difference in kind. Consultation does not give a subordinate the chance for personal achievement which he can recognize; through involvement, it subtly denies him the exercise of responsibility which would lead to his development, however humbly, as an executive in his own right. Far from being the best route to motivational change, this kind of participation is a red herring. It is hygiene masquerading as a motivator, diverting attention from the real problem. It may help to prevent dissatisfaction, but it does not motivate.

The laboratory technicians, sales representatives, design engineers, and foremen did indeed participate, but not in a consultative exercise designed to keep them happy or to help their managers reach better decisions. Nor was it participation in ambiguity—an all too common occurrence in which, although no one quite knows where he stands or what may happen, the mere fact of participation is supposed to bring success. The participation of employees involved in the studies consisted of doing things which had always previously been done by more senior people. In all cases consultation continued, but now it was consultation upward. In consultation upward there is no ambiguity; tasks and roles are clear. Both parties are motivated, the subordinate by the need to make the best decision, to satisfy himself, to justify the trust placed in him, to enhance his professional reputation; the manager by the need to develop his staff.

When design engineers consulted their more senior colleagues, it was on questions of technical difficulty, commercial delicacy, or professional integrity—all more to the point than the mere price of a piece of equipment. Foremen consulted their managers on unusual budgetary worries, or the personnel department on tricky disciplinary problems. Sales representatives consulted headquarters on matters such as the stock position on a certain product before negotiating special terms with a customer.

Participation is indeed the best route to motivational change, but only when it is participation in the act of management, no matter at what level it takes place. And the test of the genuineness of that participation is simple—it must be left to the subordinate to be the prime mover in consultation on those topics where he carries personal responsibility. For the manager, as for the subordinate, the right to be consulted must be earned by competence in giving help. Therein lies the only authority worth having.

EXPECTED CONSEQUENCES

In view of so many possible difficulties in the way, are the gains to be expected from job enrichment significant or only marginal?

We believe the gains are significant, but the evidence must speak for itself. In all, 100 people were in the experimental groups in the studies described. A conservative reckoning of the financial benefit achieved, arrived at by halving all estimated annual gains or savings, would still be over $200,000 per year. Cost was measurable in a few days of managers' time at each place.

Do the gains relate primarily to job satisfaction or to performance?

Contrary to expectation, the gains, initially at least, seem to relate primarily to performance. Wherever a direct measure of performance was possible, an immediate gain was registered. In one or two instances, performance seemed to peak and then drop back somewhat, though it stayed well above its starting point and well above the control group's performance. Elsewhere there seemed to be a more gradual improvement; if anything it gained momentum through the trial period. We have no evidence to suggest that performance gains, once firmly established, are not capable of being sustained.

In the short term, gains in job satisfaction would seem to be less spectacular. Attitudes do not change overnight. Satisfaction is the result of performance, not vice versa, and there is a long history of frustration to be overcome. When direct measurement of job satisfaction was possible, the most significant gains seemed to come when the trial period was longest. There is every reason to think that in the long term attitudes catch up with performance and that job enrichment initiates a steady and prolonged improvement in both.

What are the consequences for supervision if jobs are loaded with new tasks taken from above—i.e., does one man's enrichment become another's impoverishment?

The more subordinates' jobs are enriched, the more superfluous does supervision, in its old sense, become. Several of the studies showed that short-term absences of the experimental groups' supervisors could be coped with more easily as day-to-day concern for operational problems shifted downward. The need for the supervisor to be always "on the job" diminished; greater organizational flexibility was gained.

But though supervision may become redundant, supervisors do not. Fears of loss of authority or prestige were never realized. Far from their jobs being impoverished, supervisors now found that they had time available to do more important work. Design engineers' supervisors were able to devote more effort to technical development; production foremen's supervisors found themselves playing a fuller managerial role.

The enrichment of lower-level jobs seems to set up a chain reaction resulting in the enrichment of supervisors' jobs as well. Fears that the supervisor may somehow miss out are based on the premise that there is a finite pool of responsibility in the organization which is shared among its members. In practice new higher-order responsibilities are born.

Even when subordinates are given responsibilities not previously held by their own supervisors, as happened in the sales representatives' study and to a lesser extent in some of the others, there is no evidence that supervisors feel bypassed or deprived, except perhaps very temporarily. It soon becomes apparent to all concerned that to supervise people with authority of their own is a more demanding, rewarding, and enjoyable task than to rule over a bunch of automatons, checking their every move.

Finally, what are the consequences for management if motivational change becomes a reality? Is the manager's role affected? If so, how? And what are the implications for management development?

The main consequence is that management becomes a service, its purpose to enable, encourage, assist, and reinforce achievement by employees. Task organization and task support are the central features of the manager's new role. In task *organization* two complementary criteria emerge: (1) tasks have to be authentic—i.e., the more opportunity they give employees to contribute to business objectives, the more effective they are likely to be motivationally; (2) tasks have to be motivational—i.e., the more they draw upon the motivators, the more likely they are to produce an effective contribution to business objectives. In task *support,* factors such as company policy and administration, technical supervision, interpersonal relations, and working conditions all have to be pressed into the service of the motivators. Control of the job is achieved by providing people with the tools of their trade, with the information they require, with training as appropriate, and with advice when sought.

The job itself becomes the prime vehicle of all individual development, of which management development is only one kind. In aiding the process of development, our starting point, as always, is problem diagnosis—in this case, assessment of individual abilities, potentials, and needs. When people are underemployed, we have no way of distinguishing between those who are near the limit of their abilities and those who have a great deal more to contribute. All too often, potential has to be inferred from risky and subjective judgments about personality. Such judgments, once made, tend to be static; people become categorized. The studies show that when tasks are organized to be as authentic and motivational as possible, management receives a more accurate and a continuing feedback on individual strengths and weaknesses, ability, and potential. Task support becomes a flexible instrument of management, responsive to feedback.

If the job itself is the prime vehicle of individual development, task support is the means by which management can influence it. We still think of individual development, especially management development, far too much as something which can be imposed from outside. We pay lip service to on-the-job training but go on running courses as a refuge. We speak of self-development, but we are at a loss to know how to encourage it. Now, however, we can postulate a criterion: self-development is likely to be most effective when the task a person is engaged in is authentic and motivational and when in doing it he receives understanding, imaginative, and capable support. When these conditions are met, the job itself becomes a true learning situation, its ingredients the motivators.

Though only one study set out specifically to measure individual development, the most pervasive impression from all was one of development and personal growth achieved. The latent inspirational value of jobs appeared to have been released. People were able to demonstrate and utilize skills they already possessed, and go on to learn new ones. Each new facet of the task required a response in terms of individual development, and results suggest that that response was seldom lacking.

The best evidence of development came, however, not from the experimental groups in the studies, but from the managers who put the studies into effect. It is sometimes said that attitude change is the key to success. But in seeking to improve the performance of our business, perhaps we rely too much on efforts to change managers' attitudes. These studies went ahead without waiting for miracles of conversion first. Just as the experimental groups in the studies represented a cross section of employees engaged on those jobs, so the managers who put the studies into effect represented a cross section of managers. Enthusiasts and skeptics alike agreed to judge the studies by their results. They did, and the effect was clear for the observer to see. Success proved to be the key to attitude change. In retrospect, who would want it otherwise?

Efficiency in the military: The Hill Air Force Base project

Frederick Herzberg
and
Major General Edmund A. Rafalko

War is waste, and the military wages war. During peace time, a criticism of the military, deserved or not, is that it continues to be a wasteful organization. The military problem in peace time is how to prepare for war, an understandably wasteful enterprise in terms of more humane needs in society; but it is expected not to be wasteful in the process of accomplishing its mission of being prepared for war. With defense expenditures in the $80 to $90 billion range, however, waste can have a very large multiplier factor.

The military has a number of unique problems in its management of weapons systems and support for the armed services. The requirements of national defense place higher demands for quality and efficiency on the military than is found in civilian industries. Through improvements in weaponry, lead time has diminished so rapidly that any technical failure in weapons systems such as the Phantom F-4 fighter jet or the ICBM missile threatens our survival as a nation. The maintenance costs for such a fail-safe system are astronomical. Civilian industry does not have the same problem. An automobile, for example, has maintenance costs which are borne for protection against the inconvenience of using

Note: We would like to acknowledge the encouragement, advice, and administrative support for this project by the former Commander of Ogden Air Logistics Center, Hill Air Force Base, Utah, Lt. General Bryce Poe. The success of this project really belongs to the civilian and military executives and their employees who have brought about the actual changes and improvements.

public transport. A dead battery in your car is a nuisance and an irritation. If the car continues to be unreliable, then you rid yourself of the nuisance and buy a newer model. An ICBM, however, is fired only once, and if it will not ignite or goes off course, then you have a potential catastrophe. Efficiency in the military through increased productivity and reduced waste becomes, therefore, an extremely sensitive concern. Quality can never be compromised, as it often is in civilian industry. If there is waste, it grows and becomes scandalous; similarly, a productivity increase is within the strict guidelines for military hardware and can have an even greater payoff than in civilian organizations.

Also, our civilian organizations have had more opportunities than the military to solve the seemingly ambiguous problem of increasing employee motivation, yet remaining cost competitive in the marketplace. The management literature is replete with testimonials and case studies outlining the long, involved, many-faceted projects of this type in private industry.[1] Presented in religious-revivalistic fashion, they describe the time, effort, costs, and agony expended as horrendous, whether it be in the assembly of automobiles or in producing dog food. At the same time, the relationship between the internal training department and the consultant has flourished, and, accordingly, so have the organization's costs for these changes. Managers, with all their diversified training, try a snippet of this and a snippet of that. They hope that somewhere among all these managerial styles lies the right combination.

This is characterized as the goulash approach, where several techniques are incorrigibly packaged together to create a more "modern organizational and leadership style." Like goulash, it makes the organization "taste" good, but it often gives it indigestion.

The various branches of the Department of Defense come under continuous, close, and often diverse political observation, and pressure on all matters is exerted by external and internal auditing agencies. Civil service regulations prescribe the personnel actions available and, finally, the entire service labors under the public's general impression that military officers are primarily soldiers, and, least of all, business managers. Military organizations operate under procedures designed more for control and audit than for efficiency. Such strenuous bureaucratic control is condemned as onerous to civilian industry and, at times, even ludicrous. However, despite all the problems, there are military leader-managers who have proven most trenchant in adopting a change strategy that meets problems of both motivation and productivity. The military manager has one highly developed attribute that is particularly useful in changing organizations, a real sense for pragmatism.

---

[1] See, e.g., L. E. Bjork, "An Experiment in Work Satisfaction," *Scientific American*, March 1975, pp. 17–23.

OJE AT HILL AIR FORCE BASE

The Ogden Air Logistics Center, managing complete support (maintenance, overhaul, supplies, etc.) for such diverse commodities as fighters, bombers, ICBMs, training and simulation devices, landing gear, photographic equipment, and munitions, has succeeded where many civilian organizations have failed. It has cut through the goulash and adopted a singularly effective program of Orthodox Job Enrichment (OJE). By ignoring the jargon and concentrating on pragmatism, this OJE program has been swift in impact. In one year the program is quickly approaching its goal of becoming completely self-sufficient and sustaining. Within this time frame, the cost savings, based on productivity alone, have already begun to soar.

The design of the project ensured successful implementation, while preserving the needs for efficiency and quality that are so necessary in national defense installations. Each of the five divisions (or directorates) selected keymen in their organizations to participate in a three-week training program on Motivation-Hygiene Theory and Orthodox Job Enrichment. After these keymen received intensive training, they selected pilot projects in their own functional areas through consultation with the heads of their divisions. These pilot projects were selected to impact on areas of fragmented jobs and heavy work load requirements, typified by low job satisfaction and low productivity. Additional, different functional areas were selected in order to observe the applicability in a diverse range of activities. And, finally, middle-level management had to be competent and willing to explore changes in the work itself.

The task of these keymen was to operate as internal consultants and coordinators of training in Orthodox Job Enrichment. To do this, each keyman organized two task groups, an implementing and a coordinating group, and trained both in Orthodox Job Enrichment. The implementing group consisted of supervisors of the job under scrutiny and other supervisors from related functional areas that served complementary functions, such as quality inspectors. Their task was to generate job changes that would create more satisfying jobs, based on the principles of Motivation-Hygiene Theory.

The coordinating group approved the changes. Consisting of middle-level management, this group served as a review board for the division on the pilot project, often borrowing the talents of other managers who provided expertise from other divisions, such as personnel or supply for the production lines. Within this structure, the keyman became the catalyst for job changes by helping the supervisor generate job changes and eliciting support from middle management.

With brief yet concise overviews of the OJE strategy provided to upper-level managers, the entire organization was well informed, and

Table 1

Timetable for Orthodox Job Enrichment, Hill Air Force Base

TIME TO ACTIVATE	
Organize for OJE...	4 weeks
Appoint administrator	
Select keymen	
Orientation for OJE......................................	1 week
Executive seminar	
Union seminar	
Formal training of keymen.............................	3 weeks
Keyman pilot selection..................................	1 week
Preparation, training and preliminary OJE plan by	
supervisors..	3 weeks
Begin implementations until major changes	
implemented...	8 weeks
Measures which produce first significant trends..........	12 weeks
SUMMARY: ELAPSED TIME TO ACTIVATE OJE	
Prepare and plan for change............................	3 months
Implement changes......................................	2 months
See significant indication of results......................	3 months
Total elapsed time.................................	8 months

support of the project was generated from the top down. Table 1 shows the timetable for the first 11 projects. Within eight months these projects were fully implemented and, as Figure 1 shows, there were significant indications of success, i.e., benefits exceeding costs. Although not detailed here, most of the investments in the projects were the costs of salaries for the keymen, who were transferred from other jobs in the Air Logistics Center.

As Table 2 shows, the number of projects has grown from 11, initially, to 29, affecting a wide variety of jobs. Hill Air Force Base estimates that

Figure 1

OJE cost/benefit comparison, Hill Air Force Base

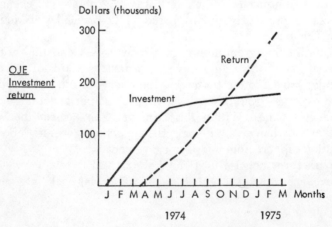

Table 2

OJE pilot projects, Hill Air Force Base

Initial projects	*New projects*
1. Avionics section	12. Contract document
2. F–4 leading-edge slat	preparation
3. Installation equipment	13. Transient alert
management (IEMO) divisions	14. Metal fabrication
4. Magnetic tape library	15. Base management systems
5. Periscope sextant	unit
6. Buyers–contract negotiators	16. Voucher examiners
(minuteman)	17. Career management and
7. Vehicle service and repair	employee relations merger
8. Minuteman downstage flight	18. Outside plant—telephone
controls and audio reproducers	maintenance
9. Refrigeration and air	19. Aerospace electronics
conditioning	section
10. Distribution control,	20. Explosive safety function
microfilm products	21. Missile maintenance
11. Merit placement function	systems and TO section
	22. Production management
	23. Card punch and Autodin
	24. Foreign military sales
	25. Item managers
	26. Key punch
	27. Packing and packaging
	28. Mail distribution
	29. Plans and programs division

Note: At the time of publication the number of new projects has grown to 56.

over 1,000 employees have been directly involved and over 260 managers have been trained in OJE during the one-year life of the project.

A detailed look at 4 of the first 11 projects may help illustrate the dynamics of Orthodox Job Enrichment in providing managerial effectiveness. Not all the projects have been unqualified successes, however, and some comments on the problems will also highlight the difficulties in managing change.

AVIONICS PROJECT

The avionics project is one of the most successful in terms of cost savings, as estimated by the Hill Air Force Base staff. The responsibilities of avionics are to test and repair all navigational equipment on the F–4 aircraft scheduled for maintenance.

The maintenance activity is separated into three production lines, each with an avionics section followed by a separate avionics flight-test section. Before Orthodox Job Enrichment, the avionics personnel on the production lines checked the 19 navigational systems on their assigned aircraft before flight test and then began work on another aircraft. Any defects found subsequently were analyzed and repaired by flight-test personnel.

Table 3

OJE case study, avionics repair project

Before OJE	After OJE	Ingredients of a good job involved
Avionics technicians separated into production-line and flight-line groups	Consolidation of flight-line and one third of production-line technicians	Own expertise, learning function
Flight-line group corrected all avionics defect	Each avionics technician handles own defects	Personal accountability, responsibility for work
Only flight-line group communicated with pilots	Each avionics technician works with pilot testing his aircraft	Direct feedback, client relationship with pilot

The supervisor in the implementing group, under the guidance of the keyman, decided to test Orthodox Job Enrichment on one of the three avionics production lines. As Table 3 shows, the mechanics on the OJE line began to follow their planes out of the hangar to flight test. The flight-line group then began training the production-line mechanics in flight-test analysis, the end result being an informal consolidation of the two groups.

The results have been dramatic, as shown in Table 4. The number of test flights has been reduced on the average of one-half flight per aircraft—an estimated savings of $85,648.88 during the test phase alone. Perhaps the most convincing evidence of the success of the project has come recently in the decision of upper-level management to institute the job changes in the other two production lines.

Table 4

OJE case study, results, avionics repair project

	Number of aircraft	Total flight rate/aircraft	Reflight rate/aircraft	Avionics-caused reflight rate/aircraft	Other defects-caused reflight rate/aircraft
Base data: October 1973–July 1974*	63	2.52	1.52	.84	.68
Test data: April 1974–December 1974*	47	1.96	.96	.33	.63
Net result		(.56)	(.56)	(.51)	(.05)
Savings due to OJE——————————————————→				$85,648.88	
			(.51 flights, 47 aircraft, $3,573.17 per flight)		

º Dates overlap because of time each aircraft is on the assembly line; the 63 and 47 aircraft are different aircraft.

WING-SLAT PROJECT

The wing-slat project was concerned with another maintenance function on the F–4 aircraft. This time the work involved a modification of the aircraft as a means of improving its maneuverability. For this particular job, a three-piece steel strip has to be fastened to the bottom side of the aircraft, wing tip to wing tip, with over 600 fasteners.

Before Orthodox Job Enrichment, there were 217 separate tasks, and the work was scheduled by the foreman and checked by him or a quality officer. When a quality error was found, the foreman reassigned the job to another mechanic. Table 5 shows the strategy of job redesign. The im-

Table 5

OJE case study, sheet-metal wing modification project

Before OJE	*After OJE*	*Ingredients of a good job involved*
217 separate tasks	1 job	Own expertise, learning function, resource control
No coordination between mechanics at shift change	Crews paired between shift to facilitate turnover of work	Personal accountability, direct communications
100 percent foreman inspections	Selected foreman inspections	Direct feedback, personal accountability
No mechanic inspections	Selected mechanic inspections	Scheduling, personal accountability
Quality inspectors worked with foreman	Quality inspectors work with mechanic	Direct feedback, personal accountability, recognition
Foreman scheduled defect work	Mechanic fixes own defects	Learning function, personal accountability

plementing group, as in avionics, chose one of the four production crews and had the mechanics begin to work directly with quality inspectors. Foremen began checking only some of the aircraft, and any defects in workmanship were the responsibility of the mechanic who made the error. In addition, the total job on an aircraft was assigned to crews, overlapping on shifts, and the crews began scheduling their own work. The result was an increase across the board on the ingredients of a good job.

The results of the project are shown in Figure 2. Prior to Orthodox Job Enrichment, considerable learning which had taken place because of the newness of the job was beginning to level off. The test group, when compared to the best of the four production crews in Figure 2, began with lower productivity, but after a few months of Orthodox Job Enrichment it had surpassed that group, with savings estimated at $89,300. As

Figure 2

OJE case study, results, sheet-metal wing modification project (learning curve approach)

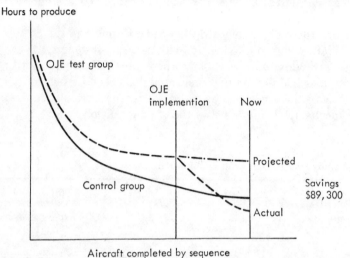

Aircraft completed by sequence

in the avionics project, the job changes introduced in the OJE group are now being built into the job for the other three production crews.

WAREHOUSEMAN–DRIVER PROJECT

The distribution division at Hill Air Force Base provides the supply support for the maintenance of the aircraft and other weapon systems, both on base and worldwide. Yet the executive planning for storage utilization and internal supply functions is often dependent upon the efficiency of the warehousemen who handle the goods. Because of productivity and quality problems in the warehouse, a pilot project was initiated in the installation equipment division to see how Orthodox Job Enrichment could benefit the supply functions.

Essentially, the job consisted of locating and delivering equipment to other divisions. The warehouseman-driver would receive his orders from a scheduler-planner, find the equipment and deliver it to the customer. Receipts on delivery were handed to an inspector, who then checked to see if they had done their jobs correctly.

The implementing group decided to give more responsibilities to the warehouseman-driver. As Table 6 shows, the employee was assigned specific customers, allowed to schedule his own work, and given his own vehicle and the responsibility for budget control and maintenance of that vehicle.

The results of these changes have been more difficult to quantify than

Table 6

OJE case study, warehouseman-driver project

Before OJE	After OJE	Ingredients of a good job involved
Scheduler-planner assigned work	Employees have own customer area of responsibility, schedule own work	Scheduling, client relationship, own expertise
Vehicle usage controlled by scheduler	Employees given responsibility for own vehicle, including maintenance	Personal accountability, resource control
Inspectors checked all work	Training provided in inspection, and some employees carry out own inspection	Learning function, direct feedback

those on the production line. However, the elimination of the inspection function and the use of less wasteful operations allowed two inspectors and one warehouseman-driver to go to a new warehouse complex, making it unnecessary to hire three new employees, with a yearly cost savings estimated at $37,900. In addition, a customer satisfaction survey revealed that 90 percent of the customers reported they had noticed a change, and 100 percent of these reported an improvement in the quality of the service.

MAGNETIC TAPE LIBRARY PROJECT

The magnetic tape library supplies all the computers within the Data Automation Branch at Hill Air Force Base, with approximately 41,000 reels in storage. The major problem that made this function a good pilot project was a problem with missing tapes. Several tapes a month would be lost, requiring a slowdown in computer processing and extra time spent on locating or reconstructing those tapes. Somewhere within the tasks of filing, pulling, and erasing tapes, as scheduled by the super-

Table 7

OJE case study, magnetic tape library project

Before OJE	After OJE	Ingredients of a good job involved
Separate tasks as assigned	Total systems responsibility, filing accountability	Responsibility, customer relationship, accountability
Pulled tapes and delivered them to meet delivery schedules	Meeting customer demand, scratching, cleaning	Customer relationship
Scratched and cleaned tapes in period-end batches	Individual feedback system on errors—must correct own errors	Feedback

visor, the librarians were misplacing tapes. Since the programmers and operators also had access to the library, the librarians could not be held solely accountable.

The implementing group, after considerable debate, decided to initiate the changes in the job shown in Table 7. The librarians were given more responsibility for each customer order, and they improved location accuracy and followed through with additional quality services.

The results were impressive. The average number of lost tapes decreased from nine to one per month, and, as Table 8 shows, this change amounted to an estimated savings of $4,216 on researching and reconstructing tapes alone. Considering the time saved in efficiency in computer usage, where time is very expensive, a large multiplier factor is

Table 8

OJE case study, results, magnetic tape library project

	Time period	Average tapes lost per month	Average cost per lost tape*	Total cost
Before OJE........................	6 months	9	$87	$4,698
After OJE..........................	6 months	1	87	482
Lost-tape savings................				4,216
Other (equipment, etc.) savings...				3,284
Total savings for project.......				7,500

* Includes average personnel cost for researching lost tape ($20) and average cost to reproduce lost tape ($67).

hidden within the computer operations. Although there is no easy way to quantify these savings, it may be expected to be very high, akin to the problems of an air traffic controller when one of his radar scopes blinks out during a busy day.

This project presently is stalled. While job design changes have increased quality and overall job satisfaction, two of the employees have left, perhaps because they were not interested in a more responsible job. Due to restrictive rehiring rates, these vacancies could not be filled, causing a work overload. Management is now able to fill those vacancies and return to its implementation plan, which calls for additional changes in the job design.

SUCCESSES AND FAILURES

Several other projects have had difficulties. One in particular, concerned with service and repair of the periscope sextant, shows a frequent managerial problem with increasing productivity demands. This job was changed through Orthodox Job Enrichment so that individual employees could perform the whole job of repairing the entire sextant rather than its components. They inspected their own work, logged their own performance rates, and tagged their names on each sextant they completed. Within one month, productivity had increased by 50 percent among those employees skilled enough to do the whole job. However, an increase in production demands caused middle-level management to increase the work force and use the skilled workers to train the new employees. As of this writing, the employees are beginning to return to the OJE approach, but it is too soon to see any measurable results in productivity.

A somewhat different problem occurred in the procurement division. The keyman, with his implementing group, decided to give contract negotiators for missiles an enriched job by allowing them more authority to develop and approve contracts with private industry. This particular section was chosen because they seemed to have a higher delinquency rate than similar groups of contract negotiators. An objective review of their work, however, showed that even before Orthodox Job Enrichment they were processing more documents than similar groups. After Orthodox Job Enrichment, this group began processing even more documents, but a change in standard time production allocation credit for production count again pushed down their productivity rates. Interviews with these

Table 9

OJE benefit summary, April 1974–January 1975 (dollar value)

Project	To-date savings	Annual savings (at same rate)
Avionics section	$ 85,649	$114,200
F–4 leading-edge slat	89,300	107,100
IEMO management division	15,800	37,900
Magnetic tape library	7,500	15,000
Periscope sextant	Intangible[1]	Intangible
Buyers–contract negotiators	Intangible[2]	Intangible
Vehicle service and repair	10,700	25,700
Minuteman downstage flight controllers and audio reproducers	Intangible[3]	Intangible
Refrigeration and air conditioning	Intangible[4]	Intangible
Distribution control, microfilm products	10,300	17,600
Merit placement function	45,300	60,400
Total	$264,549	$377,900

[1] *Periscope sextant:* Project was initially very successful. Management, however, had made a prior decision to hire additional people. The additional people came on board in the middle of the project. Project canceled to accommodate training of new people. Project never got back to the initial high success level of early job enrichment. Current status: Majority of original job-enriched employees have gone back to enriched job module. ..

[2] *Buyers/contract negotiators:* The number of contracts to be processed increased dramatically, and the standards for contract productivity for each negotiator were also changed significantly during the project period, thus providing irrelevant productivity measures.

[3] *Minuteman downstage flight controlers:* Group selected to be enriched were part of a homogeneous work force. Initially, management declined to allow changes to move throughout entire work unit and therefore created an unequal position between job-enriched and nonenriched groups. The power of motivators available was, therefore, severely restricted. Current status: Project is being expanded to include the entire unit.

[4] *Refrigeration and air conditioning:* Keyman was unable to train management and sell the concepts of job enrichment.

workers revealed that they liked their jobs more than ever but disliked the way they were being treated. As could be expected, these dislikes fell into areas of policy and procedures of allocating work assignments. They were being used well, but now wanted also to be treated well.

The successes have more than made up for these failures, however. Table 9 shows the preliminary savings from the first 11 projects during the first year of Orthodox Job Enrichment, as estimated by the staff at Hill Air Force Base headquarters. Internal expansion of projects ensures even greater savings in the future. The measurement of job attitudes, some of the softer ware of the social scientist, was, for the most part, deemphasized during the initial test phases of this project. The Air Logistics Center at Ogden needed hard productivity data to justify its costs. This requirement fits with the OJE perspective, in which the attitudes are the "fallout" of performance, and not the other way around.

What this preliminary report stresses is that the fears of a more adult management of work are not justified and in fact are counterproductive to increasing productivity in our organizations. It also stresses that the implementation of job enrichment need not be the agonizing and time-consuming ordeal that the behavioral scientist literature suggests we are to expect. Many military and civilian managers in this project deserve accolades for quickly grasping how to merge a humanistic respect for workers with the needed increase in productivity and, at the same time, manage the process of change and the many problems associated with the Civil Service Commission, the unions, and diverse organizational interests found at military bases. At Hill Air Force Base, we suffered the anguish but it did not deter us.

An American approach to job enrichment

The quality of work life is often described as a noneconomic indicator of humanism on the job. The payoffs are most frequently described in terms of better employee attitudes, and indications are also frequently given of potential "fallout" gains in productivity. It is not surprising, therefore, that corporate anxieties over the current economic crisis should lead to fiscal restraint on programs designed to improve the working life of employees. Many old-line managers have looked upon experiments in job redesign as aberrations of an affluent age which the company no longer needs, and certainly cannot afford.

In many cases, the company can do without in the short term. The or ganizational change programs offered by the behavioral scientists have often turned into political experiments on how the company can enhance its popularity. The recession has made this kind of grass-roots diplomacy in the company an improbable means of attaining the much needed economic versatility.

Today's economic problems are unlike the Great Depression of the thirties, however. A return to the carrot-and-stick approach, using job security as the harness, which has been advocated by many old-time "human" engineers will not solve the productivity problem and the stagflation that goes with it. "Why should I give a damn!" is the educated response of the workers to threats from management today.[1] Increasing the economic anxieties of the American worker would simply produce chronically ill organizations, with reduced productivity and increased costs of managing people. Severe economic penalties are attached to the mismanagement of people today. A closer examination of the types of job design that create effective organizations now and will do so ten years from now is necessary.

Many job redesigns have been conducted both in this country and in

---

[1] *The Wall Street Journal*, December 3, 1974.

Europe. Some of these experiments, such as those in participative management and industrial democracy, have attempted to increase motivation by increasing the political power of the employees (e.g., the Co-Determination Laws in West Germany and new, sweeping laws in Sweden designed to increase the worker's economic, social, and political power in company operations). It is thought that the democratic way, which has worked tumultously in politics, could enhance the quality of work life. The strategy often is reduced to an attack on boredom through an increase in the amount of employee participation in the governance of the organization. These projects, although *thought* to be very popular among employees, are now not considered to be as viable job redesign strategies as formerly, and they appear to be losing upper-level management support in many companies in the United States. At the same time, our labor unions have remained conspicuously silent or at best noncommittal in their attitudes toward humanizing work. Meeting worker demands for increased pay, saunas, physiotherapists, and social workers, as Kockums shipyard in Sweden has done,[2] seems to American management to be an unjustifiably expensive way of reducing personnel problems, yet it is the price paid for industrial democracy.

Two job-design methodologies have remained promising alternatives for the crisis-ridden economics of today's corporations. These two methodologies I call Orthodox Job Enrichment and Socio-Technical Systems.

The Volvo company in Sweden is perhaps the best known proponent of the Socio-Technical Systems approach. Some of the leading innovators and practitioners of the sociotechnical approach would have reservations that the celebrated Volvo experiments truly reflect their concepts of the sociotechnical position. The overlapping among the various approaches I described in my *Harvard Business Review* article "The Wise Old Turk"[3] gives some validity to this assertion.

Relying on group dynamics theory, this strategy emphasizes the membership needs of man. Work fragmentation is treated as primarily a problem stemming from the social organization of work, and the jobs are designed to make the employee's social life whole again. The team has become the conscious symbol of this approach and the *raison d'être* for individual motivation. As Pehr G. Gyllenhammar, the president of Volvo, has stated, "The modern working man feels the need of belonging to a team . . . to identify with the goods he produces . . . to feel he is appreciated for the work he performs."[4] Which modern working man Gyllenhammar refers to is in dispute, however. Recently six American

---

[2] *The Wall Street Journal,* October 25, 1974. Frederick Herzberg, *The Wise Old Turk,* pp. 70–80.

[3] *Harvard Business Review,* September–October 1974. Reprinted as the second article in this chapter.

[4] Pehr G. Gyllenhammar, *Volvo Press Information, 1412–LA* Göteborg, Sweden, January 5, 1973.

automobile employees spent a month working in one of the car assembly operations at Saab-Scandia, which has the same team spirit as Volvo. Five of the six Americans actually preferred the assembly line to the team. These employees reported that they would rather be left alone at the boring task, so that they could have the freedom to think their own thoughts.[5] Perhaps the assembly line, the modern whipping boy, provides some escape from extra aggravations that can arise from complex inter-personal relationships fostered in the team, as well as considerable down-time to think about what to do after work hours.

Orthodox Job Enrichment (OJE), in contrast, has focused on the work itself as a means of fulfilling *individual* motivational needs. Jobs are de-signed to maximize the opportunities for personal growth at work, and numerous experiments have been successful in demonstrating that this procedure increases both job satisfaction and productivity. The types of job changes established in companies have varied considerably, de-pending upon the investments of the company in technological hardware, which often places limits on the practicality of various job redesign strategies.

This article reports on a comprehensive OJE project currently under-way at a large engine company which provides the closest comparison with the "sociotechnical" project of Volvo. This project, which involves the entire operation of a new production plant, was initiated when top management asked themselves, "What would it take to make us a viable company in the next 10 to 20 years?"

The answer of the Engine Company (as it will be referred to) to that question was based on a direct and compelling belief in the need to foster growth and development of each individual employee, particularly since the operations call for a more educated, aware, and less passive work force in respect to decisions which affect them in their jobs. The Company's approach, based on the dynamics of Motivation-Hygiene Theory, defined a quality work environment from the outset as one in which people have a motivating job to do. Its plans for job enrichment in the new plant are being designed to meet these objectives and, at the same time, ensure that these objectives will provide for an effective organization in the future.

This approach is in some respects a marked contrast to the sociological approach taken by the Volvo company. Volvo began with the proposition that employees had a strong need for social acceptance and worker group influence on the decisions made on the shop floor. One of its first steps in job design was to ensure proper consultation with employees on the safety features of the physical plant in order to achieve, as nearly as possible, a risk-free job environment. The implicit strategy of consultation was to begin to develop *a sense of belonging and involvement in the organiza-*

---

[5] Paul Gainer, *Detroit News*, January 5, 1975.

tion. Consequently, management could expect more willingness to follow through with decisions on the part of employees who had contributed suggestions. Thus the beginning steps in the sociotechnical approach were taken in order to set the stage for improving the *sociology of work.*

As has been noted, the team is the chief characteristic of the sociotechnical approach. Teams are organized so members can provide emotional support to one another and to foster camaraderie among workers on the line, in the expectation that this group cohesiveness will also adhere to the company's goals. This objective is basically accomplished through what Volvo calls job alternation (job rotation). The work is scheduled by the team with the approval of the foreman so that each employee works a different job every day, as in the case of bumper assembly or the typing pool, or every hour, as is done on internal sealing operations. Besides adding variety to a dull job, according to Gyllenhammar, "Jobs are exchanged so that everyone learns everyone else's work . . . giving them a greater sense of affinity with their workmates." Job alternation, then, permits shared responsibility and out of necessity closer interpersonal relationships among employees.

In "One More Time: How Do You Motivate Employees?"[6] I characterized this approach to "enriching" jobs as horizontal loading of the job —not enrichment. As part of this horizontal loading the work cycle has been considerably lengthened. Volvo should also be commended for marked innovations in the mechanical engineering of its assembly lines and the hygienic appearance of its plant.

The Engine Company plant also utilizes teams, a seeming anomaly in OJE prescriptions. They do so for two reasons: First, the assembly of a whole engine, given the technology, is more than a full-time occupation of one employee. Second—and here this experiment makes its major departure from Volvo—the teams are designed to promote individual growth rather than to provide a second family for the employee.

The basic dynamics of motivation that are derived from Motivation-Hygiene Theory may help to clarify the steps to job design used at the Engine Company plant, in contrast to the practice at Volvo. At Volvo, motivation is thought to come from the attempts of employees to reduce the frustrations and anxieties arising from their monotonous work by working harder for the team. Motivation at the new Engine Company plant, in contrast, is achieved through the resurgent individual needs for personal competence. As I stated in "Why Job Enrichment?"[7] motivation is defined by the formula:

$$\text{Motivation} = f\left(\frac{\text{Ability}}{\text{Potential}}; \ \frac{\text{Opportunity}}{\text{Ability}}; \ \text{What is reinforced}\right)$$

---

[6] *Harvard Business Review* (January–February 1968), reprinted in two parts in Chapters 2 and 3.

[7] The first article in this chapter.

Potential, the raw talents that an employee brings to the job, is utilized, through training, to increase ability and opportunities to perform commensurate with ability. Rather than reinforcing togetherness, Motivation-Hygiene Theory calls for the reinforcement of personal achievement in an ever-expanding job.

ABILITY WITH OPPORTUNITY: STRUCTURING THE WORK

Orthodox Job Enrichment organizes the workplace so that both ability and opportunity can expand rapidly. The job design for the employees in the factory teams, one of the three functional areas at the Engine Company plant, demonstrates how the principles work. (There are office and management teams as well.) Lacking space, only the assembly and test groups will be described in detail, since they most clearly illustrate how the operations in the plant are formed.

The new employee first learns the basic skills of the job, the *complete* assembly and testing of the engine. The educators are the more senior members of the team. After mastering these skills, the employee begins training at the next level of competence, investigating the performance engineering aspects of engine production. This training enables the employee to troubleshoot an engine which does not pass quality performance tests. Social acceptance by other members of the team is not used as a vehicle for personal development. Teamwork translates into increased individual competence on the job. The team helps serve this goal because it is a teaching and planning unit as well as a working unit.

At each level of increasing competence, the job responsibilities expand. However, it became quickly obvious that there were differential abilities and backgrounds among team members. As a result, some learned faster than others and could take on more responsibility. This is to be expected, and while it does create certain personnel problems, it did not interfere with the basic thrust of providing opportunity for expanding ability.

A section manager covering four to five teams was installed to assist team members in developing administrative rather than technical skills. One of these section managers was promoted from the team to a managerial position. Others have been promoted to other technical staff positions. The system therefore provides a method of promotion. Eventually, as the work force's skill level increases, these section managers will be able to handle more teams.

Figure 1 shows the typical levels of training and expertise in which the employee both performs the task he has mastered and receives training at the next highest level. What has been created is a core job which meets the minimum requirements for motivating work. It is from this basic requirement of a good job that further developments for the employees have become possible.

Figure 1

Design of the individual job at the Engine Company

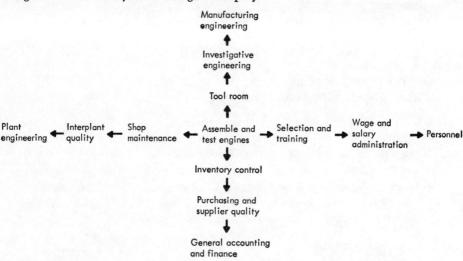

An employee begins with the basic core job, which calls for ability to assemble an engine. Second, he may learn to test, troubleshoot, diagnose, and seek out production- and quality-related problems. A third level would be the skill level necessary to do some basic production engineering and process engineering work, and the ability to cope with manufacturing engineering problems. The fourth level would be the development of overall skills and understandings across the four core areas of plant operations: assembly and test, materials, maintenance, and machining. All plant employees are to receive training in fundamental cost accounting to enable them to prepare and administer their own budgets, concomitant with their present ability and authority to set production standards for their teams.

In order to ensure continued training, each member of the factory teams at the Engine Company plant has broad-based management support. The training, for example, is conducted by adviser-consultants from management assigned to work within specific areas of the factory, as well as the newly created section manager. Adviser-consultants from manufacturing support, facilities-maintenance, and material management work with the engine assembly employees on a day-to-day basis, lending their special expertise and technical know-how to all production operations.

The key concept underlying the use of adviser-consultants is to maximize the talent and training available to individuals in the factory teams, while minimizing the use of KITA management. Power tactics are de-emphasized, and management personnel are listened to more for their competence than because of their status in the organization. Most or-

Figure 2

Organization of the plant of the Engine Company

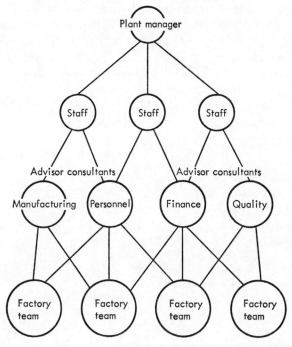

ganizations concentrate on the 10 percent of their work force who do not exhibit motivation on their jobs, attempting to coerce them to do more. The Engine Company plant directs its attention to the 90 percent of its employees who *are* motivated, providing them with the expertise necessary to increase their abilities on the job. With this procedure, management responds to the strengths of its organization—not its weaknesses.

The plant manager and his staff supervise these management speciality areas. Figure 2 shows the total organization of the plant. It is designed so that those working in the factory have as much responsibility for production rates and costs as they can handle. Eventually the employees will manage their own budgets, with the assistance of the adviser-consultants, and will become their own advisors, both within their own teams and in consulting with other factory teams. The more responsibilities they acquire, the more staff time remains for future planning rather than putting out fires on the production line.

MEETING FACILITATING HYGIENE NEEDS

The teamwork also serves the hygiene needs of employees by cutting much of the red tape that surrounds effective job performance (company policy and administration). One of the greatest sources of pain in an organization is its bureaucratic structure. The massive organization often mismanages the hygiene and motivational needs of the employees, not because of its lack of concern for employees but because of its fastidious observance of rules and procedures. The bureaucracy attempts to parcel out the jobs, ignoring talents and setting uniform procedures. These procedures mistakenly promote the lowest common denominator of expertise by slicing up the gestalt of the job and putting the necessary skills for the whole job in organizationally distinct departments.

The teams are given responsibilities extending beyond the basic skills necessary to meet production goals, including:

1. The selection of new employees.
2. The training of new employees.
3. Redesigning production procedures.
4. Work scheduling.
5. Internal team communications.
6. Plant policies relating to the above and other policies relating to the total organization.

Rather than placing these functions in separate departments, as in a personnel department, for example, those decisions that directly affect the work are made in close proximity to the job. The team, therefore, provides much of the company policy and removes a barrier to motivated performance by reducing the number of people and departments involved in making production decisions.

The team responsibilities at the plant provide what is called, in motivation-hygiene terminology, facilitating hygiene. There is no expectation that these functions actually increase employee motivation. It is the nature of the jobs that requires some teamwork. Team decisions on the job make the rules and procedures guiding production more flexible and responsive to individual needs. Volvo gains its collective strength from membership in the team. At the Engine Company plant, on the other hand, the strength of the team is in the competence of individuals. This distinction may sound like a subtle one, but it translates into emphasis on individual training and performance rather than on team building in the design of jobs.

The Engine Company plant inadvertently experimented with team building when they gave the teams responsibility for managing the vending machines, organizing recreational activities, and conducting charity fund drives. These were hygiene management tasks, and the teamwork required to arrive at decisions followed the dynamics of hygiene. The ensuing interpersonal dynamics were found to require more group development and empathic concern for equity in the solution of the multiple aggravations arising from each decision.

The broader issue involved here is what constitutes fragmented work. The mistaken impression of many managers (and this has occurred at the

Engine Company) is that they must attempt to unify the existence of their employees by putting them in control over their total work environment. In so doing, they put many elements into the job which are strictly hygiene. The management of the factory cafeteria, for example, may be motivating to a dietitian but not to an engineer. The attempt is to provide a feeling of community among employees, but the result is often a more complex and subsequently more dissatisfying hygiene environment. The primary task of the organization, to be effective by meeting the motivational needs of the employees, cannot be heard over the shouting.

Figure 3

Automobile assembly line at Volvo: A typical job rotation cycle

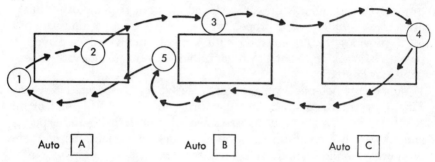

1. Rear bumper assembly.
2. Instrument dashboard work inside the car.
3. Mounting door locks.
4. Grill console.
5. Brake pipe unit installation.

Source: Adapted from L. K. Taylor, "Worker Participation in Sweden," *Industrial and Commercial Training*, vol. 5 (1973), p. 10.

Figure 3, which depicts how the production teams operate at Volvo, makes it possible to see the essential differences between the job designs at the two plants. It can be seen that in the Volvo plant, the jobs describe a rotation cycle, a computerized "Do loop," which is unidimensional. The process is like musical chairs. It provides a way for everyone to work beside everyone else, while sacrificing individual growth. For the Engine Company plant, a photograph could not capture the operations of the team; a motion picture or moving hologram would be required to represent the three-dimensional nature of the work. Such a diagram of the structure at the Engine Company plant would show the team members meeting at the beginning of the day, using a flip chart to review their assignments, and then spreading out to different jobs based on their individual skills and needs for training. For Volvo, the end result is completing the circle. At the Engine Company plant there is an upward spiral, not returning to zero but ending theoretically at the level of plant manager for those who continue to advance.

MEASURING POTENTIAL: SELECTION PROCEDURES

The effectiveness of the plant, while designed to allow for ever-increasing opportunities for satisfying work, still depends on the potential of the employees to be motivated. Volvo, which uses 50 percent immigrant labor, makes the home away from home a more important part of the job than satisfying work. The Engine Company plant sees the key to the success of the project, in the long run, as the selection of a motivated work force. The selection process provides the necessary screening of the "potential" of prospective employees. Returning to the motivational formula, the potential is the undeveloped talent of the employees in the organization which, with proper training and the opportunity to perform, provides the organization with a highly motivated employee. If potential is lacking, what the organization can do to motivate its employees is limited.

To measure potential, job applicants receive three separate interviews. First, they are asked what skills they bring to the job. This part of the selection procedure permits an assessment of prior training and expertise and previously demonstrated know-how on similar jobs. Second, the prospective employee undergoes a hygiene interview and a separate motivational interview. The hygiene interview consists of determining the painful aspects of a person's life on the job, the kinds of things he seeks to avoid, and the typical dissatisfactions he has had at work in the past. The salary plan and fringe benefits are also explained, keeping in mind any potential hygiene conflicts between the individual and the company. The motivational interview is designed to review the history of job satisfactions and the future aspirations of the job applicant. Here the interviewer is trained to pick out signs of "motivator inversion," in which the prospective employee sees himself working hard solely for hygiene purposes.

Besides intellectual potential, a chief criterion for selection is that the employee has potential to experience satisfaction. If, as in motivator inversion, the employee sees his achievements as a means of avoiding pain rather than gaining satisfaction, plans for increasing opportunities on the job would only create more painful circumstances in the working life of that employee. The redesign of the job would be wasted effort, since the work, no matter how meaningful, would fail to provide motivation to the individual who can find no personal fulfillment from his job.

Three separate interviewers conduct these three interviews. At least one interviewer is a trained team member. The decision to hire is based on their joint decisions after reviewing the job applicant's current ability, his hygiene concerns, and his potential for motivated performance in the future.

REINFORCEMENT OF PERSONAL ACHIEVEMENT: COMPENSATION

The two separate need systems of man (hygiene and motivation) require two different ways of providing reinforcement on the job. To reinforce motivational needs, the organization must reward expertise with more responsibility and advancement opportunities. The employee with ability advances quickly in the number of responsibilities he has on the job.

The hygiene needs must be met through a fair and equitable salary schedule, while reducing the complexity in the compensation system. All employees from top management down are paid a weekly salary. Newly hired employees are paid on the basis of an entry level. Six months later the employee receives a second or interim rate. After six months on the interim rate, an individual receives the third or full rate. Graduation to the full rate indicates that an employee has learned most aspects of the core job and is prepared to receive training in a new set of skills. The promise is that the company is then willing to place full confidence in that employee's ability to learn and to grow and to expand his or her job responsibilities. However, since the original compensation system was implemented, the need to establish ranges within the full-rate category has become a pressure point.

RESULTS

The Engine Company plant has been in operation for less than a year and a half. Despite major changes from previous company engine plant operations, the results have been quick to come, and these results have outlasted any temporary supposed Hawthorne effects. The following positive observations of the plant can be made with a great deal of reliability.

Positive observations

The establishment of the new plant provided an opportunity to create a new plant, to try new ideas without being restricted. Extreme freedom was given in what could be done. The restrictions were that it was necessary to produce quality engines within eight months and to hire a work force representative of all groups. The plant consisted of bare walls and no staff except an assigned plant manager. In eight months a plant layout had to be achieved, a work force hired and trained, new policies developed, the philosophy and innovations explained and implemented. There was no template.

All of this was accomplished, and the engines were produced on schedule. The directive was met. *Or, better stated, the employees of this new plant met the directive. They came into an ambitious and novel situation from their past work experience and got the show going. Maybe management had the work concepts, but the workers had the talent to respond.*

In addition, the following observations can be made:

After one year of operation, turnover in the factory and office teams has been less than 5 percent.

Employees have been observed working unscheduled overtime to finish engines or otherwise complete work assignments.

Factory team employees have a greater interest in reaching and surpassing production goals.

Employees have more interest in understanding the total manufacturing process. Employees have made frequent trips to both suppliers and customers to view their operations or participate in equipment checkouts, and so forth.

Employees have taken a much greater interest in participating in the employment process. Factory and office team members conduct the motivation and skills interviews for all new hires in their core groups.

Interestingly, on one occasion a group of factory team women challenged the men in their team because they had been given less responsible tasks to perform. A team of women completely assembled and tested an engine. The engine passed test without any problems.

In general, managers seem to be beginning to overcome their cultural biases. The old feeling that employees are not working if they are not at their machines is being dispelled. Within the first year of operation, seven factory team members have already stepped into management team positions.

In the middle of these management innovations, the plant had to switch to the assembly of a new engine. The assembly and test teams got the new engine ready, demonstrating the flexible learning-centered nature of the work force. Management sees the people as more challenged by their work. In some cases, the employees can do things now that have taken years to achieve in other plants, and with better, more open communications. There have also been better ideas, and more of them, coming from the employees.

Finally, the question of unionization. From the start, the plant was not against unions, and an organization drive was started there several months ago. The company did not discourage its employees from organizing. Rather, management dealt with unionization implications for the new work organization. The company asked that the employees review how a traditional union might interfere with the work innovations taking place at the Engine Company plant and with their newly found satisfaction with their jobs. Less than 15 percent of the employees voted for the union. The employee decision was not against unions, but for motivation on the job. They did not want to introduce any changes that might affect the satisfactions they gained from their work.

Problems

The problems that have arisen deal mostly with the motivators, not the hygiene factors. They are the kinds of problems we now applaud.

While great emphasis has been placed on the selection of the factory and office teams, time pressures did not permit adequate orientation of key managers. This has resulted in the selection of some managers, who, although technically competent, find it difficult to operate in a nontraditional work environment. This is not surprising, since key managers had to come out of more traditional plants.

It has been much easier for the factory teams to operate according to the design than it has been for the office and management teams. Members of the management teams often revert to a more traditional management style when confronted with day-to-day production pressures. This, too, is not surprising, since the status of white-collar workers and office management is often a hygiene barrier to job redesign efforts.

Although good initial training in base skills has been provided, ongoing training for other than core skills has been deficient and is now being covered more thoroughly. The implementation of the new procedures proceeded faster than expected, and the staff was not prepared for the opportunity for advanced training coming so soon.

The group process within the teams themselves has needed strengthening. The overriding goal of individual development was not made consistent with training in those managerial skills necessary to organize the individual efforts on the team.

Total company expansion requirements dictated the limitation of the number of experienced operations people that could be transferred to the new plant. This hurt efforts to train the employees and adequately document processes and policies necessary to do complete job designs.

The need for better communication and feedback systems to report on the progress of concept implementation has become evident. More frequent interteam meetings and off-site key management meetings have been needed.

The teams have some complaints. They report that they want more training, that management at times has backed off the team concept, and that they do not get enough feedback on their performance.

SUMMARY

American personnel practices and industrial relations have traditionally been more pragmatic and less ideologic than their European counterparts. With the recognition by the industries on both continents that managerial styles and the role of work in the lives of their employees have undergone dramatic change in the past two decades, new strategies, particularly those emphasizing job design, have emerged. Because of the ideologic background of European labor relations, these new strategies for humanizing the workplace have leaned more to meeting the social and political needs of employees.

The OJE projects at the new Engine Company plant are more in keeping with the American tradition of trying to humanize work by dealing with the central thrust of the pragmatism inherent in individual development needs. The experiments at Volvo and at the Engine Company plant have in common new plants, comparable work processes, and successful management and labor forces. Both of these experiments are in an early stage of development. They should provide the field of work humanization and worker motivation with an *in vivo* comparison of managerial philosophies, theories, and applications.

The managerial choice

With approximately $7\frac{1}{2}$ percent unemployment in the United States and an equally painful (though in some instances lower) overall percentage in the Western European countries, the myth of recession and unemployment as a patent stimulant for increasing worker productivity and cooperation has been thoroughly discredited.[1] The choice that I have been writing about for so many years has now become truly critical. The choice that I am referring to is whether management continues its historic penchant for trying to *make employees work* or finds means to *make employees want to work* (Figure 1).

This choice has been made more complicated as well as more critical by the heightened and dangerously militant questions of social policy we are being forced to face, as well as by the confused economics of a modern society. In this article I will comment on some of the most important aspects of this crucial choice.

MAKING PEOPLE WORK

In other articles I have described the concepts underlying the techniques used by managers to make people work.[2] In these articles I have designated these techniques as the KITA (Kick in the pants) approach. Essentially there are three forms of the KITA philosophy of management. There are the various types of negative KITAs or threats to the employees (the stick in the proverbial story of how to move a donkey). There are more numerous types of positive KITAs or ways to bribe employees (the carrot in front of the donkey). And a third, more subtle form is the ideologic KITA. In this last kind of KITA, the approach is to exhort employees to better performance by appealing to social values in

---

[1] Frederick Herzberg, "Economic Crisis and Work Motivation," *Industry Week*, February 25, 1974. An edited version is included in Chapter 1.

[2] "One More Time: How Do You Motivate Employees?" *Harvard Business Review*, January–February, 1968 (reprinted in two parts in Chapters 2 and 3) and "Moving Your Employees or Motivating Them?" *Industry Week*, May 18, 1970.

191

the form of various cultural slogans of the "apple pie" variety which have special appeal to particular segments of the work force, or to the majority of the population in times of national crises (Rosie the Riveter, successful in World War II, and WIN Buttons, unsuccessful in the 1974 war on inflation).

Ideological KITA operates on the basis of the psychological phenomenon of the "expanded ego," in which the individual sees himself as part of a larger social entity. The Marine Corps offers a familiar illustration of the successful use of the "expanded ego" concept with the effectiveness of its buddy system and unit morale policies. The psychological

Figure 1

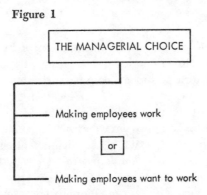

trick here is to make each Marine consider his own existence as including the existence of his unit, thereby ensuring his feeling of immortality. If he is killed, his unit lives on; so by considering his own ego as part of the unit he vicariously limits his mortality. Similarly, ideologic KITAs create the feeling among some workers that the "cause" of which they consider themselves a part transcends their own limited life and consequently reduces their own vulnerability to hurtful physical and psychological consequences.

All of the three forms of KITA for *moving* employees, as I have previously pointed out, are no longer economically sound, but now in addition we have become aware of their deleterious social policy effects (see Figure 2). These could be detailed in terms of many specifics, but I will limit myself to a few of the larger principles involved.

Negative KITAs have always culminated in *revolution*. We in this country have naively considered revolution in terms of a Russian or Chinese bloodbath or the lesser styles of periodic coups that have characterized changes in governments in so many African and South American nations. Because we have been blessed with resilient institutions and traditions, we fail to recognize that American-style revolutions have continuously occurred since the birth of the country, with, of course, the Civil War being the most pathological. In the main, our revolutions have seemed benign in comparison to the bloodletting and complete upheavals that we commonly associate with the term. However, the seemingly benign revolutions in the United States have, because of our people's expectations of normalcy, had at least an equal economic, social, and psychological impact as the more brutal forms of revolution.

The New Deal of the Roosevelt era was thought by many to be as devastating a social and political revolution as the one that occurred in Russia approximately 15 years earlier. Today we are witnessing our public servants engaged in revolution, as police, firemen, teachers, and others defy laws and court orders and threaten devastation in our cities. The point is that the threat of negative KITAs (jail terms, fines, loss of pay, loss of seniority, loss of security) leads to little in the way of positive economic benefits, and it is socially dangerous.

Figure 2

THE CONSEQUENCES OF MAKING EMPLOYEES WORK

Negative KITA	⟶	Revolution
Positive KITA	⟶	Bankruptcy
Ideological KITA	⟶	Inhumanity

Positive KITA, that is, bribing workers, has had the economic effect of making companies pay more and receive less. At the larger social level, it eventually leads to economic *bankruptcy*, as witness the condition of the great City of New York.

The use of ideological KITA can lead to "justified" *inhumanity*. The Soviet and Chinese revolutions are sufficient testimonials of the effect of heavy reliance on this approach to making people work. In this country, ideological appeals have sanctimoniously supported slavery, sweatshops, and numerous other inhumanities toward workers. Only recently have we realized the inhumanity of denying education, jobs, food, and other basic necessities to our minorities, including all the poor of our nation. Even the relatively well-off are subject to ideological exhortations to justify general environmental and specific working situations that we know to be inhuman. For the general public, polluted air and water are the most obvious result of ideological preachments that "force" the acceptance of an earlier death. The Occupational Safety and Health Review Commission has been created to protect the right of workers to humane conditions in safety and general health as they perform their jobs. The incidence of black lung disease among miners and cancer among those working with asbestos is so well documented that it is inhuman to counter these dangers with ideological slogans of debatable economic necessity.

The consequences of making people work—revolution, bankruptcy, and inhumanity—are real spectres hanging over our society. The argument still revolves around the advisability of choosing these possibilities by maintaining a discredited economic and management theory as it relates to worker performance; this is choice by default.

MAKING PEOPLE WANT TO WORK

The other choice for management is learning how to get employees to want to work, or learning how to motivate people rather than how to move them. Movement is a *short-term* strategy, while motivation requires a long-term strategy. The bases for the social barriers to motivation are rather clear.

The bases for barriers to motivation

First, because movement has worked in the past, the aphorism of "nothing succeeds like success" is used to argue against any fundamental change in management. The tragedies that have occurred in personal lives, organizational institutions, and even governments proves this aphorism wrong. It is the failure to manage success that has been the source of the most regretable failures in life.

Second, we live in a short-term society. *New* is the most overused word in the advertiser's language. Studies made on poor, and presumably therefore unsuccessful, people have attributed their condition to a short time perspective regarding the way they choose and put into practice their values and appetites. If these conclusions are reasonably valid, then we may reasonably fear that the short-term society syndrome will become normalized, so that the psychology of people is reduced to the lowest level of aspirations and commitments.

The fact is that life is a tragically short-term affair, an incurable disease that can only be managed and never cured. This fact has reached the consciousness of most people today and has reinforced the ethos for a short-term society. Although we may be living longer, we are living in shorter spurts.

This short-term psychology also leads to exaggeration of man's eternal tendency to pursue the fast buck, and this tends to decrease the time and energy allocated to the pursuit of happiness. A shorter positive life dedicated to pain avoidance is hardly a prescription for a sane and productive country. Since the motivators are a long-term affair, they become more and more crowded out of our lives.

The question, and the accompanying choice, boils down to this: Where does man get his psychological income? We have always recognized that man does not live by bread alone. In addition to his physical wants and needs there are the more human, mind-expanding wants and needs, which are of equal strength in his existence. The various metaphysical systems that have been created and the nature of man's work activity have been the primary sustaining sources for his psychological income. The former, however, are increasingly failing, and income from the latter is becoming increasingly unattainable. The less the psychological income, the more will opiatic pursuit of physical income inexorably follow.

It is this fact which is exacerbating the dual crises of commodity shortages and an exploding population. Even in countries that have managed to limit their population growth, the lack of psychological sustenance has produced a more consuming rather than a more producing society. This is tantamount to increasing the population, when it comes to the requirements for and availability of resources.

If we continue to rely on grain-fed cattle as our major source of protein, we will quickly exhaust our supply. Just as we must substitute grass-fed cattle, fish, beans, and other sources of protein to survive nutritionally, we must substitute psychic nutrition so we do not exhaust the supply of physical nutrition. There is a need to reverse the historic, accelerating trend of denying what is now being called "the quality of life" for "the quantity of life." This is not a philosophical argument; it is rather the only way to achieve any meaningful quantity of life at all.

There is an additional factor that reduces our opportunity to improve or even sustain both the quality and quantity of our lives if we continue to seek solutions via KITA. The strife it brings about in a more complicated society increases the need for the professions of intermediaries, particularly (and sadly, for the wounded) the *lawyers* and the *government*. They act in the manner of gambling establishments, skimming the poker pot on each deal, with the end result that the adversaries are contending over smaller pots, and the productive resources are consequently diminished.

Barriers to job enrichment programs

Recent attempts to implement the choice of work motivation for economic reasons, as well as to improve the quality of work life, have led to an avalanche of writings, publicity, and how-to manuals for job enrichment, and allied improvement of the work environment. The rhetoric and publicity are in sad contrast to what has actually been achieved. Since I have been called "the father of job enrichment," I feel a responsibility to suggest some of the reasons for the disparity between the promise and the reality when it comes to the area of job enrichment.

There are three general social reasons and a larger number of specific intraorganizational reasons for the failure to institutionalize job enrichment programs, even after a successful demonstration. First, we will examine the three social barriers (see Figure 3).

The first is the unending hope of people, organizations, and society for a return to "normalcy." No comment seems necessary on this perennial neurotic aspiration.

The second is, frankly, class warfare between management and the unions, in which the workers and some unions, particularly those in Europe, see the quality-of-life movement as a means of introducing socialism under the guise of improved manager/worker relationships. The behavioral scientists' contribution to this movement is disguised under the euphemisms of *industrial democracy* or *participative management.*

The third is the fact that the quality of life can be sold as a profitable business enterprise. Commercialized nostalgia is booming. Travel is no longer the relaxing, educational, mind-broadening experience it once was considered to be. "If this is Tuesday, It Must Be Belgium" parodies how

Figure 3

THREE
SOCIAL BARRIERS
TO
JOB ENRICHMENT

(1.)   The unending hope for a return to "normalcy"

(2.)   The class warfare between management and the unions

(3.)   The commercialization of quality of life

any psychological benefits of travel are stripped away for the sake of efficiency in moving people around as a more profitable business policy. In fact, we are losing our enjoyment of leisure and are merely consuming it. Garages are filled with leisure equipment that has never been enjoyed. Interpersonal relationships and intimate sex have succumbed to commercial exploitation. Little value has ensued from learning how to enjoy the company of other people or even getting along better with them, or from achieving "peace of mind" or improving sexual satisfactions. If all the how-to books and the seminars are of any help, then why have people increasingly turned to drug addiction and alcoholism to "solve" such problems? The fact is that all nonwork aspects of life are being overloaded in compensation for the loss of fulfillment in work.

When it comes to improving the quality of work life and individual worker motivation, industry is sold similar packaged and gimmick-filled programs by the behavioral scientists whose psychological tests and other questionable personnel paraphanalia were sold as a business, under the guise of responding to the social and human concerns of workers and management. The credentials of these "business humanitarians" are woeful. They do not look to any professional society for guidance, but to trade associations which serve almost any dues-paying member.

The other major reasons for the failure of job enrichment programs to become self-sustaining, continuous, and systematized in organizations, even where projects have succeeded, are the consequences of these three larger issues. The additional barriers are listed separately for the three general levels of organizations: the hands-on worker (Figure 4), middle management (Figure 5) and the higher "executive" group (Figure 6).

Figure 4

BARRIERS TO JOB ENRICHMENT

At the worker level

1. Confusion between hygiene and the motivators

2. Distrust of management's motivations

3. Among older employees—the "adaptive" life-style

4. The fear of incompetence

5. The fear of redundancy

Barriers at the worker level

1. There is an understandable confusion between hygiene and the motivators at the worker level. The worker has for so long experienced his work as only a means of meeting his economic necessities that he has difficulty in conceiving of it as a source of noneconomic satisfaction. However, when he is laid off or retired he often recognizes that doing nothing is as painful as consuming less. This barrier is reinforced by the actual absence of motivator qualities in his job. Therefore it is not unexpected that, where no opportunity to find satisfaction exists in the work itself, he cannot distinguish his feelings of no dissatisfaction from no satisfaction.

2. There is a reasonable distrust of management's motivation at the worker level. Workers are extremely prone to see job enrichment as a rate-busting procedure. This is reinforced by the unions, who also feel that job enrichment will lessen their control over the workers and limit their bargaining position for rate differentials when workers perform expanded jobs. Craft rivalries are an added barrier the worker and his union erect to the acceptance of the redesign of jobs for more intrinsic job satisfaction.

3. Many older employees who have adapted to their work life-style are often resistant to changes being made in their jobs. They have found routinized work to be a compulsive activity that provides steadiness to their lives. They no longer seek meaning—just a ritual to calm their troubles and enable them to repress their lost dreams.

4. The fear of incompetence is a quite pervasive response to attempts to start and maintain a job enrichment program, since the existing work has been generally designed for the mindless, and the selection process for workers has paralleled the nature of the jobs. This fear is found to a greater extent among minorities whose grievances overshadow their reality testing.

5. The fear of losing redundant functions is obvious to the worker, for job enrichment does attack featherbedding.

Figure 5

BARRIERS TO JOB ENRICHMENT

At middle-management level

1. Fear of incompetence, redundancy, and the "leave me alone" adaptation

2. Careerism—with its political games

3. Fear of loss of authority

4. Job enrichment—just another development program

5. Fear of improved efficiency

6. Lack of knowledge of job enrichment

Barriers at the middle-management level

1. As in the worker force, among middle managers there is fear of incompetence, fear of redundancy, and a "leave me alone" psychological adaptation.

2. Job enrichment has many organizational repercussions, and careerism, with its political games, surfaces rather quickly. Uppermost in the minds of middle managers is the question: What do these changes mean for my opportunities? This group is very susceptible to these feelings, because at this level the manager experiences the most anxiety about his values, position, and future in the company.

3. There are feelings of loss of authority. After job enrichment, middle managers may no longer feel that they are "bosses." Too many middle

managers see the boss role as their function, and, unhappily for them and the organization, this is all too true in actual fact. Job enrichment for middle managers is a crying need.

4. Many middle managers have been subjected to so many development programs aimed at making them "better managers" it is little wonder that they view job enrichment as just another product that comes along—to be tolerated but not really acted upon.

5. There is, surprisingly, a fear of improved efficiency. If the workers take more on their shoulders and do a better job, then the middle manager looks bad. It is similar to the hostility that first-line supervisors and foremen have to suggestion plans from the working force. Why didn't they think of the suggested improvements themselves?

6. Middle management is too often only peripherally briefed on the programs. They really do not know what to do. Top management says go ahead—but how? With what authority? Do they really mean it? Will I be supported? And with the consultant field pitching so many variations and procedures,[3] it is understandable that middle management is first confused and then hostile.

Figure 6

BARRIERS TO JOB ENRICHMENT

At the executive level

1. Personnel problems—another annoyance

2. Job enrichment viewed as just another PR gimmick

3. Job enrichment "complicates" the big picture

4. Fear of loss of control—the "boss" syndrome

Barriers at the executive level

1. The executive generally is concerned with "hard" matters, such as production, marketing, and finance. Personnel problems are generally relegated to the status of an annoyance stemming from irrational human nature. These annoyances are taken seriously only when they become "hard" problems, such as contract negotiations, work stoppages, or strikes. Work satisfaction is good for speeches.

2. Too many executives view job enrichment as primarily a public

---

[3] See "The Wise Old Turk," *Harvard Business Review*, September–October 1974, reprinted as the second article in this chapter.

relations gimmick. Once they have milked the PR value, they lose interest.

3. Since they are on top, executives supposedly see the complicating consequences for other parts of the organization. I feel that they use this more as an excuse than an explanation. All their activities should consider the "big picture." Job enrichment programs are not unique in requiring integration within the larger organizational programs and policies.

4. Finally, they do fear loss of control (the "boss syndrome") as well as the fear of incompetence and the loss of the security blanket of managing by obsessive-compulsive routines.

There are, of course, many other barriers, some large, such as capital investment (e.g., the automobile assembly line), some small, such as the petty concerns that crop up with any personnel project. The barriers I have listed are the major psychological ones I have encountered, analyzed, dealt with (and in many instances, failed with) in organizations large and small, of most varieties and in many different cultures.

Despite all the difficulties the choice needs to be made between making work psychologically attractive, and the predictable alternatives—revolution, bankruptcy, and inhumanity. The required choice is not beyond the reach of attainment by reasonable management attempts. It requires a better understanding and willingness to see the world of work as different from past visions, which have become illusions.

chapter 4

Motivation-Hygiene Theory and mental health

INTRODUCTION

In recent years the quest for better ways to manage people has turned inward. Managers are now searching for new meaning in their own lives, discarding the traditions that guided their behavior and values in the past as irrelevant to modern concerns. Just as the need for better management created a host of contradictory programs for better managerial techniques, the need for personal understanding has led to numerous, altogether frivolous programs designed to teach people the techniques of better living. The behavioral science market is now glutted with these human potential movements—transcendental meditation, EST, transactional analysis, rolfing, and many others. This chapter seeks to provide some understanding and perspective by returning to the basics for an understanding of mental health, the central core of Motivation-Hygiene Theory.

Motivation-hygiene conceptions of mental health and mental illness have been developed through the study of functioning populations in the pursuit of what is universally accepted as "normal" and "human" activity —work. Most definitions pertaining to mental illness and mental health which underlie the practice of psychiatry, clinical psychology, and other related behavior modification professions have their origins in the study of acknowledged abnormal populations. The motivation-hygiene concepts begin essentially with the study of what is "normal" and attempt to define "abnormal" as significant alterations from this standard, rather than the traditional abnormal-normal conceptual sequence.

Much of the disenchantment with the mental health movement in the United States can be traced to reliance on studies of the mentally ill in the development of psychological theories of human behavior. Because these patients displayed only hygiene concerns, the psychiatrist and clinical psychologist observed only the suffering aspects of human nature. Operating under an illusion similar to that embraced by industry, the helping professions hoped that consideration of the need to avoid pain would alone bring forth positive attitudes and better mental health. They were unable to recognize the personal-growth needs of the "normal" person, as these needs did not manifest themselves in the clinical population.

These psychological theories, therefore, became illness models rather than models of mental health. Characteristically, the theories have been unable to arrive at a definition of mental health other than one based on the cultural norms for the expression of pain. Psychotherapeutic successes have been unimpressive, and the wise psychotherapist has relied more on his artistic talents than his science of human behavior. The helping professions have failed both in defining the problems adequately and solving them, not because of the cantankerous nature of the human animal but rather through their reliance on a deterministic point of view about one half of human behavior.

Motivation-Hygiene Theory provides some alternative conceptions of mental health. Through the observation of mentally healthy individuals, the capacity of man to change, to grow, and to determine his own future can be recognized. This capacity forms the basis of motivation-hygiene definitions of mental health.

In the first of the two theoretical articles in this chapter, "A Motivation-Hygiene Concept of Mental Health," I and Roy M. Hamlin have developed some definitions of mental health based on my research evidence of man at work. A normal human being seeks the avoidance of pain because the pain hurts; he also seeks satisfaction, not as a relief from pain but for its own rewards. The basis for mental health, then, is defined as the realization of motivational needs rather than the absence of pain. We point out that these needs are not simply released from bondage once the pain is alleviated; they have to be developed through real opportunities for psychological growth.

We define abnormality in this article not as based on a normative assessment of human suffering, as do most psychological theories, but as the inversion of the two need systems through the use of pain avoidance as a substitute for satisfaction and fulfillment. The abnormal person, called a hygiene seeker, is chronically dissatisfied, regardless of his achievements. He at times appears highly motivated, like the Protestant ethic hygiene seeker who works to absolve himself rather than for the joy of achievement and personal growth. The singular goal of avoiding pain is, of course, unattainable because the dynamics of hygiene are cyclical, nonadditive, and escalating. The psychotherapist would need only to recall how frequently his clients enter therapy asking unanswerable questions to recognize how the dynamics of motivational inversion manifest themselves.

The concepts of growth and individual actualization, if they are dealt with at all in psychotherapy, are generally thought of as an end product of pain removal or as a bonus to a rehabilitated, damaged psyche. In a follow-up article, "The Motivation-Hygiene Concept and Psychotherapy," Herzberg and Hamlin develop a motivational approach to psychotherapy which is not dependent upon pain reduction. What is necessary in treatment is a redirection of goals, away from obsessional concerns for hygiene needs and toward motivational needs. In describing the contributions of physical therapies and depth, ego, and social therapies, we point out that many of them contain elements of motivational dynamics. However, these treatment approaches continue to emphasize the relief of suffering in their analysis of the needs of the client. This orientation undoubtedly motivates the therapist in his search for the determinants of human behavior, but it can actually reinforce the motivational inversion of the client by interpreting all of his behavior as arising from hygiene needs. More recently, the development of ego psychology appears to provide man with motivational needs but continues to promote the idea that one cannot grow psychologically in the presence of pain, a myth which has doomed most psychotherapies.

In place of these forms of clinical intervention, we present four principles to guide the treatment of motivational inversions. This motivation-hygiene approach would redirect the client toward personal growth, providing him with opportunities but not treating him as if he were a lost child in a threatening world. Instead the client is given responsibility for his actions and, therefore, the freedom to change.

Following these theoretical presentations is "Motivation and Mental Health: Some Empirical Evidence," a review of a number of empirical studies of motivation-hygiene concepts of mental health and abnormality. Most of these studies were conducted by my doctoral students while I was in charge of the Industrial Mental Health Program at Case Western Reserve University. Other research studies reported were carried out by my collaborator, Roy Hamlin, and his students. Those interested in a further detailed description of the research methods utilized in these empirical investigations should consult the original articles listed in the references for this article.

The theoretical papers and the research articles present a new look at mental health, its definitions and treatment. The concept of motivational inversion is especially fruitful, and it has good empirical validation. The analysis of other therapeutic endeavors can be extended to the newer behavior therapies, which can be helpful in the treatment of specific hygiene complaints that have gotten out of hand (phobias, for example). But when dealing with motivational problems, these therapies would reinforce achievement with hygiene. In motivator-hygiene psychotherapy, direct and active interventions are utilized to help the client recognize his motivational needs. This pragmatic, no-nonsense approach is applicable to blue-collar as well as white-collar workers, students, and others with high verbal skills. It is hoped that the ideas contained in this chapter can assist in providing direction to the overdetermined mental health client and his psychotherapist.

A motivation-hygiene concept of mental health

Frederick Herzberg
and
Roy M. Hamlin

This article presents a concept of mental health based on the study of job attitudes reported in *The Motivation to Work*.[1] The concept emphasizes the distinction between a positive mental health and a negative mental illness. These two aspects emerged as operationally distinct in the study of job attitudes, and this operational distinction may have important theoretical and research implications in the study of behavioral disorders. If two dimensions or modes of response—a positive or approach dimension and a negative or avoidance dimension—can be distinguished, new problems may arise and old confusions may disappear.

Both classical writings and recent papers suggest ideas similar to those set forth here. Although the concept is not entirely new, two contributions of the article may be new. First, the concept needs to be clearly stated. Second, the operational distinction between the factors associated with approach behaviors and the factors associated with avoidance behaviors needs to be clearly defined and clothed in some theoretical framework.

This article will include: (1) a brief review of the concept as developed in the study of job attitudes, (2) a generalization of this concept to the definition of mental health and mental illness, (3) some comment on how this concept fits with traditional analytical thinking and with newer developments in the biochemistry of emotional disorders, and (4) a comment on research implications.

---

[1] Frederick Herzberg, Bernard Mausner, and Barbara Snyderman, *The Motivation to Work* (New York: John Wiley & Sons, 1959).

REVIEW OF THE MOTIVATION-HYGIENE CONCEPT

In *The Motivation to Work* a theory of job motivation was presented which considers adjustment to work to be made up of two separate dimensions or components, the first dealing with job satisfaction and the second with job dissatisfaction. The important feature of this theory is the implication that these two components of work adjustment are not opposites; rather, they are two distinct dimensions. The theory was generalized from data obtained by examining both the subjective and the objective nature of job situations in which employees reported that they had been unusually happy and unhappy.

Two sets of factors emerged. Situations which made employees unhappy were characterized by *poor company policies and administrative practices, poor supervision, poor interpersonal relationships, poor working conditions,* and *unfair salary schedules.* The favorable sides of these factors, however, rarely were characteristic of the job situations in which the respondents considered themselves happy with their work. It seems that these factors were of primary importance in the prevention of job dissatisfaction but had little effect in altering job attitudes to a positive state of satisfaction. In addition, they were alike in that they all referred to the *environment* in which the job task was performed and not to the job itself. Because they essentially described the job environment and served primarily as preventives, they were named the *hygiene* factors, in analogy with such medical hygiene approaches as water purification, garbage disposal, smoke control, and housing control, all of which pertain to the environment and serve basically *to prevent ill health.*

As already stated, the analysis of the situations in which job satisfaction was reported rarely revealed these hygiene factors. Instead a completely different set of factors was found. The five most frequently named were *achievement, task responsibility, professional advancement, interesting work,* and *recognition for achievement.* These factors also operated in only one direction, but this time to bring about job satisfaction; they were not involved in the creation of job dissatisfaction. Because of their role in positive improvement of job attitudes and also their discovered effects in enhancing work performance, they were named the *motivators,* in line with a popular connotation of motivation. An important further distinction between the hygiene factors and the motivators was that the latter pertained to the job *content,* in contrast to the job *context* of the hygiene factors.

The major implication of the Motivation-Hygiene Theory involves this concept of two separate dimensions. These dimensions are distinct in the sense that each depends on its own separate set of factors. One set of factors leads to high satisfaction but does not contribute in any appreciable degree to dissatisfaction. Instead, it is another set of factors that determines dissatisfaction, and these factors, in turn, contribute little to high levels of satisfaction. The distinction between these two dimensions has importance for two reasons. First, the relevant factors are specified; because they are derived from research data and not from armchair speculation, they permit systematic manipulation and analysis. Second, the distinction involves a point of view, or conceptual shift. This conceptual shift will almost certainly lead to major changes in research on job satisfaction. Essentially the same shift could well lead to an equally important change in theory and research on mental health.

IMPLICATIONS FOR MENTAL HEALTH

The implications of Motivation-Hygiene Theory for mental health are best introduced by a brief summary of the subjective reactions of the employees surveyed as to why the various factors affected them the way they did. For the job-dissatisfied situation, the subjects reported they had been made unhappy mostly because they felt they were being treated unfairly, or they found the situation unpleasant or painful. On the other hand, the common denominator for the reasons for positive job attitudes seemed to be variations on the theme of feelings of psychological growth, the fulfillment of self-actualizing needs. There was an approach-avoidance dichotomy with respect to job adjustment. The need to avoid unpleasant job environments led to job dissatisfaction; the need for self-realization led to job satisfaction when the opportunity for self-realization was afforded.

A "hygienic" environment prevents discontent with a job, but such an environment cannot lead the individual beyond a minimal adjustment consisting of the absence of dissatisfaction. A positive "happiness" seems to require some attainment of psychological growth.

It is clear why the hygiene factors fail to provide for positive satisfactions: They do not possess the characteristics necessary to give an individual a sense of growth. To feel one has grown depends on achievement in tasks which have meaning to the individual. Since the hygiene factors do not relate to the task, they are powerless to do this. Growth is dependent on some achievement, but achievement requires a task. The motivators are task factors, and thus they are necessary for growth; they provide the psychological simulation by which the individual can be activated toward his self-realization needs.

To generalize from job attitudes to mental attitudes, we can specify two types of adjustment for mental health: an adjustment to the environment, which is mainly an avoidance adjustment, and an adjustment to oneself, which is dependent on the successful striving for psychological growth, self-actualization, and self-realization, or, most simply, on being psychologically more than one has been in the past.

To be sure, the

concept of self-actualization, or self-realization, as a man's ultimate goal has been focal to the thought of many personality theorists. For such men as Jung, Adler, Sullivan, Rogers and Goldstein the supreme goal of man is to fulfill himself as a creative, unique individual according to his own innate potentialities and within the limits of reality. When he is deflected from this goal he becomes, as Jung says, "a crippled animal"![2]

Such a philosophy in itself, however, fails to define self-actualization and fails to specify the factors relevant and necessary for research progress. Mental health remains too unique, individual, and vitalistic. It is a highly personal program, or urge, which can only be released by hygiene measures to remove mental illness or by passive and pious nonintervention.

Without gainsaying the inherent individuality of self-actualization, *The Motivation to Work* takes a tentative but firm step in the direction of specifying the factors essential to eliciting mental health. To paraphrase John C. Flanagan, speaking on *The Motivation to Work*, only a small number of interrelated factors is responsible for *mental health*. The key to an understanding of mental health is to be found in a sense of personal growth and of self-actualization *resulting from* the following group of factors: *achievement, responsibility, meaningful work,* and *advancement*.[3] This list of factors, admittedly tentative, nevertheless establishes a preliminary basis for the systematic research analysis and manipulation of mental health.

TRADITIONAL AND MOTIVATION-HYGIENE VIEWS OF MENTAL HEALTH

Traditionally, mental health has been regarded as the obverse of mental illness. Mental health, in this sense, is the mere *absence* of mental illness. At one time the psychoanalyst anticipated that mental health would be automatically released when the conflicts of mental illness were resolved. And currently, the biochemist hopes that mental health will bloom once serotonin and norepinephrine are properly balanced and optimimally distributed in the brain. The removal of mental illness will automatically result in mental health.

In essence, this traditional view ignores *mental health*. In general, the focus has been on mental illness—on anxiety, anxiety-reducing mechanisms, past frustrations, childhood trauma, distressing interpersonal relations, disturbing ideas and worries, current patterns of inefficiency, and

---

[2] Ibid., p. 114.

[3] J. C. Flanagan, "Leadership Skills: Their Identification, Development and Evaluation" (Paper delivered at Office of Naval Research—Louisiana State University Symposium on Leadership and Interpersonal Behavior, March 3–5, 1959).

stressful present environments. Except for sporadic lip service, positive attitudes and experiences have been considered chiefly in an atmosphere of distress and dependency.

The factors which determine mental illness, we suggest, are not the obverse of the mental health factors. Rather the mental illness factors belong to the category of hygiene factors, which describe the environment of man and which serve to cause illness when they are deficient, but which effect little positive increase in mental health. They are factors which cause avoidance behavior, but only, as we shall develop, in the "sick" individual do they activate approach behavior. The implications of the conceptual shift for job satisfaction becomes apparent at once. Traditional research has focused almost exclusively on only one set of factors, on the hygiene or job-context factors. The motivating factors, the positive or self-actualizing factors, have been largely neglected. The thesis of this article is that a very similar neglect has characterized traditional research on mental health.

Specifically, the resolution of conflicts, the correction of biochemical imbalance, and the modification of psychic defenses could all be categorically assigned to attempts to modify the hygiene or avoidance needs of the individual. The positive motivating factors—self-actualization and personal growth—have been treated in two ways. Either they have been neglected and dismissed as essentially not relevant, or they have been regarded as so individually sacred and vague as to defy research analysis. At best, the mental health factors have been looked upon as important *forces* which could be released by the removal of mental illness factors.

The motivation-hygiene concept stresses three points regarding mental adjustment. First is the proposition that mental illness and mental health are not on the same dimension. Contrary to classical psychoanalytical belief, the degrees of adjustment do not scale from sickness to positive health; rather, there are degrees of sickness and degrees of health. The degree of sickness reflects an individual's reaction to the hygiene factors, while the degree of mental health represents his reaction to the motivator factors.

Second, the motivator–mental health aspect of personal adjustment has been sadly neglected in theory, research, and application. The positive side of personal adjustment has been considered to be a dividend or consequence of successful attention to the negative-maladjustment side.

Third is a new definition or idea of mental illness which we should now like to develop and propose. The new definition derives from the first proposition that mental illness is not the opposite of mental health and also is suggested by some data obtained in the job attitude studies.

While the incidents in which job satisfaction was reported in the survey for *The Motivation to Work* almost always contained the factors which related to the job task—the motivators—there were a few individuals who reported receiving job satisfaction solely from hygiene factors, that is from some aspect of the job environment. Commenting on this reversal in *The Motivation to Work,* Herzberg et al. suggest that "there may be individuals who because of their training and because of the things that have happened to them have learned to react positively to the factors associated with the *context* of their jobs."[4] These hygiene seekers are primarily attracted to things that, in the majority of the working population, serve only to prevent dissatisfaction and are not a source of positive feelings. The hygiene seeker has not reached a stage of personality development wherein self-actualizing needs are active. From this point of view he is fixated at a less mature level of personal adjustment.

An implied admonition to industry in *The Motivation to Work* is that the lack of motivators in jobs will increase the sensitivity of employees to real or imagined bad job hygiene, and consequently the amount and quality of hygiene given to employees must be constantly improved. There is also the reported finding that the relief from job dissatisfaction through hygiene factors is only a temporary effect, and thus the need for more frequent attention to the job environment is increased. The hygiene factors partake of the quality of opiates for meaningless work. The individual becomes unhappy without them but is relieved only temporarily with them, for their effects soon wear off, and the hygiene seeker is left chronically dissatisfied.

A hygiene seeker is not just a victim of circumstances but is *motivated* in the direction of temporary satisfaction. It is not that his job offers little opportunity for self-actualization; rather, it is that his needs lie predominantly in another direction, that of satisfying avoidance needs. He is seeking positive happiness via the route of avoidance behavior. His resultant chronic dissatisfaction is an illness of motivation. Chronic unhappiness, a motivation pattern that ensures continual dissatisfaction, a failure to grow or to want to grow—these characteristics add up to a neurotic personality.

We would like to suggest that the neurotic is an individual with a lifetime pattern of hygiene seeking, and that the definition of a neurotic in terms of defenses against anxiety arising from early psychological conflicts (if valid) at best represents the *origin* of his hygiene seeking. The motivation-hygiene view of a neurotic adjustment is free of ties with any theory of etiology, and our thesis is therefore made independent of conceptualizations regarding the traditional dynamics of personality development and adjustment. In fact, we suggest that the neurotic motivation pattern of hygiene seeking is mostly a learned process which arises from the value systems endemic in society. Our social critics appear to be closer to the fundamental problems of our mental health crisis than the more dogma-minded behavioral scientists.

---

[4] Ibid., p. 103.

Categories of adjustment

Since total adjustment depends on the satisfaction of two separate types of needs, we can attempt a rough operational categorization of adjustment by examining the sources of a person's satisfactions. A first category is characterized by *positive mental health*. Persons in this category show a preponderance of lifetime satisfactions coming from situations in which the motivator factors are paramount. These factors are necessary to provide a sense of personal growth. They can be identified as directly involving the individual in some task, project, or activity in which achievement or the consequences of achievement are possible. Those factors found meaningful for industrial job satisfaction may not be complete or sufficiently descriptive to encompass the total life picture of an individual; other factors may be necessary to describe the motivators in this larger sense. Whatever they may be, the criteria for their selection must include activity on the part of the individual—some task, episode, adventure, or activity in which the individual achieves a growth experience and without which the individual *will not* feel unhappy, dissatisfied, or uncomfortable. In addition, to belong to this positive category, the individual must have frequent opportunity for the satisfaction of these motivator needs. How frequent and how challenging the growth opportunities must be will depend on the level of ability (both genetic and learned) of the individual and on his tolerance for delayed success. This tolerance, too, may be constitutional, learned, or governed by dynamic conflicts; the source does not really matter to the argument.

The motivation-hygiene concept may seem to involve certain paradoxes. For example, is all achievement work and no play? Is the individual of limited ability doomed to be a nonachiever, and therefore a hygiene seeker? The answers should be obvious already.

In regard to work and play, achievements include all personal growth experiences. The book *The Motivation to Work* does focus on industrial production, which is demanded by society or company policy. The satisfying sequences reported, however, are rich in examples of creativity and individual initiative. Artistic and scholarly interests, receptive openness to new insights, true relaxation, and regrouping of growth potentials (as contrasted with plain laziness) are all achievements or elements in achievement. Nowhere is the balanced work-play growth element in achievement more apparent than in the mentally healthy individual.

In regard to limitations resulting from meagre ability, the motivating history of achievement depends to an important degree on a realistic attitude. The individual who concerns himself largely with vague aspirations, completely unrelated to his abilities and to the actual situation, is simply one variety of hygiene seeker. He does not seek satisfaction in the job itself; rather he seeks it in those surrounding conditions which include such cultural noises as "any native-born American can be President" or "every young person should have a college degree." The previous quotation may be repeated: "the supreme goal of man is to fulfill himself as a creative, *unique* individual according to his own *innate potentialities* and within the *limits of reality*." (Italics have been added.)

A final condition for membership in this most adjusted group would be a good life environment or successful avoidance of poor hygiene factors. Again, those factors necessary for the work situation may not suffice for all the environments of the individual.

Three conditions, then, will serve to define a mentally healthy individual. Seeking life satisfaction through personal growth experiences (experiences defined as containing the motivator factors); sufficient success commensurate with ability and tolerance for delay, to give direct evidence of growth; and finally, successful avoidance of discomfort from poor hygiene.

The second category of adjustment is characterized as *symptom-free adjustment*. Individuals grouped in this category also seek and obtain their satisfactions primarily from the motivator factors. However, their growth needs will be much less reinforced during their life because of the lack of opportunity. Such individuals will not have achieved a complete sense of fulfillment because of circumstances extrinsic to their motivation. Routine jobs and routine life experiences attenuate the growth of these individuals, not their motivation. Because their motivation is "healthy" we do not place these persons on the "sick" continuum. In addition, those in this category must have sufficient satisfactions of their hygiene needs.

The third category of adjustment represents a qualitative jump from the mental health dimension to the mental illness dimension. We may call this category the *maladjusted*. The basic characteristic of persons in this group is that they have sought satisfaction in life primarily from hygiene sources. There is an inversion of motivation away from the approach behavior of growth to the avoidance behavior of comfortable environment. This is the hygiene seeker. His maladjustment is defined by the direction of his motivation and is evidenced by the environmental source of his satisfactions.

Many in this category have had a significant number of personal achievements, but since their motivation pattern emphasizes hygiene desires, their achievements result in no growth experience. We have commented before that hygiene satisfactions are short-lived and thereby have the characteristics of opiates. The environmental satisfactions for persons whom we call *maladjusted* must be rather frequent and of substantial quality.

It is the satisfactions of their hygiene needs which differentiate the maladjusted from the final category in our system—the *mentally ill*. The mentally ill are lifetime hygiene seekers with poor life environments (as perceived by the individual). This poor environment may be realistic or may reflect mostly an accentuated sensitivity to hygiene deprivation because of their inversion of motivation.

The motivation-hygiene concept holds that mental health depends on the individual's history or past experience. In his history the healthy individual has succeeded in growth achievements. In contrast, mental illness depends on a different pattern of past experience. The unhealthy individual has concerned himself with surrounding conditions; his search for satisfaction has focused on the limitations imposed by objective reality and by other individuals, including society and the culture.

In the usual job situation these limitations consist of company policy, technical supervision, interpersonal relations, and the like. In broader life adjustments the surrounding conditions include cultural taboos, social demands for material production, and limited native ability. The hygiene seeker devotes his energies to concern with the surrounding limitations, to "defenses" in the Freudian sense. He seeks satisfaction, or mental health, in a policy of "defense." No personal growth occurs, and his search for health is not only fruitless, it leads to ever more intricate maneuvers of defense or hygiene seeking.

No one definition of mental illness, or of mental health, is likely to satisfy all readers. Rather than define mental health, it might be better to state an initial and tentative hypothesis. In brief, the hypothesis inherent in the motivation-hygiene concept is: Psychological income from predominantly hygiene sources will characterize the mentally sick.

RESEARCH DEVELOPMENTS

At present, the two major developments in research on mental health center around (1) biochemistry and (2) the activation and social restoration of psychotic patients. It may well be argued that drugs do not, and will not, restore patients to mental health. To paraphrase again from the job attitude studies: certain conditions may be established to alleviate mental illness, but these conditions have *little positive effect* in developing mental health.

Since the introduction of major tranquilizers (phenothiazines and their derivatives) there has been a steady decline in the number of patients in mental hospitals. Have drugs cured more patients? Probably not. The effect of drugs seems so far to have been an indirect one. The best of the tranquilizers has been less effective than insulin coma. To date, tranquilizers and antidepressants have achieved two important results. One is that hospital management has been revolutionized by an overall diminishing effect on social disturbance within the institution, and this change has freed time and energy for effective social and personal attention to the motivation of patients. The other is that the promise of drugs has once more lent optimism and enthusiasm to the possibility of activating and socially rehabilitating long-neglected patients. Drugs, and with them motivators, are being administered to withdrawn and depressed patients who had been in mental hospitals from 9 to 26 years. Furthermore, the long-time interest in practical techniques for social restoration of mental patients has only recently begun to have effect. Whatever favorable results prove valid and lasting should not be hastily attributed to hygiene factors alone. The dual feature of the motivation-hygiene concept deserves careful consideration. Hygiene factors may alter the degree of mental illness, but motivating or self-actualizing factors may be the *only* factors effective in developing mental health.

We recognize that the stress on positive health factors is in keeping with the current zeitgeist. *Traditional* research on mental health neglected these factors, but more recently they have received strong support in a variety of developments: research around the concept of creativity, the developing theme of behavior primacy drives, and the activation studies of schizophrenic patients. The motivation-hygiene concept of mental health will not initiate such research, which has already appeared from a variety of sources. Nevertheless, the two-dimensional theory and the tentative but specific group of factors under each dimension may prove important as a step toward an effective conceptual model.

The motivation-hygiene concept and psychotherapy

Frederick Herzberg
and
Roy M. Hamlin

In the preceding article in this chapter,[1] the authors of this article presented a theory of mental health which arose out of some recent research findings in the area of job satisfaction. It is our purpose now to comment on how this theory would alter present concepts and practices in the treatment of mental disorders.

To guide the reader, we shall first synopsize the *motivation-hygiene concept of mental health.* Then we shall suggest the implications this theory has for psychotherapy. Following this, we shall relate our suggestions for therapy to the premises and practices of current approaches to treatment—specifically, physical therapies for mental illness and dynamic, ego, and social psychotherapies. Finally, we shall offer a few principles for a psychotherapeutic approach more in tune with the conceptions offered in the motivation-hygiene concept of mental health.

SYNOPSIS OF THE CONCEPT

The motivation-hygiene concept grew out of a study of job attitudes.[2] In that study, as we noted in the preceding article, engineers and accountants reported two kinds of experiences: a period in their professional career when their job satisfaction was very high, and a period when it was very low. They reported the *factors* which caused this satis-

---

[1] Frederick Herzberg and Roy Hamlin, "A Motivation-Hygiene Concept of Mental Health," *Mental Hygiene,* vol. 45 (July 1961), pp. 394–401.

[2] See Frederick Herzberg, Bernard Mausner, and Barbara Snyderman, *The Motivation to Work* (New York: John Wiley & Sons, 1959).

faction or dissatisfaction, their *attitudes* at the time, and the effects on their adjustment.

In general, they talked about one set of factors leading to satisfaction and a distinctly different set leading to dissatisfaction. To summarize, the satisfaction or motivator factors included achievement, responsibility, and goal-directed effort. The dissatisfaction or hygiene factors included supervision by others, interpersonal relations, working conditions, salary, and company policy and administrative practices.

When the respondents reported feeling happy with their jobs, they most frequently described factors related to their tasks to events that indicated to them that they were successful in the performance of their work, and to the possibility of professional growth. Conversely, when feelings of unhappiness were reported, they were associated with conditions that surrounded the doing of the job. These events suggest to the individual that the context in which he performs his work is unfair or disorganized and as such represents an unhealthy psychological work environment.[3]

The motivation-hygiene concept of job attitudes suggests that satisfaction on the job depends on *task-oriented factors,* whereas dissatisfaction depends on context factors or *surrounding conditions.* The factors that lead to satisfaction do not influence dissatisfaction, and vice versa. One set of factors is not the opposite of, or the absence of, the other set. Nor is one set primary to the other. Each of the factors serves different functions—one to avoid unpleasantness and the other to actualize the individual self.

Reproduced as Figure 1 is the figure from *The Motivation to Work* which led to the construction of the above hypotheses. Much more substantiating data describing the study is presented in the book; this figure, however, does portray the essentially dual nature of job attitudes. The factors listed in this figure are a kind of shorthand for summarizing the "objective" events that each respondent described.

The length of each box represents the frequency with which each factor appeared in the events reported, and the width of the box indicates the duration of time the good or bad job attitude lasted, in terms of a classification of short duration or long duration. A short duration was usually not longer than two weeks, while a long duration attitude change may have lasted for years.

A further word is required on the factor of recognition. When it appeared in a sequence of events describing a job-satisfied period, it usually referred to recognition for a task rather than recognition as a human relations tool divorced from any accomplishment. This latter type of recognition does not often serve as a *satisfier.*

The importance of the two distinct sets of factors to research in job

---

[3] Ibid., p. 113.

Figure 1

Comparison of satisfiers and dissatisfiers

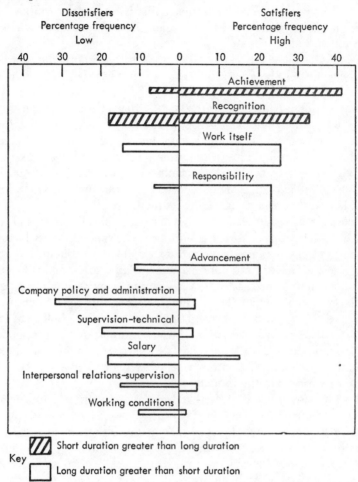

satisfaction can hardly be overestimated. Traditional research in job attitudes has consistently emphasized the betterment of surrounding conditions, largely neglecting the self-actualization factors. On the other hand, there are a number of reservations to the job study. These include:

1. The study depends on verbal reports of past events.
2. The reports considered satisfaction in the work situation only.
3. The respondents were limited to engineers and accountants.

A number of studies have subsequently been completed on a variety of different populations and with significant alterations in methods, suggesting that the motivation-hygiene concept has a considerable degree of general validity. The two sets of factors have emerged with air force personnel,[4] nonprofessional workers,[5] general managers,[6] schizophrenic patients,[7] and physical rehabilitation patients.[8] Age, job tenure, place of work, and other demographic variables show no substantial effect on these relationships.

In our preceding article, we undertook to generalize the motivation-hygiene concept to broader problems of mental health. Briefly, that article makes the following points:

First, it suggests a break with the tradition of a single continuum of mental illness to mental health and argues that we should properly think of each—i.e., mental illness and mental health—as two distinct continua. It defines the mental illness continuum in terms of the success with which an individual avoids unpleasantness in his life. The mental health continuum, in contrast, is defined in terms of the success with which an individual *approaches* psychological growth.

Second, it lists distinct factors which determine the potential adjustment of an individual on each continuum. The mental illness factors describe essentially the environment or extraindividual stimuli. Included in environmental factors are interpersonal relationships and such social-psychological influences as status, as well as the more tangible aspects of the physical environment. The mental health factors refer to occurrences which provide opportunity for self-actualization or psychological growth —task challenges, task achievements, responsibilities. The former factors essentially describe the attractiveness of the context of an individual's life space, and the latter factors describe what is happening to the psychological capabilities of the individual.

Third, the theory indicates that the environmental factors can only provide for the absence of mental illness, and they have no power to bring forth mentally healthy states. They also only help to avoid mental illness for a short time and must constantly be replenished and improved in order to keep the individual from being sick. This description of the factors as environmental and preventive has led us to use the term "hygiene factors" in analogy with its medical meaning of environmental and preventive.

Fourth, the mental health factors serve primarily to promote mental

---

[4] Paul Schwartz, *Attitudes of Middle Management Personnel* (Pittsburgh: American Institute for Research, 1951).

[5] John Gibson, "Sources of Job Satisfaction and Job Dissatisfaction as Interpreted from Analyses of Write-in Responses" (Ph.D., dissertation, Western Reserve University, Cleveland, 1962).

[6] Schwartz, *Attitudes of Middle Management Personnel.*

[7] R. M. Hamlin and R. S. Nemo, "Self-Actualization in Choice Scores of Improved Schizophrenics," *Journal of Clinical Psychology*, vol. 18 (January 1961), pp. 51–54.

[8] Ranette Fantz, "Motivation Factors in Rehabilitation" (Ph.D., dissertation, Western Reserve University, Cleveland, 1962).

health while having little effect in producing mental illness. No one is made sick by lack of growth potential, just as no one is made healthy by an abundance of hygiene factors. In order to emphasize the individual's active responsibility for psychological growth, in contrast to the passive avoidance nature of the response to hygiene factors, we choose to call mental health factors the motivators.

Fifth, while all organisms seek to satisfy both their avoidance-hygiene needs and their approach-motivator needs, the mentally ill person seeks to achieve positive meaning in life via the hygiene factors. Since the hygiene factors do not possess the qualities to provide for psychological growth, such individuals have a pathological inversion of their motivations. It is this inversion which defines the mentally ill rather than the actual environmental circumstances or growth opportunities.

IMPLICATIONS FOR PSYCHOTHERAPY

What are the implications of such a theory for psychotherapy? It seems to suggest that therapy has emphasized hygiene factors and mental illness. The motivator factors and mental health have been consistently neglected. It becomes apparent that therapy oriented toward the removal of unpleasantness coming from either environmental sources or inter-psychic sources can achieve only a temporary nonillness state. The task of therapy is more fundamentally the correction of an inversion of motivation—specifically, the redirection of a person's goals for proper satisfaction away from the hygiene factors to the motivator factors.

It is not necessarily the achievement of psychological growth that is the primary goal of therapy, but the instilling within the patient of the desire to seek growth. It is this motivational change that is essential. Perhaps circumstances make it impossible for the patient to achieve growth, and consequently he will not achieve a place on the mental health continuum. However, if the desire for growth is there and he seeks his satisfaction from growth, an adverse hygiene will only have a noxious effect on him, rather than the mental illness effect.

The mental illness stems from the combination of the noxiousness and the desire for happiness from its avoidance. If therapy can eliminate the latter—the seeking of happiness from avoidance of unpleasantness—it will serve first to vitiate the effects of unpleasantness, and, second, it will bring the individual to a state whereby it becomes possible for him—given the opportunity—to become mentally healthy, as distinct from rising merely to the state of no mental illness. We suggest that neither the resolving of psychological psychic conflicts or the environmental counterparts nor the achievement of psychological growth is the primary goal of psychotherapy.

Instead, the primary goal is to bring about a motivational pattern which corresponds to the expectations that the two-dimensional motivation-hygiene concept of mental health suggests—i.e., the satisfaction of the hygiene needs to serve only the avoidance, defensiveness, and negative results. Only in the hygiene seeker is there a pathological dependence on hygiene needs and a lack of striving for a positive approach, happiness, and growth results. It is only the satisfaction of the motivator needs that will bring about these latter consequences. The task of psychotherapy is to bring about this nonoverlapping, two-dimensional motivational pattern within the patient.

Let us use an analogy here. A child learning to ride a bicycle perhaps offers an illustration of what we mean. We can provide the most sanitary conditions where the child attempts to master the riding of a bicycle. We can also provide as much encouragement and love as the most conscientious parent has to offer. But the fact is that the child will never learn to ride a bicycle unless you give him a bicycle! He needs the substance of the task to achieve this growth; hygiene improvement will not do it. Safeguarding him from injury, from failure, or from loss of parental affection serves no effective purpose without the means by which he can accomplish the achievement—the bicycle, in this case.

It is so obvious in this illustration, but think for a moment of the lack of tasks that is endemic in so many life situations (particularly the job) and in which we expect the person to behave in mentally mature, self-actualizing ways. This over obvious point has major implications for mental health, for we tend to forget the ingredients necessary for health by overworshipping the ingredients necessary for avoiding ill health. We expect the hygiene factors to accomplish both goals.

Now let us give the child his bicycle. He wants to learn to ride because he will avoid the unpleasantness of dad's disappointment, the unpleasantness of peers' derision, the unpleasantness of his inability to participate in play activities. What is the child's motivation to learn and grow? Avoidance! Is he seeking happiness because by learning to ride he avoids unpleasantness? Which factors are involved in his satisfaction? Good relationships, acceptance, or satisfactions with being more capable than he was before he learned to ride? From a child we expect mostly the former and hope for some of the latter. We accept the transitory nature of most of his hobbies, interests, and play. But for an adult, the significance of the task should have a much greater meaning.

Music lessons for children provide another good example, for they are rarely complied with because of the intrinsic maturational potentialities, but rather because of the satisfactions derived from the avoidance of unpleasant consequences. The child who complies because he delights in the task and achieves satisfactions from accomplishment and mastery is so very psychologically different. We say that he has a healthy approach to his music lessons, as opposed to the avoidance of unhealthy consequences from failure to comply. Now should we wish to instill love and desire for his music, can we be effective by increasing the hygiene surrounding his practice? All that this would accomplish is to make the task *less unpleasant—not more rewarding.*

By reinforcing those factors that serve the avoidance-hygiene needs, we do *not* reinforce the growth-motivator needs. The child may become accomplished on the piano by attention to hygiene needs alone because he happens to have talent and is capable of learning with negative motivations. The point is that his accomplishment represents no psychological growth.

If the aim of the music lesson is accomplishment for accomplishment's sake, to provide a mechanism for psychological growth, then the purpose of the lessons must be the channeling of his motivation to seek satisfactions from piano playing, rather than seeing the accomplishment as a means of satisfying avoidance motivations. The attempt to do just this is psychotherapy, as defined here. Whether the child achieves satisfactions from piano playing or not is a specific matter. Not all children's activities must lead to growth; however, for proper health, the distinction of what motivations lead to growth and what motivations lead to the avoidance of difficulty must eventually become internalized by a child before he can become an actualizing adult.

THERAPY PHILOSOPHIES

We have said that the goal of psychotherapy is the reorientation of an individual's sources for satisfaction. We hasten to emphasize that hygiene needs are important, but we recognize what their limitations are. At this point, perhaps it might be helpful to review some major therapy philosophies within the framework of the comments already made. The presentation will cover: (1) physical therapies for mental illness, (2) dynamic, ego, and social psychotherapies, and (3) some guiding principles for psychotherapy based on the motivation-hygiene concept.

Physical therapies

The physical, or organic, therapies have achieved a few impressive successes with mental illness. Paresis and cretinism stand out as classical examples, and recent progress with phenylketonuria follows the classical model. Shock, lobotomy, and tranquilizers represent newer electrical, surgical, and chemical approaches.

The basic premise involves a therapist who takes responsibility, solves a problem, and performs a cure. The motivator factors of achievement, responsibility, and goal-directed effort lie clearly with the therapist, not with the patient. Procedures, as well as the premise, foster the patient's passive hygiene role. The patient can only concern himself with factors over which he has no control—hygiene factors. His self-actualization tendencies are neglected or even systematically extinguished. The chains that Pinel struck from his charges are replaced by even stronger bonds, and the unhealthy mental condition is perpetuated, becomes fixed and chronic. At best, the patient's capacity for mental health is taken from him at the same time that his mental illness is alleviated.

The physical treatment of certain physical conditions accords more attention to motivator considerations than is the case in most psychotherapies. Two of these physical conditions serve to illustrate the point.

First, progressive methods of treating the physically disabled, such as paraplegics and the blind, have placed responsibility with the patient and have emphasized motivator factors. Even here, a certain reluctance and lack of explicit acceptance have characterized the shift to positive self-actualization. The label "rehabilitation" sets the procedures apart from psychotherapy. Therapy comes first and is basic; rehabilitation comes later and enjoys less status. The possibility that the motivator factors play a major role from the beginning clashes with the organic approach to mental illness. Yet, particularly with neuroses and psychoses, this possibility (of deficient "ego strength" as a major consideration) deserves attention.

The second physical condition—not generally regarded as disease—which deserves mention is pregnancy. Here the patient retains responsibility, achievement, and goal-directed labor. The therapist ranks somewhere along with the husband, often indispensable but not the star performer in self-actualization. The model may serve for much of psychotherapy. The focus is on bringing forth healthy life, rather than on removing disease. Only the mental patient can take responsibility for and achieve mental health. The therapist eliminates or lessens hygiene interference along the way.

With physical therapies for mental disease, the extensive use of tranquilizers in schizophrenia over the past six years provides the best single illustration of the motivation-hygiene thesis. In our preceding article we refer briefly to the research picture in regard to chemotherapy and motivator therapy. Since that paper was published, Hordern has presented a scholarly and thoughtful review on the tranquilizers, reaching remarkably similar conclusions.[9]

The ataractic drugs (tranquilizers) have had striking success, chiefly in larger hospitals, with limited staff, where little attention could be given to activating and socially stimulating long-neglected patients. The drugs have tremendously lessened social disturbance on hospital wards and have favorably altered the attitude of staff toward patients. At the same time, the tranquilizers do not deprive patients of the capacity to respond. In well-staffed, progressive hospitals the value of the newer drugs has been less apparent: in these settings, self-actualization had already been

---

[9] Anthony Hordern, "Psychiatry and the Tranquilizers," *New England Medical Journal*, vol. 265 (September 1961), pp. 584–88, 634–38.

fostered. The major contribution of the drugs may well be that they create a situation which frees time and energy for motivator therapy: emphasis on personal responsibility, achievement, purposeful effort, and progressive advancement.

The physical therapies focus on alleviating mental illness. They establish conditions which lessen distress-hygiene conditions. These conditions, however, have *little positive effect* in developing mental health, which depends on motivator or self-actualization factors. The importance of psychotherapy along with physical therapies has been repeatedly emphasized, as with the various shock therapies. The psychotherapies that have been advocated, however, have put the same overemphasis on hygiene factors—surrounding conditions which determine the patient's behavior. The patient's own self-actualization has been relatively neglected. These traditional models for psychotherapy will be considered next.

Depth, ego, and social therapies

The basic premise of the dynamic or depth therapies holds that the patient attains mental health by resigning himself to determinants. Two classes of determinants govern behavior: biological constitution and childhood experience (instincts and the unconscious). These are hygiene factors—surrounding conditions under which the individual must perform his life tasks. No healthy, positive action can change the past.

The method of these depth therapies, as well as the premise, focuses on hygiene. The therapist directs the patient's attention to infantile conflicts, to defenses against anxiety, and to interpersonal relations. The classical techniques of free association, dream analysis, and transference parallel these hygiene aspects. The patient learns to seek satisfaction in surrounding conditions, and by escaping from stress. The positive health factors of responsibility, achievement, and purposeful effort receive secondary attention.

At best, self-actualization is a bonus which automatically follows once the individual resigns himself to his sexual drives and the mistakes of his mother. At worst, and more typically, initiative and action are seen as evidences of pathology. The individual has not yet resigned himself to the determinants of his behavior. He is still sick because he is still trying to achieve, take responsibility, and impose purpose on his efforts. This hygiene bias in depth therapies leads to the embarrassing necessity of labeling effective behaviors with negative terms: the well-adjusted man who earns a million dollars is overcompensating; the star professional football guard is a masochist; and the man who loves his wife is reliving an Oedipus complex.

The concept of scientific determinism molded early psychotherapy. Essentially, the thesis is that biological drives and unconscious urges control the individual. He in turn has little control over these forces or over his own destiny. The individual person's achievement, responsibility, and effort have insignificant importance. They are, indeed, an illusion stemming from the outmoded Age of Reason and the idea of the Rational Man —"science" demonstrates that evolution and irrational forces determine man's behavior. Man's responsibility and achievement are myths. His efforts are healthy and free of anxiety only when they conform to biological and cultural forces. Any deviation, originality, or initiative represents mental illness.

The degradation of the individual came about in logical steps. Galileo destroyed the illusion that man's world was the center of the universe. Darwin exploded the myth of man's divine origin. Finally, Freud debunked the idea of man's rational mind. Rather rapidly, man lost his world, his soul, and his mind. Science reduced man to a puppet. In effect, man was no longer responsible for his behavior, for his thoughts, for his soul, or for his fellow man. Laws of physics, evolution, and unconscious instincts ruled the individual.

Dynamic therapy developed under the influence of such scientific determinism. The tremendous impact of psychoanalysis on literature, art, and cultural institutions speaks for itself. As psychotherapy, the contribution has been less astounding. Yet, in spite of the lack of firm evidence, there can be no serious doubt that psychoanalytic therapy has helped many individual patients. It may well be that these successes occur only with patients who are highly motivator oriented to begin with. These strong egos *persistently seek satisfaction in responsibility, achievement, and effort.* The prolonged focus on hygiene during the course of psychoanalysis does not undermine their basically healthy orientation, and it does alleviate hygiene stresses. Thus, analysis succeeds chiefly with educated, financially solvent neurotics, not merely because they can pay the fees but also because they have positive assets initially. With psychotics, and with those neurotics where motivator factors and ego strength are primary considerations, the results of psychoanalysis are disappointing.

Two recently completed investigations lend support to this thesis. The first, by Hamlin and Nemo, was conducted on a population of chronic schizophrenic patients at the Danville Veterans Administration Hospital in Illinois.[10] Twenty-three improved subjects were compared with 23 unimproved subjects on a test presumed to measure a motivator v. hygiene orientation. Scores were obtained by a manifest content analysis of the verbally stated reasons given by each patient for his choice of 40 activity preference items. The results and conclusions were as follows:

The improved subjects obtained higher motivator scores than the unimproved ($p < .001$). These scores reflect a tendency to seek satisfaction in self-actualizing behaviors: achievement, responsibility, and goal-directed efforts.

---

[10] Hamlin and Nemo, "Self-Actualization of Improved Schizophrenics." Details of this study are given in the next article.

The improved subjects also obtained lower hygiene scores ($p < .001$). An incidental comparison showed that college students obtained higher motivator and lower hygiene scores than either schizophrenic group.

The second study concerned patients in a rehabilitation hospital.[11] Each patient was given a motivator-hygiene score based upon the factors which he used in describing events when he felt exceptionally happy or unhappy in the hospital. The patients were divided into two groups— the motivator seekers and the hygiene seekers—based upon the number of sequences which were classified as motivator oriented and the number of sequences which were classified as hygiene oriented. Predictions were made as to which of the two groups would have more patients in an improved category after physical therapy training. The criterion was an index of improvement in activities of daily living. The results showed a significant difference ($p < .02$) between the two groups in favor of the patients classified as "motivators."

Depth therapies today employ techniques so diverse and eclectic that they encompass most of the self-actualization and motivator factors. However, two difficulties impede progress. First, the concept of determination holds on, like the Old Man of the Sea riding the back of Sinbad. Second, the basic approach fosters a hygiene orientation: the patient *learns to seek satisfaction by escaping* from surrounding stress, rather than by achievement or self-actualization. The motivator person grows in new behaviors of which he was formerly incapable: the hygiene person develops insight into stresses of which he was formerly not aware. The dynamic therapies not only appeal to the hygiene seeker; they make hygiene seekers out of more healthy motivator seekers.

From the very beginning, the psychoanalytic movement carried the seeds for motivator therapy. "The highest mental achievement that is possible in a man is that of struggling successfully against an inward passion for the sake of a cause to which he has devoted himself." This line from Freud's *The Moses of Michelangelo* has not caught on among his disciples.

Only when the hygiene bias began to submerge the individual, the self, and the motivator factors did Adler go off on a separate course. His individual psychology passed through stages of depth therapy, ego therapy, and social therapy in a somewhat wavering fashion. For convenience, his approach may be considered an ego therapy, although his early emphasis on inferiority was more dynamic and his later concept of social interest more social.

The guiding feature of Adler's psychotherapy centered around the individual—the self or ego. His major thesis clashed with Freud's from the beginning. This clash can be stated simply: Freud saw man as the victim of determinism, whereas Adler saw man as capable of determining events.

---

[11] Fantz, "Motivation Factors in Rehabilitation." Details of this study are given in the next article.

Freud's patient could only resign himself to his fate. Adler's patient could do something.

Adler's ego or self-actualization psychology, however, never threw off the hygiene considerations of 19th-century determinism. Context conditions had to explain any positive tendencies in the individual. Organ inferiority, masculine protest, order of birth, and a "style of life" based on childhood experiences cause the individual to strive and to develop purpose. Man never achieves or puts forth effort except as a reaction to maladjustment or distress. Only in his later writings did Adler move toward the obvious possibility that life is a positive force in itself, that man has the potentiality for achievement, responsibility, and purposeful effort as a fundamental characteristic.

The problems of self-determination, "free will," and teleology turned Adler to philosophy. The relatively recent emphasis of science on cultural evolution as distinct from gene evolution had only an early glimmering of influence on Adler's concepts. Integrators of scientific thought today suspect that the species of man has discarded biological evolution and has replaced this all-oppressive determinant by culture, accumulative knowledge, and science.

Man does not evolve wings; he builds planes. He does not breed diabetes out of the species; he discovers drugs. So potent are the achievements of his ingenuity that they *prevent,* or cancel out, biological evolution. Bodily wings offer no survival value. The fittest, who do not have diabetes, survive and breed no more successfully than the diabetic. Some see the Götterdämerung of the species in this violation of nature. An equally tenable view holds that man, as a species, has assumed responsibility for his own destiny. Like the second stage of a space rocket, cultural evolution has taken off on its own, dropping behind the burned-out launching equipment of Darwinian evolution.

This cultural evolution, or science, incorporates the contributions of an increasing number of individuals. Nevertheless, it is the achievement, responsibility, and purposeful effort of single individuals that determine man's behavior. These are the motivator factors. No longer can man adjust by resigning himself to the powerful determinants imposed upon him. He can only attain mental health, and survive, insofar as he achieves and takes responsibility. The accomplishments of one individual are still insignificant in terms of 10 million years, or of cosmic distances. Yet cultural evolution draws its strength from no other source than individual achievement, responsibility, and purpose.

If there is one self-contained energy unit in the known universe that can lay claim to something comparable to the outmoded concept of free will, it is the individual person. The whole idea of determinism is, of course, circular; but the individual human, as a small unit in a tremendous force, can well hold his own with any other determinant of his own size.

It was logical that Adler should grope toward a somewhat hazy concept of "social interest." He saw this, however, not so much in its relationship to cultural evolution, but more as another hygiene factor: man's behavior is determined by social forces. The individual is still a puppet, dependent on society and culture for his mental health.

The obverse of this view may state the situation more appropriately: society and culture are determined by the achievements and deviations (maladjustments, to Freud) of human individuals. Be that as it may, Adler moved tentatively toward the social psychotherapies, loosely identified with the Harry Stack Sullivan group, and also foreshadowed the laissez-faire ego psychology of such therapists as Carl Rogers. The latter may be set aside for the sake of brevity: in his clearest formulation, Rogers advocated an encouraging situation (nondirection, simple reflection of affect, etc.) which relied on lessening hygiene pressures so as to let the individual grow on his own, *with no specific techniques* for introducing positive achievement, responsibility, and effort. The social therapies require more comment.

The social psychotherapies have developed steadily toward motivator emphasis, but largely within the traditional hygiene premise: mental health depends on escape and resignation. Thus, Fromm and Horney extend depth therapy by adding one more determinant of man's behavior. The individual cannot afford to spend his life in appeasing only evolution and the unconscious; he must also watch out for a new monster, Culture. Interpersonal relations generate conflict, and the healthy person is, at best, one whose distress is minimal. Man creates society to satisfy hygiene needs (instincts, unconscious).

However, the society which he has created turns on him and makes demands contrary to his nature; society warps and frustrates man. The "creative individual" does, indeed, play an increasing role, but chiefly in a futile struggle to alleviate surrounding conditions.

Sullivan employs two intriguing strategies to break even further with depth therapies: a completely new vocabulary and a definition of the "person" in terms of interpersonal operations only. He succeeds in de-emphasizing past determinants by stressing current realities. He also eliminates the individual as a person in his own right. Social variables do not determine the individual's behavior; the person is nothing more than a way of looking at interpersonal events. Sullivan's overall view need not conflict with a realistic balance between motivator and hygiene considerations in therapy. The basic premise, however, emphasizes surrounding conditions. Achievement and action, Sullivan's "energy transformations," serve only to reduce the threat of nontask factors.

Although the basic premise of social therapies stresses hygiene, to the neglect of self-actualization, these therapies do move away from historical determinants and toward present *action*. This trend has led inevitably to motivator elements in technique. The progress toward a motivator-hygiene balance is clearly illustrated in group therapies. It is common practice to divide group procedures roughly into two major classes: depth and activity.

The former emphasize the value of group interaction in alleviating conflicts, interpersonal stresses, and other anxieties stemming from surrounding conditions. The activity group, on the other hand, often centers procedures around a task. Achievement, role responsibility, and productive effort play a major part.

Typically, the distinction between alleviating stress and fostering self-actualization is not sharp. In role playing and psychodrama, for example, action and output of effort are exploited, but they are seen as a means to hygiene ends. The participants develop insight into surrounding persecutions and practice new defenses appropriate for the long-suffering puppet. Indeed, when an activity group is specifically so labeled, it is not generally regarded as psychotherapy. Anker and Walsh, for example, compare group psychotherapy with a "special activity program"; the implication is that only hygiene therapy is psychotherapy.[12] By traditional definition, psychotherapy excludes task-oriented self-actualization.

In line with the same hygiene bias, other activity programs are called milieu therapy. That is, the milieu or surrounding conditions are improved; this is traditional or hygiene therapy. The focus on achievement, responsibility, and effort is often obvious, but these positive health factors are not formally recognized as part of psychotherapy.

The results of Anker and Walsh deserve a further comment. Within the limits of the study, group psychotherapy (hygiene therapy) accomplished essentially nothing with chronic schizophrenic patients. The activity program produced changes "with compelling strength and consistency."

The group activity task was chosen to meet the following criteria:

1. The group should have a definite goal or finished product which may be *achieved* in a relatively short period of time.
2. The goal should be *periodic* so that once the immediate goal is achieved, another similar one—but one presenting new challenges—takes its place.
3. There must be a sufficient range of demand so that patients at all levels of adjustment may *contribute meaningfully* to the goal.
4. The activity must be complex enough so that it will pose meaningful problems to be resolved by the group.
5. This activity must be of such a nature that patients are capable of maintaining it with a *minimum of staff intervention*, particularly professional staff.

---

[12] J. M. Anker and R. P. Walsh, "Group Psychotherapy, a Special Activity Program, and Group Structure in the Treatment of Chronic Schizophrenics," *Journal of Consulting Psychology*, vol. 25 (December 1961), pp. 476–81.

In these criteria, we find the motivator factors specifically spelled out: achievement, responsibility, goal-directed effort, and continuity of growth. That self-actualization takes place in a social setting and receives social *recognition* is clearly recognized in the job attitudes book, *The Motivation to Work.*

Certain developments in the social psychotherapies have moved toward consideration of the motivator factors, at least in *techniques.* Basic *premises* cling stubbornly to a hygiene bias. This discrepancy between (isolated) practices and theory retards development of an effective motivator-hygiene balance in psychotherapy. It is a balance that is called for. Certainly, stress, anxiety, biological constitution, traumatic childhood experiences, and the demands of culture and society cannot be dismissed as unimportant. But psychotherapy does not cure ten million years of evolution, ten thousand years of culture, or six years of childhood long since past.

Therapy changes the behaviors of rather insignificant individuals, now and in the immediate future. In this context, the insignificant person becomes significant. His achievements, his responsibilities, and his efforts should be accorded at least as much respect as the *other* (rather hazy) determinants which furnish a background against which he performs his life tasks. Therapy can help him evade stress or move toward self-actualization. His mental illness can be alleviated or his mental health fostered.

There is much evidence that healthy positive achievement reduces anxiety as effectively as avoidance of stress and adroit defenses. There is no reason to suppose that hygiene considerations come first and are primary, and that self-actualization comes later and is secondary. In fact, psychotics and severely impaired neurotics may be the patients most in need of a motivator focus. These are the individuals whose "ego strength" is least.

Motivation-hygiene therapy

It is premature to specify a detailed model for motivation-hygiene therapy, but at least a tentative sketch can be offered. From what has already been said, four principles for psychotherapy emerge. First, the objective of therapy should be the reorientation of the individual's motivation to seek satisfactions from psychological growth, and not the alleviation of psychological distress.

Sensitivity to psychological stress is as much a function of the orientation of the person as it is of the nature of the stress itself; and a hygiene orientation can only magnify and constantly create new stresses. Some psychological discomfort must be borne—not so much in the stiff-upper-lip tradition, but rather in the sense that it does not need to bar growth activities. We have already emphasized that the satisfaction of avoidance needs does not necessarily precede the satisfaction of actualizing needs.

Second, satisfaction from experiencing growth can only arise when there is opportunity to achieve on some task. The concept of "task" needs to be more broadly interpreted than in the job situation: the healthy organism "responds to that which, through past experience, is immediately significant."[13] The task at hand may be recovery from psychosis, obtaining food, or making friends. The distinction is not a difference in goals or needs but lies rather in the approach—a task-oriented approach in the face of difficulties, or a difficulty-oriented approach in the face of a task.

Third, the therapist must make absolutely clear the distinction between hygiene therapy and motivator therapy. Hygiene therapy can provide alleviation for some pain—some supportive base to *maintain* the individual while he climbs aboard a task. It cannot, however, make him mentally healthy. The motivator side of therapy stresses that the firepower and the growth urge has to come from the patient: but the therapist does more than reassure, explain, sit and wait, provide affection and acceptance. This is where the early Rogerians fell into the "self-actualization is a bonus" trap.

The major shift calls for specifying what the therapist can do to bring about a self-actualizing need within the individual. The therapist cannot do the patient's behaving for him; but he can set, program, and manipulate the motivator factors—responsibility, effort, and sequence of achievement steps. He can orient his perceptions to the positive assets of the patient, at least in addition to surveying all that is warped, bound, and sick. In order to direct the patient to task achievement and growth, it is essential that the therapist see the *potentials* that exist.

Fourth, as a corollary to the third principle, the therapist must avoid teaching or encouraging the patient's view of his illness as determined by forces beyond his control. Psychodynamic explanations of symptomatology, focusing on the early origins of emotional problems and the repeated assertions that the patient is a *victim* of unconscious and infantile needs, can only serve to reinforce his resigned attitude toward his difficulties and lead to a personal definition of an avoidance organism.

How these principles are formed into a specific technology of psychotherapy is the task and challenge for the mental health professions. The ingredients for the technology lie dispersed among all the current approaches; and perhaps what is required is not new methods, but a rebuilding of psychotherapy out of planks from the many structures that have proved architecturally unsound.

---

[13] Robert Cohn, "Language and Behavior," *American Scientist*, vol. 49 (December 1961), pp. 502–8.

Motivation and mental health: Some empirical evidence

As noted in the lead article of this chapter, Motivation-Hygiene Theory defines mental health as arising from the recognition of motivational needs. The "abnormal" case, the hygiene seeker, does not manifest these concerns, and the hygiene seeker can be identified by the absence of motivational content in his descriptions of the kinds of events and choices that markedly influence his life. Justification for discerning the phenomenon of motivational inversion in hygiene seeking comes most convincingly from the ability to reliably measure differences in motivational needs among individuals, on the basis of which it is possible in some meaningful fashion to predict differences in their behavior. This procedure follows the traditions of scientific investigations in psychology, which have their major origins in the study of individual differences.

This article presents several of the studies which have tested the relationship between mental health indicators and the realization of motivational needs. The review is not confined to investigations of the most dysfunctional members of our society because individual recognition of motivational needs is expected to be a meaningful characteristic of human behavior, whether among successful businessmen (see the article, "Motivational Types," in Chapter 2), college students, or schizophrenic groups. It should also be noted that an attempt has been made to describe a few of the many investigations which as yet are unpublished and therefore are not readily available to the public, other than through university libraries.[1]

The most logical beginning of an empirical inquiry into the relevance of motivator inversion is within clinical populations. Simply put, do individuals hospitalized for mental disorders display a different motivational pattern? Roy Hamlin, a collaborator in the two preceding articles in this section, and one of his students, Robert Nemo, sought an answer

---

[1] Some of these studies were previously reported in my book *Work and the Nature of Man* (New York: Thomas J. Crowell Co., 1966).

to this question in one of the first published articles on motivation and mental health (Hamlin & Nemo, 1961). They compared improved with unimproved schizophrenics, and a third group of college students was used as an additional control. To determine motivational patterns the *Choice-Motivator Scale* developed by Hamlin was used. In this test subjects are asked to make choices between two comparable occupations and to describe the reasons for their choices. These reasons are then classified as either hygiene or motivational by independent raters (reliabilities are above 90 percent), and each subject is given a score based on the number of motivation and hygiene reasons he used to explain his choices.

Hamlin and Nemo hypothesized that college students would give the greatest number of motivator choices, followed by the improved schizophrenics, with the least number of such choices given by the group classi-

Table 1

Numbers of motivator and hygiene reasons given by three groups (Hamlin & Nemo, 1961)

Group	Motivator	Hygiene
Students	44	22
Improved	29	29
Unimproved	16	47

fied as unimproved schizophrenics. Table 1 shows the results of their investigation in terms of the average percentage of motivator and hygiene reasons given by the three groups (the percentages do not sum to 100 percent because some responses were not usable). One look at the table shows that the college students did, in fact, give more motivator reasons than the schizophrenics, and the improved schizophrenics did better in this respect than those classified as unimproved. The differences were all highly statistically significant.

This study by itself does not confirm that mental health depends upon a motivational orientation. Surely one could ask many questions about the other differences among the groups which could account for the Hamlin and Nemo results, and the method left much to be desired. Herzberg, Mathapo, Wiener, and Wiesen (1974) report two studies which provide more conclusive evidence of the motivation-hygiene distinction between mental health and mental illness.

In most studies of Motivation-Hygiene Theory which use the critical-incident method, a proportion of the data (estimated for normal samples to be around 19 percent) does not appear to fit the model; that is, some hygiene events are called satisfying and some motivational events are called dissatisfying. These data are called slippages in Motivation-Hygiene Theory (and disconfirmations of the theory by critics). I have suggested in the article on organizational profiles ("Motivation-Hygiene Profiles," Chapter 2) that some of this slippage is due to experimental error and some is due to organizational abnormalities. What Herzberg et al. (1974) did in their two studies was to show that some of the slippage is also due to motivational inversions of the people interviewed, rather than to problems of the organization, experimenter biases, or Motivation-Hygiene Theory.

The authors collected five positive critical events, along with two negative events, from their subjects, 123 newly admitted patients of a Veterans' Administration hospital. Each of these patients received a motivation inversion score based on the number of times they described a hygiene event as the cause of positive feelings. The next step was to define a criterion for mental disorder, a difficult problem in any study which attempts to differentiate clinical and normal populations. Instead of identifying groups based on professional judgments alone, as Hamlin and Nemo did, Herzberg et al. used a series of indicators, all of which had been used successfully in the past to distinguish severity of mental disorder.

For paper-and-pencil tests, the authors relied on three *Minnesota Multiphasic Personality Inventory* subscales,[2] Barron's *Ego Strength Scale*,[3] and adapted forms of a *Personal Report Checklist Questionnaire* by Langner and Michael[4] and a *Physical Correlates Questionnaire* developed by Gurin, Veroff, and Feld.[5] For historical data, often reported to be the best predictor of future problems, the authors used *severity of diagnosis*, the *number of hospitalizations*, and the *total length of hospitalizations*. There would be debate on whether any one of these measures was a truly valid criterion of mental disorder. Taken together, however, we can assume that the principal manifestations of mental disorder are represented, at least as far as our current understanding of these disorders permits.

The results confirmed the hypothesis in every case. Motivator inversions were related to illness scores on each of the criteria. Table 2, reproduced from the Herzberg et al. study, summarizes the data for five of the criteria.

These authors also reported a second study which replicated the Hamlin and Nemo results with a different group—50 schizophrenic outpatients. To assess motivation, they used the critical-events method of

[2] S. R. Hathaway and J. C. McKinley, *Manual for the Minnesota Multiphasic Personality Inventory* (New York: Psychological Corporation, 1967).

[3] Frank Barron, "An Ego Strength Scale Which Predicts Response to Psychotherapy," *Journal of Consulting Psychology*, vol. 17 (1953), pp. 327–33.

[4] T. S. Langner and S. T. Michael, *Life Stress and Mental Health* (New York: Free Press of Glencoe, 1963).

[5] Gerald Gurin, Joseph Veroff, and Sheila Feld, *Americans View Their Mental Health* (New York: Basic Books, 1960).

the previous study. Also, they modified the *Choice-Motivator Scale* used by Hamlin and Nemo in order to obtain a higher percentage of scoreable responses. They selected a single criterion of what they called "global disorder," the *number of days the patients had been hospitalized,* and divided their sample into high and low groups based on records of internment. They found that the less hospitalization, the less evidence there was of motivator inversion and the higher the scores on motivator orientation.

Beginning with the Hamlin and Nemo study, these research projects were able to make finer and finer distinctions between mentally healthy and mentally ill, based on the predictions of Motivation-Hygiene Theory.

Table 2

Relationships between motivator inversions and average scores on five measures of global mental disorder (Herzberg et al., 1974)

Global mental disorder measures	Number of inversions				
	0–1	2	3	4	5
Ego strength......................	42	42	39	34	35
Personal-problems checklist......	43	45	46	50	55
Psychosomatic symptoms........	33	35	41	44	46
Number of hospitalizations.......	2.5	2.1	2.8	3.8	4.3
Length of hospitalizations (in months).....................	9.0	5.5	10.2	16.9	15.4

Note: All relationships are statistically significant.

Differences in motivational patterns were found among college students and improved and unimproved schizophrenics, and varying degrees of mental disorder were found among hospitalized and outpatient groups. These studies demonstrate that motivational orientation and its counterpart, motivational inversion, are closely linked with concepts of mental health and mental illness.

Going beyond this demonstration, however, a question often asked is whether other conditions in the immediate environment of the patients could account for the differences both in motivator inversion and degree of disorder—that is, living or having lived in a hospital environment. There is a dilemma here because one of the most acceptable indicators of severe mental disorder is hospitalization. The problem is akin to defining criminality based on the length of time in prison. From a theoretical perspective, changes in the motivational opportunities of the setting can affect the motivations of the person. Mental health, in terms of Motivation-Hygiene Theory, develops out of enriched environments which provide positive experiences in achievements, responsibility, advancement, and the like. Further, we can expect these elements to be frequently missing in institutional settings.

In addition to their two studies reviewed here, Herzberg et al. (1974)

tested for differences between hospital and work environments by asking the patients to describe two kinds of critical events, those that occurred in the hospital and those that occurred at work. Of the positive work experiences of the patients, 64 percent were motivators. For these same patients, only 30 percent of the positive hospital experiences also contained motivational content. The environment of the hospital clearly emphasized hygiene. We would expect that, regardless of the severity of the mental disorder, the longer a person stayed in the hospital, the fewer opportunities he would have for motivation and the more likely he would be to display motivator inversions. The hospitalization of patients, therefore, cannot be distinguished from the effects of deep-rooted differences in motivational patterns in these studies.

These problems are typical in the psychological sciences whenever attempts are made to prove the causes of any phenomenon such as mental disorder. They are resolved only through numerous experiments in a variety of settings in which scores on one variable, such as motivator inversion, can be shown to predict future behavior, while holding constant other potential influences. Usually this is done in one of two ways: either the environment is changed, with the expectation that it will change behavior (as in job enrichment studies, which predict more motivated performance from the better jobs), or future performance is predicted based on individual differences such as the number of motivator inversions.

A number of studies have used these procedures to test hypotheses derived from Motivation-Hygiene Theory concepts of mental health. Ranette Fantz (1962), in her doctoral dissertation under my direction, reported a predictive study using patients who had been hospitalized for severe physical disabilities. She reasoned that those patients with a motivator orientation would show more progress in rehabilitation than those who showed a hygiene orientation. These patients were not classified as mentally ill and came from numerous occupational backgrounds. For some of them it was their first major hospitalization.

Fantz used the critical-incident survey technique to collect six positive events, four from hospital experiences and two from previous work experience. Each of the 21 patients was classified as a hygiene seeker if more than three of the six events were hygiene; otherwise, he or she was classified as a motivator seeker.

Progress in rehabilitation was measured with independent ratings of six functions: bathing, dressing, going to the toilet, locomotion, continence, and eating. The occupational therapy department made these ratings two times; once when the patients were given the critical-incident interview and later just before they left the hospital (or three months after the first rating if they were still hospitalized).

The results of the study are reproduced in Table 3. Eight of the nine patients classified as motivator seekers were rated as improved. Only 3

Table 3

Relationship of motivational pattern to improvement in rehabilitation
(Fantz, 1962)

	Improved subjects	Not Improved	Total
Motivation seeker..........................	8	1	9
Hygiene seeker............................	3	9	12
Total.................................	11	10	21

of the 12 hygiene seekers showed similar improvement. These differences were statistically significant. Fantz also classified the patients using only work events and obtained the same trend in the data, as shown in Table 4. Because of the small number involved, however, those results failed to reach statistical significance.

The physically handicapped have an exceedingly difficult task to perform and, in most cases, it is a task for which they have received little preparation. What Fantz has shown through her results is that reliance on the motivators, such as achievement, responsibility, and personal growth, for satisfaction may be the chief characteristic of the person who strives successfully to recover as much as possible from his physical disability. Once again, the results favor a definition of mental health based on individual differences in motivational orientation.

Kenneth Sanvold (1962), a student of Hamlin's, asked a similar question from a slightly different perspective. He reasoned that a motivator orientation depended upon approaching rather than avoiding tasks, but the tasks had to be meaningful, containing opportunities for real achievement. He hypothesized that if he constructed meaningful tasks for even schizophrenic patients, their experiences of achievement would show up in higher scores in motivation orientation. Sanvold used a complex research design in which three different groups, improved and unimproved schizophrenics and normals (volunteers from a nursing aide program), performed either an exceedingly simple or a difficult task. He also varied the "purpose" of the tasks by telling half of the people in each group that their performance would determine whether they would be selected for future tasks. He then looked at before and after scores on the *Choice-*

Table 4

Relationship of work motivations to improvement in rehabilitation
(Fantz, 1962)

	Improved subjects	Not improved	Total
Motivator seeker on the job...............	11	6	17
Hygiene seeker on the job................	0	4	4
Total.................................	11	10	21

Motivator Scale used by Hamlin and Nemo to see if the effort of the task and its purpose would influence motivator orientation. He also used another measure of motivation, verbal responsivity. This measure was obtained by assessing verbal performance of subjects when they were asked to relate stories based on two *Thematic Apperception Test* pictures.[6]

His results were impressive. The tasks that required effort and had purpose improved both verbal responsivity and motivator orientation for all groups. He also found individual differences. The normal subjects were affected only by the degree of effort in the task. For the unimproved schizophrenics, and the improved schizophrenics to a lesser degree, the task itself was not sufficient. For them higher motivation also depended upon receiving more instructions about the purpose of the task.

There appeared to be two separate influences on motivator responses, both of which confirm Motivation-Hygiene Theory concepts. First of all, a task which is meaningful, when approached, increases motivator orientation. Second, people differ on their needs for outside sources of information about the task, in addition to the work itself. The unimproved schizophrenics and the improved schizophrenics seemed to rely on the context surrounding their efforts in order to define the value of their achievements. Training for mental health would then require a gentle guidance toward more self-recognized achievement and a reduction in attention to the context (and its built-in dependencies).

One of the frequently overlooked points of Motivation-Hygiene Theory is that a meaningful task which requires effort is also stressful, and stress is usually seen as prompting avoidance behavior, not motivated performance. In terms of Motivation-Hygiene Theory, however, stressful conditions often provide opportunities to grow psychologically, even though they may be approached with apprehension. It is only the hygiene seeker who attempts to avoid all stressful conditions because of their potentially painful consequences.[7]

H. C. Haywood and Virginia Dobbs of Peabody College explored this relationship between tension-producing situations and motivation orientation. Instead of using patients, Haywood and Dobbs (1963) selected a group of 100 juniors and seniors in high school for their investigation. They asked whether, among normal high school students, there were differences in motivator orientation that could account for why some students seemed to approach stressful situations while others avoided them.

The authors used the *Choice-Motivator Scale* to determine the motivational orientation of the students. An anxiety inventory was used to

---

[6] See J. W. Atkinson (ed.), *Motives in Fantasy, Action and Society* (Princeton, N.J.: D. Van Nostrand, 1958).

[7] This statement is not exactly accurate for some types of hygiene seekers. See Chapter 2.

measure the attitudes of the students toward a number of different tension-producing situations, such as going out on a date or mountain climbing.

The findings supported Motivation-Hygiene Theory predictions. Those who were oriented toward the motivators reported a preference toward approaching rather than avoiding stressful conditions.

Albert Sheridan, under my direction, studied the same phenomena in an experimental study with a slightly different twist. Sheridan (1969) reasoned that unstructured college classrooms would produce stress and opportunities for personal growth which would be ideally suited for those students with a strong motivator orientation. Those with a hygiene orientation could be expected to avoid the stressful conditions and would necessarily do poorly in the unstructured classes.

For this study, 247 students from Case Western Reserve University, all with at least one year of college, were administered the *Job Motivator Inventory*. This test consists of a series of paired comparisons which includes my 16 job attitude factors. Each choice made by the subject is considered either motivator or hygiene oriented. A motivator score for the subject is obtained by determining the number of times a motivator was chosen over a hygiene item. Subjects were classified into two groups based on their scores. Since intelligence could be a factor in this study, it was controlled by comparing the *Scholastic Aptitude Test* scores (used in the selection procedures of most colleges) of the subjects.

The degree of structure of the classes the students had taken was evaluated by trained academic counselors. The counselor rated each course as containing either a greater degree of ambiguity or a greater degree of structure. The performance of the students was measured by their *grade point average* in each of the two different course structures.

The results showed that motivator orientation was significantly related to higher performance in the less structured courses. Also, it was discovered that those students with a hygiene orientation performed better in structured classes than in the ambiguous situation. In these structured classes the hygiene-oriented group performed at the same level as the motivation-oriented group. Those students with a motivation orientation apparently performed reasonably well when told what to do and excelled in the ambiguous classroom situation. The hygiene-oriented students were able to obtain reasonably good grades (in comparison to the motivator group) only when they were given clear instructions.

In another investigation I studied college graduates entering the world of work.[8] The focus of the study was whether motivator orientation could predict the success of the college graduate in a management development program. This program was designed to be tough, and

---

[8] Frederick Herzberg, special study conducted for the College Recruitment Section of AT&T, 1965.

"screening" was based on performance during the training. Motivation orientation was measured in two ways. The *Choice-Motivator Scale* was administered, along with a rating scale containing five motivator and five hygiene factors. The recruit was asked to recall a positive and a negative critical event occurring in his training and check which factors were involved. Job performance assessments, made by the supervisors, were expected to be influenced by these measures of motivation.

The results again substantiated the predictions. High motivation scores on both scales predicted success in the management development program.

This training program, like many others in industry, generated considerable anxiety among the youthful employees. Organizations are well known for creating anxieties, especially in hygiene areas such as job security, status, and supervision. There are also anxieties associated with a challenging job, what I call motivator anxieties. Unfortunately, most companies concentrate on reducing these anxieties by removing the need for talent on the job. The training program provided both kinds of anxieties, but only those graduates who opted for the intrinsic satisfactions from a challenging job assignment were successful.

The distinction between motivator and hygiene anxieties were investigated further by John Taylor in his doctoral dissertation under my direction. Taylor (1976) reasoned that enriched jobs would produce more anxieties about the work itself and fewer hygiene anxieties than would jobs that were not enriched.

At the time of Taylor's study an Orthodox Job Enrichment program underway at a large Air Force installation provided an excellent opportunity to test these hypotheses.[9] Using a questionnaire with a critical-incident format, he asked employees at the base to recall events in their present jobs which made them apprehensive and to describe how they felt about the events and why they felt the way they did.

He first tested whether he could distinguish two kinds of anxieties, motivator and hygiene. He classified the events as either motivators or as hygiene, based on the original factors, achievement, recognition for achievement, and so forth, and then looked at their reasons for the apprehensions. If the employees reported that they were apprehensive because of the job context, such as loss of status or a demotion, the reason was classified as hygiene. On the other hand, if they reported apprehensions because they were unsure how well they were performing the work itself, the reasons were classified as motivators. His results showed that the employee faced with apprehensions about the task saw his anxieties as a challenge to his performance. The employee faced with

---

[9] Frederick Herzberg and Major General Edmund A. Rafalko, "Efficiency in the Military: The Hill Air Force Project," *Personnel*, November–December 1975. This article is reprinted in Chapter 3.

apprehensions about supervision or some other hygiene problem was more concerned about the hygiene consequences.

The next step, and the crucial one, was to compare those people who had enriched jobs with those with comparable but unenriched jobs. Taylor used employees who had experienced changes on their jobs due to the Orthodox Job Enrichment program as the test group and selected a central group from those employees who had the same job classifications but who were not in the program. This test was a strict one, since the job enrichment projects were conducted in places where there had been motivational problems.

The results of this comparison are reproduced in Table 5. These findings showed clearly that the test group reported more motivator anxieties, while the controls reported more hygiene anxieties. The employees in-

Table 5

Total number of motivator anxiety and hygiene anxiety events reported by enriched and nonenriched groups (Taylor, 1976)

	Enriched group	Nonenriched group
Motivator anxiety events......................	23	8
Hygiene anxiety events.......................	12	16

volved in job enrichment were more concerned about how well they were doing their jobs. The employees in the control groups were more concerned with how well they were being treated by their supervisors, their peers, or the company.

The successful use of these studies of high school and college students as well as adult workers to test motivation-hygiene concepts of mental health is of great significance. First, the results show that motivation-hygiene predictions about individual differences hold for other groups besides those who enter hospitals and clinics for mental health services. Second, college students are a critical population. At work, learning is sometimes divorced from the jobs, but for college students their business is learning. Such a growth process is basic for the development of a motivator orientation. The results raise further issues about the quality of our educational institutions, which often appear to be concerned with structuring credits but are circumspect regarding whether they should challenge their students to perform. Hygienic classrooms often mean failure in management development programs for students who do not have the necessary motivation to get the job done.

The importance of motivational needs is not confined to our colleges and universities, nor is it expected to diminish with age and experience. As the Taylor study demonstrated, motivator concerns arising out of needs to do a good job are present in our organizations long after formal schooling has ended. These challenges inherent in the task can be suppressed or enhanced. Too often management chooses to suppress them. Perhaps one of the greatest tragedies in life is represented by the man who is forced to retire because of company policies. There are enough stories of the once healthy executive who turns senile a year or two after retiring, and of the boredom and frustrations of the man or woman cut off from any opportunity to achieve.

I will conclude this review with reports of two studies which investigated some of the problems of those about to retire. In terms of Motivation-Hygiene Theory, a healthy attitude toward retirement is a negative one. Shoukrey Saleh, in his dissertation at Case Western Reserve University, asked this question: Are managers approaching retirement who have high motivator orientations less favorable toward retirement than hygiene-oriented managers? Saleh (1963) used a group of 85 managers, ages 60 to 65, from 12 companies with forced retirement plans to test this hypothesis.

In order to assess motivation he used the *Job Motivation Inventory*, a paired-comparison test in which subjects are asked to choose between hygiene and motivator items.[10] A single motivator score is obtained by counting the number of motivator choices the subjects make. Attitudes toward retirement were obtained by asking the managers how satisfied they were with their upcoming retirement.

Saleh next defined highest and lowest groups based on their motivation scores and tested which groups were the most favorable toward retirement. His results showed clearly that those lowest in motivation were most likely to be pleased with their retirement. Three times as many people in the high-motivator group as in the low-motivator group did not want to retire.

Saleh also looked at the motivator scores of the entire group of pre-retirees and compared them with a younger group. Those approaching retirement showed a marked hygiene orientation, in contrast to the more youthful employees. This result appears to reflect the realities of increasingly fewer and fewer opportunities for motivated performance. On their way out of the business they have less and less to do and are allowed to take on fewer challenging job assignments. The preparation for retirement appears to be an increased hygiene orientation toward working life.

Saleh followed up his study by testing the self-rated job productivity of 350 civil service employees in Canada who were about to retire (Saleh, 1964). He found that those people who still felt that they were productive were unwilling to retire, while those who felt they were contributing little on the job were willing to end their careers.

---

[10] Robert Kahoe, "Development of an Objective Factorial Motivation-Hygiene Inventory" (Ph.D., dissertation, George Peabody College for Teachers, 1966).

Yet, retirement is an inevitable consequence of the aging process, and workers are encouraged to cross this threshold "gracefully." Robert Schiebe, in his doctoral dissertation at Case Western Reserve University, asked how well prepared managers were in adapting to this change. Schiebe (1968) interviewed 65 industrial managers, ranging in age from 50 to 64, and asked them to describe favorable and unfavorable retirements, using a modified critical-incident technique. He also administered a rating scale concerning specific attitudes they had about retirement.

The results of the critical-incident interviews were consistent with Motivation-Hygiene Theory. Favorable retirement was described with motivator items, and unfavorable retirement was discussed with reference to hygiene items. These results are similar to those found by others, confirming the hypothesis that motivator and hygiene factors are important off the job as well as at work. Most preretirees showed a favorable disposition toward retirement (Saleh found this also) and rated their own retirement and those of people in general as pleasant. The motivators were seen as important to successful retirement, along with an acceptance of the inevitable change in their own working lives.

When asked about their plans, however, the managers saw financial planning as more important than planning for what to do. These ratings were much the same, even though the same group rated specific cases of unfavorable retirement as due to inadequate planning for activities. When asked to relate his own plans, the preretirees either gave no plans for activities or the plans they gave were incomplete and unspecified. They recognized their motivational needs and the importance of planning for their satisfaction, but they had not followed through on their own planning.

In the preceding article in this chapter, Herzberg and Hamlin (1963) pointed out that real opportunities must be provided to assist in the development of motivation. It appears that preretirees are not given these opportunities; retirement planning seems to be limited to hygiene factors, such as financial assurance, and does not include the motivators. It is incorrect to assume that even a highly motivated person can figure out what to do without assistance. He has not been educated in this new phase of his life and does not know the alternatives open to him. How often do we find our colleagues expressing dreams of doing all those things they never had time for during their working lives? Yet without training and the time provided by the organization before retirement to learn new skills, the dream of sailing the seven seas may take place from a rocking-chair world. Schiebe's findings not only confirm some of the motivation-hygiene conceptions of mental health, they also suggest a need for major changes in our social policy in order to meet the mental health needs of the retired population.

The studies reviewed in this section confirmed the value of distinguishing among individuals on the basis of their motivational patterns. These findings do not suggest, however, that personnel decisions should be based on motivator scores on the *Choice-Motivator Scale,* for example. These instruments provide only rough estimates of the degree of recognition of motivational needs. The use of such tests to determine careers would not only be an unethical managerial practice, it would be inaccurate and riddled with error. Rather, these studies demonstrate the importance of recognizing motivational needs, both for the individual and for the company. The next step to take in research in this area is in the development of better diagnostic tools for monitoring motivational inversion, and such instruments are currently under development. Of even greater significance is the need to develop specific treatment techniques for individual motivational inversion which can be used by mental health professionals in promoting mental health with their clients.

REFERENCES

Fantz, R. Motivational factors in rehabilitation. Doctoral dissertation, Western Reserve University, 1962.

Hamlin, R. and **Nemo, R.** Self-actualization in choice scores of improved schizophrenics. *Journal of Clinical Psychology,* 1961, *18*, 51–54.

Haywood, H. C. and **Dobbs, V.** *Motivation and anxiety in high school boys.* Peabody Papers in Human Development, vol. 1, no. 9, 1963.

Herzberg, F., and **Hamlin, R. M.** The motivation-hygiene concept and psycotherapy. *Mental Hygiene,* 1963, 47, 384–397.

Herzberg, F., Mathapo, J., Wiener, Y., and **Wiesen, L.** Motivation-hygiene correlates of mental health: An examination of motivational inversion in a clinical population." *Journal of Consulting and Clinical Psychology,* 1974, *42*, pp. 411–419.

Saleh, S. *Report of pre-retirement study.* Ontario Department of Civil Service, 1964.

Saleh, S. A study of attitude change and its effect in the pre-retirement period. Doctoral dissertation, Case Western Reserve University, 1963.

Sanvold, K. The effect of effort and task orientation on the motivator orientation and verbal responsibility of chronic schizophrenic patients and normals. Doctoral dissertation, University of Illinois, 1962.

Schiebe, R. A. The psychological impact of impending retirement of management personnel. Doctoral dissertation, Case Western Reserve University, 1968.

Sheridan, A. J. Behavioral consequences of motivational orientation. Doctoral dissertation, Case Western Reserve University, 1969.

Taylor, J. N. Anxiety concepts in the Motivation-Hygiene Theory. Doctoral dissertation, George Washington University, 1976.

chapter 5

Criticism and defense of Motivation-Hygiene Theory

INTRODUCTION

Since its introduction in published form, Motivation-Hygiene Theory has had a great impact on the field of job attitudes and motivation. It has affected the thoughts and practices of management while stimulating the interest and curiosity of behavioral scientists. Perhaps inevitably, it has also attracted hostile critics. This circle of critics has been relatively small in numbers and range of influence. It has been, however, very vocal and persistent, and it has enjoyed an easy access to the one or two psychological journals dealing with work behavior. Consequently, a major controversy in the history of industrial psychology has been created. While constructive scientific controversy and criticism may refresh thinking, stimulate new ideas, and generally contribute to the dissemination of knowledge, the Motivation-Hygiene Theory controversy has been anything but that. The criticism directed at the theory and its supportive research has been loaded with bitter, destructive, personal overtones. The confusion in the critical literature has been surpassed only by the passion underlying it. It has indeed become a difficult task to separate substance from irrelevance and polemic in much of the critical literature.

This chapter presents two comprehensive articles, one by David Whitsett and Erik Winslow and a second by Benedict Grigaliunas and Yoash Wiener, which review the research critical of Motivation-Hygiene Theory. The latter article has been augmented by the inclusion of the results of two additional studies completed after the publication of the article.[1] The Whitsett and Winslow article deals with studies up to 1966, and the Grigaliunas and Wiener paper analyzes critical research which has appeared in the literature since that time. The two articles are similar in the types of problems they deal with and in their conclusions, and the interested reader will find in them a detailed and analytical presentation of numerous problems relevant to the literature critical of Motivation-Hygiene Theory. As a means of introducing these papers, the discussion which follows roughly outlines some of the most prevalent criticisms and the responses to them given in this chapter.

One of the first criticisms of Motivation-Hygiene Theory to emerge has been that only one method—the critical-incident method—can provide empirical support to the theory. When the critics employed another method—different variants of the rating-scale procedure—to test the theory, the results were not supportive. Since their own method has not supported Motivation-Hygiene Theory, the critics have claimed that the theory is wrong. This claim, of course, is illogical. The fact that another method of testing Motivation-Hygiene Theory has not supported it is meaningless unless it can be demonstrated that such a method is valid and appropriate. One cannot logically employ, for example, a typing skill test to measure IQ and use the results to evaluate a theory of intellectual development.

The rating-scale procedure is not appropriate for testing Motivation-Hygiene Theory because it has several serious limitations. First, since in this procedure employees are forced to rate job factors that have been determined by the researchers and not by themselves, *ratings* of attitudes and feelings may be obtained when none in *reality* may exist. This, of course, produces irrelevant, artificial, and invalid data. Second, cultural-noise responses, value systems, and socially expected responses are too often the product of the rating-scale procedure. Such responses prevent the investigation of basic psychological processes, since they almost always reflect only the influences of a given situation and not the operation of more universal and fundamental processes. Third, the rating-scale procedure has been acknowledged in most textbooks of industrial psychology to suffer from a large array of additional disadvantages: it is easy to fake; it is global and undifferentiating in its assessment; and it is quite unreliable. These problems are especially crucial when the rating-

---

[1] Yoash Wiener, Rimantas Vaitenas, and Frederick Herzberg, "Social Desirability, Repression, and Sensitization as Factors in the Critical Incidents Methods of Motivation-Hygiene Theory" (*Human Resources Management Publication* 75–101, University of Utah, 1975), and Yoash Wiener, Rimantas Vaitenas, Kenneth Klein, and Frederick Herzberg, "Motivation-Hygiene Theory: An Alternative Classification System and Its Relationship to the Defensiveness Hypothesis" (*Human Resources Management Publication* 75–101, University of Utah, 1975). A review of Benedict S. Grigaliunas and Frederick Herzberg, "Relevancy in the Test of Motivation-Hygiene Theory," *Journal of Applied Psychology*, vol. 55 (1971), pp. 73–79, has also been added.

scale procedure—often with a one-item rating scale—is used to investigate sources of highly involved and complex emotional reactions. Motivation-Hygiene Theory, it may be recalled, is concerned with just such job reactions.

Since the rating-scale procedure has been shown to be a highly deficient alternative for the testing of Motivation-Hygiene Theory, the argument that this theory must be supported by more than one method if it is to be considered valid has become clearly unconvincing. New avenues of attack had to be sought by the critics. The focus of their criticism has shifted from singling out the critical-incident method as the *only* method to support Motivation-Hygiene Theory to presenting it as a *biased* method that produces biased results. The critics now claim that the critical-incident method supports Motivation-Hygiene Theory only because of a bias and an artifact imbedded in it, namely "defensive responding."

According to these critics, the critical-incident method tends to pick up specific defensive reactions from people, such as attributing the cause of good work events to themselves and the cause of bad work events to others. This reaction happens to coincide with results that support Motivation-Hygiene Theory. Thus, the critics assert, the supportive results of Motivation-Hygiene Theory are misleading. They do not reflect the motivational nature of man as presented by Motivation-Hygiene Theory but are instead an artifact of ego defensiveness. Therefore, Motivation-Hygiene Theory has no real research support.

The "defensiveness" criticism of Motivation-Hygiene Theory has been the most widespread and the most vocalized. Fortunately, this criticism does not have to remain in the realm of speculation or accusation. Grigaliunas and Wiener review the specific research relevant to this question and discuss two basic empirical investigations of the "defensiveness" criticism, showing clearly that the critical-incident method does not suffer from the "defensiveness" bias.

Even though the "defensiveness" argument has clearly been rejected by empirical tests and investigations, Motivation-Hygiene Theory criticism has not subsided. Instead, it has undergone yet another twist and shift. The critical-incident method itself is not being blamed anymore for being biased or artifactual. On the contrary, it has been hailed—now also by critics—as a very effective research method. The new line of criticism is now directed toward the classification system I used to code the critical incidents. The critics have claimed that this system is not logical and consistent in that it classifies incidents on the basis of both "events and agents" (i.e., what happened in the incident, and who made it happen). They have asserted that had the incidents been classified only by "events," the results would not have supported Motivation-Hygiene Theory. However, the recent investigation by Wiener, Vaitenas, Klein, and Herzberg discussed in Grigaliunas and Wiener shows that the proposed classification system had flaws, not the Herzberg system.

Other issues in the Motivation-Hygiene Theory controversy are also dealt with in detail in this chapter. For example, many critical studies made conclusions about the validity of Motivation-Hygiene Theory by testing hypotheses that could not be logically derived from this theory (e.g., "overall" satisfaction and "importance" hypotheses). Some critical investigations misinterpreted their own results, and alternative interpretations of these results are often supportive of Motivation-Hygiene Theory. In addition, the questions of individual differences and Motivation-Hygiene Theory, the reliability of the critical-incident method, and the performance implications of Motivation-Hygiene Theory will be touched upon.

The conclusion that clearly emerges from the review and analysis of the critical studies is that, on the whole, their design, rationale, and findings provide a very unconvincing case against the validity of Motivation-Hygiene Theory.

In evaluating the Motivation-Hygiene Theory controversy, perhaps the tone and style of the critical papers are more revealing than their substance. It is quite likely that no other theory throughout the history of psychology has attracted so many critical investigations, merely to show that it is void of any merit whatever. Such overkill reflects more on the practices and motivations of some of the critical investigators than on the validity of Motivation-Hygiene Theory. Too often the pre-occupation of the critics has been to "lay to rest" the theory, rather than to clarify issues. For example, two of the more vocal critics of Motivation-Hygiene Theory concluded their 1967 study with the following statement: "Little more can be said. The authors join with Dunnette, Campbell and Hakel in hoping that the two-factor theory can be laid to rest with a minimum of fanfare."[2]

The reality is, of course, that subsequent to 1967, as well as preceding it, Motivation-Hygiene Theory attracted perhaps more interest than any other single issue in industrial psychology. Industrial psychology has been, nevertheless, the one big loser in this controversy. Progress in this field has not been enhanced by the large number of articles criticizing Motivation-Hygiene Theory. Effort and energy seem to have been wasted; there has been no increase in substantive knowledge. One cannot really say upon reading this literature that indeed one knows and understands work motivation better than one ever did before reading it.

Critical attack, quite clearly, has not prevented Motivation-Hygiene Theory from contributing both to a theoretical understanding of work and human motivation and to practical applications and action research.

---

[2] C. L. Hulin and P. A. Smith, "An Empirical Investigation of Two Implications of the Two-Factor Theory of Job Satisfaction," *Journal of Applied Psychology*, vol. 51 (1967), p. 401.

It is realized, however, that a strong need still exists for further theorization and research. Progress in this area will be facilitated with the increased constructiveness of much of the research effort.

This chapter serves one other purpose, apart from increasing understanding of Motivation-Hygiene Theory research. The chapter is also a handbook of documented answers to the criticisms. It provides some needed ammunition to the manager who has seen motivation-hygiene applications work for him and his company but has had to deal with a persistent yet altogether pedestrian critic who enjoys doing armchair surveys from his seat in the bowels of the personnel department.

David Whitsett, Erik Winslow, and Benedict Grigaliunas all received their doctoral degrees under me. Yoash Wiener was an assistant professor in the Industrial Mental Health program I directed at Case Western Reserve University. Professor Wiener succeeded me as director of this program when I left to assume my new position as University Distinguished Professor at the University of Utah.

An analysis of studies critical of the Motivation-Hygiene Theory

David A. Whitsett
and
Erik K. Winslow

The publication of *The Motivation to Work* (Herzberg, Mausner, & Snyderman, 1959) presented the field of industrial psychology with a new way of looking at job attitudes. Indeed, it was hailed as "an important step forward in our efforts to understand human motivation." (Dunnette & Kirchner, 1965, p. 148). The study and the theoretical concepts which emerged from it have not been without critics. The purpose of this article will be to review the history of the theory, to present an oversimplified version of the complex motivator-hygiene theoretical formulation, and to evaluate studies reporting results which are in apparent disagreement with the theory.

HISTORY OF THE THEORY

Following an extensive review of the literature on job attitudes (Herzberg, Mausner, Peterson, & Capwell, 1957) covering some 2,000 articles spread over a period of approximately 50 years, Herzberg, Mausner and Snyderman (1959) undertook a study to investigate a puzzling phenomenon. One of the important findings that emerged from *Job Attitudes: Review of Research and Opinion* (Herzberg et al., 1957) ". . . was the fact that there was a difference in the primacy of factors, depending upon whether the investigator was looking for things the worker liked about his job or things he disliked."

Note: The authors would like to acknowledge the contributions of Dr. William Paul to this review. We further express our gratitude to Professor Frederick Herzberg for his valuable comments on this paper.

The study reported in *The Motivation to Work* was designed to test the implication that certain factors were satisfying, while other, different factors were dissatisfying. The study attempted to specify attitudes, identify factors in these attitudes, and investigate the effects of these attitudes. A semistructured interview was used to allow these three components to emerge from the subject's own experience and to ensure that an actual event and a change in feelings had occurred. This interview asked the respondent to describe sequences of events related to times when he was exceptionally satisfied and exceptionally dissatisfied with his job. The importance of this procedure has been lauded by Dunnette and Kirchner (1965, p. 152):

Although these conclusions are important, a more fundamental contribution of the study is that the job factors so identified were allowed to emerge from descriptions of actual job situations rather than being based exclusively on responses to check-lists or sets of statements developed ahead of time by the investigator. The job factors derived by Herzberg's classification are more likely, therefore, to reflect things in the job environment leading to employees' approach and avoidance behaviors. As such, the factors seem to be a logical starting point for developing the measures of job motivation we discussed in the previous section.

The study used as subjects 200 engineers and accountants. The details of the study can be found clearly spelled out in either the original (Herzberg et al., 1959) or the most recent statement of the theory (Herzberg, 1966).

Using content analysis of the sequences elicited through the interviews, a clear picture emerged of the fundamental distinction between two sets of factors. One set of factors revolved around the actual doing of the job, the job content, or the intrinsic aspects of the job. The other set of factors revolved around the environmental setting of the job, the surrounding conditions, the job context, or the extrinsic aspects of the job.

The intrinsic factors which emerged from the content analysis were: achievement, recognition, work itself, responsibility, advancement. The extrinsic factors were: company policy and administration, supervision-technical, salary, interpersonal relations–supervisor, and working conditions.

The results indicated that certain factors contributed more than others to periods of great satisfaction. These factors were related to the doing of the task, to the feelings of psychological growth, and to more positive attitudes toward the work. Since these factors were also related to periods of superior performance and effort, they were labeled *motivators*.

Distinct and separate from these were a group of factors which had to do with the conditions that surround the doing of the job. These factors, when at a low level, serve to bring about poor job attitudes and are related to a psychologically poor work environment. However, when these factors are at a high level they serve to prevent poor job attitudes but they neither push the individual to continuing superior performance nor lead to job satisfaction. These factors were given the name *hygiene factors*. This is analogous to the medical use of the term "hygiene," in which health hazards are removed from the environment to prevent diseases rather than to cure them.

Subsequent to the publication of these findings, the authors were criticized for generalizing the results beyond the narrow range of jobs investigated. While this may have been a valid criticism at one time, at least 15 replications using a wide variety of populations have since been completed, making the original study the most replicated study in the field.

EXPLANATION OF THE THEORY

A brief encounter with the theory is necessary to allow easy discussion of the relevant points covered below in dealing with the studies. The

Figure 1

Traditional (A) and motivator-hygiene (B) attitude models

(A)

Dissatisfaction ---------------------------------- Satisfaction

(B)

Dissatisfaction ←----------- Hygiene ----------- No dissatisfaction

No satisfaction ----------- Motivators -----------→ Satisfaction

basic distinction to be drawn is that between those factors that lead to satisfaction on the job and superior performance, the *motivators*, and those that prevent dissatisfaction but contribute neither to satisfaction nor to lasting motivation,[1] the *hygiene* or maintenance factors.

This distinction presents a problem in semantics in that we normally think of satisfaction and dissatisfaction as opposites, that is, what is not dissatisfying must be satisfying and vice versa. One of the crucial understandings must be that in the Motivation-Hygiene (M–H) Theory, dissatisfaction and those factors that contribute to dissatisfaction are *separate and distinct* from those factors that contribute to satisfaction. Satisfaction is *not* opposite from dissatisfaction, for they operate on separate continua. The opposite of satisfaction is *no satisfaction,* while the opposite of dissatisfaction is *no dissatisfaction* (Figure 1–B). This is different from traditional thinking of satisfaction and dissatisfaction as simple opposites (Figure 1–A).

Operating here are two extremely different needs of man. One set of needs may be thought of as stemming from man's animal nature; these

[1] By motivation we mean here the internal generator which makes the individual want to grow and achieve on his own, rather than an external pressure which simply induces movement.

drives are related to the need to avoid pain. This set of needs can be seen as comparable to Maslow's (1955) deficiency motives, or what White (1959) calls tension reduction drives. These needs are the ones upon which hygiene factors act. However, since these needs serve only to reduce pain, they do not lead to growth, nor do they provide for growth. The growth needs, which are like Maslow's growth motives and White's competence or effectance motives, are those that have to do with the uniquely human push toward self-realization, or, very simply, to be psychologically more than one was yesterday. Since psychological growth can only be achieved through successful completion of *meaningful* tasks, only the factors having to do with the intrinsic aspects of the job—the motivators—can influence these inherent growth needs. These motivator factors are not able to relieve pain nor to satisfy the avoidance needs, just as the hygiene factors cannot satisfy the growth needs. (For a more complete treatment of this idea, see Herzberg & Hamlin, 1961, 1963; Herzberg, 1962a, 1962b, 1965, 1966.)

To sum up, because of the independent and distinct characteristics of these two needs, we find two distinct groups of factors contributing to the fulfillment of these needs. With the above ideas in mind, we can now return to our discussion of job satisfaction and job dissatisfaction.

The hygiene factors, maintenance factors, extrinsic factors, job context factors, or dissatisfiers[2] operate on the continuum running from dissatisfaction to no dissatisfaction. These factors are supervision, co-workers, company policy and administration, status, working conditions, and security. Salary is included in this group, but this is a confounded factor since it is so often tied to advancement or recognition, which are motivators. The basic criteria for inclusion as a hygiene factor are that the factors should have short-term effects, contribute more to dissatisfaction, and be cyclical in action—that is, need frequent replenishment.

The motivator factors, intrinsic factors, job content factors, or satisfiers (see footnote 2) operate on a distinct and different continuum which runs from no satisfaction to satisfaction. These factors include achievement, recognition for achievement, advancement, possibility of growth, work itself, and responsibility. These factors provide satisfaction for the human need of psychological growth or competence and act as reinforcement for the "built in" generator that we usually call motivation.

The above discussion will provide a basis for understanding the concepts with which the following review will deal. In reviewing the studies which appear critical of the Motivation-Hygiene Theory, we have found three basic kinds of errors to be prevalent: (1) misinterpretation of the Motivation-Hygiene Theory, (2) methodological weaknesses, and (3)

---

[2] The present authors object to the use of the dichotomy satisfiers-dissatisfiers. This confuses the basic distinction and frequently becomes an exercise in semantics which does not allow a clear discussion of the insights of this theory. For the remainder of this article we will use the terms "motivator" and "hygiene" factors.

misinterpretation of results. We will review these studies within the framework of these three types of errors.

REVIEW OF THE STUDIES

One of the most common and persistent misinterpretations of the Motivation-Hygiene (M–H) Theory is the attempt to use measures of overall job satisfaction to make statements purporting to be derived from the theory. The theory does not, and purposely does not, make statements about overall job satisfaction. The separateness of the sets of factors makes it apparent that job attitudes must be looked at twice—once to see if the needs fulfilled by the hygiene factors are indeed fulfilled, and again to see if the needs fulfilled by the motivator factors are met. Friedlander (1964) has concluded, "Since there are strong indications that satisfaction and dissatisfaction are not negatively related poles of a single continuum, it is probable that one is not justified in converting (by combining) the two constructs into a single scale or a single construct" (p. 391).

The clearest instance in which this error in interpretation has been made is in a study by Ewen, Smith, Hulin, & Locke (1966). In the study the authors made and tested predictions based both on the M–H Theory and on what they call "traditional uni-dimensional theory." In so doing, these authors have made two errors in interpretation. First, they have interpreted H–H Theory as saying that hygiene contributes nothing to overall job satisfaction. The problem here is one of semantics. The essence of the motivation-hygiene concept is that motivator factors and hygiene factors are independent, operate on different needs, and cannot be combined. Therefore, M–H Theory makes no predictions about overall anything. But let us suppose, for the sake of discussion, that M–H Theory did make predictions about overall job satisfaction. What would it predict? If we avoid the semantic error made in equating satisfaction in the M–H sense and satisfaction in the overall job satisfaction sense, it becomes evident that M–H Theory would predict that both motivator factors and hygiene factors contribute to overall satisfaction. It makes no sense to say that if a man is unhappy with his working conditions, this will not have a negative effect on his overall feeling toward his job. M–H Theory would not predict this and neither, we hope, would anybody else.

Their second error involves the use of the term "neutral." Within the structure of M–H Theory there is no neutral point on the motivator continuum because the motivators contribute only to satisfaction; thus a person is, with respect to the motivators, either more or less satisfied, but never neutral. The same is true of hygiene—a person is either more or less dissatisfied, never neutral. It is evident that man lives his life as a unity and consequently combines his feelings of satisfaction and dissatisfaction. He thus may "feel" neutral. However, M–H Theory contends that this neutral feeling is made up of some amount of satisfaction (derived from motivators) and some amount of dissatisfaction (derived from hygiene).

These two errors have led Ewen et al. to make completely incorrect predictions from the M–H Theory. The authors state (p. 545): "There exist several straightforward hypotheses for which the Herzberg two-factor theory and traditional unidimensional theory make diametrically opposed predictions."

Let us examine their hypotheses. Hypothesis I states: If there is one group of employees (group A) who are neutral with regard to the motivators and a second group (group B) who are dissatisfied with the motivators, and the two groups are equal with regard to hygiene, M–H Theory would predict that the two groups would be equal in overall job satis-faction, while traditional theory would predict that group A would have higher overall job satisfaction than group B.[3]

Hypothesis II is similar to Hypothesis I, but this time the authors are holding motivators constant and are dealing with the effects of hygiene. The authors hypothesize that M–H Theory would predict no differences in overall job satisfaction between those neutral with regard to hygiene (group A) and those satisfied with hygiene (group B). They further hypothesize that traditional theory would predict that group B would have higher overall job satisfaction than group A.

Hypothesis III states that M–H Theory would predict that being dis-satisfied with hygiene should lead to greater overall dissatisfaction than being dissatisfied with the motivators. They state that traditional theory would predict no differences in overall dissatisfaction.

Hypothesis IV states that M–H Theory would predict that being satis-fied with the motivators should lead to greater overall satisfaction than being satisfied with hygiene. Finally, they hypothesize that traditional theory would predict no differences.

In all four cases, the authors have predicted incorrectly from the M–H Theory. By forcing the M–H Theory to make predictions about a concept (overall job satisfaction) which negates its very nature, they have reduced its dimensions to exactly those of traditional unidimensional theory. Within this restrictive framework, M–H Theory would make exactly the same predictions as traditional theory. Under these circumstances it could make no other predictions.

The fact that the results of this study partially support M–H Theory and partially support traditional theory is probably due to weaknesses in the methodology. For example, the authors used as their criterion a measure of overall job satisfaction—The General Motors Faces Scale (Kunin, 1955)—which is "a one-item graphic scale, consisting of six faces varying from a large smile to a large frown" (Ewen et al., 1966,

---

[3] We have taken the liberty of modifying the wording of these hypotheses to remain consistent with the terminology of this paper. We are certain that the meaning of the hypotheses remain the same.

p. 547). The subject is asked to check the face which most closely represents his feelings toward his job—in general. The authors admit that this particular scale has not been validated, but they point out that other similar scales, when used for particular job satisfaction dimensions, have shown "good discriminant and convergent validity" (p. 547).[4] The magnitude of their error is increased by the fact that the score on this one item is used as the sole criterion measure for their entire study.

It is difficult to understand why the authors of this study would choose to measure Herzberg's factors with the Job Descriptive Index (JDI), which they say Vroom (1964) has called "without doubt the most carefully constructed measure of job attitudes in existence today" and then base all their results on a single-item unvalidated criterion score.

Even their choice of the JDI was unfortunate in this case, because it led them to use only 3 of Herzberg's 16 factors. They used the work itself and promotional opportunities and policies as motivators, and pay as the only hygiene factor. The inadequacy of using only these three factors to test the M–H Theory is illustrated by the results of Graen's (1966a, p. 554) reanalysis of their data, in which he showed that they had accounted for only 20 percent of the variance in overall satisfaction. In addition, two of the three factors that they used were of questionable relevance to the M–H Theory. Their first factor, the work itself, is unquestionably a pure motivator factor. Their second choice, promotional opportunities and policies, is a factor apparently designed to tap advancement or possibility of growth, but it is contaminated with aspects of company policy and administration, which is a hygiene factor. It is also unfortunate that they used pay as their only hygiene factor, since it is probably the most marginal and complex of all Herzberg's factors. This choice of factors, when added to their single-item measure of overall job satisfaction, leads to further obscurity of the clarity of their results. In spite of all this, the authors report that the results of three of their eight tests support the M–H concept of job attitudes as opposed to traditional theory but, due to the serious misinterpretation of the M–H Theory and the methodological weaknesses of this study, it is probably not wise to claim support or refutation of either point of view.

A study frequently cited as being critical of the M–H Theory is Ewen's (1964) investigation of the job attitudes of 1,021 life insurance agents. Responses to a 58-item four-point attitude scale were factor analyzed, yielding six clearly interpretable factors: general morale and satisfaction, manager interest in agents, company training policies, salary, the work

---

[4] They refer here to a study by Locke, Smith, Hulin, & Kendall (1963) in which the Faces Scale was found to have the best discriminant and convergent validity of the four graphic rating methods tested. However, this article concludes, "This does not mean that it [the Faces Scale] would necessarily show convergent and discriminant validity when compared to maximally different methods of measuring satisfaction" (p. 319).

itself, and prestige or recognition. Unfortunately, Ewen then chose to measure each of these factors with only one item, with the exception of general morale and satisfaction, for which he used two items.[5] Even though he chose the items having the highest loadings on the respective factors, the inadequacy of a one- or two-item measure of any attitude should be obvious.

Ewen classified three of his factors as hygiene: manager interest in agents, company training policies, and salary. It is difficult to determine the adequacy of Ewen's factors since he does not present his items, but we have already discussed the contamination of the salary factor. It is highly probable that the factor manager interest in agents contains aspects of recognition or other motivators; company training policies are almost certainly contaminated with aspects of the possibility of growth, which is also a motivator.

Ewen's two motivator factors, work itself and prestige or recognition, also require some comment. Prestige or recognition appears from its title to contain elements of the hygiene factor prestige or status. Work itself seems to be the most clearly interpretable factor he has used and is probably a pure motivator.

The results indicated that work itself operated as a motivator, as M–H Theory would predict. The other factors operated both as motivator and hygiene factors, a result also predictable from M–H Theory due to their contaminated nature. However, any conclusions leading to support or refutation of the M–H Theory are probably unwarranted, due to the fact that the results are based on an overall general morale and satisfaction factor. We find it perplexing that this study is so often cited as a clear refutation of the M–H Theory (Wernimont, 1966; Malinovsky & Barry, 1965; Burke, 1966), especially in light of the fact that Ewen himself concludes, "A more extensive research design is necessary in order to adequately test the Herzberg theory" (1964, p. 163).

Malinovsky and Barry (1965) report a study in which they investigated the job attitudes of 117 blue-collar workers to test the applicability of the M–H Theory to this population. The authors performed a factor analysis of responses to their 40-item work attitude survey and found that both motivator and hygiene factors correlated positively with overall job satisfaction. They conclude that this is contrary to predictions made from the M–H Theory. This conclusion is incorrect, due to their use of a measure of overall job satisfaction. That is, the authors imply that M–H Theory would predict a negative relationship between hygiene factors and overall job satisfaction. This erroneous assumption is, once again, a result of the semantic confusion involved in equating satisfaction in the "overall" sense with satisfaction as used in the M–H Theory.

---

[5] The reader will not find this fact mentioned in Ewen's article (1964). However, he did make this clear in a paper presented at the 71st Annual Meeting of the American Psychological Association, Philadelphia, 1963.

A more important finding is Malinovsky and Barry's report that "The job attitudes of blue collar workers could be separated into two relatively independent sets of variables, comparable to motivator or hygiene variables" (p. 446). We feel, then, that the net effect of this study is clearly supportive of the M–H Theory.

Wernimont (1966) reports a study in which he obtained responses to both forced-choice and free-choice items from 50 accountants and 82 engineers in self-descriptions of past satisfying and dissatisfying job situations. The author reports that the correlations obtained between overall present satisfaction and present feelings about various job factors "may be contrasted with the findings of Herzberg et al. (1959), who felt that extrinsic [hygiene] factors could not contribute much to an individual's positive feeling about his job" (p. 47). It is true that M–H Theory says that hygiene does not contribute to positive satisfaction. However, Wernimont did not measure positive satisfaction; he measured overall satisfaction, which is made up of both those things that are satisfying and those things that are dissatisfying. The error committed here should by now be apparent to the reader.

Wernimont constructed two forced-choice checklists, each made up of 50 pairs of items with each pair consisting of one motivator and one hygiene item. One set of 50 was written in a positive tone and the other in a negative tone. The pairs were equated for social desirability. Each subject was asked to describe briefly some situation that had occurred on his job which made him feel very happy with his job—some situation that made him feel he had just about the best job anyone could have. He was then asked to check the one statement in each of the 50 positive pairs of statements which best described how he felt in that situation. This process was then repeated for a past very unhappy, negative situation with the 50 negatively worded pairs of items. Unfortunately Wernimont, after asking his subjects to think of a particular time in the *past* when they felt they had just about the best (worst) job anyone could have, gave them items to rate which were worded in the *present* tense, many of which were essentially neutral! For example:

1. My boss is fairly reasonable in dealing with me.
2. I feel that the responsibilities I have in my job are okay.
3. I have an average amount of interest in the kind of work I do.
4. My boss is about average in competence in his job.

It is difficult to see how there is any connection between the respondent's ratings on these essentially neutral items and the extremely happy or unhappy incident he has just described. To begin with, the items should have been written in the past tense and they should have been stronger, either more positive or more negative. But even if this had been done, the biggest problem would still remain. It is inconceivable that all 50 items could have been relevant to the incident described.

Wernimont himself realized this, and in his dissertation (on which his article was based) he commented, "Since each respondent was obligated to choose one statement from each of fifty pairs of statements by placing a check mark in front of that statement, it can readily be seen that some of the items chosen might have little or nothing to do with a given specific situation. In other words, the individual would be forced to choose between two statements neither of which would be relevant to the situation he had just described" (Wernimont, 1964, p. 41). Nevertheless, in his published article he apparently ignored this problem and concluded that, since both motivator and hygiene items had been checked with respect to both happy and unhappy situations, both factors contribute to satisfaction and dissatisfaction. The probability that an individual will endorse all 50 motivator items for a happy event and all 50 hygiene items for an unhappy event is minute. This is especially true when the respondent is asked to check essentially neutral items, written in the present tense, many of which are irrelevant to the situation he has just described. Because of these conditions, this part of Wernimont's study is probably nothing more than a present-tense attitude survey.

In the second part of the study, Wernimont attempts to remedy the situation of having the respondents check irrelevant items by asking them to "check again the 10 items which best describe the satisfying (dissatisfying) situation on your job." He notes that this then made the respondents *"free* to choose all 10 statements pertaining to 1 job factor or 1 statement from 10 different job factors or any proportion in between." In this instance he obtained results very much like those of Herzberg's (1959) original study. Wernimont concludes, ". . . The [forced choice] techniques used in this study for eliminating the suspected sources of bias (respondent defensiveness) had a substantial effect on the obtained results." We would agree with Wernimont that his method substantially affected his results. However, we question whether the effects of this method operated to clarify or to obscure the nature of the job attitudes of his subjects.

Dunnette (1965) used 12 of Herzberg's 16 job dimensions to prepare a pool of 143 pairs of statements descriptive of different job situations. Each pair of statements consisted of the same item worded to describe first a satisfying job situation and then a dissatisfying situation. The statements were judged for social desirability, and on this basis the pool of items was reduced to 150, 75 worded favorably and 75 worded unfavorably. These items were administered to a group of subjects who were asked to describe how well each statement described a past job situation. A factor analysis of these results led to Dunnette's final choice of two sets of 36 statements with highest factor loadings on each of the 12 job dimensions.

These items were then presented to six groups of subjects who were asked to think back to previously satisfying and dissatisfying job situations and to describe the elements of these situations by Q-sorting the two sets of statements. One extremely important point must be noted here. The subjects were instructed to sort these statements along a seven-point scale of importance in the situation they had just described, in accordance with a quasi-normal forced distribution. The requirement of this distribution was that the subjects had to place the two most important items in category 7, the two least important in category 1, five items in categories 6 and 2, then seven items in categories 5 and 3 and, finally, eight items in category 4. It should be immediately apparent, as it was in Wernimont's (1966) study, that all 36 items could not possibly be relevant to the situation the subject had just described. We might conceive of a hypothetical extremely satisfying (dissatisfying) situation in which as many as four or five factors might be relevant. Since there is an average of three items per factor, this would mean that a maximum of 15 of the 36 items would have some relevance to the situation. Assuming these 15 items are sorted correctly, the frame of reference the subject uses for sorting the remaining 21 items is uncertain. We might expect that social desirability and the respondent's present feelings about his job would operate to dictate his choices.

It would seem logical to allow the subject to respond in a free-choice manner, as in Wernimont's (1966) study, to indicate those items he felt were important to the extreme situation he had described. Since the original purpose of the study was to determine what people felt were important contributors to their feelings of extreme satisfaction and dissatisfaction in their jobs, it is unfortunate that the reality of their feelings was obscured by the necessity of having to respond to many items with no relevance to this situation.

Dunnette found that an analysis of the mean differences and their direction argued in favor of a two-factor view of satisfaction-dissatisfaction. That is, the means for motivator factors were greater in satisfying situations than in dissatisfying situations, while the means for hygiene factors were higher in dissatisfying situations than in satisfying situations. However, in ranking job dimension means separately for satisfying and dissatisfying situations, there was some indication that motivator factors are more important than hygiene factors in both satisfying and dissatisfying situations.

We feel that the direct data of this study are supportive of the M–H Theory and what the author feels is nonsupportive is a misinterpretation of the underlying structure of the M–H Theory.

There are four studies by Friedlander (1963, 1964, 1965, 1966) which have sometimes been cited as nonsupportive of the M–H Theory. In his 1963 study, Friedlander factor analyzed questionnaire responses of over 9,000 employees of a large midwestern manufacturing company. Three factors emerged. The first factor, labeled social and technical environment, was made up entirely of hygiene items, which is supportive of

M–H Theory. Likewise supportive was the second factor, which was called intrinsic self-actualizing work aspects. This factor was made up entirely of motivator items. The third factor, recognition through advancement, was made up of four motivator items plus an item reading, "I was expecting (or received) a merit increase." Friedlander interprets this item as a hygiene item and thus says the factor is not a pure motivator factor. We feel that *merit* increase, since it serves as recognition, should be interpreted as a motivator. With this interpretation, the makeup of all three factors is clearly supportive of the theory.

The results of Friedlander's 1965 study also support M–H Theory. Friedlander concludes (p. 173), "The results of this investigation would seem to add empirical weight to earlier studies suggesting a dual motivation theory." His findings in this study, based on questionnaire responses of 1,935 government employees, show that one set of factors contributed primarily to dissatisfaction and that another, and separate, set of factors contributed to satisfaction.

With a single exception, Friedlander's 1964 study is also supportive of M–H Theory. In administering two questionnaires in which the importance to satisfaction and dissatisfaction of various job characteristics were compared, Friedlander concluded:

1. "Herzberg's findings that satisfiers and dissatisfiers were not opposite ends of a common set of dimensions were substantiated by the current study" (p. 391).
2. Motivator factors seemed to be important to both satisfaction and dissatisfaction, while hygiene factors appeared to be generally less important. (This finding, concerning the importance of the motivators, will be discussed in the summary section of this article.)

Friedlander's 1966 study is not intended as a "test" of M–H Theory but rather is an investigation of the relationship between motivation and job performance. The findings (p. 147) include the result: "Within the white-collar groups, low performance employees place significantly greater importance than do high performance employees upon the social and interpersonal characteristics of their work environment. . . ." Such findings need not be interpreted as supportive or nonsupportive of M–H Theory but rather should be thought of as valuable and fruitful outgrowths of the framework provided by that theory. It is this type of study that we consider most valuable.

Graen (1966b) appears to have a working understanding of the M–H concepts. He reports a study in which he attempts to develop psychometric measures of the motivator-hygiene factors by means of factor analysis. A 96-item questionnaire was developed, based on the motivation-hygiene scheme. The respondents (153 engineers) were asked to rate the importance of each item to their overall satisfaction or dissatisfaction on a scale from 1 to 5 (see Figure 2).

Figure 2

Overall satisfaction-dissatisfaction scale

Very important to my job satisfaction				Not important				Very important to my job dissatisfaction
5	0	3	2	1	2	3	4	5

At first glance this scale appears to be a two-dimensional scale, but the fact that "the numerical values shown on the scale were used as scores" (Graen, 1966b, p. 564), with no apparent use of algebraic sign, reduces this to a simple 1 through 5 scale of importance. Thus the distinction of whether a given item contributes to satisfaction or dissatisfaction is lost. As a result, the intercorrelations of the 96 items and the factor analysis of the resulting matrix have bearing only on the importance of the items and not on their content. Therefore, Graen's conclusion that the M–H factors "do not constitute homogeneous groupings of job content in the factor analytic or correlational sense" (p. 566) is in error. The misinterpretation of his results lies in the fact that he did not analyze homogeneity of content but rather analyzed homogeneity of importance. The scaling of these items simply on importance, and the factor analysis performed on importance scores, lead us to conclude that the results of this study bear no relevance to the underlying factor structure of the M–H Theory.

Lindsay (1965) has attempted to analyze the underlying dynamics of the M–H Theory. He made hypotheses concerning the amount of variance in overall job satisfaction accounted for by motivator and hygiene variables taken together, the contribution to the total variance by interaction effects between the two, and the independent contributions of motivator and hygiene variables taken separately. Even though Lindsay realizes that his work involves a modification or a reformulation of the M–H Theory, his apparent lack of understanding of the nature of the dynamics of the theory has led him to distort it into a unidimensional model. As a result, this study does not constitute a valid test of the M–H Theory. To begin with, he has made the interpretative error we have seen committed in several other studies reviewed here; that is, he has attempted to evaluate the M–H Theory within the framework of overall job satisfaction. Second, he attempts to test the theory using only 2 of the 16 factors, one motivator factor (achievement) and one hygiene factor (company policy and administration). In any study purporting to test the M–H Theory, it would be considered inadequate to use only two factors. However, in this case it is an especially unfortunate choice, since the study aims at measuring the amount of variance contributed by these factors.

Another methodological error which leads us to question the results obtained is the nature of the task imposed on his subjects. An example of the type of items used appears below:

10-A I really accomplished something in a job I was doing.
10-B I was working in a group that was disorganized and operated inefficiently due to a change in management practices.

Degree of Satisfaction

1   2   3   4   5

The subjects were required to "Read each of the *pairs* of statements carefully. Then indicate, on the basis of your experience, your degree of satisfaction with both of the situations" (Lindsay, 1965, p. 74). Reading the pair of items above, it is apparent that combining one's feelings into a single rating based on these two disparate items is a difficult task. Therefore, it is not surprising that Lindsay found in a pilot study that "some workers had difficulty in responding to pairs of items" (p. 32).

The results of the study indicated that the two variables (achievement and company policy) accounted for nearly 75 percent of the variance in overall job satisfaction, which Lindsay interprets as supportive of the M–H Theory. He had stated that the M–H Theory would predict no interaction effects between motivator and hygiene variables, and, since he found a statistically significant interaction effect, he interpreted this as nonsupportive. However, the actual amount of this contribution is *0.8 of 1 percent,* which Lindsay (1965, pp. 52–53) admits "may be in that grey area of 'practical' versus 'significant' differences."

The results pertaining to the third hypothesis indicated that the motivator factor contributed more of the variance in overall satisfaction than the hygiene factor, a situation which will be discussed in more detail in the summary of this article.

In general, then, due to the interpretative and methodological weaknesses of this study, we cannot construe it as an adequate test of the utility of the M–H Theory.

Ott (1965) administered a 115-item job attitude questionnaire to 350 telephone operators and factor analyzed their responses by the principal-axis method. Ten factors were extracted, the first five of which accounted for most of the variance. Three of these five factors are made up primarily of items relating to supervision, a fourth has mostly to do with relationships with customers, and a fifth with company policies and benefit programs. Ott (1965, Abstract, p. 3) indicates, "The major conclusion of this research was that Herzberg's theory was shown not to be general from an occupational standpoint. Further, the validity of his theoretical constructs was demonstrated to be questionable."

We feel there are two important points to be noted here. First, the fact that all five of Ott's most important factors were made up primarily of hygiene items is predictable from an examination of his questionnaire.

Ninety out of 115 items deal with hygiene or context, while 25 are content or motivator items. As Graen (1966b, p. 564) has noted, "A major determinant of the factors resulting from a factor analysis is the sampling of items." Second, it should be evident, from the following examples, that the author's choice of items as representative of "extreme incidents" leaves something to be desired.

1. When sitting down to work and finding pencil dust all over your work space.
2. Using the bulletin boards for showing the progress of "contests."
3. When an operator next to you sprawls all over your work space. (Ott, 1965, Appendix I)

We feel that to interpret the results of this study as refuting the utility of M–H concepts would be without foundation.

A particularly interesting study has been done by Centers and Bugental (1966) in which they investigated the strength of intrinsic (motivator) and extrinsic (hygiene) job factors in a sample of 692 individuals from all occupational levels. It was their prediction that individuals in higher occupational levels would place a greater value on intrinsic job factors than would individuals at lower occupational levels. Individuals at lower levels were expected to place a greater value on extrinsic job factors. Their results, as originally interpreted, support these predictions. However, a closer examination of their study reveals that they have made a rather serious interpretational error. Their subjects were presented a card on which were written six items (three motivators and three hygiene items). They were then asked, "Which of these things is most important in keeping you on your present job?" (p. 194). The authors found that individuals in the higher occupational groups tended to choose the motivator items, while those in the lower occupational levels chose the hygiene items. They interpret this to mean that the motivators are more "valued" among those in the higher occupational levels and that hygiene is more "valued" among those in the lower occupational levels. The fact that this is a misinterpretation becomes clear if we focus on the question asked in this study. That is, the investigators did not ask, "What do you *value* in your job?" but "What *keeps* you on your job?" What they measured here is not their subjects' values but rather what is available in the jobs. The motivators are, for the most part, available at the higher occupational levels and so are chosen as "important in keeping me on my present job." However, it is highly probable that the motivators are *not* available to those individuals in the lower occupational levels and thus cannot operate to "keep them on their jobs." The point here is that this study probably demonstrates not that the motivators are not valued by people in lower occupational levels, but that the motivators are not available to these people.

A unique misinterpretation of the M–H Theory has been made by

Burke (1966). In this study he tested the "unidimensionality" of the motivator and hygiene concepts and concluded that, for his sample of 187 college students, the concepts are not unidimensional. The key here is the meaning he attributes to the word "unidimensional." He apparently means having a fixed order. That is, he was testing whether his subjects would, with some consistency, rank his five motivator factors in some preferential order, e.g., opportunity for advancement first, challenges ability second, etc., and whether they would do the same thing with his five hygiene factors, e.g., good salary ranked consistently first, job security consistently second, etc. This was not the case. He found that his subjects' feelings about the relative "importance for self" of these factors varied widely. From this he concludes, "Herzberg's two-factor theory may be an oversimplified representation of job satisfaction" (Burke, 1966, p. 317). We do not understand this conclusion, since M–H Theory makes no claim that there should be any fixed order of importance among either motivator or hygiene factors. In fact, individual differences make it difficult to imagine this being the case. For this reason we cannot see how Burke's results are in any way damaging to the validity of the M–H concept.

SUMMARY AND CONTENTS

What can we conclude from the results of the studies reviewed here? It would appear, because of the numerous misinterpretations of the M–H Theory, the general weaknesses in methods, and the frequent misinterpretations of results, that taken as a group the studies reviewed offer little empirical evidence for doubting the validity of the theory. We conclude that the theory has clearly retained its utility and viability. In fact, it is interesting to note that the results of some of the most critical studies (Dunnette, 1965; Ewen, 1964; Ewen et al., 1966; Malinovsky & Barry, 1965; Wernimont, 1966) actually support, in part, the M–H Theory. These studies serve to illustrate that findings in the direction of those of the original study (Herzberg et al., 1959) are obtainable through a variety of methodologies.

There is one consistent finding (Burke, 1966; Centers & Bugental, 1966; Dunnette, 1965; Ewen et al., 1966; Friedlander, 1964; Graen, 1966a, 1966b) which focuses on the issue of the relative importance of motivator and hygiene factors. These studies report, in general, that the motivators appear more important in rankings of factors in job attitudes than the hygiene factors. One possible explanation for this result becomes evident in examining the populations used in these studies. The subjects, for the most part, have been drawn from higher occupational and educational groups. The finding that these groups regard the motivators as more important is by no means a new one. In *Job Attitudes: Review of Research and Opinion,* Herzberg et al. (1957, p. 54) reported:

The factor preferences of workers are affected similarly by employee occupational level and education. One of the most consistent findings is that intrinsic aspects of the job are more important to employees with greater education and to employees at higher occupational levels.

Another possible explanation lies in the methods used. The studies reviewed here have used several types of "rating" methods, i.e., the procedures have required that subjects rate or rank or assign importance to the various job factors. That a rating or ranking procedure leads to results which indicate the motivators to be more potent determiners of job attitudes is also not a new finding. Herzberg et al. found exactly this in the original *Motivation to Work* study (1959). In the portion of the study in which a rating scale was used, the motivators were rated higher on how seriously they affected feelings about the job. Thus, it may be that rating or ranking methods lead to results of this kind. The long duration of the motivators' effects and their effects on attitudinal correlates led Herzberg to call attention to the potency of the motivators (Herzberg et al., 1959, pp. 90–96). However, M–H Theory has gone beyond the ranking of importance to an understanding of the basic dynamics of the factors. The M–H Theory has led us away from fruitless arguments as to which single drive, need, or interest is more important. That is, the M–H Theory makes statements about the nature of man. It says that he operates on two equally important basic needs: the need to grow and the need to avoid pain. Thus, the finding that some of the factors underlying one need appear to take precedence does not diminish the importance of the other need. The essence of the theory is that the two are served by independent and different groups of factors, that *both* sets of needs must be met and that an overemphasis on *either* may lead to serious personnel problems. It should be obvious that an overemphasis on hygiene, to the exclusion of motivators, cannot result in superior performance, while ignoring hygiene and concentrating solely on the motivators will lead to dissatisfaction. This distinction between intrinsic and extrinsic (motivator and hygiene) factors has been a major contribution of the theory, and it has been clearly upheld even by the articles reviewed here.

The M–H Theory has made many contributions. The best way to demonstrate these is to examine it in terms of the generally accepted criteria of the value of a theory.

First, a theory should provide resolving power. That is, it should bring into focus and clearly identify the variables important in the problems to which it addresses itself. The M–H Theory has clearly demonstrated its ability to identify and clarify the underlying sources of job attitudes.

Second, a theory should have explanatory power. M–H Theory does not deny the findings of past research but rather integrates and explains results previously thought to be contradictory. Prior findings had indicated that different factors emerged as important to job attitudes, depending on whether subjects were asked what they liked or what they disliked about their jobs. The M–H Theory was the first to account for these disparate results through its explanation of the basic underlying need structure of man.

Third, a theory should generate research. The volume of research generated by the Motivation-Hygiene Theory makes it one of the leading topics for investigation in the field of industrial psychology. This current emphasis on M–H research may be directly related to the theory's superior ability to define the relevant variables in job attitudes and motivation.

Finally, a theory should offer a basis for useful prediction. The predictive ability of the Motivation-Hygiene Theory has been demonstrated not only in the field of job attitudes, but also in the field of mental health (see Hamlin & Nemo, 1962; Graglia & Hamlin, 1964; Haywood & Dobbs, 1964; Sandvold, 1962; Haywood & Wachs, 1966). We hope that the M–H Theory will continue to generate predictive research. However, we should like to emphasize that, in testing a theory, an investigator is obligated to interpret that theory correctly, to use adequate methods, and to interpret his results carefully. He should also consider, "A theory is only *useful or not useful* and those qualities are defined mostly in how efficiently the theory generates predictions or propositions. . . . It is only the derivations or propositions or ideas derived from the theory which are open to empirical test. The theory itself is assumed and acceptance or rejection of it is determined by its utility, not by its truth or falsity" (Hall & Lindzey, 1957, pp. 11–13).

REFERENCES

Burke, R.   Are Herzberg's motivators and hygienes unidimensional? *Journal of Applied Psychology,* 1966, *50,* 317–321.

Centers, R., & Bugental, D.   Intrinsic and extrinsic job motivation among different segments of the working population. *Journal of Applied Psychology,* 1966, *50,* 193–197.

Dunnette, M.   Factor structure of unusually satisfying and unusually dissatisfying job situations for six occupational groups. Paper read at Midwestern Psychological Association, Chicago, April 29–May 1, 1965.

Dunnette, M., & Kirchner, W.   *Psychology applied to industry.* New York: Appleton-Century-Crofts, 1965.

Ewen, R. B.   Some determinants of job satisfaction: A study of the generality of Herzberg's theory. *Journal of Applied Psychology,* 1964, *48,* 161–163.

Ewen, R., Smith, P., Hulin, C., & Locke, E.   An empirical test of the Herzberg two-factor theory. *Journal of Applied Psychology,* 1966, *50,* 544–550.

Friedlander, F.   Underlying sources of job satisfaction. *Journal of Applied Psychology,* 1963, *47,* 246–250.

Friedlander, F.   Job characteristics as satisfiers and dissatisfiers. *Journal of Applied Psychology,* 1964, *48,* 388–392.

Friedlander, F.   Relationships between the importance and the satisfaction of various environmental factors. *Journal of Applied Psychology*, 1965, *49*, 160–164.

Friedlander, F.   Motivation to work and organizational performance. *Journal of Applied Psychology*, 1966, *50*, 143–152.

Graen, G.   Addendum to "An empirical test of the Herzberg two-factor theory." *Journal of Applied Psychology*, 1966, *50*, 551–555. (a)

Graen, G.   Motivator and hygiene dimensions for research and development engineers. *Journal of Applied Psychology*, 1966, *50*, 563–566. (b)

Graglia, A., & Hamlin, R.   Effect of effort and task orientation on activity preference. Paper delivered at Eastern Psychological Association meeting, Philadelphia, 1964.

Hall, C. S., & Lindzey, G.   *Theories of personality*. New York: John Wiley & Sons, 1957.

Hamlin, R. M., & Nemo, R. S.   Self-actualization in choice scores of improved schizophrenics. *Journal of Clinical Psychology*, 1962, *18*, 51–54.

Haywood, H. C., & Dobbs, V.   Motivation and anxiety in high school boys. *Journal of Personality*, 1964, *32*, 371–379.

Haywood, H. C., & Wachs, T. D.   Size-discrimination learning as a function of motivation-hygiene orientation in adolescents. *Journal of Educational Psychology*, 1966, *57*, 279–286.

Herzberg, F.   New approaches in management organization and job design. *Industrial Medicine and Surgery*, 1962, *33*, 477–482. (a)

Herzberg, F.   Basic needs and satisfaction of individuals. Proceedings of Industrial Relations Research Counselors Symposium on Advanced Research in Industrial Relations. *Industrial Relations Monograph*, 1962 (21). (b)

Herzberg, F.   The new industrial psychology. *Industrial and Labor Relations Review*, 1965, *18*, 364–376.

Herzberg, F.   *Work and the nature of man*. Cleveland: Thomas Y. Crowell Co., 1966.

Herzberg, F., & Hamlin, R.   A motivation-hygiene concept of mental health. *Mental Hygiene*, 1961, *45*, 394–401.

Herzberg, F., & Hamlin, R.   The motivation-hygiene concept and psychotherapy. *Mental Hygiene*, 1963 (47), 384–397.

Herzberg, F., Mausner, B., & Snyderman, B.   *The motivation to work* (2nd ed.). New York: John Wiley & Sons, 1959.

Herzberg, F., Mausner, B., Peterson, R., & Capwell, D. E.   *Job attitudes: Review of research and opinion*. Pittsburgh: Psychological Service of Pittsburgh, 1957.

Kunin, T.   The construction of a new type of attitude measure. *Personnel Psychology*, 1955 (8), 65–77.

Lindsay, C. A.   Job satisfaction: An examination and test of a modification of the Herzberg theory. Unpublished doctoral thesis, Pennsylvania State University, 1965.

Locke, E. A., Smith, P. C., Hulin, C. L., & Kendall, L. M.   Cornell Studies of

Job Satisfaction: V. Scale characteristics of the Job Descriptive Index. Cornell University, 1963. (Mimeographed)

Malinovsky, M. R., & Barry, J. R. Determinants of work attitudes. *Journal of Applied Psychology,* 1965, *49,* 446–451.

Maslow, A. Deficiency motivation and growth motivation. In M. R. Jones (Ed.), *Nebraska Symposium on Motivation.* Lincoln: University of Nebraska Press, 1955.

Ott, C. D. The generality of Herzberg's two-factor theory of motivation. Unpublished doctoral thesis, Ohio State University, 1965.

Sandvold, K. The effect of effort and task orientation on the motivation orientation and verbal responsivity of chronic schizophrenic patients and normals. Unpublished doctoral thesis, University of Illinois, 1962.

Vroom, V. H. *Work and motivation.* New York: John Wiley & Sons, 1964.

Wernimont, P. F. Intrinsic and extrinsic factors in job satisfaction. Unpublished doctoral thesis, University of Minnesota, 1964.

Wernimont, P. F. Intrinsic and extrinsic factors in job satisfaction. *Journal of Applied Psychology,* 1966, *50,* 41–50.

White, R. W. Motivation reconsidered: The concept of competence. *Psychological Review,* 1959, *46,* 297–334.

Has the research challenge to Motivation-Hygiene Theory been conclusive? An analysis of critical studies

Benedict Grigaliunas
and
Yoash Wiener

Since its introduction in Herzberg, Mausner, & Snyderman (1959), Motivation-Hygiene (M–H) Theory has had a wide impact on the field of job attitudes and motivation. The theory, with its implications, has produced a large following of proponents as well as a significant number of critics and has created a major controversy in the history of industrial psychology. For the first article reprinted in this chapter, Whitsett and Winslow (1967) performed a detailed analysis of research studies critical to M–H Theory. They pointed out that many investigations were characterized by methodological flaws, misrepresentation of results, and gross misunderstanding of M–H Theory.

In the past several years, the number of critical articles has not declined. Some old flaws pointed out by Whitsett and Winslow have persisted, and new issues have emerged. Many of the critical studies have concluded that M–H Theory is not valid. Korman (1971), discussing it in a textbook, stated: "Conclusions by Dunnette, Campbell, and Hakel (1967) based on their work, as well as that of Ewen, et al. (1966), among others, seem to have effectively laid the Herzberg theory to rest in terms

Note: The authors (listed in alphabetical order) would like to acknowledge the helpful comments of Dr. Frederick Herzberg on this paper. A few paragraphs have been deleted to remove some redundancy from previous articles, and a review of the two new articles mentioned in the introduction has been added.

of the degree to which it is supported by well-designed studies." (p. 149).

This analysis will attempt to show that such definitive and unqualified conclusions are not warranted on the basis of the research from which they were derived. Several other reviews of M–H literature have appeared recently (e.g., King, 1970; Bockman, 1971). By and large, they have classified and summarized methods, findings, and conclusions. This article will *analyze* conclusions, data, and procedures.

We will deal primarily with studies critical of M–H Theory that have been published subsequent to the Whitsett and Winslow paper. We would like to make it quite clear that defending M–H Theory per se is not our purpose. The support of any theory and the maintenance or improvement of its utility can be effected only through further research and the elaboration of new theoretical and methodological ideas. Our goal is, by reviewing analytically the large number of critical studies which have appeared in the past four or five years, to permit a more balanced view of M–H Theory and its research base. The issues to be discussed and analyzed are as follows: (1) the methodology of measuring the two feeling dimensions on separate continua, (2) the "overall" job satisfaction concept, (3) individual differences and M–H Theory, (4) the reliability of the critical-incident method, (5) the concept of the "importance" of job factors, (6) performance implications of M–H Theory, and (7) the social desirability criticism.

A STATEMENT OF M–H THEORY

The following is a brief statement of M–H Theory. A detailed statement can be found in several sources (e.g., Herzberg et al., 1959; and Herzberg, 1962, 1966, 1968). M–H Theory makes a distinction between two *types* and *sets* of job factors. One set revolves around the actual doing of the job, the job content or the intrinsic aspects of the job. These factors, which are called *motivators*, include achievement, recognition for achievement, work itself, responsibility, advancement, and growth. The other set revolves around the environmental setting of the job. These factors are extrinsic to the job; they include company policy and administration, supervision, salary, interpersonal relations, working conditions, status, and security. They are called *hygiene* or maintenance factors.

The motivator factors and the hygiene factors relate differentially to two separate *sets* of human needs: pain avoidance and growth. The common element of the pain-avoidance needs is that their satisfaction can bring about an elimination of either physical or psychological deficiency, pain, or discomfort. However, they cannot lead to a growth experience. The growth needs are those that have to do with the uniquely human push for self-actualization (Maslow, 1955).

The basic proposition of M–H Theory is that the motivator factors can act as incentives in the satisfaction of growth needs and the hygiene factors in the satisfaction of pain-avoidance needs. From this proposition M–H Theory derives its attitudinal-affective and motivational-performance implications.

Attitudinal-affective implications

M–H Theory proposes a distinction between the affective states resulting from growth and pain-avoidance needs. The affective experience resulting from the satisfaction of pain-avoidance needs is relief. When the needs are unfulfilled, the affective experience is discomfort or pain. In M–H literature, this feeling dimension of discomfort–relief has been most often labeled the dissatisfaction dimension, with the end points labeled "No dissatisfaction–Dissatisfaction." The affective experience resulting from the satisfaction of growth needs is *qualitatively* different from the feeling dimension, discomfort–relief. It is a feeling dimension of positive satisfaction, conceived as a feeling continuum of fulfillment–emptiness. In M–H literature, the end points of this dimension are most often labeled "No satisfaction–Satisfaction. Hygiene factors cannot cause fulfillment. When at a high level they will bring about relief; when at a low level they will cause discomfort. Motivator factors, on the other hand, cannot cause discomfort. They can bring about fulfillment or the absence of it (emptiness), depending on whether they are at a low or high level.

In M–H Theory, job feelings are bidimensional. One group of job factors—the motivators—is most likely to affect one type of job feelings—fulfillment–emptiness—and another group of job factors—the hygiene factors—is most likely to affect another type of job feelings—discomfort–relief. If a job is to contribute to the mental well-being of a worker, both types of needs have to be satisfied, and both types of feelings should exist, originating in the appropriate job factors.

Motivational-performance implications

Hygiene factors, when acting as incentives for pain-avoidance needs, are forces external to the individual himself which either pull or push him toward an action or movement. Action or performance caused by such forces can be characterized as movement performance. The individual can be moved—*pulled* to act by an incentive (e.g. better work conditions) which can reduce an existing pain, or *pushed* by the incentive of avoiding a threat of pain (avoiding being fired). In either case, these forces move the individual by acting upon him from the outside. The pain-avoidance needs themselves have the basic characteristic of being cyclical in nature. The feeling of deprivation is recurring, and it progressively requires an increase in incentives for its satisfaction. The performance implications are as follows: the effect of hygiene factors is short term, and the level of performance will never be above the minimum effort necessary to eliminate a state of psychological or physical pain or discomfort. In order to get performance (movement) one must create a pain situation or play upon an already existing pain. Otherwise there is no reason to expect movement.

The motivational dynamics of performance brought about by a manipulation of motivator factors is entirely different. Contrary to the movement performance caused by hygiene factors, motivator factors cause motivated performance. The underlying motivational processes are activated by an internal generator rather than by extrinsic forces that push or pull. The underlying needs to be fulfilled are growth needs, which are positive-approach drives, in contrast to the pain-avoidance nature of hygiene needs. The incentives to satisfy such needs *are actions by the individual himself*—knowing more than before, creating more and being more competent than in the past. Motivator factors provide for such incentives. The performance implications here are clear too: motivator factors are long lasting in their effects and can lift performance to approach the maximum potential of an individual.

Empirical support for M–H Theory

The two major aspects of the theory that have received empirical support are the distinction between the two sets of factors as they relate to job feelings, and the performance consequences of motivator and hygiene factors.

In M–H Theory the feeling dimension of discomfort–relief (dissatisfaction) and those factors that contribute to these feelings (hygiene factors) are *separate and distinct* from those factors (motivators) that contribute to the feeling dimension of fulfillment–emptiness ("satisfaction"). Empirically demonstrating this fundamental distinction is indeed a difficult methodological issue. Herzberg, Mausner, and Snyderman (1959) suggested a procedure and a strategy to tackle it. They attempted to specify job feelings and attitudes and to identify the factors in these feelings by using the critical-incident method in the form of a semistructured interview. This allowed these components to emerge from the subjects' own experiences and ensured that an actual event and a change in feeling had occurred. The interviewer asked the respondent to describe sequences of events related to times when he was exceptionally satisfied and exceptionally dissatisfied with his job. Two hundred engineers and accountants were used as subjects. A content analysis showed a clear-cut distinction between two sets of factors. Job context factors—hygiene— were most often mentioned as contributing to dissatisfaction (low feelings), and job content factors—motivators—were most often mentioned as causing satisfaction (high feelings).

This study provides support for the proposition that the motivator and hygiene factors are dynamically distinct, since they underlie different affective states. It also provides support for the proposition that satisfaction is not an opposite feeling from dissatisfaction. If satisfaction is the opposite of dissatisfaction, then they should have both been caused by the same factors (a high level of any factor would cause satisfaction, and a low level of the same factor would cause dissatisfaction).

The methodological approach of Herzberg et al. (1959) seems to be a logical approach for the investigation of the dimensionality of affective states. It allows dimensionality to emerge when the types of events or factors associated with a given feeling state are *different* from the factors and events associated with a different feeling state. In addition to providing a criterion for dimensionality, this method is a source of information about the dynamic association of feeling states with actual underlying events and factors. Such information can only add to the understanding of affective processes and their possible antecedents. The Herzberg et al. study has been replicated in different job situations with different types of subjects and even in different cultures. In most of these studies the pattern of results has been the same. This methodology has been the target of much of the criticism of M–H Theory.

The second source of empirical support for M–H Theory comes from studies investigating the performance consequences of motivator and hygiene factors. An appropriate procedure for testing the performance implications of the theory should consist of manipulating job factors as independent variables and measuring their effect on objective criteria of job performance. Recently a series of such studies has been carried out (Ford, 1970; Paul, Robinson, & Herzberg, 1969[1]). The findings show increased productivity as a result of introducing more motivators into a job under constant hygiene conditions, where previous changes in hygiene did not produce any productivity changes. The different behavioral consequences of motivator and hygiene manipulations indicate the existence of different motivational processes.

The above described "performance" research—the job enrichment research—has not been criticized as a source of empirical support for M–H Theory. It has been altogether ignored in the critical literature.

THE METHODOLOGY OF MEASURING THE TWO FEELING STATES ON SEPARATE CONTINUA

Perhaps the most critical methodological issue confronting M–H Theory treats the question of bidimensionality of job attitudes and feelings. The existence of the qualitative difference between the feelings of satisfaction and dissatisfaction is the essence of M–H Theory and any of

---

[1] This article is reprinted in Chapter 3.

its derivations. If any theory is to be adequately tested, then its premises must be assumed correct and the hypotheses derived. In M–H Theory, one must assume the bidimensionality underlying the feelings of satisfaction and dissatisfaction. Few of the critical studies have begun with this assumption. One study that has followed this requirement of theory testing was conducted by Hulin and Smith (1967). They made the point quite clearly: "it must be assumed that it [M–H Theory] is correct and that satisfaction is qualitatively different from dissatisfaction, and overall satisfaction and dissatisfaction must be measured on different scales."

Hulin and Smith, then, attempted to devise a procedure which would achieve a meaningful separation of the two feeling states. However, closer examination of their method indicates certain deficiencies. They used the General Motors Faces Scale which has been used in the past to measure overall job feelings. This scale consists of five faces with varying smiles, a neutral face, and five faces with varying frowns. In order to separate qualitatively the feelings of satisfaction and dissatisfaction, Hulin and Smith broke at the neutral point and called them two separate scales: the "smiling" scale to measure satisfaction and the "frowning" scale to measure dissatisfaction. As a result, the authors obtained on paper two scales with a common end point (neutral) in each. In reality, two qualitatively different scales have not been attained; rather a unidimensional scale was broken into two parts. To be at least formally consistent with M–H Theory, the end points should consist of faces representing satis-faction–no satisfaction and dissatisfaction–no dissatisfaction, rather than satisfaction–neutral and dissatisfaction–neutral.

More crucial than these formal difficulties is the psychological mean-ingfulness of the above procedure. We question the procedure of having a person rate himself on cognitive labels denoting an affective state as a means to elicit or measure this feeling state. The following example will help to clarify the difficulties involved. Consider love and hate which, intuitively, can be considered to be qualitatively different, not opposite, feelings, and largely independent.

Suppose you ask a child if he loves his daddy and ask another child if he hates his daddy. Can one expect the two children to respond to these questions on the basis of two different feeling states just because one question used the label "love" and the other "hate"? The difficulty can be only compounded with the feeling states of satisfaction and dissatis-faction. In addition to this basic psychological question of the degree to which cognitive labels represent affective states, obvious semantic and linguistic difficulties are inherent in distinguishing the constructs of satis-faction and dissatisfaction from each other. Such a procedure has further questionable utility because often the cognitive labeling of emotions is dependent upon broad cultural mores and specific temporary situa-tional cues (Schacter & Singer, 1962). In general, the self-rating procedure to assess a complex feeling state suffers from the disadvantages common to all rating-scale instruments: it is easy to fake; it is global and undifferentiating in its assessment (Blum & Naylor, 1968, p. 295); and it is quite unreliable (Tiffin & McCormick, 1965, p. 256).

The possibility of a certain predictive utility in employing a rating scale to assess a simple emotional state should not be denied. However, the rating-scale procedure does not seem to lead to a better understanding and explanation of dynamic processes involved in affective reactions. A very frustrating experience for most visitors in foreign countries is being faced with the global, undifferentiated, and practically impossible question: "Do you like our country?" Presenting a scale of smiling and frowning faces to adults and asking them: "How much do you like your job?" seems to be problematic.

Hulin and Smith's own data illustrate the difficulties that subjects had in responding to their supposedly separate measures of satisfaction and dissatisfaction. All but two assigned to respond to the dissatisfaction scale actually checked only the top two faces out of the possible five. Hulin and Smith then state, "Due to the *satisfaction* levels encountered in this company, the JIG *dissatisfaction* scale was essentially a three point scale" (italics ours). This factual statement indicates two points: (1) the feelings-state labels of "satisfaction" and "dissatisfaction" were used interchangeably, showing that the meaning of the concept "two different feeling dimensions" remained ambiguous, (2) subjects, when asked to rate their feeling of dissatisfaction, could scarcely do so (they checked just the top two faces out of a possible five). This reinforces our argument that simply providing a person with a verbal label indicating a feeling state and asking him to rate himself with regard to it does not necessarily provide a psychologically meaningful datum. Hulin and Smith's procedure, then, does not seem to be an appropriate alternative technique for measuring meaningfully and independently the two separate feeling states of satisfaction and dissatisfaction.

Yet this technique was used in another study (Graen & Hulin, 1968) to further "test" M–H Theory. Subjects were asked to check on the "faces" scale the degree of their satisfaction or dissatisfaction with the "total" job. According to M–H Theory, it is meaningless to expect only one kind of feeling, whether it is satisfaction or dissatisfaction, since the total job consists of different experiences (motivators, hygiene factors), producing different feeling states (satisfaction, dissatisfaction). The Graen and Hulin study did not test any hypothesis derived from M–H Theory.

Additional support indicating that Hulin's method failed to provide meaningful separate measures of satisfaction and dissatisfaction comes from two studies by Waters and Waters (1969) and Waters and Roach (1971). In these studies, the procedure to measure separately the two feeling states was similar to the Hulin and Smith method. The 1969 study reports the following intercorrelations: satisfaction −.61 with dissatisfaction, while these two scales, respectively, correlated .78 and −.69 with satisfaction–dissatisfaction (overall satisfaction). These high correlations point to the possibility that all three scales measure pretty much the *same thing*, whatever it is. The high correlation can support the contention that subjects employed the same (or a very similar) affective frame of reference in making the three ratings of satisfaction, dissatisfaction, and satisfaction–dissatisfaction. These correlations seem to refute the premise of successful separate measurement of the two feeling states upon which the conclusions are based.

All the above studies sought to measure the two feelings on separate continua. But they took a unidimensional scale of satisfaction–dissatisfaction and broke it at the neutral point into two scales. On paper they indeed obtained two scales (with a common end point—neutral—in each). Psychologically meaningful separate measurement of the two feeling states requires more than merely dividing a unidimensional scale into two halves.

Another, somewhat different attempt at separate measurement of satisfaction and dissatisfaction was that of Lahiri and Srivastva (1967). They presented subjects with 26 job factors, 13 motivators and 13 hygiene factors, with the following instructions: "Think of a time when you felt exceptionally good about your job. . . . The following are some of the factors which may have contributed to your feeling of satisfaction at that time. Indicate by checking (✔) the extent to which *each factor* contributed to your feeling of satisfaction on the scales given below" (p. 256, italics ours). This constituted the method of measuring satisfaction. For measuring dissatisfaction, the instructions were identical, except that "dissatisfaction" was substituted for "satisfaction" and "bad" was substituted for "good." The same 26 factors were presented for rating. Apart from the questionable meaningfulness of labeling emotional experiences, subjects were asked to rate *both* motivator and hygiene factors on *both* dimensions of satisfaction and dissatisfaction! If M–H Theory is assumed as correct, this is impossible, since motivator factors underlie satisfaction and hygiene factors underlie dissatisfaction. Lahiri and Srivastva forced subjects to ascribe inappropriate factors to their job feelings. The resultant ratings are meaningless in terms of M–H Theory, for two reasons: (1) their procedure did not provide for a real separation of the two feeling dimensions, and (2) the data generated cannot test the theory.

We acknowledge the desirability of testing M–H propositions by an assessment of affective states. The techniques proposed so far by critics have relied upon rating-scale methods, which presume a single continuum. The critical-incident method is not restricted in this way and can tap dynamics underlying affective states which are qualitatively separate. Other possibilities would be welcome.

THE "OVERALL" JOB SATISFACTION CONCEPT

A major source of confusion and misunderstanding in the research history of M–H Theory has been those studies that have "derived" hypotheses from the theory, employing "overall" job satisfaction as a basic construct. In spite of repeated attempts for explanation on the part of Herzberg and his colleagues (i.e., the Whitsett and Winslow article above), this approach to "testing" M–H Theory has continued.

A widely quoted study by Hinrichs and Mischkind (1967) falls in this category. Their report opens with an overview of the theory: "Briefly stated, the [M–H] notion proposes that two distinct sets of factors account for overall job satisfaction . . ." (p. 191). This statement is a clear misunderstanding of the major premise of M–H Theory. A most unique contribution of M–H Theory is its view of job feelings as bidimensional phenomena rather than one overall feeling state. Two distinct sets of factors (motivators, hygiene factors) account not for "overall job satisfaction" but for *two qualitatively distinct* feeling states (satisfaction and dissatisfaction, respectively).

Hinrichs and Mischkind asserted that one could predict from Herzberg's theoretical statements that people with high *overall satisfaction,* when asked to specify things that influence them in *positive and negative* ways concerning their job, would mention in *both* cases primarily motivator factors, whereas people low on overall job satisfaction would mention in *both* cases primarily hygiene factors. This is erroneous. M–H Theory cannot make differential predictions as to levels of overall satisfaction because there is no such concept in M–H Theory. The Hinrichs-Mischkind hypothesis clearly implies an association of *both positive and negative* feelings with either motivator or hygiene factors, depending on the level of "overall satisfaction." Such a hypothesis cannot be derived from M–H Theory and cannot be used to "test" the theory.

Hinrichs and Mischkind did not employ in their conclusions the only analysis of their data relevant to M–H Theory. This analysis deals with the total group (the other analyses dealt with the high and low overall satisfaction groups). The prediction from the total group would be that when subjects respond to the request, "List one or two specific things that most influence your feelings in a positive (negative) way about your employment" (p. 193), they would mention primarily motivator factors for the positive feelings, and primarily hygiene factors for the negative feelings. The results obtained from this analysis are precisely in line with the M–H Theory hypothesis. The authors themselves refer to the particular chi-square (the type of "motivation" factor associated with positive and negative reasons) most relevant to the above hypothesis as the analysis that produced the "result [that] accounts for the greatest proportion of the total chi-square" (p. 196). Specifically, this analysis indicated that:

(*a*) a greater proportion of hygiene factors are mentioned as negative as opposed to positive reasons ($p < .0001$); (*b*) a greater proportion of motivator factors are mentioned as positive as opposed to negative reasons ($p <$ .0001); (c) a greater proportion of money factors are mentioned as negative as opposed to positive reasons ($p < .0001$). (p. 196)

When the data are analyzed for the total group, without regard for the level of overall job satisfaction, M–H Theory is supported.

When the data are analyzed with regard to levels of overall job satisfaction (JS), a strong association between types of factors (motivator, hygiene) and positive and negative "reasons" (feelings) is found in accordance to M–H Theory for the high overall JS ($n = 455$). Only a weak tendency in the predicted direction, however, can be observed for the low JS ($n = 158$) (money being considered hygiene; Hinrichs and Mischkind, Table 3, p. 195). The distinction between high and low overall satisfaction is meaningless in the conceptual framework of M–H Theory. This analysis, therefore, is not relevant for reaching conclusions concerning the theory.

Does the distinction between high and low overall satisfaction in terms of the operations used in the Hinrichs-Mischkind study have psychological meaningfulness? Their measure for overall JS is: "Considering everything, how would you rate your present satisfaction as an XYZ employee? (Circle one number on the scale below which best expresses how you feel)" (p. 193). The subject was then presented with a list of 11 numbers from 0 to 10 (the zero being designated "completely dissatisfied" and the ten "completely satisfied"). This scale seemed to provide for very little variance ($SD = 1.82$, $M = 7.04$). Also, 74 percent of the sample (455 subjects) marked the top four points of the scale, while only 24 percent fell in the seven lower points. Since the mean rating was 7.04, an extremely high number of subjects must have checked the point seven. The scale did not provide for fine discrimination throughout its total range.

The authors, indeed, had difficulties in determining what was "high overall satisfaction" and what was "low." Their decision about a cut-off point was post hoc and arbitrary. Subjects circling the top four numbers were considered high-satisfaction subjects; they consisted of the larger majority ($n = 455$). A much smaller group ($n = 158$) marked the seven bottom numbers and were considered the low-satisfaction group. The justification given was: "five percent of the respondents checking 'seven' indicated they had 'no negative feelings' about their job, whereas not a single respondent checking 'six' failed to mention at least one negative reason" (p. 194). How many subjects marked the numbers 0–4, which are the points below the neutral point of the scale? To consider these subjects as low-satisfaction subjects would seem to be a more appropriate procedure, if one uses such a rating scale.

Several other recent studies (Wolf, 1967; Kosmo & Behling, 1969; Armstrong, 1971) investigate hypotheses that deal with direct relationships between overall satisfaction and specific job factors, claiming that these hypotheses are a test for M–H Theory.

An examination of Wolf's (1967) procedure shows its inadequacy for making conclusions concerning M–H Theory. The following is a main item from his questionnaire: "What do you feel caused your *job satisfaction* to increase, stay the same, decrease during the last year?" (p. 123). On the basis of this question, he related different job factors to satisfaction, concluding that M–H Theory cannot be fully supported, since even though motivators were found to be associated mostly with satisfaction, "the context factors were related to both satisfaction and dissatisfaction." The above item asks subjects to relate to changes in their overall job satisfaction. It taps a unidimensional property, whatever it is. It equates "decreased satisfaction" with Herzberg's construct of dissatisfaction and equates "increased satisfaction" with Herzberg's construct of satisfaction. Wolf's study is typical of the traditional job satisfaction model. It employs M–H terminology, but not the conceptual framework of M–H Theory.

Kosmo and Behling's study (1969) suffers from the same weakness. The aim of this study was to test predictions of the effect of various combinations of perceived levels of motivators and hygiene factors on overall satisfaction with the job. By confirming such predictions, the authors assumed that "the compatibility of the Herzberg duality with a logically-derived scalar format" could be established. The subjects, on the basis of their perceived level of motivators and hygienes, were divided into four groups: High motivators–High hygiene (HH), High motivators–Low hygiene (HL), Low motivators–High hygiene (LH), and Low motivators–Low hygiene (LL). The dependent variable was overall JS. The hypothesis was that HH subjects would be highest in overall satisfaction; then in decreasing order, HL, LH, and LL. The hypothesis is a typical "job satisfaction" hypothesis, based on the "traditional" model. In a general form it would state that the higher the perceived level of all kinds of positive factors, the more the individual would be satisfied with the job. The results are in line with the hypothesis and thus with the traditional model. They do not reflect one way or the other on M–H Theory.

Armstrong (1971) investigated the role of "occupational level" as a moderator variable in the conceptual framework of M–H Theory. He stated two hypotheses: (1) for the high occupational level, motivators contribute more to overall job satisfaction than do hygiene factors; (2) for the low occupational level, hygiene factors make the greater contribution. These hypotheses have nothing to do with M–H Theory, even though they use its terminology. In M–H Theory "overall satisfaction" is a meaningless concept. One should not attempt to draw conclusions about the theory employing this concept in making the hypotheses purporting to test it.

Another aspect of Armstrong's study is also questionable. He wanted to show that the "proposed content-context dichotomy for the job factors was not empirically supported at either occupational level." To demonstrate this he obtained "satisfaction" ratings for each of the factors and then intercorrelated them. There were no more significant correlations within the motivator and hygiene sectors of the matrix than between them. This was taken as evidence against the bidimensional notion of M–H Theory. The problem here and in other studies using correlational and factor analytical approaches (e.g., Levine & Weitz, 1968) is that they try to test the idea of bidimensionality of job feelings by assuming a priori unidimensionality of feelings. This is done by having all job factors, whether they be motivators or hygiene factors, rated on the *one* feeling dimension of "overall satisfaction." On the basis of what logic or psychological process should one expect an intercorrelation matrix based on a unidimensional feeling rating to produce evidence for *two* different feeling states associated with different kinds of factors?

Two additional studies (Weissenberg & Gruenfeld, 1968; Gruenfeld & Weissenberg, 1970) investigated relationships between the variables job involvement, field independence, and articulation and "job satisfaction." The procedure involved the following two steps: (1) measuring *all* job factors (i.e., both hygiene factors and motivators) on one feeling dimension (scale by Wernimont, 1966); (2) correlating these factors with a measure of overall satisfaction (nine-point scale). Conclusions about M–H Theory from such procedures are unwarranted.

Finally, Graen's (1968) study should be mentioned. His ideas, design, and hypotheses are similar to the well-known Ewen, Smith, Hulin & Locke study (1966). This latter investigation was criticized by Whitsett and Winslow in the first article of this chapter, and the criticism was acknowledged by the investigators (see Hulin & Smith, 1967). They admitted that

. . . unfortunately, both the Ewen et al. and the Graen (1966) articles have what could be considered a serious shortcoming. They measured overall job satisfaction by means of the General Motor Faces Scale, which assumes that job satisfaction–dissatisfaction is a continuum. . . . If, as the two-factor theory suggests, satisfaction and dissatisfaction are qualitatively different, the use of such a continuum could raise some doubt about the conclusions and the criticism of Herzberg resulting from these analyses. (p. 396)

In spite of this acknowledgment of a serious shortcoming, Graen replicated it in his 1968 study and concluded that M–H Theory was invalid.

The "overall satisfaction" studies do not pit traditional theory and M–H Theory predictions against each other. Rather, the hypotheses and predictions they make are all based on traditional models. These studies employ M–H *terminology* but do not test its *propositions*.

INDIVIDUAL DIFFERENCES AND M–H THEORY

Several researchers (Dunnette, Campbell, & Hakel, 1967; and Schwab & Heneman, 1970) claim that the association between high (satisfying)

and low (dissatisfying) job experiences and motivator and hygiene factors predicted by M–H Theory is not supported. What is being asked of M–H Theory is seldom demanded of other theory—perfect prediction. As Dunnette et al. state: "Clearly the first five job features . . . are more often associated with satisfying stories, and another five job features . . . are more often associated with dissatisfying stories. But it is also apparent that the association is far from perfect" (p. 145). Schwab and Heneman express similar sentiments. Anything less than perfect prediction indicates "lack of confirmation" for the M–H Theory.

This absence of perfect prediction is used to charge that Herzberg "chose to ignore . . . individual differences in favor of stating a general theory of job motivation" (Dunnette et al., 1967, p. 145). They seem to say that one is justified in proposing a "general theory" only if the data fit a perfect prediction. Proposing a "general theory" when the data show individual differences is unwarranted and only points out that individual differences have been ignored. Such arguments indicate a confusion between deviation of data from perfect prediction and a theoretical failure to account for individual differences. They oversimplify the dilemma involved in attempting to construct "general laws" in psychology.

The fact that data do not perfectly support a prediction does not automatically mean that the prediction "ignored individual differences." Very possibly, the imperfect prediction was caused by errors of measurement inherent in any psychological procedure. One will be hard pressed to find even one psychological study that has produced results conforming "perfectly" to prediction. The Dunnette et al. and Schwab and Heneman contention that Herzberg's results were "misleading" because they were not "perfect" is itself misleading. Herzberg is no more guilty of ignoring individual differences than any other researcher whose work produced or supported a "general law" on the basis of results which include variance.

More specifically, this question of individual differences in M–H research data is a major issue in the report by Schwab and Heneman (1970). They attempted to show that many of the subjects in a typical M–H critical-incident study deviate from the expected response. There was no need to conduct a special study to show this. A cursory glance at any M–H replication shows it immediately. Motivator factors are sometimes mentioned in low (dissatisfaction) stories and hygiene factors are sometimes mentioned in high (satisfaction) stories. This would not have happened if a number of subjects had not responded in a way different from that expected. Schwab and Heneman's study does not really add any new information. However, the way they present their conclusions exemplifies another case of misinterpretation of data.

Having obtained their data by the conventional M–H methodology, they looked at the frequency with which subjects gave one of the four possible combinations of motivator-hygiene responses to "high-low" stories. These combinations are: motivator-hygiene (M–H) responses,

M–M responses, H–M responses, and H–H responses. The percentage of subjects in each of these categories was 43.5, 41.2, 4.7, and 10.6, respectively. Perfect prediction would be the combination M–H, a motivator response to a satisfying event and a hygiene response to a dissatisfying event. Totally wrong prediction would be H–M, a hygiene response to a satisfying event and a motivator response to a dissatisfying event. M–M and H–H are "partially" correct.

What conclusions did Schwab and Heneman draw from these data? They state: "One could more accurately predict *individual* responses to favorable and unfavorable events by betting against the two-factor theory." It is indeed true that the chances to win a bet that the theory is *perfectly correct* are 43.5 percent, but the chances to win a bet that the theory is *totally wrong* are 4.7 percent. In general, 95.3 percent of the individual responses were either totally or partially correct. Schwab and Heneman's conclusion is not in line with all their data.

Their data in its "aggregate" form (i.e., as in the original M–H studies) has not provided for a good replication. They reported that 46 percent of the responses to unfavorable events were motivators. In a typical M–H study this percentage is much less (averaging about 30 percent). The "typical" M–H study would show even better predictability of individual responses than did the Schwab and Heneman study. (For further treatment of an M–H Theory of individual differences, see Herzberg, Mathapo, Wiener, Wiesen, 1974, and Herzberg, 1966.)

THE RELIABILITY OF THE CRITICAL-INCIDENT METHOD

The criticism of the reliability of the critical-incident method consists of two aspects: (1) the reliability of the coding process and (2) the consistency of the data.

As regards the first aspect, criticism is laid against the subjectivity of the method. The argument states, with a negative implication, that data produced by the critical-incident method depend on judgmental decisions. Furthermore, the "possibility of experimenter-biasing effects in analyzing the data" has been brought up (Dunnette et al., 1967, p. 147). The available evid·nce however, refutes these contentions. Almost all M–H studies using the critical-incident method report a high degree of agreement between coders. Even Schwab and Heneman (1970) concede coding reliability. They assessed reliabilities for all coding steps, concluding that "high inter-coder reliability was obtained in each of the four procedural steps" (p. 55).

Existing research shows that good reliability is obtained in the use of the sequence-of-events method (a variation of the critical-incident method) or the critical-incident method in M–H research. There has been no research to show otherwise. The criticism that subjectivity is present in the critical-incident method apparently assumes that other traditional methods cannot be accused of the same fault. Experimenter subjectivity exists, however, wherever an a priori decision is made on what factors or variables are to be measured by any questionnaire or rating scale. Dunnette himself makes the point: "a more fundamental contribution of the study is that job factors so identified [by the critical-incident method] were allowed to emerge from descriptions of actual job situations rather than being based exclusively on responses to checklists or sets of statements developed ahead of time by the investigator" (Dunnette & Kirchner, 1965, p. 152). Why should judgments of social desirability and content classification of 286 statements describing job events (Dunnette et al., 1967) be less subjective than judgments involved in M–H methodology? Yet the judgments in Dunnette et al. are the cornerstone of a study that attempts to demonstrate the subjectivity of the judgments involved in M–H methodology.

The second aspect of the reliability issue is concerned with the *consistency* of the generated data, which is criticized in Hinton's widely quoted study (1968). He requested a sample of college students to relate, on two separate data collections, one good and one bad sequence of events that had occurred within the past 18 months and a good and bad sequence that had occurred more than 18 months ago. If the data generated by M–H methodology are to be considered reliable, the factor profiles obtained from the sequences occurring within the past 18 months should parallel those obtained from the sequences occurring 18 months or more ago. The author apparently intended to use the test-retest method to obtain a reliability index. His method does not constitute such an index. By intentionally manipulating the time variable of incident occurrence, he introduces an additional variable which has to be taken into account in interpreting the generated data.

Recent research (Davis & Allen, 1970; Grigaliunas, 1970) shows that there are differences in the time a given feeling associated with a factor lasts. Some factors are of short duration, while others are long-duration factors. When one taps sequences that occurred 18 months or more ago, one capitalizes on the long-duration factors and tends to eliminate the short-duration factors. Hinton also introduced a situational variable, because with a three-year time span, it is highly probable that a significant number of his college subjects were in a totally different environment during the last year as opposed to a year, or two, or three years ago, when some of them were in high school. Hinton forced differences between profiles and defeated his original intent to measure test-retest reliability.

If one wants to measure the reliability of the sequence-of-events methodology, one should keep all possible variables constant. A possible way to do this would be to use a large sample of subjects under identical conditions (same job, organization, time period, demographic data, etc.), split the sample into two groups, and compare profiles. These profiles should then be very similar, not only in the relationship between motivators and hygiene in general but in specific rank order and relative frequency of factor occurrence. The fact that one gets differences between profiles with respect to relative frequency and rank order of factors when a time or situational variable is introduced indicates not lack of reliability but the sensitivity of the method. One is correct to expect the general relationship between motivator-hygiene factors and high-low (satisfaction-dissatisfaction) sequences across situations and time periods, but not correct to expect the same specific rank ordering and relative frequency of factors.

Hinton's concern in being fair to assess the reliability of M–H data led him to use the sequence-of-events methodology. Though claiming close adherence to the original Herzberg method, he obtained data dissimilar to Herzberg's and the other numerous replications utilizing this method. He failed to obtain the typical relationship between motivator and hygiene factors and high (satisfaction) and low (dissatisfaction) sequences. Based on part of his own data, he obtained approximately 52 percent motivator factors and 48 percent hygiene factors in the high sequences and 44 percent motivator factors and 56 percent hygiene factors in the low sequences. These data were for the sequences that occurred 18 months or more ago. A similar percentage distribution is found in the sequences that occurred within 18 months. Most replications show a much stronger relationship.

Hinton's failure to attain a typical replication is a serious shortcoming, because the reliability or validity of a method cannot be assessed by using data that is atypical for that method. This probably happened because of the coding of sequences (apart altogether from questions of time and situation). Closer examination of his data shows that the average number of different factors coded per sequence under all his conditions was 3.79 (data based on Hinton, 1968, Table 4). Herzberg, in his original study, obtained an average of 1.84 different factors for each of the sequences of events reported by respondents. Most replications do not significantly deviate from this average. An average of four different factors coded per sequence is unreasonably high and sheds doubts on the nature of the coding. Hinton's problematic data and his procedure seem unable to clarify either methodological or theoretical issues.

There is strong evidence for high reliability in the coding of the content-analyzed data (see replication studies as well as Schwab & Heneman, 1970). The challenge to the consistency of results in Hinton's work has been shown to be far from well based. Consistency of results is best indicated by the numerous replications that have been already performed on a wide variety of populations, geographic locations, and jobs, as well as other demographic variables. Hinton's error was to confuse consistency of factor profile with test-retest reliability. That profiles should differ in factor occurrence and rank order for various situations and conditions is

an index of the strength of the method. This allows for individual differences to manifest themselves across differing populations and situations,
while the general relationship between motivator-hygiene factors and
high-low sequences maintains itself.

THE "IMPORTANCE" OF THE JOB FACTORS CONCEPT

A number of researchers continue to make a rather common error of
theoretical interpretation in testing M–H Theory; they suggest that motivator factors should be rated more important than hygiene factors when
an individual evaluates a total job. The logic rests on the assumption that
since motivator factors, when present, lead to job satisfaction, they should
be rated as the more important. Hygiene factors should not be rated as
important, since they can only be determinants of job dissatisfaction. This
thinking clearly implies that M–H Theory places a value on motivators as
being "good" and hygienes as being "bad." This is not correct. Hulin and
Smith (1967) exemplify such thinking:

> The two-factor theory would predict that if the work were very interesting
> or if there were good opportunities for advancement on jobs, then these jobs
> would be seen as very good. . . . However, if the work were very uninterest-
> ing or if there were no opportunities for advancement, these jobs would not
> necessarily be *judged* as being bad jobs. . . . Low pay, on the other hand,
> should lead to a job being *judged* as being relatively bad, but high pay should
> not necessarily lead to a job being judged as being good (p. 399, italics ours).

Hulin and Smith assumed they were testing M–H predictions about the
causative origins of feelings arising from specific job situations. What they
were primarily concerned with was the general issue of how individuals
judge or evaluate jobs as being good or bad. To the extent that M–H
Theory can be applied to this question, it would not agree with the Hulin
and Smith hypotheses. Both motivators and hygienes, if present, can be
determinants of a job being evaluated as good, as well as both, if lacking,
can be determinants of a job being evaluated as bad. When an individual
evaluates a total job, M–H Theory would state that feelings of dissatisfaction are just as "important" as feelings of satisfaction. Consequently, motivators and hygienes are equally "important" for any given job. An individual's pain as well as an individual's satisfaction are very real and
equally important feeling states, even though their causative origins and
natures differ drastically. Certainly an employee may state that he has a
great job if he gets paid very well but does not have to do anything.
Likewise, a dedicated teacher may feel he has a good job even though he
earns very little.

Hulin and Smith made the mistake of equating good with satisfaction,
and bad with dissatisfaction. This is logically unjustified, and definitely
unwarranted on the basis of M–H Theory. Furthermore, they also violated
the basic premise with which they began their own study: the need to

measure the two feeling states separately. They placed the good and bad as the ends of a single scale—a continuum—and related responses to this scale to job factors.

The general error in asserting that M–H Theory predicts that motivator factors are more important than hygiene factors has been made in other recent studies. Armstrong (1971) stated:

> Since the *judged* importance of the two types of factors was found to be a function of occupational level, . . . those (predictions) derived from Herzberg's model were refuted . . . it logically follows that content aspects should be *judged* most important because they are asserted to be the primary contributors to job satisfaction . . . (p. 64, italics ours).

In the second half of his study, Hinton (1968) makes the same error. His procedure was simply to give a list of 14 of the Herzberg factors, along with their definitions, to the subjects. He then asked them to "rank order these 14 factors according to the *importance* the factors held for them personally." He assumes that M–H Theory would predict "a monotonically decreasing magnitude of responses in the 'motivator' column and a monotonically increasing magnitude of responses in the 'hygiene' column." Obviously his results did not show this, nor would M–H Theory have made such a prediction.

There is nothing in M–H Theory that suggests that motivators are "good" and hygienes are "bad," or that motivators are more "important" and hygienes are "less important." Both motivators and hygienes are equally important for any given job. Nevertheless, groups of people do differ with respect to their value systems, and many situations in life provide different degrees of both motivators and hygienes. Individuals as well as groups differ with respect to their own values and the situations where they find themselves. The "importance" question, itself, is a value-system question.

Grigaliunas and Herzberg (1971), in their article "Relevancy in the Test of Motivation-Hygiene Theory," demonstrated the fallibility of ratings of importance.[2] In this experiment subjects were asked to describe two critical incidents and then were instructed to rate the importance of 20 factors defined a priori (10 hygiene and 10 motivational) in determining how they felt about what happened. After replicating the original findings, using content analysis, the authors analyzed those factors that subjects had judged to be "extremely important" or "very important" in determining their feelings about the incidents. As expected, the subjects rated both hygiene and motivator factors as highly important for "good" and "bad" incidents, similar to the results obtained by Hinton (1968).

Grigaliunas and Herzberg went one step further, however. After checking to ensure against rater biases, five independent raters were instructed

---

[2] Material on this study in this and the next paragraph was added after this review had been published.

to code the critical incidents by matching the descriptions of the incidents with the same 20 factors used by the subjects. These content analyses revealed that the ratings of importance made by the subjects did not agree with their own descriptions of what happened in the critical event. Furthermore, the rater judgments confirmed M–H Theory once again; satisfying events came from motivator factors, while dissatisfying events arose out of hygiene factors. Apparently, the ratings of importance provoked value-system judgments from the subjects on what "ought" to be important rather than on what actually happened during the critical event.

Value systems and their measurement can provide a great deal of predictive information in many settings. However, value-system research should not be misconstrued as testing the original hypothesis of M–H Theory.

PERFORMANCE IMPLICATIONS OF M–H THEORY

M–H Theory is a theory of human motivation. When applied to industrial settings it has performance implications. Only one critical study (Schwab, Devitt, & Cummings, 1971) has dealt with this aspect of the theory. This stated the M–H Theory position on performance as follows: "Specifically, the theory states that performance effects are more likely to be associated with the satisfiers . . . than with the dissatisfiers. The latter serve merely to maintain performance level" (p. 294). This statement, although not incorrect, is an oversimplification.

M–H Theory does not deny performance consequences arising from hygiene factors. Its concern is not so much with quantitative differences in performance consequences between motivator factors and hygiene factors as with differences in the motivational dynamics underlying "hygiene" and "motivator" performance. The motivational performance implications of M–H Theory were briefly presented at the beginning of this article. A more detailed treatment can be found in Herzberg (1966, 1968).

The Schwab et al. (1971) hypothesis missed the broader motivational implications of M–H Theory. The authors also seem to have failed to establish an appropriate design to test their version of the performance hypothesis. The hypothesis they attempted to test stated that performance effects are associated more with motivator than with hygiene factors. Their testing procedure was characterized by two steps. First, subjects were asked to respond to the original pattern of Herzberg's interview; by coding only one factor for an incident it was possible to classify subjects according to type of factor (motivator or hygiene) they associated with each type of incident (satisfying, dissatisfying). Second, subjects self-rated the level of their performance during the time of the incident on a seven-point semantic-differential scale. Mean scores on this scale were

compared for groups of subjects classified on the basis of the type of incident and type of factor associated with the incident.

This procedure seems to be based on the assumption that the *one*
factor extracted from the incident is the *only*, or at least the major, cause
for the general level of performance at the time of the incident. No logic
or evidence can support such an assumption. Very rarely, if at all, can a
single factor account for a general level of performance. Furthermore, the
factors emerging from the incidents in the M–H critical-incident method
reflect *directly* on the dynamic only of job feelings, not of job performance. In any case, it is precarious to reach conclusions about *causal* relationships between job factors and performance on the basis of the performance self-rating of an individual and the *one* factor emerging from
the incident he gave.

Schwab et al. indicated that they employed this procedure because
Herzberg et al. (1959) did so. Herzberg and his colleagues have gone
far beyond this procedure. In fact, the data obtained by this procedure
served more as a source of theoretical ideas than as a test of these ideas.
An appropriate test for the performance hypothesis should consist of
manipulating job factors as independent variables and observing their
effects on objective performance measures. Herzberg and his colleagues
performed a whole series of such studies (Ford, 1970; Paul, Robinson, &
Herzberg, 1969). These investigations have initiated the job enrichment
movement, which is a widely accepted practice in organizational settings.
The findings of these studies demonstrate increased productivity as a result of introducing more motivators into a job, under constant hygiene
conditions, where previous changes in hygiene did not produce any productivity changes.

The point Schwab et al. attempted to make was that since there was no
difference in self-rating of performance between motivators and hygiene
factors within either type of sequence (dissatisfying or satisfying) performance should be viewed as related to the type of sequence rather than
to the type of factor. Hence the conclusion that the M–H Theory performance hypothesis is unsupported "by its own methodology." We
contend that this conclusion is not justified. Table 1, upon which the
conclusion is based, includes data from Schwab et al. for subjects who
belong to the favorable-hygiene and to the unfavorable-motivator groups.
Subjects who responded in such a way deviated to begin with from the
basic prediction of M–H Theory with regard to the relationships between
job factors and job feelings. It is unreasonable to use them for the testing
of other hypotheses derived from M–H Theory—in the present case, a
performance hypothesis.

It is unreasonable to pick up and isolate subjects who obviously do not
behave according to a basic prediction of a theory and employ them to
disprove further related hypotheses of the same theory. However, this is
exactly what Schwab et al. did. Had they disregarded the subjects who

belonged to unfavorable-motivator and the favorable-hygiene groups, the results would have been in line with the M–H notion. Furthermore, the "performance hypothesis" could gain some support even if the "deviate" subjects were to be included. Focusing in Table 1 on the main effect of job factors (motivators, hygienes) can illustrate this immediately. But any results, supportive or unsupportive of the performance

Table 1

Performance effects of motivators and hygienes within favorable and unfavorable sequences

Sequence and job factor	N	Self-rating of performance
Favorable		
Motivators..........................	66	6.18
Hygienes............................	14	6.36
Unfavorable		
Motivators..........................	40	3.60
Hygienes............................	40	3.80

Source: This table is based on Table 4, Schwab et al. (1971), p. 301.

hypothesis using the Schwab et al. procedure, would have been weak results, because their procedure is weak.

THE "SOCIAL DESIRABILITY" ARGUMENT AS AN ALTERNATIVE EXPLANATION TO M–H THEORY

M–H Theory has been widely criticized on the grounds that it is methodologically bound. It can be verified, it is claimed, only by one methodology, the critical-incident method. Other methodologies (always based in one way or another on rating scales) do not support it. The critics assert that the support the theory receives from the critical-incident method is simply a result of an artifact involved in this method. As Dunnette et al. (1967) state:

interviews provide no safeguard against defensive replies from the respondents; many respondents might quite naturally tend to attribute good job events to things they themselves had done (e.g., achievement, recognition, responsibility) and bad job events to things outside or extrinsic to themselves (e.g., working conditions, supervision, company policies and practices). If such were the case, the findings of Herzberg, et al. speak more clearly to a basic aspect of human nature (the tendency to want to "look good" in the eyes of others) than to the motivational or satisfying effects of different types of job situations or environments (p. 148).

This "social desirability" argument (see also Vroom, 1964) has been, perhaps, the most widely quoted criticism against either the theory or the methodology. However, this argument has not been supported empirically. The available relevant data—including research by the critics —tends to refute the reasoning behind the social-desirability criticism.

If the assertion by Dunnette et al. that individuals tend to attribute positive events and consequences to themselves and negative ones to "outside" environmental factors is correct, it should be expected that very few respondents in a critical-incident type interview would attribute negative events and consequences to themselves. Obviously, such an expectation would be in line with their proposition that a "basic aspect of human nature" is "the tendency to want to 'look good.' " Empirical results contradict this expectation completely. Relevant data are available in Table 1, adapted from Schwab et al.: 50 percent (40 out of 80 subjects) of those who described unfavorable events ascribed these events to themselves rather than to the environment. The social-desirability argument does not hold for these subjects, and it should not be used as a universal "basic human nature" argument to explain away results which support M–H Theory. (The Schwab et al. data regarding the distribution of the cases that deviate from perfect M–H prediction—slippage—is quite in line with other replications, even though the degree of absolute slippage is larger.)

Another indication that the social-desirability argument may not be valid is available from the data in Dunnette et al. They report the following mean social-desirability values of statements comparing intrinsic and extrinsic groupings for positive and negative events (p. 152):

	Positive events	Negative events
Intrinsic job dimension	5.93	2.97
Extrinsic job dimension	5.21	3.36

Dunnette et al. did not present tests of significance, but it seems safe to assume that the only meaningful differences are between the social-desirability values of positive and negative events. No meaningful differences are apparent between intrinsic and extrinsic job dimensions as a main effect or as an interaction with "type of events." The social-desirability argument calls, if at all, for just such differences in job dimension. The failure to obtain the expected differences supports our contention that the social-desirability hypothesis cannot be used as an alternative explanation to M–H Theory.

Two recent studies deal directly with the issues of social desirability and defensive responding as an alternative explanation of M–H Theory results. In one study by Bobbitt and Behling (1972), situational variables were manipulated to enhance the social-desirability demands of the experiment. Three groups of supervisors were subjected to two experimental conditions: In condition 1 respondents to the critical-incident method were led to believe that their responses might affect their futures within the organization for which they worked, and in condition 2 respondents were led to believe that their responses would have no effect on their futures. The goal was "to test the effects of varying opportunities to 'look good' on the patterning of motivator and hygiene responses. . . ." The hypotheses stated that the results would resemble the typical M–H replication more closely under condition 1 than under condition 2. The results showed that there were no statistically significant differences between the data obtained under both conditions. The authors concluded that the contention "that individuals attribute satisfaction to their own actions and dissatisfaction to those of others in order to appear in a favorable light to significant others is not supported by the results" (p. 26).

Another study recently conducted by Wiener, Vaitenas, and Herzberg (1975) investigated the effects of individual differences in defensiveness and social desirability on M–H responses to a critical-incident survey.[3] The authors reasoned that if M–H Theory results were due to social desirability and/or defensiveness, as critics maintained, then people who typically gave socially desirable or defensive responses should conform more with M–H predictions than other subjects. In this study 153 students in night classes who came from a variety of occupational fields were administered the Marlowe-Crowne Social Desirability Scale (Crowne & Marlowe, 1964) and the revised Repression-Sensitization Scale (Byrne, Barry, & Nelson, 1963), along with a paper-and-pencil version of the critical-incident survey. These subjects were then divided into high and low groups, based on their social desirability scores, and repression, normal, and sensitization groups, based on their scores on defensiveness. If criticisms of the theory were correct, then the groups scoring high on social desirability and/or high on repression would give responses on the critical-incident survey that conformed more closely with M–H predictions.

The findings did not support the criticisms and, in fact, suggested that the opposite was true. Subjects high on social desirability gave critical-incident responses which conformed less with M–H Theory predictions than those low on social desirability. Those subjects utilizing repression as a defense were no different from normals, and both conformed with M–H Theory predictions. In addition, the sensitizers, who were least likely to use repression as a defense, gave critical-incident responses which were more closely aligned with M–H Theory predictions. Therefore, M–H Theory predictions were most likely to be supported when subjects were not defensive or giving socially desirable responses. The classification of satisfactions as motivators and dissatisfactions as hygiene was distorted

---

[3] This study was published by the University of Utah after this review had been completed. Material on this study in this and the next two paragraphs has been added.

by such defensive responding, not created by it, as critics have claimed.

It is not much of a surprise that the social-desirability argument as applied to the critical-incident method has not received empirical support. This procedure is less amenable to a social-desirability response predisposition than the traditional "objective" rating methods. Two obvious reasons may account for that: (1) the critical-incident method focuses on *real* and actual events and behaviors, and (2) it possesses some "projective" elements, in that it is very difficult for a subject to establish expectations as to "what the experimenter is up to." These basic characteristics of the critical-incident method are absent in most rating procedures. In order to cope with the social-desirability biases, rating-scale procedures must adopt restrictive steps such as the forced-choice techniques, which further increase the artificiality and nonrelevancy of response.

Schneider and Locke (1971) and Locke (1973) asserted that Herzberg's classification system of critical incidents confuses two levels of analysis, events (what happened) and agents (who made it happen). They claimed that this confusion produces artifactual results and that if incidents were classified only according to events the results would not support M–H Theory. They devised a new event classification system and reported nonsupportive results. The fact, however, is that Herzberg's system does classify incidents only by events. An incident that cannot be classified on the basis of "what happened" is unacceptable. Inspection of Appendix II in Herzberg et al. (1959) would clearly show that event classification is the backbone of the system. Why then did Schneider and Locke's new event classification not confirm M–H Theory predictions? Two factors may account for this. First, they "translated" incorrectly their categories into motivator and hygiene factors. For example, they considered "amount of work" as a motivator. Second, an examination of their data reveals that the data would fail to replicate M–H results even if they had classified their incidents by Herzberg's system. It is not surprising, then, that they could not replicate M–H results employing a different system. To date, all other studies employing the critical-incident method and the Herzberg coding system always replicated M–H predictions.

Wiener, Vaitenas, Klein, and Herzberg (1975)[4] discovered a major flaw in the Schneider and Locke classification system that appears to be at least partially responsible for these contradictions. These investigators noticed that the "event" classification system used by Schneider and Locke coded many more responses as motivators and fewer responses as hygiene than the Herzberg system. They surmised that a hygiene category for coding interpersonal relations in the performance of the job was missing in the Schneider and Locke classification system and may have caused such hygiene responses to be inappropriately labeled as motivators. Data

---

[4] Published by the University of Utah after this review had been completed. Material in this paragraph on this study has been added to this review.

from a paper-and-pencil critical-incident survey was recoded, using the Schneider and Locke system with the addition of one new hygiene category, "interpersonal atmosphere work related." With the inclusion of this category, the data confirmed M–H Theory predictions. The authors concluded, therefore, that alternative classification systems such as the one they investigated would support M–H Theory, provided those systems were inclusive and properly differentiated between hygiene and motivational factors.

The question still can be asked why methods other than the critical-incident method do not provide results that support M–H Theory. We have attempted to answer this question in the sections on measuring the two feeling dimensions and overall job satisfaction. The basic point made was that the simple rating-scale methods cannot meaningfully separate the two feeling states of satisfaction and dissatisfaction; they actually measure just one "overall" state. They measure characteristics which— whatever they may be—are different from the distinct feeling states that M–H Theory deals with. The fact that the variety of rating-scale methods has not come up with results similar to those of the critical-incident method only points out the need to keep looking in different directions for psychologically and logically valid alternatives. Projective techniques may constitute one possibility.

Arbitrariness in discarding the critical-incident method because it does not provide the same measure as "traditional" procedures can be demonstrated in a recent study by Soliman (1970). One of his main objectives was "to subject the M–H Theory to an empirical test to find out whether it is a function of its own specific methodology or not." Accordingly he tested his subjects twice, using two different techniques, the "Herzberg instrument" being one of them and the Job Description Index (Smith, in Fleishman, 1967) the other. The reasoning was that similarity of responses to the two instruments would indicate that M–H Theory is not a function of its own methodology, whereas dissimilarity would indicate that it is. Soliman correlated the M–H factors from the critical-incident method with "corresponding" factors of the JDI. (He has not made clear how he obtained from the "Herzberg instrument" the values to be correlated.) The correlations were not significant, and his conclusion was that "the M–H Theory was not substantiated." The conclusion could also be that the traditional "linear" job satisfaction theory "was not substantiated." Soliman's reasoning is typical of quite a few critics (e.g., King, 1970). It would have had a degree of justification if Herzberg's "job satisfaction" concept was the same as Smith's (in Fleishman, 1967). As it is not, the correlations between the "Herzberg instrument" and the JDI could scarcely be anything else but zero.

In the literature critical of M–H Theory, a usual procedure has been to require subjects to rate the importance that each of the 16 Herzberg job factors held for them personally. These ratings are then related to measures of overall job satisfaction, occupational level, or other demographic variables, and it is found that individuals or groups have different values. The procedure of having subjects rate factors as to their importance reflects value-system research and is itself inherently loaded with social desirability (Grigaliunas & Herzberg, 1971). It is inconsistent for research of this type to criticize a different methodology on the grounds that it produces "socially desired" biased data.

CONCLUSION

Our conclusion is that, as a whole, the design, rationale, and findings of the critical studies do not provide a strong case for refuting M–H Theory. The following main problems have been revealed:

1. An apparent lack of success in developing an appropriate technique to measure or demonstrate bidimensionality of job feelings as an alternative to Herzberg's critical-incident approach. The research critical of M–H Theory has relied upon the rating-scale score—often a one-item scale—to assess complex motivational and emotional phenomena.

2. Conclusions about the validity of M–H Theory were made by testing hypotheses that could not be logically derived from this theory (e.g., "overall" satisfaction and "importance" hypotheses).

3. The results of several studies are inconclusive and can be interpreted in alternative ways that are not unsupportive of M–H Theory.

It can be argued that M–H Theory is indeed not an easy theory to test and that its constructs are not readily amenable to operational definitions. Such a claim may have a degree of validity. The critical studies, however, have not made this claim. They have contended that research "seems to have effectively laid the Herzberg theory to rest in terms of the degree to which it is supported by well-designed studies" (Korman, 1971, p. 149). This review has objected to this contention and has shown that its justification is scant.

We realize that merely rejecting and refuting criticism is not sufficient to maintain the usefulness and utility of an explanatory system. It has not been the intention of this review to place M–H Theory in a position of an "untouchable" status. We are aware of the need for further explorations. They call for constructive efforts in M–H research, theoretic and applicative.

REFERENCES

Armstrong, T. B. Job content and context factors related to satisfaction for different occupational levels. *Journal of Applied Psychology*, 1971, 55, 57–65.

Blum, M. L., & Naylor, J. C.   *Industrial psychology.* New York: Harper & Row, 1968.

Bobbitt, H. R., & Behling, O.   Defense mechanism as an alternative explanation of Herzberg's motivator-hygiene results. *Journal of Applied Psychology,* 1972, 56, 24–27.

Byrne, D., Barry, J., and Nelson, D.   Relation of revised repression-sensitization scale to measures of self-description. *Psychological Reports,* 1963, 13, 323–334.

Bockman, V. M.   The Herzberg controversy. *Personnel Psychology,* 1971, 24, 155–189.

Crowne, D., & Marlowe, D.   *The approval motive.* New York: John Wiley & Sons, 1964.

Davis, K., & Allen, G.   The duration of motivator and hygiene factors. *Personnel Psychology,* 1970, 23, 67–76.

Dunnette, M. P., Campbell, J. P., & Hakel, M. D.   Factors contributing to job satisfaction and job dissatisfaction in six occupational groups. *Organizational Behavior and Human Performance,* 1967, 2, 143–174.

Dunnette, M. P., & Kirchner, W.   *Psychology applied to industry.* New York: Appleton-Century-Crofts, 1965.

Ewen, R., Smith, P., Hulin, C., & Locke, E.   An empirical test of the Herzberg two-factor theory. *Journal of Applied Psychology,* 1966, 50, 544–550.

Fleishman, E. A. (Ed.).   *Studies in personnel and industrial psychology.* Homewood, Ill.: Dorsey Press, 1967.

Ford, R. N. *Motivation through the work itself.* New York: American Management Association, 1970.

Graen, G. B.   Addendum to "An empirical test of the Herzberg two-factor theory." *Journal of Applied Psychology,* 1966, 50, 551–555.

Graen, G. B.   Testing traditional and two-factor hypotheses concerning job satisfaction. *Journal of Applied Psychology,* 1968, 52, 366–371.

Graen, G. B., & Hulin, C. L.   Addendum to "An empirical investigation of two implications of the two-factor theory of job satisfaction." *Journal of Applied Psychology,* 1968, 52, 341–342.

Grigaliunas, B. S.   Duration and its relationship to slippage in motivator-hygiene research. Unpublished doctoral dissertation, Case Western Reserve University, 1970.

Grigaliunas, B. S., & Herzberg, F.   Relevancy in the test of Motivation-Hygiene Theory. *Journal of Applied Psychology,* 1971, 55, 73–79.

Gruenfeld, L. W., & Weissenberg, P.   Field independence and articulation of sources of job satisfaction. *Journal of Applied Psychology,* 1970, 54, 424–426.

Herzberg, F.   Basic needs and satisfaction of individuals. Proceedings of Industrial Relations Research Counselors Symposium on Advanced Research in Industrial Relations. *Industrial Relations Monograph,* 1962, 21.

Herzberg, F.   *Work and the nature of man.* New York: Thomas Y. Crowell Co., 1966.

Herzberg, F.   One more time: How do you motivate employees? *Harvard Business Review*, January–February, 1968, pp. 53–62.

Herzberg, F., Mathapo, J., Wiener, Y., & Wiesen, L. E.   Motivation-hygiene correlates of mental health: An examination of motivational inversion in a clinical population. *Journal of Clinical and Consulting Psychology*, 1974, *42*, 411–419.

Herzberg, F., Mausner, B., & Snyderman, B.   *The motivation to work*. New York: John Wiley & Sons, 1959.

Hinrichs, J. R., & Mischkind, L. A.   Empirical and theoretical limitations of the two-factor hypothesis of job satisfaction. *Journal of Applied Psychology*, 1967, *51*, 191–200.

Hinton, B. L.   An empirical investigation of the Herzberg methodology and two-factor theory. *Organizational Behavior and Human Performance*, 1968, *3*, 286–309.

Hulin, C. L., & Smith, P. A.   An empirical investigation of two implications of the two-factor theory of job satisfaction. *Journal of Applied Psychology*, 1967, *51*, 396–402.

King, N.   A clarification and evaluation of the two-factor theory of job satisfaction. *Psychological Bulletin*, 1970, *74*, 18–31.

Korman, A. B.   *Industrial and Organizational Psychology*. Englewood Cliffs, N.J.: Prentice-Hall, 1971.

Kosmo, R., & Behling, O.   Single continuum job satisfaction versus duality: An empirical test. *Personnel Psychology*, 1969, *22*, 327–334.

Lahiri, D. K., & Srivastva, S.   Determinants of satisfaction in middle-management personnel. *Journal of Applied Psychology*, 1967, *51*, 254–263.

Levine, E. L., & Weitz, J.   Job satisfaction among graduate students: Intrinsic versus extrinsic variables. *Journal of Applied Psychology*, 1968, *52*, 263–271.

Locke, E. A.   Satisfiers and dissatisfiers among white-collar and blue-collar employees. *Journal of Applied Psychology*, 1973, *58*, 67–76.

Maslow, A.   Deficiency motivation and growth motivation. In M. R. Jones (Ed.), *Nebraska Symposium on Motivation*. Lincoln: University of Nebraska Press, 1955.

Paul, P. J., Robinson, R. B., & Herzberg, F.   Job enrichment pays off. *Harvard Business Review*, March–April 1969, 61–78.

Schacter, S., & Singer J. E.   Cognitive, social and physiological determinants of emotional state. *Psychological Review*, 1962, *69*, 379–399.

Schneider, J., & Locke, E. A.   A critique of Herzberg's incident classification system and a suggested revision. *Organizational Behavior and Human Performance*, 1971, *6*, 441–457.

Schwab, D. P., Devitt, H. W., & Cummings, L. L.   A test of the adequacy of the two-factor theory as a predictor of self-report performance efforts. *Personnel Psychology*, 1971, *24*, 293–303.

Schwab, D. P., & Heneman, H. G., III.   Aggregate and individual predictability of the two-factor theory of job satisfaction. *Personnel Psychology*, 1970, *23*, 55–66.

Soliman, H. M.   Motivation-hygiene theory of job attitudes: An empirical investigation and an attempt to reconcile both the one- and two-factor theories of job attitudes. *Journal of Applied Psychology,* 1970, *54,* 452–461.

Tiffin, J., & McCormick, E. J.   *Industrial psychology.* Englewood Cliffs, N.J.: Prentice-Hall, Inc., 1965.

Vroom, V. H.   *Work and Motivation.* New York: John Wiley & Sons, 1964.

Waters, L. K., & Roach, D.   The two-factor theory of job satisfaction: Empirical tests for four samples of insurance company employees. *Personnel Psychology,* 1971, *24,* 697–705.

Waters, L. K., & Waters, G. W.   Correlates of job satisfaction and job dissatisfaction among female clerical workers. *Journal of Applied Psychology,* 1969.

Weissenberg, P., & Gruenfeld, L. W.   Relationship between job satisfaction and job involvement. *Journal of Applied Psychology,* 1968, *52,* 469–473.

Wernimont, P. F.   Intrinsic and extrinsic factors in job satisfaction. *Journal of Applied Psychology,* 1966, *50,* 41–50.

Whitsett, D. A., & Winslow, E. K.   An analysis of studies critical of the Motivation-Hygiene Theory. *Personnel Psychology,* 1967, *20,* 121–132.

Wiener, Y., Vaitenas, R., & Herzberg, F.   Social desirability, repression and sensitization as factors in the critical incidents method of Motivation-Hygiene Theory. *Human Resources Management Publication,* 75–101, University of Utah, 1975.

Wiener, Y., Vaitenas, R., Klein, K., & Herzberg, F.   Motivation-Hygiene Theory: An alternative classification system and its relationship to the defensiveness hypothesis. *Human Resources Management Publication,* 75–101, University of Utah, 1975.

Wolf, M. G.   The relationship of content and context factors to attitudes toward company and job. *Personnel Psychology,* 1967, *20,* 121–132.

chapter 6

Questions and answers

INTRODUCTION

There is no way for a theoretician, particularly a theoretician who is equally a practitioner, to fully explain himself in direct prose. His unwarranted presumption is always that the answers to any specific questions are contained in the broader concepts he writes about. Either the theoretician reduces his ideas down to the step-by-step approach of programmed learning, and leaves his audience missing the forest for all the trees, or he can hope that the reader can translate the answers to the specifics for himself—and this is indeed an unrealistic expectation.

In addition, the theoretician cannot anticipate all the areas in which he is not completely comprehensible. In this chapter I will try to narrow the gap between what I believe I have communicated and what is realistically communicated in any book by answering many specific questions.

The questions that are posed are primarily those that I frequently have found to be bothersome to my readers, audiences, and particularly my academic colleagues. The first article in this section, reproduced from *Management Review* and entitled "Managers or Animal Trainers?" is one of the many published interviews I have given on my work. It provides the best format of these interviews and serves as a good introduction to the larger question-and-answer section which follows.

This article is followed by a more extensive question-and-answer section in the hope that many remaining unanswered questions at least will be clarified and the many misinterpretations of the Motivation-Hygiene Theory may be dispelled. The first part of this question-and-answer exercise deals with Motivation-Hygiene Theory in its broadest aspects. The second part relates to the process of job enrichment.

I am grateful to my assistants, Drs. John Taylor and Alex Zautra, for compiling most of the list of these additional questions and evaluating the adequacy of my responses to them. I realize that gaps will remain because of the limited range of questions that can be reasonably entertained at any one time. Quite frankly, in some instances I am as yet unable to give appropriate answers.

Managers or animal trainers?

An interview with
Frederick Herzberg
by
William F. Dowling

Question: Maybe the best place to start is with the title of one of your Harvard Business Review *articles, "One More Time: How Do You Motivate Employees?"*

Answer: Historically, we have to begin with a grant I received to investigate the whole area of job attitudes when I was at Psychological Services in Pittsburgh. This particular interest originated during my days in the Graduate School of Public Health. After I got my Ph.D., I went to Public Health School and received an M.P.H. in what's called Industrial Mental Health—it's never been properly defined. When I went to Psychological Services as research director, I was interested in aspects of mental health, which certainly included job attitudes. The first stage of this research program, obviously, was to review the literature in the field, and my staff and I did a very comprehensive review of that literature. We had a bibliography of 3,000 books and articles. The result was a book called *Job Attitudes: Review of Research and Opinion*, a scholarly review of what was known on attitudes from 1900 to 1955.

However, when we had finished *Job Attitudes: Review of Research and Opinion* we could make no sense out of it. It seemed that the human being was forever debarred from rational understanding as to why he worked.

We looked again at some of the data describing what people wanted from their jobs and noticed that there was a hint that the things people said positively about their job experiences were not the opposite of what they said negatively about their job experiences; the reverse of the factors that seemed to make people happy in jobs did not make them unhappy. So what happens in science, when your research leads to ambiguity? You begin to suspect your premises. In my Public Health School days I had conceived the concept that mental health was not the opposite of mental illness; that mentally healthy people were just not the obverse of mentally sick people. So I took a stab on the basis of mental health not being the opposite of mental illness and came up with a new concept.

Question: *That was your core insight?*

Answer: That was the core insight. I said, perhaps we're talking about two different modalities. Job satisfaction, let's use that term, and job dissatisfaction are not opposites; they are completely separate continua, like hearing and vision. If this is true, if we recognize that they are separate continua, then they must be produced by different factors and have their own dynamics. That was the stab I made.

Then I said, O.K., let's test this idea. Obviously, what had to be done was to find out what made people happy separately from finding out what made people unhappy. And you couldn't just ask people, "What do you like about your job?" That's like asking, "How do you feel?"—a nonsensical question. In fact, two questions must be asked: What makes you happy on the job? And, equally important, What makes you unhappy on the job?

Question: *Your methodology was different, too, as I recall.*

Answer: Yes, people respond for the sake of responding. And they tend to give the answers that will win the approval of the people asking the questions. You ask people a lot of questions in a public opinion poll and you get a lot of answers without any real feelings about them. Instead of asking people what makes them happy or unhappy, I thought it would be better to get at the kinds of experiences that produced satisfaction or dissatisfaction with a job. By doing these two things—by asking two questions where one was usually asked and by obtaining my data from analysis of the kinds of experiences people had rather than what they say makes them happy and unhappy—I found that the two systems existed.

With the appearance of the two systems, my thinking that what makes people happy and what makes people unhappy were not the same things was verified. In analyzing the commonalities among the factors that make people definitely unhappy or definitely happy, I found that the factors which make people happy all are related to what people did; the job content. Contrariwise, I found that what made people unhappy was related to the situation in which they did their job: job environment, job context —what I called hygiene factors. So now you have a finding that makes much more sense. What makes people happy is what they do or the way they're utilized, and what makes people unhappy is the way they're treated. That pretty much summarizes my second book, *The Motivation to Work*

Question: *Then in your third book,* Work and the Nature of Man, *you searched for the psychological underpinnings for your theory.*

Answer: Why does job content make people happy? Yes. I had to ask that question. Further research and experience suggested what makes people unhappy is pain from the environment. We have this in common with all animals. We're all trying to adjust to the environment—to avoid pain. On the other hand, man is also different from an animal and what makes him different is that he is a determiner, whereas the animal is always determined. What man does determines his human characteristics—I cannot become psychologically taller unless I do things.

So I developed the Adam and Abraham concept, the two natures of man. As Adam, he's an animal, and as an animal he tries to avoid pain from the environment as all animals do. As Abraham, he's a human being, and as a human being he's not the opposite of an animal, he's qualitatively different. His dynamic is to manifest his talents, and the only way he can manifest his talents is by doing things that allow him to develop his potential. In short, *Work and the Nature of Man* provided the rationale for the findings of what motivated men to work.

In summary, you had a three-step sequence. First, what we knew about job attitudes from the past made no sense, so we had to look at the problem differently. Second, when the problem was redefined, a very different research result was obtained. Third, I had to explain the research results. Now I have a theory, documented with research and supported by an understanding of why the theory worked. You ask, how do you apply it? Now we come to "One More Time."

Question: *How do you apply the theory? That was also the subject of the last chapter in* Work and the Nature of Man.

Answer: "One More Time" does two things. First, it suggests that you can get people to do things as Adam, and you can get people to do things as human beings—but the ways you get them to do things are very different. To get people to do things as animals, you move them. When I respond as an animal because I want to avoid being hurt, that's movement. I called it KITA, for "kick in the ass." When a human being does something, he's motivated. The initiative comes from within. Further, I showed how the various techniques of human relations are just different forms of positive and negative KITA.

Second, I went on to demonstrate the difference between management by movement and management by motivation or job enrichment. How, by changing what people do, you motivate them to do better work. I described how job enrichment paid off handsomely in one company—AT&T, although it wasn't identified as such in the article. Since then, many other companies have applied job enrichment with equal success. That's what happened in the past.

Most of my work now consists of looking at the total problem of mankind living in society through Motivation-Hygiene Theory. Not only must we reorient our management thinking in terms of how you motivate people for a better P&L statement, but of how we apply the same theory to develop a sane society. AT&T faces not only problems with dial tones and profits, but the central and more crucial problem of whether or not it can survive as a social institution in our society. Of course, the problem is not unique to AT&T. It faces every institution.

That pretty much summarizes Motivation-Hygiene Theory, what it is, how it came to be, and where it is going.

Question: It certainly does. But let's dwell a bit longer on some features of the theory. One fact that I found very significant was that your motivators had a much more positive and long-term impact on performance than did your hygiene factors, and this was true even in the relatively rare instances in which the hygiene factors had a positive influence.

Answer: We have just completed a study replicating that perfectly. The hygiene factors are always short term, like the length of time you're not dissatisfied with your salary. It takes about two weeks for the effects of a raise to wear off.

Question: I think I've had experiences where I've been happier a little longer than that. But I buy your general point.

Answer: Also, the hygiene factors go back to zero. No matter how many times you have told your wife you love her, if you fail to tell her you love her, she says, "You never tell me you love me." The hygiene factors are all subject to the "what have you done for me lately" syndrome. A colonel bucking for general in the Army feels as deprived status-wise as a private bucking for corporal. A colonel is the zero point. If you get a $4,000 increase in salary and the next year they give you a $2,000 increase in salary, psychologically you have taken a $2,000 cut. By contrast, the motivators are long term and don't go back to zero. I write a book and I achieve some growth. If I don't write another book, I don't get back to where I was before. When I achieve, that achievement never disappears. Of course, if I write a book and then write an article, I haven't developed as much as I did with the book, but it's still an addition. You see, with the hygiene factors, you've got to have as much as, or more than, you had before to notice any difference, but with the motivators, you do not have to have as much as before to know the difference and feel the growth.

Question: *Another point that struck me was the fact that your dissatisfier or hygiene factors very seldom appear as satisfiers. One exception I recall were the lower-level supervisors in the Midwest utility who felt happy about getting along with their employees.*

Answer: That's what in Motivation-Hygiene Theory we call a pathology. The pathology can be either in the individuals or in the company. Let's take one in the company. I have people tell me what made them happy and unhappy, their experiences, and then draw a profile and tell you what's going on in that company. Take, for example, the lower-level supervisors in the utility industry. The hygiene factors became so important that relief from them gave people the false feeling of being happy. For example, if you hit yourself over the head, you say you feel good when you stop doing it. Actually, it is not that you feel good, but that you don't feel as bad. There's nothing positive about the way you feel. If this were true, then the mechanism for feeling good would be to hit yourself over the head so that you could stop. Do you see the idiocy of it? However, because many people say, "I feel better" or "I feel good" when hygiene factors improve, they get the mistaken notion that they're feeling good; sometimes the relief from pain can be so great that you mistake it for a satisfaction feeling.

Now in any company where hygiene factors are so important for individuals that their relief gives people the mistaken report that they feel good, what they're really saying is, "I stopped hitting myself over the head with a hammer and I felt good." If this happens in a company, you know that the company's so damn hygiene oriented that people find their only happiness in relief from pain.

Question: *You at least hinted that this probably was true of this utility company.*

Answer: Oh, it was. And we have other examples where utility companies were hung up on hygiene factors.

Question: *In your first study, the one "swing factor" was the factor of money. At least, it appeared with almost equal frequency as a satisfier and a dissatisfier.*

Answer: Let me explain money to you. Money is a hygiene factor. However, because it is associated with so many other factors, it's included with them. For example, advancement is a motivator, but correlated with advancement is usually a salary increase, so money gets pulled along. Increased responsibility is a motivator, right, but more money is frequently associated with increased responsibility. So money hides in different concepts and becomes a ubiquitous factor. But dynamically, the fact is that money isn't what you do, it's what you get for what you do or how you're treated for what you do. By definition that is a hygiene factor.

Another reason for the confusion is that money is the biggest KITA available, and what many people do is to mistake movement for motivation. I say money is not a motivator; it's a good mover.

Question: In talking about one electric utility and its extraordinarily large bonuses, you made the distinction between ordinary wages and money earned as recognition for extraordinary performance, and you said that the latter could be called a true motivator.

Answer: I've changed my mind, because at that time I hadn't clarified the concept of movement in relation to motivation. At that time I had to explain why the company got such impressive production, and the easiest explanation was that money was recognition for achievement. Now I recognize that it's the biggest KITA they have. What they're getting is not motivation, but movement.

Question: Considering that their workers outproduce workers in competing companies by two to one—or at least they used to—you certainly got a lot of movement.

Answer: If you can afford to move people, move them. But don't forget that KITA costs more and more to move people less and less. In many cases, we're getting a negative return on our investment with such things as profit sharing and fringe benefits.

Question: You had a very striking analogy between heroin and hygiene: You need to provide more and more of both to get less and less effect. In other words, your suggestion is that most managements are not using their resources properly when they concentrate on the hygiene factors, in many instances almost to the exclusion of the motivators.

Answer: There are two ways of getting people to do things. One way is to play on their pains. It's no great effort to find out what makes people hurt; play a tune on it and they will tell you where the gold is buried— right? The trick may be money, fringe benefits, security, or human relations, which is the most vicious form of KITA.

Question: Why do you call human relations "vicious"?

Answer: Because it says, "I will be decent to you if you work harder." I say, "You be decent to me to be decent to me." You say, "You know, I'll be a nice guy if you work harder." That's like saying "I took the old lady across the street, give me my reward!" This is why I'm so critical of sensitivity training and of human relations programs. They prostitute human relations and prostitute human decency.

Now, there's another way of getting me to do things—not because you want me to do it or because I just want the reward. Remember, a reward is something I get for doing something I wouldn't ordinarily do if it weren't for the reward. Motivation is another way of getting me to do something. Motivation says do this because it's very meaningful *for me* to do it. This is where management has missed out.

Question: *The reward is intrinsic?*

Answer: The reward is the personal satisfaction in what you do. What management has failed to do—incredibly failed to do—is capitalize on the human desire for achievement. Managements have always looked at man as an animal to be manipulated with a carrot and a stick. They found that when man hurts, he will move to avoid pain—and they say, "We're motivating the employees." Hell, you're not motivating them, you're moving them. What I've been advocating is, for God's sake, only to give hygiene to solve hygiene problems or because people hurt. Another and far more efficient way of getting people to do a good job is to give them the opportunity to get satisfaction out of doing a good job. That's the area management misses. I love the term "delegation" That's the most bastard technique I know—that's letting someone borrow your job for a while.

Question: *Why has management been so derelict in using motivators?*

Answer: Because of the obviousness of man's pain. Man's achievement motivation is not as visible as man's pain—it has to be discovered. Second, it's easier to manage with hygiene factors. You can have lousier managers. It doesn't take many brains to hold up a jellybean and get a guy to do something. Every dog trainer knows the trick. But it takes a lot of talent to manage people through their abilities, and because this is so, we don't have managers; what we have, by-and-large, are animal trainers. All you have to do is go into the typical corporation and see the managers at work with their bags of jellybeans and their whips.

Question: *You had another suggestion. A lot of managers are afraid to encourage employees to actualize themselves because in the process they might buck the organization, challenge authority, and infringe on what managers regard as their prerogatives.*

Answer: Let me give you another reason. Most organizations are manager-proof. What I mean by manager-proof is that in most organizations you don't need creative managements. What you need are good police-men. And I could paraphrase Lincoln on this: You can fool all of the people some of the time, and that's enough to make a profit. What most organizations ask about their people is "How well housebroken are they?" rather than, "How creative are they?" Most organizations are very un-imaginative. The only substantial use of imagination in organizations takes place in marketing. There's some in R&D, but it's pretty much sup-pressed. For the rest, top management wants the housebroken guy.

Question: What about jobs that allow no real room for creativity or growth?

Answer: Mickey Mouse jobs.

Question: Ideally, maybe you ought to automate them and get rid of them. But that may be too expensive in many instances.

Answer: There are a lot of Mickey Mouse people. So put the Mickey Mouse people in Mickey Mouse jobs, okay?

Question: It's as simple as that?

Answer: No, unfortunately, it's not that simple. Intrinsically, very few people are Mickey Mouse people. They're made that way. However, you live with reality, and there are a lot of people who will not be unhappy in Mickey Mouse jobs, and who can be moved into them.

Question: In other words, it's a matter of selection, of fitting the Mickey Mouse jobs to the Mickey Mouse people.

Answer: In a sense. I don't approve of it, but until you get rid of the Mickey Mouse jobs, I see the logic of it.

Question: I'm thinking of people who are really only suited for the simplest, most monotonous tasks, performing outstandingly on them, like the example you cite from Argyris where people who were actually men-tally defective turned in outstanding performance on routine tasks.

Answer: I'm more concerned not with biological morons but the more frequent cases where industry has psychologically extirpated the brain. It's a very sad thing when you have a college graduate performing like a moron in a Mickey Mouse job.

Question: *That's quite different. What do you do about the college graduate in a Mickey Mouse job? Presumably you enrich the job. However, the term "enrichment" in itself is a kind of slogan. What does it mean when you apply it within an organization?*

Answer: It would take me two hours just to go through the hygiene factors and describe how you manage them.

Question: *I would be more interested in how you manage the motivators.*

Answer: You can't manage one without considering the other. I come into a company and I ask two basic questions: What kind of talent do they have? If they have low talent, but who are well housebroken, the company can't go anyplace because you can't be motivated if there is no know-how. All you can do is fall back on a lot of slogans. This is why all demagogues substitute slogans for talent.

The other thing I ask is how they use the talent they have. If they haven't used the talent, then the talent is considered to be scrap in that company. To the degree that you consider talent "scrap" in your company, it spills over into many of the hygiene factors and your people become psychological amputees.

Now, when a man has a leg amputated, you fit him with a prosthetic device and you say he's made a good adjustment. But despite the adjustment he is sick, because he's still only got one leg—normal is two legs. Psychologically, the same thing is true on the job. The attitude that these people have on the job is as normal an attitude as that of the amputee or as normal an attitude as that of a guy who's been kicked in the ass all his life. They simply adjust. You have the attitude of seduced people, of a woman who lost her virginity but doesn't want to admit it.

Question: *You talk about jobs where lower-level supervisors have spent their time checking on performance. You would enrich the supervisors' jobs by assigning these jobs to someone else and releasing them for higher-level jobs of training and managing.*

Answer: When you have a supervisor checking a man on a job, he's not a supervisor, he's a checker. You have a manager checking the supervisor. He's not a manager, he's a checker. What happens in the typical company is that people are overchecked and undermanaged. When this has happened, two people are doing the same job and neither takes responsibility. What we get is the ludicrous situation of bawling out the supervisor for the mistake of a subordinate.

Question: Job enrichment, in other words, doesn't come by giving the guy a human relations course or any kind of training. It comes about only through redesigning his job and making it more meaningful to him.

Answer: When a production supervisor is told to stop hanging over an employee, that usually accomplishes nothing. The approach that works is to make it impossible for him to hang over the guy. If two guys don't get along with one another, you can send them to five years of psychotherapy or you can separate them. You see the point.

Management has this God-awful belief that you can change attitudes in people, and that attitudes lead to behavior. Nonsense! Behavior leads to attitudes. Attitudes are the confirmation of your behavior; attitudes are the rationalizations of your behavior. If you were forced to behave as if you believed in segregation, you would have attitudes that conform to that kind of behavior. The attitudes enable you to read the environment. Then you choose arenas or ball parks where your behavior is again acceptable. This then leads you to go to a school that practices discrimination, and that behavior therefore is acceptable. There you develop other behaviors that lead to other attitudes that correlate with them. You build up a whole system of attitudes that confirm the various behaviors that you manifest, and this constellation of attitudes becomes your value system. Your value system, then, is a confirmation or rationalization for your behavior. What determines your behavior on the job is primarily two things: What kind of talent you have, and what you're permitted to do—the degree of job initiative.

Question: The degree of initiative allowed by the organization.

Answer: That's right. What really tells me whether or not I'll play the piano are two things: Do I have a piano, and can I play the piano? If I can play the piano and have a piano, then I'll have an attitude that's favorable to piano playing. If I can dance and get an opportunity to dance, then I'll have an opportunity to develop an attitude favorable to dancing: If I can't dance, I'll say, "Who wants to dance?" Do you see the point?

Question: Yes.

Answer: Many of my colleagues are saying, "Let's change the attitudes of people" and I say you cannot—you're getting things backwards. These colleagues have the best of all possible worlds—they have a value system substituting for science. That is, they're trying to change people's attitudes to proper attitudes. The proper attitude for a man in a Mickey Mouse job is a Mickey Mouse attitude. Second, because the attempt never works, they never have to face up to the reality of accomplishing anything and being held responsible for the results.

Question: *I can see that job enrichment leads to increased growth and self-actualization, but the connection between job enrichment and improved performance isn't nearly as clear. Isn't job enrichment more likely to take the form of an improved interest in quality instead of productivity?*

Answer: Yes, much more of an interest in quality, for two reasons. One is an industrial engineering reason: Productivity is more determined by the technology than by the individual. The productivity of many factory workers, salesmen, telephone operators is determined by so many different factors. Quality, however, is much more determined by the individual. Therefore, the employee who is motivated to do a better job improves the quality of his work.

Another reason for the emphasis on quality is that quality has more nuances to it than productivity. Productivity is on a single continuum. Quality is on many continua. There's more possibility for a man to actualize his talents by emphasizing one of the many facets quality has.

You can always improve productivity at the expense of quality. The Russians are masters at this. If you were a Russian manager and were given a quota for turning out so many tons of sewing machines, what would you do? You'd make them out of the heaviest cast iron, wouldn't you? We laugh at the Russians because they get productivity at the expense of quality this way, but so do we. How many companies over here are more concerned with indexes than with the total performance? In more than one company the productivity indexes are all high, but the quality stinks.

Question: *You mentioned in* Work *and the* Nature *of* Man *that the Motivation-Hygiene Theory had been confirmed by 10 studies in 17 populations.*

Answer: Now it's over 50 studies.

Question: *How many of the additional studies deal with lower-level employees—where you logically would expect to find the most exceptions to the theory?*

Answer: We've got a lot of lower-level ones. I will give you this flat statement: The theory has held up from the lowest-level job to the highest-level job. The only differences between workers in various groups is the kind of pathology they normalize. It doesn't change the basic nature of man. My colleagues, you know, say that lower-level workers don't want achievement. Well, lower-level workers don't want achievement because they never have been allowed to experience it. My colleagues are following a kind of circular, self-confirming hypothesis: You don't give the black a good education, so he doesn't show up bright, so you say he's stupid and make it unnecessary for him to get a good education. Similarly, your lower-level workers have no chance to do anything, and since they can't do anything, my colleagues say—see, they don't want to do anything. Of course, they have attitudes appropriate to people who don't do anything—they have adapted.

Question: In light of their adapting, it's surprising to find that they still express a preference for motivators as things that make them feel happy on the job. Apparently they treasured these opportunities, no matter how rare they were.

Answer: My book points out what the basic needs of these people are, not what they checked off in opinion surveys. You see, the difference is that I get the kinds of experiences that affect people, not the kinds of rationalizations dealt with in rating scales.

Go out and interview the hard hats. So many Mickey Mouse behavioral "scientists" would talk to them to get them to confirm their sociological concepts of stratification. I'd want to talk to these people like human beings. Many psychologists don't know people. They know what happens to people, they know the cultures of people, but they don't know people.

Question: Have you ever gone into an organization that you felt recognized the true potential of motivators and was doing something about realizing them?

Answer: There is no organization that I would say was a perfectly motivated organization. Take the Bell System. Some parts are marvelous; other parts are bad. I can characterize the leadership of an organization in terms of KITAs as opposed to motivation. But a company that makes a good use of motivators—there isn't any. I can talk in terms of a division at best, but usually about a section, a group, or a man.

I believe in organizations based on mutual respect through mutual distrust in the hygiene area and mutual trust in the motivator area. That's more real and sane. When two people trust each other in the hygiene area, the guy who trusts most loses. I don't want to sound cynical, but I didn't make this world, I just report on it.

Question: You talked a while back about applying Motivation-Hygiene Theory to the larger problems of society. Where do you begin?

Answer: The major problem in our society is that we don't know how to manage success. Throughout history, the great tragedies of cultures or organizations have not been in the failure to produce success but in the failure to manage it once it's been achieved. Managing success needs a different managerial style than producing success. We can produce success with KITAs, but once people have success they no longer are moved by KITAs. They begin to ask the question consciously and in ever-increasing numbers, "How do we spend our lives?"

In producing success, you treat people as animals, hoping that the end result will be a human being—this just doesn't work. We have to start treating people as human beings and not as KITA objects if we're going to be able to manage our society successfully. If you fail to produce success, you don't get something, but if you fail to manage success you produce catastrophe. Personally, I've abandoned the possibility of developing a sane society through hygiene. You're only going to develop a sane society through giving more satisfaction to people, not less dissatisfaction.

Question: *How does this relate to a specific problem like the blacks in our society and giving them more satisfaction?*

Answer: There are so many problems related to the blacks, and so little time in which to solve them. If any nation could have solved this problem, I think this nation could have. Look at the three problems facing the United States today—nation building, in Vietnam; people building here, the blacks and other minorities; and earth building, the ecological problem. That's just too much. We can't nation build, earth build, and people build simultaneously. We don't have much ingenuity or time.

Let me add that I think you can only solve the race problem in terms of whites behaving toward blacks as their equals and developing attitudes to accompany their behavior.

What really bothers me, and where I get pessimistic, is the competence problem. You can't motivate anybody to do a job if he can't do it. We can set up all kinds of job corps programs, but that's a drop in the bucket—there are 22 million blacks, and the overwhelming majority are incompetent to do a job in which it's realistic to talk about motivation and satisfaction.

People say, "Why don't the blacks begin to pull themselves up by the bootstraps?" The answer to this question lies in the recognition that it is an inappropriate question to ask. The background and initial experience of the black in the United States cannot be equated to those of *any* other ethnic group. As such, it is only within recent memory that the legal and extralegal barriers to entry into the institutions of our society have been lowered to permit the opportunities to gain competence. In other words, the black has had further to go than other nonracial ethnic groups to develop competence.

Competence and the opportunity to use that competence are prerequisites to motivation. If I'm motivated, I'll achieve, but if I've never achieved, I can't be motivated. It will necessitate the spending of a lot of expensive KITA before the black will develop the intrinsic achievement to feel equal on the motivation–happiness continuum as well as minimizing the "less than" feelings on the hygiene–unhappiness continuum. I don't think we're going to lick the competence problem immediately—certainly not in our lifetime, and maybe not in the lifetime of our children.

Questions and answers pertaining to Motivation-Hygiene Theory

Question: There is some confusion in understanding Motivation-Hygiene Theory regarding the relative importance of the motivator and hygiene factors. Which are more important, and, within each group, what is the rank order of their importance?

Answer: As was seen in the preceding chapter on criticisms of Motivation-Hygiene Theory, this is one of the places that most academicians go off in misunderstandings. It would seem abundantly clear that the motivators and the hygiene factors are not comparable. The whole essence of the theory is that they are two different attitudinal feelings based upon different dynamics and different origins, and they serve different purposes.

So, in a sense, asking which one is more important is trying to compare oranges and apples. More important for what? Motivators are more important as a source for personal meaning as it is derived through the process of psychological growth. The hygiene factors are important when you hurt, to relieve the pain. I don't know which is more important, eating or writing a book. It is as if you would ask me which one you would want me to kill, your son or your daughter. They are noncompetitive questions. For example, when someone who is very hungry is given food and finds satisfaction, the misunderstanding occurs if you use the term in the sense of being relieved from the pangs of hunger and confuse that sense with the same satisfaction one gets from the pride of achievement. Pride in accomplishment is not equatable with relief from hunger.

Within the factors, the hygiene factors generally have equal importance overall. This is because we cannot equate types of pain. One of the reasons you can never tell anyone your troubles is that no one can evaluate the pain you feel by the objective source of the pain. Pain is a subjective experience, and therefore the usual response you would get, verbally or nonverbally, is "You have troubles? Wait until you hear mine!" The relative importance attributed to the various hygiene factors which is so commonly reported in the literature, and in a sense is given some theoretical support by Maslow's need hierarchy, really represents a cultural, normative, public opinion poll. Simply put, there are some hygiene factors that are more commonly experienced than other hygiene factors. As I pointed out in the article on organization profiles in Chapter 2, an unpleasant experience with your boss will occur much more frequently than the unpleasant experience of being fired. Because of the differential frequency with which hygiene factors occur in life, we mistake frequency for importance.

When it comes to the motivators, there is a hierarchy, and surprisingly, the hierarchy is in inverse proportion to the frequency of the individual factors. The reason for this is that the underlying dynamic in hygiene factors is to avoid pain, and, as I have said, there is an infinite source of pain in the environment of man which he will experience. In the motivator factors, the underlying dynamic is psychological growth. It is the human source for happiness. Since psychological growth is the end point of man's achievement, his goal as a human being, the initial factors and the more frequently occurring factors, such as achievement and recognition for achievement, are preparatory to the more lasting goal of psychological growth.

A further explanation of this hierarchy can be found in my book *Work and the Nature of Man,* particularly in the chapter dealing with the definition of the various stages of psychological growth. It is obvious that there are more opportunities for achievement in life than there are opportunities for increased responsibility and advancement. Many of these achievements do not lead to psychological growth, so of all the achievements that man can put under his belt, only a few are metabolized into growth. Most are sort of wasted achievements. They do not enter into his experiential bag of wisdom which enables him to act taller after he realizes any one specific achievement than he did before. Philosophically speaking, I would consider loneliness as the most important hygiene factor and boredom as the most important motivator.

Question: Your theory has been frequently compared to Abraham Maslow's theory of the need hierarchy. Just what is the relationship between these two theories?

Answer: This is one of the most common questions I receive, primarily because textbook writers have a tendency to put together and compare theories, not because there is a natural connection between them, but because they are forced to provide some of their own input into their books, since they are writing about other people's work. It is to be hoped that our textbook writers would be more perceptive than journalistic in their writings. It is true that Maslow's lower-order needs can be equated in some fashion to my hygiene needs and his higher-order needs in some fashion to what I call the motivation needs of man. However, that is about as much connection between the two theories as is really relevant and pertinent. The attempt to combine the two theories into one, I really believe, is an exercise in the "creativity" of textbook and review writers.

Question: *What do you feel about Maslow?*

Answer: You can name very few psychologists who have captured the imagination of both professionals and the general public. Freud, Skinner, Binet, Rogers, are a few; Abraham Maslow was among them. As it is with scientists and scholars who achieve both professional and public acclaim, these psychologists suffered from intense criticism, being caught in a cross fire between two parties that have a great dislike for each other, the academicians and the general public. As for Maslow, he was criticized in industry for talking "gobbledygook" (humanism) and praised by the same industrial audience for talking about their lives rather than their job specifications. Academic psychologists, on the other hand, saw Maslow's humanism only as gobbledygook especially since he did not do "basic" research. But professional psychologists saw Abraham Maslow as enabling them to investigate outside of Mickey Mouse laboratories and giving them something to do besides evaluating the responses of under-graduate students in psychology. Maslow had a brilliant mind and a Lincolnesque style which attracted many thinkers, as he released the study of man from the haunts of Freudian psychology.

Maslow's writings were better than the basic theory that is commonly taught as his, which was wrong. His theory gained great popularity, however, and all of the things that the man was saying were lost; therein lies the tragedy of Abraham Maslow. His basic theory can be summarized in two parts. The first is a complete tautology in the style of Gertrude Stein—a need that is not a need is not a need. The second and most important part of his theory, which has tremendous face validity, failed to hold up to critical analysis through either empirical investigations or conventional wisdom. He rank ordered man's needs in a hierarchy such that the satisfaction of higher-order needs awaited the satisfaction of lower-order needs. By conventional wisdom we can see clearly the difficulty with this conception of man; we would have no art if man needed to have a full belly in order to be creative. What Maslow forgot were the rising expectations. Lower-order needs are never satisfied; they are only replaced by psychologically equivalent needs which are qualitatively or quantitatively more demanding. Simply put, status needs are never satisfied. The graduate student looks for an office in which to do his work, the assistant professor needs a window, and the associate professor needs a private secretary.

Maslow was accepted, particularly by industry and students, because he was a humanist and he provided a theory which was, first, a self-evident truth, which automatically ensures great popularity (as do all self-evident truths). Second, and contrary to the basic theme in his works, his hierarchy exonerated the failure of man to grow rather than elevating him. The hierarchy became an excuse for non-self-actualization. Since lower-order needs are never satisfied (they need to be replenished), the results of his efforts were a most "scientific" and "humanistic" theory that became, in reality, an excuse for the failure of humanism in man.

Question: What is your relationship to the work of Chris Argyris?

Answer: In depth, I believe that both Argyris and I have diagnosed the essential problem of management of people in a postindustrial society in the same manner. We have both seen that the individual is not given the opportunity in organizations to live up to his human potential and that management continues to consider what I call the workers' motivation needs as secondary to the organization's hygiene needs. We both protest, in essence, the Tayloristic concept. The basic difference between Argyris and me is the approach with which we try to meet the dilemma of the individual versus the organization, as Argyris puts it. The approach of Argyris is to change, by semitherapeutic procedures (training laboratories), the attitudes and values of the managers. As a psychologist I would seem to be prone to take that approach also, but, perhaps because I am a psychologist, I have witnessed the futility of changing people's personalities and values. This is particularly evident since so much of the personality and values of people really concerns questions of ethics, for which we have had to rely on law and not psychotherapy. Witness the tragic results in the attempted rehabilitation of criminals.

I approached the problem at the more organic and substantive level. I felt that most of people's behavior is dictated not only by their early experiences and the expectations from these experiences but by the geography of the life space in which they have to operate. The changing of the consequences of personal experience, as I have said, has a very sad record. We *should* continually devote ourselves to these psychiatric approaches. But from public-health training I have found that environmental sanitation has prevented and thereby really "cured" more diseases than the therapeutist. I have looked at the job as an environmental sanitation engineer would look at a ditch and say, "If the ditch breeds mosquitos, I am not going to educate people to stay away from ditches, I am going to change that ditch so it is not a breeding ground for mosquitos." Similarly, if people have to work on Mickey Mouse jobs, I am not going to try to educate the managers as to their proper attitude and approach to these people, I am going to change the Mickey Mouse jobs. So, in essence, I suspect the basic difference between Argyris and me would be in these two different approaches—(1) a therapeutic approach and (2) a public-health engineering approach.

Question: *How does your theory relate to other theoreticians such as Rensis Likert, David McClelland, and Douglas McGregor?*

Answer: I am glad that you combined all three. All three of these theoreticians have made specific contributions of tremendous value. Likert has pointed out two things—(1) the need of individuals to be a part of what is happening to them, which is the participative management concept, and (2) the need to call attention to the cost of human resources. McClelland has really raised the concept of the achievement motivation out of the propaganda field of the sermon and the Protestant ethic and into the area of specific scientific investigations. And McGregor finally provided, by an oversimplified dichotomy, the concepts of managerial styles in such a way that he got the donkey's attention.

I don't see any of these three theoreticians providing an overall new concept or theory, but rather specific contributions to larger theories. These have been, of course, major contributions. For example, in my own theory, McClelland's achievement motivation is only a step toward the larger goal of man. Also I find in McClelland's work that what he calls achievement may be what I have relegated to the Protestant ethic type of achievement, which could be practiced by psychopaths. This type of achievement was evidenced in the earlier days of rampant individual capitalism and entrepreneurship, and it has emerged again in today's exposé of unethical practices which have tainted the public's view of industry.

Question: *What about the more psychiatrically oriented theoreticians?*

Answer: I have always believed that psychiatry is an amateur profession, and those psychologists and educators and parapsychologists who pass themselves off as psychiatrists are really amateurs practicing an amateur art. Most of their knowledge consists of clever insights into the frailties of human nature, blown up in psychiatric terminology to be no more than any observant person already knows. There have been experiments in which housewives used as psychotherapists have shown themselves to be equal to the most professionally trained practitioner. I do not deny or deride psychiatric insights (or housewives). But I do feel that psychiatry is open to rip-off, or over-the-counter remedies disguised as medicine. What psychologists and their allied pretense professions are practicing reminds me of pop art equating itself with Chagall.

Question: What you call slippages and inversions in Motivation-Hygiene Theory have been claimed by your critics to be disproof of your theory.

Answer: If I had come out with results that showed perfect profiles everybody would know that I was lying. An experiment that comes out with absolute perfect results is lying; even the measurement of Einsteinian concepts is not exact to its predictions. This is the silliest argument I know of. The problem, particularly in dealing with measurement in human behavior, is that the amount of error is going to be great. However, the amount of error always has to be seen in context with the value of the nonerror part. For example, if I make a mistake of a milimicron in an electronic communication system on a satellite, it could mean a catastrophe. If I make a mistake of 10 points above the average IQ or in the low levels of IQ the result would just be meaningless.

Now, when I first observed the profiles that emanated from the original motivation-hygiene study there were slippages—that is, motivators were on the hygiene side and hygiene factors were on the motivator side. But like any theoretician, I looked at my plot of data and asked: What makes the most sense out of this—all the deviations, or is there something underlying it? We do this all the time when we write regression equations. That is exactly what I did—I ran a regression equation and asked what would be the most sensible reason for the plot. The next point was to take the slippage, the fact that there were dots outside my regression equation, and attribute how much of these deviations could be due to error (and there was some because of the unreliability of the measures) and how much in addition had to be accounted for. It is much better to try to account for these variations than it is to say that since you do not have a perfect result, you should throw away your whole theory. I tried to account for these deviations in terms of individual differences among normal people as they experience their daily lives, in terms of the circumstances in which they find themselves and also in terms of their normalcy and abnormalcy.

In conducting studies related to these issues I found I could account for so much of the slippage that the regression equation got closer and closer to all the dots. What I am saying is that we should look at the theory and how the theory explains deviations, rather than looking at the deviations without explanations for them and stopping at that point and, on that basis, throwing out a theory.

Question: Why is your Motivation-Hygiene Theory so controversial?

Answer: Even among my critics it has been acknowledged that the theory is controversial because it upset all previous thinking related to job attitudes.[1] It is the nature of the game that a theory that comes along and cannot be incorporated into everybody else's work will be controversial, not only at the professional level but also, obviously, at the ego level. Scientists are no more immune (and perhaps much more susceptible) to feelings of jealousy than anyone else. Perhaps I should use an euphemism for the word "jealousy," but in plain talk, that is what it is.

Second, the theory not only upset a lot of theoretical and experimental work, it also questioned the tools of the psychologist and behavioral scientist. The most precious tools they had were their little instruments —the rating scales and morale questionnaires. In essence, most people make a living on the basis of their skills with tools more than their intellectual understanding. For example, surgeons are paid much more than primary-care physicians because they perform procedures, they use tools. While the primary-care physician might keep people in better health for a longer period of time, the public may not appreciate this because nothing has been done to them with an instrument or a hands-on kind of intervention.

I suspect that much of the criticism of Motivation-Hygiene Theory stems from its questioning of the behavioral scientist's tools. I am reminded of the tremendous hostility Sigmund Freud met with because he denied the electric therapies that at that time were used to treat all kinds of ailments, based upon completely fallacious understandings of the physiology and neurology of the body. Freud stripped practically every current neurologist of his profitable instrument. It may be a forgotten chapter in Freud's history, but sex, particularly in that era (which was probably the most sexy era in our history), was not the primary cause of his colleagues' rejection of Freud. It was his taking away the security blanket of their instruments. You know my theory has hit such things as the use of rating scales, morale surveys, psychological testing—these are all big business. I am not questioning the intellectual thoughts of these people—that they could accept. I am questioning the instruments they are using for their operations—that hurts.

Question: *There have been numerous tests of your Motivation-Hygiene Theory. Many have purported to disprove the two-factor concept mathematically. How do you view this criticism?*

Answer: The most dangerous thing that happened to psychologists is that they learned how to count. Factor analysis and other sophisticated mathematical tools, applied to mushy data, indeed comprise the crime of

---

[1] For example, see R. M. Steers and L. Porter, *Motivation and Work Behavior* (New York: McGraw-Hill Book Co., 1975), p. 88.

the century when it comes to behavioral science. The use of mathematical models and procedures by the so-called dismal science of economics is surpassed by their use in the more hopeless science of psychology.

Question: What is the relationship between the critical-incident methodology and Motivation-Hygiene Theory?

Answer: One of the most surprising criticisms has been that a theory can only be proved by the use of more than one method. In the philosophy of science this is ridiculous. All theories are methodologically bound, all experiments are methodologically bound. You don't try to produce steel by the Haber process and say I can't produce it by a process that produces aluminum. That a theory must be proved by more than one method is the most unscientific statement made by those in psychology, who unfortunately, know nothing about science or its philosophy. Second, the critical-incident procedure, for which, of course, I am indebted to John Flanagan, and which I modified to the sequence-of-events approach, was developed to get away from the tremendous amount of criticism that had been leveled at the rating scale—questionnaire approach. It is amazing to me that the literature is replete with examples of the inadequacies of dealing with people's verbal responses to prepared questions, and yet that is used as an argument against another approach. That is, an acknowledgedly inefficient approach is used as a reason for calling another approach inefficient. The logic escapes me; the psychology I am quite aware of.

As I pointed out in my first book, *The Motivation to Work*, what I wanted to do was to find out about people, not from what they told me they felt but from what happens to them. It goes back to the comment I made before—if I am going to change people, I am going to have to change the geography of their life space. If I want to know what people feel, I want to know what the geography of their life space is. The critical-incident method of determining people's attitudes was to look at the geography of their life space, not their rationalizations of their feelings. We already know from the dynamics of psychology that these are fraught with all the errors of defense mechanisms and so on.

Question: What about the criticism that people are more willing to give credit for success to themselves (that is, the motivators) and to blame others, including organizations (that is, hygiene) for failure, and this affects your results?

Answer: This is one of the initial criticisms; it has never been supported, and it is counter to the logic of the results. Both the logic of the results, as previously reported in *Work and the Nature of Man*, and the experimental evidence since have never justified this criticism. Can we ever escape substitutions by the opposite and double substitutions by the opposite and convoluted thinking to explain any psychological phenomenon ad infinitum? The answer is no. When dealing with human beings, to say that they have purposely or unconsciously been doing things that bring about a result provides no adequate response, unless it can be proven to me empirically, and it has not. I can review my answer to this question in more specific detail, but I am frankly bored with it because it is more of a canard than it is a legitimate question.

Question: *Do you see Motivation-Hygiene Theory in the future facing major changes or additions?*

Answer: I certainly hope so.

Question: *Motivation-Hygiene Theory is often criticized as being too simplistic, while man is complex. Would you comment?*

Answer: If it takes me two years to teach the theory at a university, and the students come out only partially understanding it, and I only partially understand it as well, and its ramifications go from mental health to job enrichment and encompass the societal questions that have already been discussed in this book, I am amazed at those who offer this "too simplistic" criticism. They offer instead extremely simplistic but psychologically tight and invulnerable counterproposals. Many of these counterproposals, like expectancy theory, are mere tautologies. I really believe that the simplistic criticism comes from simple minds and simple understanding rather than from the theory. I wish the theory were more simplistic, in keeping with the law of parsimony in science; I would be far ahead if it truly were more simplistic.

Question: *Can you explain the statement that hygiene deprivation can cause hygiene shock?*

Answer: My theory is based upon a living organism. It is obviously ridiculous to talk about happiness needs for a dead organism. If a man is in a coma, it is ridiculous to talk about his wanting to achieve. The theory holds up within the realm of reasonably functioning individuals. If we take the old laws of psychophysics and the Weber-Fechner fraction, those ratios dealing with man's ability to differentiate between changes in stimuli are pretty accurate and very functional in the design of equipment. Of course, it breaks down when you ask a man to differentiate between one ton and two tons, because he can't lift them. Similarly, in Motivation-Hygiene Theory, if there is not a viable organism there is no sense in talking about any theory. Hygiene shock explains that the theory will break down when the organism is no longer capable of functioning.

Question: When people duplicate your research, what are the most frequent problems they encounter?

Answer: This can be found in Chapter 5 on the criticisms of Motivation-Hygiene Theory, but in terms of my own personal view, the major, overall reason is that they just don't understand the theory or don't want to understand it.

Question: Does the age of a person have any significance under Motivation-Hygiene Theory?

Answer: The answer is yes and no. As I commented in one of my books, Verdi wrote *Falstaff* at the age of 80, and I am sure he suffered from tremendous hygiene ailments at this age. If I look at the mature genius of Michelangelo, Sibelius, Churchill, on and on, I find that older people still behave with motivator-hygiene dynamics. There are individual differences in the aging process, and this has to be considered.

More important, I believe, is the cultural norm in regard to aging, which deprives older people of the opportunity for motivators so that the correlation between age and Motivation-Hygiene Theory is substantially reduced, not by the innate nature of man but by the culture and its negative reinforcement of older people. Many psychologists who look at empirical findings and report symptoms and ailments rarely have gotten into the physiological and psychological dynamics underlying cultural instigations of behavior. Therefore, much of the test results on older people is a self-fulfilling prophecy which society creates. My objection is that psychologists should be aware of such self-fulfilling prophecies, since they are in their domain of investigations, and they should stop using such results as their primary data.

Question: Do you believe that the principles of Motivation-Hygiene Theory are not applicable to particular types of organizations, such as the military?

Answer: The article on the Hill Air Force Base projects in Chapter 3 certainly would answer that kind of question. The differences in organizations have been characterized too much in terms of X–Y Theory rather than in terms of the basic nature of man—he hurts, and he can gain satisfactions. Certainly an excellent rifleman can gain satisfaction by being an excellent rifleman. It is surprising how little the pride of accomplishment is based upon social value rather than upon individual psychological growth. For example, young people might say that it is much more psychologically rewarding, in the motivator sense, to use their chemistry background to produce a new antibiotic rather than a perfume. But the challenge of producing a perfume of superior quality is as much a challenge as producing a new antibiotic. The difference would be at the hygiene level, in terms of a person's own value system as regards what hurts him less in terms of cultural systems.

Question: *Why is the concept of psychological growth so important in your theory?*

Answer: I would recommend reading my book *Work and the Nature of Man,* which explains historically and in greater detail the dynamics underlying the meaning of growth in a human being. As I explained there, growth is synonymous with life. When you stop growing, you start to die. Man can come to grips, using many defense mechanisms, with his inevitable physical dying process. But handling the psychological dying process is indeed a challenge to managers.

Question: *What about the people in our organizations who fit the abnormal profiles? Whose fault is it that they are that way, and can anything be done to help these people?*

Answer: Motivation-Hygiene Theory is mostly a theory of pathology and treatment, not a theory of etiology. In fact, as a theoretician I accept most of the work that has been done in the etiology of behavioral disease. There are biological, psychological, and environmental roots to all behavior. This hasn't been the focus of my attention. However, in general, as I said in one of my films for the Bureau of National Affairs, it is harder to resurrect than to give birth, and therefore the therapeutic process is extremely expensive. In application, Motivation-Hygiene Theory has been promulgated and practiced as an attempt at management by prevention rather than management by correction. Perhaps that is another source of criticism of the theory, because there are more practitioners who are willing to correct problems and treat people in trouble than there are people who are trying to prevent human misery and suffering. If we just look at the expenditures that are made in terms of aspirin tablets to cure headaches as opposed to the research to determine the cause of headaches, the difference is astronomical.

Question: *There has been a change from your early works to your later works in the factor of recognition to recognition for achievement as a motivator. Why?*

Answer: As in all theories and research, revisions are made as new knowledge comes in. Recognition puzzled me for a long time as a motivator, although empirically it appeared on the right side as a satisfier more frequently than it did on the left side as a dissatisfier in the Motivation-Hygiene profile chart. The fact that it had much slippage to the left side, and the fact that the dynamics of the motivators would suggest that recognition is not what you do, it is what you receive for what you do, so that it would have to be a hygiene factor, puzzled me for some time. In reviewing motivation-hygiene incidents where recognition was coded, it was found that where recognition appeared on the dis-satisfier side it most often appeared along with another hygiene factor, and where recognition appeared on the positive side it was most often related to an incident which included other motivators.

Therefore, in fact, we have two factors, recognition for achievement and what I have termed the "attaboy" or hygiene recognition. This has immense importance, and as I have written, it is essential to use recognition sparingly. Recognition for achievement is to reinforce achievement, and when recognition is not used to reinforce a person's *performance* it is really a human relations device. When you use the human relations device, the "attaboy," you must recognize what you are doing. It is the difference between these two types of recognition, which have been subsumed under the one type of recognition, that has so contaminated our therapeutic processes. I think that many of our procedures would work better if we understood that we are dealing with two meanings of the same word which have different effects.

Question: Under the Motivation-Hygiene Theory, do poor working conditions (hygiene) cause mental health problems?

Answer: In Motivation-Hygiene Theory I try to throw out the whole mental health terminology and ask you what you mean by the term "mental health." Do you view mental health in terms of a positive aspect and its opposite as having no positive aspect, or is mental health viewed as opposed to being mentally sick? Poor working conditions (hygiene) can create mental illness. Poor motivator conditions can create the absence of mental health. The point is, the absence of mental health is not mental sickness. It is a difficult concept for many people who are brought up with the adjustment theory of mental illness—mental health, believing that there is a continuum from being sick to being healthy. In Motivation-Hygiene Theory there are two continua, the continuum of how much sickness you have and the continuum of how much health you have. Therefore, two questions have to be asked. As in all Motivation-Hygiene Theory, you cannot constantly ask one question, which is a habit we have grown into, when two questions need to be asked.

Questions and answers regarding job enrichment

Question: *Can all jobs be enriched?*

Answer: Often when someone asks this question he wants to know if Orthodox Job Enrichment is once and for all a panacea for all non-motivating work. On that, let me reiterate that job enrichment does not solve all the problems that management has. Some jobs are so "nothing" that they should be automated. In other cases, the short-term effects of job redesign could be dangerous—for example, with long-distance airline pilots. In such a situation, Orthodox Job Enrichment must embrace a broader scope of activities, as in introducing managerial aspects allowing for more planning and other duties not confined to the cockpit. This question is also asked by resistant managers or those first- and second-line supervisors who are too close to the job to see the potential for job changes. To these people I recommend that they look closely at what they can do to enrich the job rather than arguing about what they cannot do.

Question: *Do all people want job enrichment?*

Answer: The answer is definitely no. There are individual differences among employees in their basic abilities and motivations, as well as in their learned abilities and motivations. Job enrichment will not work for everyone. However, experience has shown that there are many more people on the healthy side of the ledger who want their jobs enriched than there are people on the diminished side who cannot accept enriched jobs. We have a choice, therefore, of structuring work for the vast majority of healthy, capable, motivated individuals and suffering or otherwise dealing with the smaller percentage of those who prefer or are only capable of Mickey Mouse work.

In essence, what we have done in the past is to structure work to meet the needs of this minority of employees. With today's social and psychological conditions, an ever-decreasing proportion are in this minority, and yet we continue to sacrifice the capabilities and motivations of the majority of our employees. Strangely enough, this decision to build work around the least capable and least motivated workers has been reinforced by the behavioral scientist, whose experience, conceptions, and "milieu" have been with the mentally sick or mentally impoverished. The cost today of alienating the healthy individual is too great. We no longer have the resources to compensate for this mistake. It has become not only uneconomical but also too psychologically damaging to our employee population. In job enrichment we are attempting the reverse strategy, that is, catering to the needs of the capable and motivated. The overall efficiency of the organization is greater with this strategy.

Question: Are the effects of job enrichment long-lasting, or is it really just another Hawthorne effect?

Answer: Let me attempt to answer this question on two levels, first theoretically, then practically. On the theoretical level, according to Motivation-Hygiene Theory, the motivators are long-term factors, while the hygiene factors are short-lived. Because the latter are based on avoidance of pain, they can only provide a short-term and temporary relief. The motivators are based on the need for individual growth, and growth is a more long-lasting quality. Think back in your own history, say for a couple of years, to when you got a pay increase. Do you still feel good about it? I doubt it very seriously. Think back an equal length of time to when you experienced a growth event, say an achievement on your job. As you think back, you probably still feel very good about that event. Achievement and growth stick to your ribs. Therefore, you can expect that job enrichment, which is based on the introduction of motivators into the work that people do, will have a much longer performance and attitudinal effect than improvement in hygiene.

Now at the practical level, what does happen? A good job enrichment program should enrich the job up to a level at which the average person will have to extend himself in order to be successful. This means that for most people the job will be challenging for a long period of time. However, some people will fail, while others will quickly master the new job and want more opportunities. The highly successful you promote, and you promote them on the basis of demonstrated ability and motivation. You then have a good criterion for promotion, whereas today most jobs have been reduced to the lowest common denominator, and no real performance differential exists on which to judge the potential for promotion. In truth, most of these judgments today are based not on performance but on how well housebroken the individual is.

Many of today's jobs do not permit the jobholder's performance to demonstrate itself. For those who fail, you have three choices. First is a training program to enable them to succeed, and this must be a substantive training program rather than the type of program which minimizes human talent and which is so common in industry. Second, you can place them in another job in which they can achieve. A person who is not achieving on a job is no good to the company and certainly no good to himself. Third, you can continue to employ him at his current job and accept the quality of work that he is capable of performing. Everyone in the same job classification does not have to do the same level of work. This differentiation will create some hygiene problems, but not any greater hygiene problems than those you already have. In one job enrichment program we continued to pay the person who could not manage the enriched job at the same rate as those who had taken on more responsibility. One of the workers performing at the enriched level complained that the limited worker was getting as much money as he was. I agreed that this was unfair, but until the project had been shaken down, I was not prepared to deal with the hygiene equity situation. I told that individual that we would be prepared for him to do the Mickey Mouse level of work and pay him the same, if he chose. He declined! He was a mature individual. He understood Motivation-Hygiene Theory—if he had reverted to the Mickey Mouse job, he would have been shortchanged twice. He would have continued to be dissatisfied with his hygiene, and he would have given up the satisfactions that he was getting from his meaningful job.

Question: What happens to the supervisors?

Answer: If you take a real hard look at the position of supervisors in terms of what they do rather than in terms of all the exalted rhetoric surrounding their job descriptions, I am sure most of you would unhappily find that they are not supervisors—they are checkers! What happens in job enrichment is that the supervisor-checker is no longer necessary. If there is a supervisory function such as planning, organizing, or teaching remaining, then, in effect, the supervisor becomes that—a true supervisor. Job enrichment does not get rid of supervision—it gets rid of checking, which in essence, is a redundant activity. The worker performs the job and the supervisor in a sense performs it again. They are both doing the same job. Why the checker? Because the individual worker is assumed not to be responsible for doing the job right in the first place!

But again, let me remind you that you cannot hold anyone responsible for being an idiot. In job enrichment we are removing the excuse for lack of responsibility and substituting the obligation of personal accountability on the part of the worker himself. Of course, this is antithetical to the role of a checker. If this makes the organization that much more profitable, our historical labor relations would justify increased payment, because this would be the right and hygienic thing to do. Remember also that an aim of job enrichment is to provide a bigger work module than the employee is expected to perform, in order to avoid the awful hygienic wage problem of constantly paying for every activity as if it were optional equipment the worker may or may not provide in his work.

Question: *What about the role of management development, management style, or organizational development as a necessary precursor to or concomitant program with job enrichment?*

Answer: My answer is to point out that these activities are all extremely beneficial and worthwhile, but they are hygiene programs. In Motivation-Hygiene Theory they should be instituted in order to minimize job dissatisfaction. But they are not motivating. It is what people do that is the essence of motivation and, therefore, it is the actual change in jobs that will do the motivating. Werner von Braun produced excellent rockets for the Germans under a vicious authoritarian style of management, and then he produced equally good rockets under the democratic system of American management. In both instances, he had the ability and the opportunity to use that ability. I am sure that under the Nazi system of management Von Braun was more unhappy, but I doubt that he was less motivated.

The dangers in the attitude-change programs being heavily linked with job enrichment are two. First, it confuses the issue. Changed attitudes do not lead to change in job behavior or the structure of the job, but changing behavior via a job structure does lead to changes in worker attitudes. Experience seems to show that the amount of job redesign that takes place when priority is given to organizational development is small indeed when compared to the effort, time, and cost expended.

Second, organizational development provides an escape hatch for managers who are more hesitant to make organizational changes in the work than they are to play around with people development. Remember, job enrichment is dealing with the content of the job, and this is where the critical focus in such programs should be. Again, I should repeat that organizational and management development and team building are worthwhile in themselves, but they are not motivation or job enrichment. My basic fear is that, although they are good hygiene programs, they masquerade for motivation programs.

Question: *What about the unions?*

Answer: Historically, the unions have been given the hygiene job, and the content of the work (the motivators) has become management's prerogative. Unions, therefore, have built in an organizational hierarchy and a constituency based on hygiene needs. The newer emphasis by the unions is on worker control, and socialistic and syndicalistic ideas such as those now prevalent in European companies. They will creep into the United States, and this will bring the ultimate demise of capitalism.

Question: How do you measure the success of job enrichment? With managerial indexes?

Answer: When you redesign the content of a job, you are often required to change what is measured for a performance appraisal. For example, if you want to measure absenteeism and you let the employee schedule his own work, you will not find the results you are looking for. The post-measures often differ from the premeasures, and the job enrichment team needs to be sensitive to that problem.

Most managerial indexes are largely inaccurate, for several reasons. First, employees will fake reports; they have been doing this for ages. Second, many of the measures are worthless. Due to advanced technology we are now able to include many measures in our computers. Before we used to think about what to measure, making sure it was theoretically meaningful; now we dump it all into a factor analysis. This gives us garbage in and garbage out.

What we really want to measure is flexibility to change rather than static productivity measures. Of course, there should be measurement of the quality of work and the other usual personnel indexes which affect productivity. These results will be self-evident; you should not need an index with statistical tables to prove it.

The most significant change, however, will be in the flexibility of the organization. With the responsibilities identified, you will get a realistic appraisal of job performance from the workers. This information helps planners see more clearly what changes are on the horizon. The supervisors will be overseeing changes, not looking for the mistakes made by his workers. These kinds of dynamics are what keep an organization creative.

Question: Should employees participate in enriching their own jobs?

Answer: Participation for participation's sake is another manipulative management device, but participation as a part of the job enrichment process can be a rich source of additional technical knowledge of jobs, while at the same time fulfilling individual needs. Employees want a sense of feeling that they have some say over their own destinies. For my observations about participation in the process of job enrichment, see the article in Chapter 3, "Job Enrichment Pays Off," which answers this question in more detail.

Question: Job enrichment has become a popular movement among industrial consultants. Will it remain so, or is there a "coming demise"?

Answer: Personnel products, like any other products, have a way of peaking and then settling down to on-the-shelf merchandise—only to reappear again (like hula hoops) when some enterprising personnel man comes up with a new slogan to revive its popularity and management has forgotten that it has been around this track before. Assessment centers are a good example. I predict that the how-to sex books have already peaked, but in ten years they will be rediscovered, with all the "ohs" and "ahs." The interest in job enrichment will probably follow the same cycle.

Question: What are the long-term effects of Orthodox Job Enrichment on the total organization?

Answer: The implementation of Orthodox Job Enrichment in an organization will also have some beneficial fallout on the adaptiveness of that organization and on the social institutions surrounding it. First of all, many of the extra hygiene problems will diminish. A boring job often leads to hypersensitivity to the work context (and at home), a point frequently overlooked by so-called OD people. Many interpersonal problems or "personality" problems will disappear when people have more competence in the organization and the opportunities to learn new jobs and skills. There will also be less psychological trauma on leaving the organization. Most trauma revolves around questions of competence. When personal confidence is raised by positive work experiences, this trauma is reduced, providing a more healthy situation for the organization as well as the individual.

With the elimination of the checking of each other's work, and built-in competence and autonomy, there will be more management by prevention because people will be planning ahead rather than correcting errors. These changes lead naturally to a more horizontal organization and one which is more flexible and responsive to changes affecting the company from the outside in.

There are some problems downwind from Orthodox Job Enrichment which make the future hard to predict. Behavioral scientists have begun to turn it into a product, and like sensitivity training, it is being packaged and sold as a "miracle drug." A recession can aggravate the hygiene concerns of a society. The result can be "we don't have time or the resources for Orthodox Job Enrichment." But in the long run, there will be no choice but to enrich jobs. The costs of managing alienated workers are astronomical.

There is one more comment I would like to make regarding the broader social issues. Everyone asks whatever happened to the work ethic. The problem is we never had a work ethic. We did have a Protestant ethic, a KITA ethic, a consumer ethic. Now we really need a work ethic. Orthodox Job Enrichment can help create one.

BIBLIOGRAPHY
OF THE WORKS OF
FREDERICK HERZBERG

Books

Job Attitudes: Research and Opinion. Psychological Service of Pittsburgh, 1957 (with B. Mausner, R. Peterson, D. Capwell).

The Motivation to Work. New York: John Wiley & Sons, 1959 (with B. Mausner and B. Snyderman).

The Motivation to Work. Osaka, Japan: Japanese Safety Council, 1965.

Work and the Nature of Man. New York: Thomas Y. Crowell Co., 1966.

Work and the Nature of Man. Japanese ed. Tokyo: Toyo Keizai Shimpo, 1968.

Le travail et la nature de l'homme. Paris: Enterprise Moderne d'Edition, 1971.

Women: The Emerging Resource. Coordinator Guide, vols. 1 and 2. Elk Grove Village, Ill.: Advanced System, Inc. 1972 (with Barbara Boyle).

Work and the Nature of Man. New York: New American Library, Mentor paperback, 1973.

Motivation: The Management of Success. Coordinator Guide, vols. 1, 2, and 3. Elk Grove Village, Ill.: Advanced System, Inc., 1973 (with B. Grigaliunas).

The Motivation to Work, Danish edition, Laursens Bogtrykkeri Tonder, 1974.

Job Enrichment. Coordinator Guide, vols. 1 and 2. Elk Grove Village, Ill.: Advanced Systems, Inc., 1974 (with R. Walters and B. Grigaliunas).

The Managerial Choice: To Be Efficient and To Be Human. Homewood, Ill.: Dow Jones–Irwin, 1976.

Articles and monographs

1952

A Study of the Psychological Factors in Primary Dysmenorrhea. *Journal of Clinical Psychology,* 1952, 8.

The Detection of Deviant Sexual Practice from Performance on the Rorschach Test. *Journal of Projective Techniques*, 1952, *16* (with G. Pascal).

1953

The Effects of Experience and Change of Job Interest on the Kuder Preference Record. *Journal of Applied Psychology*, 1953, 37 (with D. Russel).

1954

An Analysis of Morale Survey Comments. *Personnel Psychology*, 1954, 7.

Prognostic Variables for Electro-Shock Therapy. *Journal of General Psychology*, 1954, 50.

Psychological Service Morale Surveys. Psychological Service of Pittsburgh, 1954.

Temperament Measures in Industrial Selection. *Journal of Applied Psychology*, 1954, 50.

Further Studies of the Stability of the Kuder Preference Record. *Educational and Psychological Measurement*, 1954, *14* (with A. Bouton).

Studies of the Stability Preference Record. *Educational and Psychological Measurement*, 1954, *14* (with A. Bouton and B. Steiner).

Sex Differences in the Primary Mental Abilities Test. *Educational and Psychological Measurement*, 1954, *14* (with M. Lepkin).

1955

Mental Health in Industry. Psychological Service of Pittsburgh, monograph of 59 pages, 1955.

The Prevalence of Job Dissatisfaction. Psychological Service of Pittsburgh, monograph of 67 pages, 1955.

Vocational Selection and Job Attitudes. Psychological Service of Pittsburgh, monograph of 42 pages, 1955 (with D. Capwell).

Effect of Job Attitudes. Psychological Service of Pittsburgh, monograph of 51 pages, 1955 (with B. Mausner).

Supervision and Job Attitudes. Psychological Service of Pittsburgh, monograph of 75 pages, 1955 (with B. Mausner).

Factors Related to Job Attitudes. Psychological Service of Pittsburgh, monograph of 108 pages, 1955 (with R. Peterson).

1959

Book review of *Mental Health in Industry*, by A. McLean and G. Taylor, in *Personnel Psychology*, 1959, *12.*

Psychology and Work Simplification. Paper presented at Workshop on the Simplification of Dental Procedures, Western Reserve University, 1959.

The Psychology of the Unemployed. Address given at Case Western Reserve University, Cleveland, 1959. (Copies available at University of Utah, College of Business.)

Faculty Attitudes toward Experiences with a Revised Program of Medical Education. *Journal of Medical Education,* 1960, *35* (with M. Horowitz).
Some Effects on the Clinical Faculty of a Critical Incident Study of the Performance of Students. *Journal of Medical Education,* 1960, *35* (with S. Inkley and W. Adams).

1961

A Motivation-Hygiene Concept of Mental Health. *Mental Hygiene,* 1961, *45* (with R. Hamlin).

1962

Basic Needs and Satisfaction of Individuals. Industrial Relations Monograph No. 21, Industrial Relations Counselors, New York, 1962.
Comment on *The Meaning of Work* in *The Worker in the New Industrial Environment.* Foundation for Research on Human Behavior, University of Michigan, monograph, 1962.
The Mental Health Effects of the Work Environment. Foundation for Research on Human Behavior, University of Michigan, monograph, 1962.
New Approaches in Management Organization and Job Design. *Industrial Medicine and Surgery,* 1962, *31.*

1963

Motivation-Hygiene Concept and Psychotherapy. *Mental Hygiene,* 1963, *47* (with R. Hamlin).

1964

Motivation-Hygiene Concept and Problems of Manpower. *Personnel Administration,* January–February, 1964.

1965

Are You Confined by Outmoded Motivational Theories? *Occupational Hazards,* October 1965.
Comparison of Work Motivation, U.S.S.R.–U.S.A. *Soviet Life,* 1965.
Job Attitudes in the Soviet Union. *Personnel Psychology,* Fall 1965.
Motivation-Hygiene Theory of Job Attitudes. In *Proceedings of the International Congress of Social Psychiatry,* London, 1965.
Motivation to Work. *Manage,* January 1965.
Motivation to Work among Finnish Supervisors. *Personnel Psychology,* Winter 1965.
The New Industrial Psychology. *Industrial and Labor Relations Review,* 1965, *18.*
Problems of Providing Motivation in Technical Areas. In *Proceedings of the Executive Study Conference,* April 20–21, 1965, Educational Testing Service, Princeton, N.J.

Salary—A Dissatisfier. In *Proceedings of the American Compensation Society,* 1965.

1966

Ivan vs. Joe. *Newsweek,* January 24, 1966.

Motivation-Hygiene Theory. In *Proceedings of International Congress of Psychology,* Moscow, 1966.

1967

The Motivation to Work. In *Studies in Personnel and Industrial Psychology,* ed. E. Fleishman. Homewood, Ill.: Dorsey Press, 1967.

1968

Job Motivation: Money Isn't Everything. *Reader's Digest,* July 1968.

Motivating People: Money Isn't Everything. *Newsweek,* April 22, 1968.

Motivation, Morale, and Money. *Psychology Today,* March 1968.

One More Time: How Do You Motivate Employees? *Harvard Business Review,* January–February 1968.

To Motivate: Challenge the Man. *National Safety News,* May 1968.

1969

Herzberg's 10 Steps to Becoming a Successful Businessman. *Newsletter,* BNA Communications, Inc., 1969.

The New Kid in the Company. *Innovation,* No. 8 (December 1969).

To Be Efficient and to Be Human. In *Plant Engineering and Maintenance Year Book,* vol. 20 (1969).

Job Enrichment Pays Off. *Harvard Business Review,* March–April, 1969 (with W. A. Paul and K. B. Robertson).

Motivational Engineering for Pilot Training. *Technical Report AFHRL,* October, 1969 (with E. K. Winslow and Lt. Col. M. S. Majesty), Wright Patterson Air Force Base, Ohio.

1970

Be Efficient and Be Human. *Industry Week,* June 8, 1970.

Black and White of Hostility. *Industry Week,* September 21, 1970.

Does Money Really Motivate? *Purchasing,* vol. 69, August 6, 1970.

Does Your Job Bore You, or Does Professor Herzberg? (interview with Frederick Herzberg). *The Economist,* London, June 1970.

Innovations in Motivating Salesmen. In *The Marketing Road to Greater Member Firm Profitability.* New York: New York Stock Exchange, June 1970.

La Detaylorisation est en Marche (interview with Frederick Herzberg). *France et Monde,* May 1970.

Management of Hostility. *Industry Week,* August 24, 1970.

Man of the Moment: Switched on to the Behavioral Scene (interview with Frederick Herzberg). *Personnel Management,* London, July 1970.

Moving Your Employees or Motivating Them? *Industry Week,* May 18, 1970.

No People Shortage, Just . . . Turn Your People On. *Industry Week,* January 19, 1970.

People Are Polarizing. *Industry Week,* July 27, 1970.

What People Want from Their Jobs. *Industry Week,* October 19, 1970.

Work and the Two Faces of Man. *Industry Week,* November 9, 1970.

1971

Are Have-Nots Entitled to Automatic Equality? *Industry Week,* March 15, 1971.

Humanity and Efficiency. *Ulster Businessman,* April 1971.

Management of Motivators. *Industry Week,* February 15, 1971.

Managers or Animal Trainers (interview with Frederick Herzberg) by William F. Dowling. *Management Review,* vol. 60 (July 1971).

More on Avoiding Pain in Organizations. *Industry Week,* January 18, 1971.

Motivation in an Advanced Technological Society . . . To Be Efficient and To Be Human. In *Agent of Change: Technology's Impact on Management,* report on the 19th National Management Conference, Killarney, Ireland, 1971.

The Negro and His Bootstraps. Case Western Reserve University, Cleveland, 1971.

Relevancy in the Test of Motivation-Hygiene Theory. *Journal of Applied Psychology,* 1971, 55 (with B. Grigaliunas).

1972

The End of Obligation. *Industry Week,* October 16, 1972.

The Equality of Ignorance. *Industry Week,* October 9, 1972.

Swapping Managerial Garbage. *Industry Week,* October 2, 1972.

1973

Frederick Herzberg's Recipe for Motivation (interview with Frederick Herzberg). *International Management,* September 1973.

The Inimitable Herzberg (interview with Frederick Herzberg). *People & Profits,* vol. 1, no. 3 (1973).

Why Bother to Work? *Industry Week,* July 16, 1973.

1974

Commentaries in *R&D Productivity.* Study report conducted by Hughes Aircraft Co., 1974.

Coping with Change: Some Blind Alleys for the Perplexed and Some Pessimisms for the Dismayed. *Hospital Forum,* December 1974.

The Economic Crisis and Work Motivation. *Industry Week,* February 25, 1974.

Managing People in an Era of Hopelessness. *Industry Week,* November 11, 1974.

Motivation-Hygiene Profiles: Pinpointing What Ails the Organization. *Organizational Dynamics* (American Management Association), Autumn 1974.

New Perspectives on the Will to Work. *Personnel Administrator,* July–August, 1974.

The Wise Old Turk. *Harvard Business Review,* September–October, 1974.

Work, Satisfaction and Motivation-Hygiene Theory. *Book Forum,* vol. 1, no. 2 (1974) (special issue).

Motivation-Hygiene Correlates of Mental Health: An Examination of Motivational Inversion in a Clinical Population. *Journal of Consulting and Clinical Psychology,* vol. 42, no. 3 (1974) (with Y. Wiener, J. Mathapo, and L. Wiesen).

1975

Job Enrichment—Ogden Style. In *Productivity Enhancement in Logistical Systems,* U.S. Department of Commerce, May 1975.

Job Enrichment's "Father" Admits: Disparity Between Promise and Reality. *Industry Week,* November 25, 1975.

Para quem quer motivar seu pessoal e nao sabe como (interview with Frederick Herzberg). *Supermercado Moderno,* Sao Paulo, Brazil, March 1975.

Efficiency in the Military: Cutting Costs with Orthodox Job Enrichment. *Personnel* (American Management Association), November–December 1975 (with Maj. Gen. E. Rafalko).

Social Desirability, Repression and Sensitization as Factors in the Critical Incidents Method of Motivation-Hygiene Theory. Human Resources Management Publication 75–101, University of Utah, December 1975 (with Y. Wiener and R. Vaitenas).

A New Classification System for Critical Incidents: Implications for the Defensiveness Hypothesis and White Collar–Blue Collar Job Feelings. Human Resources Management Publication No. 75–101, University of Utah, December 1975 (with Y. Wiener, R. Vaitenas, K. Klein).

1976

Commentary on Maslow. In *Great Writings of Marketing.* Plymouth, Mich.: Commerce Press, January 1976.

Making Work Work Better Symposium. *The Rotarian,* May 1976.

Types of Job Enrichment. *Proceedings of First International Congress of Labor and Psychology.* Asociacion de Psicologos Industriales, Mexico City, 1976.

Films

1965

This Matter of Motivation. Dartnell Company, 1965.

1966

More Than a Living: The Theories of Frederick Herzberg. American Telephone and Telegraph Company, New York, 1966.

Test Case—Treasury (Consultant). *American Telephone and Telegraph Company,* New York, 1966.

1967

Motivation through Job Enrichment. BNA Communications, Inc., Rockville, Md., 1967.

1969

The ABC Man: The Manager in Mid-Career. BNA Communications, Inc., Rockville, Md., 1969.

Building A Climate for Individual Growth. BNA Communications, Inc., Rockville, Md., 1969.

Job Enrichment in Action. BNA Communications, Inc., Rockville, Md., 1969.

The Modern Meaning of Efficiency. BNA Communications, Inc., Rockville, Md., 1969.

What Have You Done for Me Lately? BNA Communications, Inc., Rockville, Md., 1969.

1970

Motivational Engineering for Undergraduate Pilot Training. Air Force Documentary, SPR–6–70.

1971

Advantages and Obstacles to Job Enrichment. Videotape series, Video Learning Centers, Chicago, 1971.*

Clinical Case: Directory. Videotape series, Video Learning Centers, Chicago, 1971.*

Clinical Case: Keypunch. Videotape series, Video Learning Centers, Chicago, 1971.*

Defining the Model Job. Videotape series, Video Learning Centers, Chicago, 1971.*

Implementing Job Enrichment. Videotape series, Video Learning Centers, Chicago, 1971.*

---

* Not available.

Initiating the Job Enrichment Effort. Videotape series, Video Learning Centers, Chicago, 1971.*

The Job. Canadian Television Documentary, 1971.

Management by Hygiene. Videotape series, Video Learning Centers, Chicago, 1971.*

Management by Motivation. Videotape series, Video Learning Centers, Chicago, 1971.*

Motivation to Work Studies. Videotape series, Video Learning Centers, Chicago, 1971.*

Pre-Implementation. Videotape series, Video Learning Centers, Chicago, 1971.*

Refining the Greenlight Items. Videotape series, Video Learning Centers, Chicago, 1971.*

Undertaking Job Enrichment. Videotape series, Video Learning Centers, Chicago, 1971.*

Why Jobs Die. Videotape series, Video Learning Centers, Chicago, 1971.*

1972

Documentary on Job Enrichment. RAI Corporation, Italian television, 1972.

How to Restore the Will to Work. Penton, Inc., Cleveland, 1972.

1973

Jumping for the Jellybeans. British Broadcasting Corporation, 1973.

Management by Movement. Advanced Systems, Inc., Elk Grove Village, Ill., 1973.

Management of Hostility. Advanced Systems, Inc., Elk Grove Village, Ill., 1973.

Management of Hygiene. Advanced Systems, Inc., Elk Grove Village, Ill., 1973.

Management of the Motivators. Advanced Systems, Inc., Elk Grove Village, Ill., 1973.

Motivational Types. Advanced Systems, Inc., Elk Grove Village, Ill., 1973.

Motivation-Hygiene Theory. Advanced Systems, Inc., Elk Grove Village, Ill., 1973.

Myths About Your Employees. Advanced Systems, Inc., Elk Grove Village, Ill., 1973.

The Nature of Man. Advanced Systems, Inc., Elk Grove Village, Ill., 1973.

To Be Efficient and To Be Human. Advanced Systems, Inc., Elk Grove Village, Ill., 1973.

What Happened to the Work Ethic? Advanced Systems, Inc., Elk Grove Village, Ill., 1973.

Women: The Emerging Resource: Counseling Women. Advanced Systems, Inc., Elk Grove Village, Ill., 1973 (with Barbara Boyle).

---

* Not available.

Women: The Emerging Resource: Why Be Concerned? Advanced Systems, Inc., Elk Grove Village, Ill., 1973 (with Barbara Boyle).

Women: The Emerging Resource: Why Women Work. Advanced Systems, Inc., Elk Grove Village, Ill., 1973 (with Barbara Boyle).

1974

Implementing Job Enrichment. Advanced Systems, Inc., Elk Grove Village, Ill., 1974 (with Roy Walters).

Ingredients of a Good Job. Advanced Systems, Inc., Elk Grove Village, Ill., 1974 (with Roy Walters).

Job Enrichment: A Pragmatic View. Advanced Systems, Inc., Elk Grove Village, Ill., 1974 (with Roy Walters).

Starting a Job Enrichment Program. Advanced Systems, Inc., Elk Grove Village, Ill., 1974 (with Roy Walters).

What Is Job Enrichment? Advanced Systems, Inc., Elk Grove Village, Ill., 1974 (with Roy Walters).

1975

Filmed discussion between Professor Herzberg and Professor Kalevsky (U.S.S.R.) on *Encuentro,* cultural television program, Instituto Mexicano del Seguro Social and Televisa, Mexico City, May 1975.

Filmed documentary on Job Enrichment Research Program, OJE–Ogden Style. Odger Air Force Logistics Command, Hill Air Force Base, Utah, 1975.

Some bibliographic references to selected reprinted articles

Article: "One More Time: How Do You Motivate Employees?" *Harvard Business Review* January–February, 1968 (in Chapters 2 and 3).

In *Readings in Human Relations,* ed. Keith Davis. New York: McGraw–Hill, 1968.

In *AAFES Management,* Army and Air Force Exchange Service, Dallas, Texas, 1968.

In *Psychodynamics of Management,* by Richard M. Greene. Homewood, Ill.: Dow Jones–Irwin, 1968.

In *Operations Management: Selected Readings,* ed. Gene K. Groff. Homewood, Ill.: Richard D. Irwin, 1968.

In *Personnel Administration: Principles and Cases,* by Alva F. Kindall. Homewood, Ill.: Richard D. Irwin, 1968.

Note: This list of reprinted articles is selected and incomplete because, unfortunately, courtesies are not always extended in informing me when articles of mine have been reprinted. In some instances I have knowledge of the place of reprint but have not seen the reprint and cannot locate the exact reprinted source. Therefore I have included only those of which I am 99 percent sure of exact reference and those that I am sure have actually been reprinted, even though permission to reprint has been given to others.

In *Managing People at Work: Readings In Personnel,* ed. Dale S. Beach. New York: Macmillan, 1969.

In *Industrial Launderer,* ed. Harry Kincaid, 1969.

In *Organizational Behavior and Administration: Motivation and Control in Organizations,* by Gene Dalton. Homewood, Ill.: Richard D. Irwin, 1970.

In *Concepts and Controversy in Organizational Behavior,* by W. Nord. Pacific Palisades, Cal.: Goodyear Publishing Co., 1970.

In *Readings in Organizational and Industrial Psychology,* ed. K. Wexley. New York: Oxford University Press, 1970.

In *Training and Developing Today's Work Force,* by Paul M. Diesel. American Management Association Extension Institute, 1970.

In *Readings and Cases in Management,* by Frank Paine. New York: Crowell-Collier and Macmillan, 1973.

In *Design of Jobs,* ed. Louis E. Davis and James C. Taylor. London: Penguin Books, 1973.

In *Studies in Personnel and Industrial Psychology,* ed. Edwin A. Fleishman and Alan R. Bass. Homewood, Ill.: Dorsey Press, 1974.

In *Personnel Management for Family Planning Programs.* Community and Family Study Center, The University of Chicago, 1974.

In *Motivation and Work Behavior.* By Richard M. Steers and Lyman W. Porter. New York: McGraw-Hill, 1975.

In *Concepts and Controversy in Organizational Behavior,* by W. Nord. 2d ed. Pacific Palisades, Cal.: Goodyear Publishing Co., 1976.

In *Harvard Business Review—On Management,* ed. R. F. Lewis. New York: Harper & Row, 1976.

Translations: "One More Time: How Do You Motivate Employees?"

In *Organization Development,* by F. Balvig. Copenhagen, Denmark, 1970.

In *Ediciones Contabilidad Moderna S.A.I.C.,* by R. Dealecsandris. Buenos Aires, Argentina, 1971.

In *Business Consultants.* Tokyo, 1971.

In *Esso Standard Italiano.* Rome, 1971.

Una vez mas ¿Como motivar a sus empleados? In *Biblioteca Harvard de Administracion de Empresas.* Mexico, D.F., 1974.

Article: "Job Enrichment Pays Off," *Harvard Business Review,* March–April, 1969, (with W. J. Paul and K. B. Robertson; in Chapter 3).

In *Organizational Issues in Industrial Society,* by Jon Shepard. Englewood Cliffs, N.J.: Prentice-Hall, 1969.

In *Management and Organizational Behavior,* ed. Henry Tosi. Chicago: St. Clair Press, 1974.

In *Design of Jobs,* ed. Louis E. Davis and James C. Taylor. London: Penguin Books, 1973.

In *Organizational Behavior and Industrial Psychology,* by Kenneth N. Wexley and Gary A. Yukl. New York: Oxford University Press, 1975.

In *Personal Awareness: A Psychology of Adjustment,* by R. Warga. New York: Houghton Mifflin Co., 1975.

Translations: "Job Enrichment Pays Off"

In *Business Consultants.* Tokyo, 1971.

In *Ediciones Contabilidad Moderna S.A.I.C.,* Buenos Aires, Argentina, 1971.

Article: "The Wise Old Turk," *Harvard Business Review,* September–October, 1974 (in Chapter 3).

In *Fortschrittliche Betriebsführung und Industrial Engineering.* February 24, 1975.

Translations: "The Wise Old Turk"

Inter Kibbutz Economic Advisory Unit. in Hebrew. Tel Aviv, Israel, January, 1975.

Article: "Why Bother To Work," *Industry Week,* July 16, 1973 (see "Reasons for Success," Chapter 11).

In *Association Management,* November 1973.

Article: "Management of Hostility," *Industry Week,* August 24, 1970 (see consolidated article in Chapter 1).

How Do You React to Hostility? *Management Magazine* (Bank of America), vol. 3 (May 1973).

Article: "Managers or Animal Trainers: An interview with Frederick Herzberg," by William F. Dowling. *Management Review,* July 1971 (in Chapter 6).

In *Organizational Behavior: A Book of Readings,* by Keith Davis. New York: McGraw-Hill Book Co., 1974.

Article: "The New Industrial Psychology" *Industrial and Labor Relations Review,* vol. 18, (1965).

In *Outlook,* Spring 1965.

Article: "New Approaches in Management Organization and Job Design." *Industrial Medicine and Surgery,* 1962, *31,* 477–482.

Chapter in *Management in Perspectives,* ed. William E. Schlender. New York: Houghton Mifflin Co., 1965.

Chapter in *Management and the Behavioral Sciences,* by Maneck S. Wadia. Boston: Allyn & Bacon, 1968.

Article: "Motivation, Morale and Money," *Psychology Today,* Spring 1968.

In *Psychologie Heute* (Germany), March 1975.

In *Readings in Psychology Today,* ed. CRM Books editorial staff. New York: CRM–Random House, 1969.

In *psicologia dosmil,* Spanish affiliate of *Psychology Today,* January 1976.

Index